Dreams for Dead Bodies

CLASS : CULTURE

SERIES EDITORS
Amy Schrager Lang, Syracuse University, and Bill V. Mullen, Purdue University

RECENT TITLES IN THE SERIES:

Marcial González, *Chicano Novels and the Politics of Form: Race, Class, and Reification*

Fran Leeper Buss, Editor, *Moisture of the Earth: Mary Robinson, Civil Rights and Textile Union Activist*

Clarence Lang, *Grassroots at the Gateway: Class Politics and Black Freedom Struggle in St. Louis, 1936–75*

Pamela Fox, *Natural Acts: Gender, Race, and Rusticity in Country Music*

Carole Srole, *Transcribing Class and Gender: Masculinity and Femininity in Nineteenth-Century Courts and Offices*

Lorraine M. López, Editor, *An Angle of Vision: Women Writers on Their Poor and Working-Class Roots*

Matthew H. Bernstein, Editor, *Michael Moore: Filmmaker, Newsmaker, Cultural Icon*

John Marsh, *Hog Butchers, Beggars, and Busboys: Poverty, Labor, and the Making of Modern American Poetry*

Mark W. Van Wienen, *American Socialist Triptych: The Literary-Political Work of Charlotte Perkins Gilman, Upton Sinclair, and W. E. B. Du Bois*

Liam Kennedy and Stephen Shapiro, Editors, The Wire: *Race, Class, and Genre*

Andreá N. Williams, *Dividing Lines: Class Anxiety and Postbellum Black Fiction*

Clarence Lang, *Black America in the Shadow of the Sixties: Notes on the Civil Rights Movement, Neoliberalism, and Politics*

Benjamin Balthaser, *Anti-Imperialist Modernism: Race and Transnational Radical Culture from the Great Depression to the Cold War*

M. Michelle Robinson, *Dreams for Dead Bodies: Blackness, Labor, and the Corpus of American Detective Fiction*

Dreams for Dead Bodies

BLACKNESS, LABOR, AND THE CORPUS OF AMERICAN DETECTIVE FICTION

M. Michelle Robinson

University of Michigan Press
Ann Arbor

Published in the United States of America by the
University of Michigan Press
Manufactured in the United States of America
⊗ Printed on acid-free paper

2019   2018   2017   2016   4   3   2   1

A CIP catalog record for this book is available from the British Library.

Library of Congress Cataloging-in-Publication Data

Names: Robinson, Michelle, 1979–author.
Title: Dreams for dead bodies : blackness, labor, and the corpus of American detective fiction /
    Miriam Michelle Robinson.
Description: Ann Arbor : University of Michigan Press, [2016] | Series: Class : culture | Includes
    bibliographical references and index.
Identifiers: LCCN 2015041733 | ISBN 9780472119813 (hardback : acid-free paper)
Subjects: LCSH: Detective and mystery stories, American—History and criticism. | African
    Americans in literature. | Working class in literature. | Slavery in literature. | Work in
    literature.
Classification: LCC PS374.D4 R625 2016 | DDC 813/.087209—dc23
LC record available at http://lccn.loc.gov/2015041733

Contents

Acknowledgments vii

INTRODUCTION:
The Original Plotmaker 1

CHAPTER 1: Reverse Type 28

CHAPTER 2: The Art of Framing Lies 62

CHAPTER 3: To Have Been Possessed 95

CHAPTER 4: The Great Work Remaining before Us 131

CHAPTER 5: Prescription: Homicide? 163

CONCLUSION:
Dream within a Dream 201

Notes 215

Bibliography 233

Index 251

Acknowledgments

A number of people have been important in the writing of this book. It is a great pleasure to express my gratitude to John T. Matthews and Charles Rzepka as well as Marilyn Halter, Nina Silber, and Roy Grundmann for their guidance. I am much indebted to the Institute of Arts and Humanities at the University of North Carolina at Chapel Hill for a Mellon Book Manuscript Workshop, and to Sean McCann and Robert Reid-Pharr, who graciously and generously participated. Eliza Richards, Sharon Holland, Priscilla Wald, John McGowan, and Ian Baucomb also provided words of encouragement and much-appreciated feedback that guided my revisions. Librarians at the John Hay Library at Brown University helped me navigate the Rudolph Fisher Papers. Sohini Sengupta at the Center for Faculty Excellence and Jennifer Ho offered a lift when the challenges of writing a book proposal seemed insurmountable. I am also indebted to the two anonymous readers for the University of Michigan Press who provided extensive and valuable comments on the manuscript. And I am so appreciative of LeAnn Fields and Christopher Dreyer at the University of Michigan Press for their enthusiasm and for their dedication to publishing this book.

This work would not have been possible without the support of Joy Kasson, Bernie Herman, and a long roster of my magnificent colleagues in American Studies and elsewhere at UNC–Chapel Hill. I am truly grateful to Tim Marr and Rachel Willis for their emboldening intellectual and moral support. Jenny Tone-Pah-Hote, Ben Frey, Laura Halperin, Heidi Kim, Pat Parker, Angeline Shaka, Heidi Kim, Ariana Vigil, Nadia Yaqub, Morgan Pitelka, and Rachel Pollock were great friends and sometimes disciplinarians-by-proxy during this process, as were the optimists Joe Campana, Chris Holmlund, and Michael Mallory.

My thanks go to Deedie Matthews, Ian Morse, Mariah Voutilainen, and the rest of my close and extended family for their unwavering support. Finally, I am deeply grateful to my parents, Brooks Robinson and Wylma Samaranayake-Robinson. I am lucky to be their daughter.

Introduction

The Original Plotmaker

> She was sitting on the terrace with Proust's *Remembrance of Things Past* open in her lap, but instead of reading she was looking across her sunny acres with a dreamy expression.
>
> "If I may be so bold as to ask, what are you thinking, madame?" I asked.
> "About sausage."
> "What about sausage, madame?"
> "About how good it is."
> It made me happy to see her happy, and the hogs were happy to see us both happy.
>
> —CHESTER HIMES, *THE END OF A PRIMITIVE*

In Chester Himes's book *The End of a Primitive*, an African American author named Jesse Robinson dreams of reading a book titled *Hog Will Eat Hog*, "a soft sweet lyrical and gently humorous account" of a cook who discovers one need not slaughter hogs to make sausage (193). Instead, he makes an arrangement with his pigs: each day they will volunteer some quantity of sausage "neatly stuffed in their intestines," which the man has merely to collect and turn over to his customers. This mutually agreeable bargain is botched, however, when a single hog among them claims he is all out of sausage and refuses to turn over his daily portion. "I knew by his hang-hog expression and the guilty manner in which he avoided my eyes," the narrator explains, "that the sausage manufacturers had bribed him":

> "But it is true," he contended. "Besides which I have no more guts."
>
> "Would you rather be slaughtered and butchered by the sausage manufacturers, or give us, your friends, a little bit of sausage each day?" I asked bluntly.
>
> "I don't know why I hate you so when you've been so good to me," he squealed pathetically, lard drops streaming from his little hog eyes. (194)

It is a curious pact, to be sure, between a high-strung hog, some sort of sausage broker or cook, and a Jimmy Dean–loving aesthete, which turns sour when the pig "cries lard." But it is also a heavy-handed fable in a novel about a bitter African American novelist. A writer is expected to generate a sort of formula fiction—agglutinate, mass produced, serialized, even pulp— to suit the public, we are led to believe; he is supposed to make hash of his work to fit specs negotiated by a publisher with an axe, so to speak, up against the author's neck. Or perhaps the livestock and, in particular, that pathetic pig, is meant to recall the transformation of the body into a commodity, the extraction of a black man's blood and guts for another's profit— slavery redacted, an all-American edition of *Remembrance of Things Past*. Or it is some combination of the two.

Long before Himes became celebrated as an author of hard-boiled detective fiction, his first, gorgeous, semibiographical novel, *Yesterday Will Make You Cry*, was thoroughly bowdlerized: third-person narration was swapped for first; its sober prison story was sanctified with slang (the 1972 Signet Edition called its protagonist, James Monroe, "a cool cat," and described the book as "a ruthlessly honest novel of a young black's agonizing discovery of his own emotions, his own identity"—never mind that the main character was white); and it was rechristened as the more lurid *Cast the First Stone* (qtd. in Van Peebles 19). This was "swinging of the pendulum towards pulp," laments Melvin Van Peebles, who writes, "What stomach-turning irony, forced to mutilate your work and then, adding insult to injury, having that mutilation become the map to greater fame and fortune" (19–20).

Whether the subject of Jesse Robinson's dream is a précis of Himes's scuffles with the literary establishment or a cartoon adaptation of *Dialectic of Enlightenment* is of less consequence, however, than that the subject of the dream is the subject of a book. And a most unusual one since, if we take its allegorical freight seriously, Jesse dreams of a book that capitulates the conditions of its own production, and of its failure to "give the goods." It is a book that is, quite literally, full of itself (and of its failure to be itself)—and therefore quite appropriately titled *Hog Will Eat Hog*—and it is something like the subject of Russell's paradox, a "self-including statement" in which "one confronts a mirror image of the self, a figure of an individual consciousness that is constituted precisely by its mutually reflective relationship to a self-included (mental) representation of its own representational (symbolic/linguistic) status" (Irwin, *Mystery to a Solution* 23). This was, in fact, the kind of book Himes would regularly produce when he began writing detective novels for Marcel Duhamel's La Série Noire, soon after the tepid reception of *The End of a Primitive*. Writing genre fiction was a humiliating chore the intermittently down-and-out Himes was induced to perform by Duhamel's promise of a cash advance, though Himes finally came to regard his "Harlem novels" as a unique and significant contribution to American literature. In his detective fictions, which feature a sordid assortment of violent crime, rampant corruption, and harebrained con games in a destitute Harlem, Himes plays fast and loose with the letter of the law and the "laws" of the detective genre. Moreover, his Harlem detectives Grave Digger Jones and Coffin Ed—whom Himes often referred to as plow hands and, on one occasion, as "two hog farmers on a weekend in the Big Town" (qtd. in Sallis 299)—frequently sabotage both.

Like Jesse Robinson's *Hog Will Eat Hog* in Chester Himes's *The End of a Primitive*, this study aims to get at the guts of a literary genre by delving into texts that commandeer detective fiction, turn it in its tracks, and refuse to "give the goods." *Dreams for Dead Bodies* studies the ways that American authors appropriated the analytical tactics and tools of the detective fiction while flouting its formula prescriptions. In the stead of corpses, deerstalker hats, and meerschaum pipes—what we take as the meat and gravy, so to speak, of classical detective fiction—this study constructs an alternate genealogy of precursor and "peripheral" genre texts that incorporated and exploited specific puzzle-elements. Yet each of the texts in this revisionary genealogy opens up something important about detective fiction's inner workings and our now perpetually murky grasp of its genesis and evolution over the course of a century, from the 1830s to the 1930s.[1] I treat these "outsider" literary artifacts as indispensable archives of generic "intelligence" that illuminate the social questions and concerns that motivate the genre. My aim is not only to elucidate the genre's historical contexts and the material base from which detective fiction's discursive logics arise, but also to clarify detective fiction's operations *as* historiography. I argue that American authors developed and drew on an anatomy of genre conventions associated with the clue-puzzle mystery to access and represent a sociology of racialized labor, to challenge public fictions of racial separation, and to plumb prospects for interracial sociability.

Detective fiction's narrative-analytical tools—the stimulating elements of the clue-puzzle, the cogs and wheels of detection—generate self-referential discourse whose most basic effect is to dramatize how social knowledge becomes accessible via narrative. Among the genre's principal devices is the compulsion toward *backward construction* (narrative retroversion): the temporal displacement of the crime and investigation recruit the reader, often alongside a detective figure, to a process of narrative retrieval and chronological sequencing that would arrange fragments of the past into a plausible causal sequence and a cohesive logico-temporal whole. This pursuit of narrative unity, moreover, gives rise to a paradoxical operation, the "anticipation in retrospect" that structures our reading activity (Pyrhönen, *Mayhem* 11). Detection texts commit their reader to analepsis and prolepsis simultaneously, as they invite us to imagine a future moment when the events of the past will be disclosed in their entirety. Then, the adhesion of any speculative accounts of a crime depends on *metonymy*, the rhetorical figure enlisted in our interpretations of a "clue." Metonymy, which relies on contiguity, substitutes a trace or part for its whole, or an effect for a cause and vice versa. For the reader, these partial objects (metonymic traces) conjure an assortment of possible accounts of a crime that must be whittled to a single solution.[2] Metonymy is in productive tension with *metaphor*, which requires an ingenious leap from one domain to another and, in detective fiction, typically takes the form of "imaginative identification" between doubled, oppositional figures (the detective and the criminal, for instance, or the reader and the author) as the former attempts to inhabit the sensibilities of the latter, if only to intuit his or her next move. In addition to these primary devices, the genre wields an assortment of other tools. There is the "locked room" paradox, an apparently irrational system of spatial arrangement that appears intact but has nevertheless been inexplicably violated by the criminal. Selective focalization (often through a dim-witted narrator) manipulates perception; narrative fragmentation, distraction, and ambiguity pose further interpretive challenges for the reader; and devices of disguise confound attempts to locate the culprit of the crime. Finally, there is the declaration of a solution and the detective's final "exposition of evidence" that brings the investigation to a halt. *Dreams for Dead Bodies* strives to open up the social functions of detective fiction's component parts. Each of the works I examine in this study illuminates how one or more of its repertoire of generic elements are embedded in historical conditions of production and processes of racial formation.[3]

The central argument this book advances is that the genesis of detective fiction in the United States is fundamentally entwined with the possibility of interracial sociability. Building on historians David Roediger and Elizabeth Esch's insight that race was "a difference made in the world of production" (6), this study explores how detection's devices intersect with the structures of socioeconomic life. I provide a complex account of how industrial consid-erations and racial categories were and are interarticulated, negotiated, and rehearsed through the formal mechanisms we now recognize as standard properties of detective fiction.[4] In the antebellum period, writers fashioned the formal equipment we routinely associate with classical detective fiction to parse the social effects of racial differentiation that were part and parcel of an industrially oriented market economy. I argue that the genre's narrative-analytical tools emerged in conjunction with historical factors that include the joint production of racial knowledge and managerial techniques, and a displacement of indigenous peoples that reshaped the geography and the meaning of labor. As detective fiction assumed recognizable forms in the late nineteenth century, American authors continued to avail themselves of the genre's narrative tactics in order to excavate the psychodynamically re-pressed, systematically occluded logics at the heart of the "hard facts" that regulated industrial production and the very possibilities for human com-munity.[5] Authors appropriated the genre's narrative-analytical tools to con-front the emergence of racial competition, black codes, and "convict" labor as secondary effects of "race management," as well as prospects for collective action that attempted to surmount such divisions of labor. Finally, I sug-gest that the "ethnic" dimensions that surface in well-known classical detec-tive fictions during the genre's golden era (1920s–1930s) and beyond are not anomalous but continuous with American writers' earlier uses of the genre's signifying and plotting strategies to offer a sociology of race and labor. The conventions that coalesced in classical detective fiction constituted a mode of inquiry at the level of form, one that ingeniously modeled the intrica-cies of economic dependency and its effects on interracial sociability in the United States.

In proposing a revised history of the genre in its American context, this study takes a first step toward establishing that the genre of detective fic-tion is an *interracial genre*. I use the term "interracial" not to authenticate or reinforce biological notions of race or to treat terms like "white" and "black" as natural, self-evident distinctions between peoples, but to call attention to how detective fiction's formation and subsequent developments in the genre are, in an American context, entangled with the prospect of interra-cial sociability. In *Neither Black nor White yet Both: Thematic Explorations of Interracial Literature*, Werner Sollors employs the expression "interracial" to designate literary and historical characters that we might, under other circumstances, refer to as "biracial." For Sollors, interraciality is the (sometimes repressed, sometimes championed) effect of *sexual* intercourse between races. By contrast, my use of "interracial" (paired as it is with notions of sociability) attaches to a scene or a population rather than a person. In this study, I use "interracial" as a descriptor that might designate a historical context, the character of a social space (a workplace, a neighborhood, or a family, for instance), or a thematic *content* of a text whose characters contend with a reality of racial heterogeneity. This terminology is not ideal, I realize. Nevertheless, we remain at the mercy of such historical *bizarreries* as "mixed blood," "miscegenation," "black," and "white." Sollors judiciously concedes that "despite their histories and inaccuracies, such terms may be unavoidable and even useful and helpful at times, as they have also been adopted and reappropriated for a variety of reasons, including their specificity, their ability to redefine a negative term from the past into one positively and defiantly adopted in the present, or simply the absence of better terms" (3).[6]

In turn, *Dreams for Dead Bodies* uses the term "interracial sociability" to open up the expansive associations a term like "sociability" implies: mutuality, reciprocity, dependency, and kinship between individuals, classes, or publics, as it materializes in the content and form of fictional texts. In the case of detective fiction, the genre's intriguing capacity to create and cultivate a sociability of intelligence with its readers provides yet another facet of this investigation. In his groundbreaking study *To Wake the Nations*, literary scholar Eric Sundquist proposed that any broad examination of nineteenth-century intellectual and literary culture must assume an integrated character if it is to make sense of an American literary tradition. In this vein, *Dreams for Dead Bodies* maintains that reading an integrated literary canon alongside popular detective fictions allows us to reconsider the significance of detective fiction to U.S. literary production.

Along these lines, *Dreams for Dead Bodies* extends Toni Morrison's well-known insight that white-authored literary production in the United States has continuously featured an Africanist specter as a "dark and abiding presence, there for the literary imagination as both a visible and an invisible mediating force" (46). This Africanist idiom establishes difference, suggests illicit sexuality, or represents class distinctions, and it depicts tension between speech and speechlessness with its "estranging dialect" (52). In the nineteenth century, white authors relied upon Africanist narratives, that is, stories of "black" people, to flesh out the boundaries and implications of whiteness and to meditate on their own "humanity": to think about suffering or rebellion, to discover the limits of "civilization" and "reason." While literary criticism has increasingly shifted away from this emphasis upon "blackness" or an "Africanist presence" as *the* central preoccupation of U.S. literary production to adequately historicize a populace that was infinitely more complex than black and white, this project takes for granted the importance of "blackness" to exploring the psychic life of race in U.S. literary productions.[7] Without disqualifying the complexity of class and racial formations and the fraught constructions of gender, ethnic, and national identities in the multitextured fabric of U.S. literary history, *Dreams for Dead Bodies* begins by surveying the intricacies of "black and white," given its objective is to parse a psychodynamics of interracial dependency and a discursive logic of interracial sociability that found its primary coordinates in notions of "blackness" and "whiteness" that were not themselves static. Perhaps the most important implication of this integrated analysis is its indication that we are dealing with a genre that is, to borrow a phrase from Sollors, neither white nor black yet both.

Though some might object that a distinct expression such as "interracial sociability" is superfluous or distracting, I nevertheless insist upon this peculiar phrase to describe a textual dynamic for which I find there is not yet a succinct or adequate vocabulary. Again, I use interracial sociability to refer to the ways peripheral detective fictions explicitly negotiate the realities of racial heterogeneity. It is, additionally, a term that describes form. It gestures at possibilities suggested by the kind of literary analysis Edward Said designates the contrapuntal mode: a critical recognition of the "counterpoint, intertwining and integration" of multiple, coexistent literary perspectives in the case of the "metropolitan" and "peripheral" geographic and literary relations imposed by a global-imperialist project. Said's proposed methodology eschews the "rhetorical separation of cultures," allowing for something more than "a blandly uplifting suggestion for catholicity of vision" or "retrospective Jeremiahs" (38, 259, 18). Interracial sociability, in turn, is a descriptor that distinguishes *contrapuntal writing*, writing whose particular narrative-analytical tools capture interracial animosities and comminglings and affinities in an American context, writing that leverages the distinct insights of literary detection. Furthermore, contrapuntal writing cultivates *contrapuntal reading*, steering us to the serpentine course that is "counterpoint, intertwining and integration" within American texts, rather than sending us after exiled and extratextual textual agents—without, of course, undercutting the importance of seeking out such works as well. The utility of potentially *distracting* terminology such as interracial sociability is, in this regard, its capacity to disrupt commonplace notions of genre and established literary histories, as well as to alter our everyday habits of reading and engagement with literary works.

If interracial sociability supplied the cargo and contours of detection's devices, moreover, I want to emphasize that both are bound to the textualization of labor relations. Narrative devices we now recognize in the clue-puzzle became mechanisms for shouldering an exceptionally cumbrous task: plotting something like the "generative labor trauma" that Richard Godden ascribes to white slaveholders in the American South (3–4), or registering what Alexandre Kojève has characterized, in his elucidations of Hegel's *Phenomenology of Spirit*, as "an existential impasse" experienced by the master (9). In the antebellum era, this psychic crisis was the master's parasitic enjoyment of the products of slave labor, which gave rise to "the unthinkable and productive episode during which the master both recognizes and represses the fact that his mastery is slave-made, he and his are blacks in whiteface" (Bull 227). The vicissitudes of production are not separate from sociability in the nineteenth and twentieth centuries. It is instead the texture of labor relations, I argue, and the fluctuating systems of race management on which they relied that are the structuring conditions for interracial sociability. Labor and class histories are no mere backdrop to literary investigation. Instead, they inevitably provide sites of interracial sociability that are implicated in the formal architecture of the fictions I examine.

To distinguish the ways that American authors experimented with the formal machinery we associate with literary detection, *Dreams for Dead Bodies* adopts an original methodology. As it reframes the history of detective fiction to emphasize the genre's early investment in questions of interracial sociability and economic interdependencies, this study detects generic concerns by way of a "crooked" genealogy. I propose migrating to meta- and marginal texts to historicize the formal conventions of a "formula" fiction. In this way, my work supplements previous studies by examining classical detective fiction as a genre that does something more than illuminate the disciplinary gaze of the state and the biopolitical dimensions of the law, or dramatize tensions inherent to the liberal ethos—ideas that have been powerfully advanced in works by Dennis Porter, D. A. Miller, Ronald Thomas, Karen Haltunnen, and Heather Worthington, among others.[8] I show that stylistic tactics and narrative strategies we associate with detective fiction migrated beyond generic precincts to theorize interracial dependency and sociability in peripheral and extrageneric contexts. While my recruitment of certain texts and authors regarded as "canonical" in other contexts may be regarded as presumptuous or predatory, my expectation is that this approach will yield a richer understanding of cross-fertilization in the literary landscape. For instance, the works of Pauline Hopkins (which Oxford and Rutgers University Press, among others, have reissued in recent years) are now standard fare in African American literary studies; (re)affiliating her serialized magazine fiction *Hagar's Daughter: A Story of Southern Caste Prejudice* (1901–2) with the popular detective genre may be perceived as a demotion of sorts. From the vantage point of this study, however, the appropriation of detection's devices by an author such as Hopkins underscores the significance of the detective genre to the whole of U.S. literary production at the turn of the century. My objective is to demonstrate that American literature has been and is (and American authors were and are) broadly engaged with the mechanisms of detective fiction. These mechanisms, which American authors used to capture the acceptable limits and prospects for interracial sociability over the course of the long nineteenth century, coalesced in a genre whose ostensible aim was, by the 1930s, to secure a satisfactory account of a dead body.

What a crooked genealogy demands, moreover, is an inquiry that is neither chronological nor anachronistic, but can account for those depictions of social relations that come into historical focus and formal precision no earlier than upon a second encounter. In the case of "temporal doubling," John Irwin has remarked, "the second act paradoxically appears to attain primacy while the first instance of an event (which can be understood as 'first' only after its repetition), becomes ancillary to subsequent iterations" (69). In retrospect, Irwin points out, an earlier fiction might be another's "textual echo rather than its antecedent" (*Doubling* 69). This is less epistemological tangle than a methodological proposition: that atemporal analysis is a crucial historiographic practice when it comes to tracing the lineage of the detective plot. Like the form of classical detective fiction, whose narrative clockwork depends precisely on two temporal frames and the practice of backward construction, genre history casts its shadow headlong *and* operates in hindsight. The clue-puzzle winds up its (second) story of investigation only once it has reassembled an earlier "story of the crime" that was, up to this point, always "absent but real" (Todorov 46). Along these circuitous lines, a tractable literary chronology supplies the interpretive force required to penetrate the surface of social relations and deliver an account of a past whose socioeconomic configurations are a very messy affair indeed. In other words, if we resist whatever teleological impulse certain brands of historicism foist on our sleeves, we better capture the dynamic social stakes of generic devices and the irregular contingencies and contexts that gave rise to detection's narrative-analytical tools.

For this reason, this study begins with an examination of Mark Twain's posthumously published, unfinished novel *No. 44, The Mysterious Stranger* (1897–1908). The other chapters of this study orbit around my analysis of this text, which is suffused with questions of temporal misalignment, cause and effect, and racial disguise, and follows its own mercurial chronology to accommodate the upheavals of an industrial age and the fragile forms of interracial sociability that it brought to the threshold of visibility. Chapter 1 identifies the serial charades, habits of visual indeterminacy, and always-suspect character of the sleuth-imposter in the turn-of-the-century dime novel as puzzle elements in Twain's novel, and shows how the text marshals detection's devices to grasp the dynamics of industrial life. I argue that No. 44, Twain's cosmic detective, borrows tactics from these dime-novel sleuths (who frequently appeared among the dramatis personae in "true to life" and fictionalized accounts of Pinkerton detectives and nineteenth-century labor disputes), and reimagines detective fiction's reparations of chronology to contend with late nineteenth-century anxieties about race, labor, and governance.

Chapters 2 and 3 draw back to the early nineteenth century and present detective fiction conventions as emerging from an antebellum literary culture, navigating questions of interracial dependency at a moment when ideas about race were in flux and the scope and effects of technology and industry shifted dramatically. In an era when the Nullification Crisis instigated by South Carolina's John Calhoun prompted President Andrew Jackson to announce that "America was not a compact of loosely bound states but an enduring union of people" and that "succession was equivalent to insurrection"(Reynolds 101–2), reconciling the body politic to some kind of order was not a simple task. I have touched on several of the principal issues above: appropriations of Indian lands and contentious efforts to extend the institution of slavery into these commandeered territories; a "free" and "white" workforce subjugated and absorbed by the new corporate industrial economy yet set apart from slave labor in the South on the basis of race; and, of course, a slaveocracy that championed liberty, banked on bound labor, was terrified of its own dissolution, and found itself at an impasse when faced with what Sharon Holland calls the "enslaved-now-freed person," the black emancipated subject (*Raising* 15).

Under such circumstances, strategies for narrative retrieval and reconstruction in proto-detective fictions functioned as an analogue for nation building, while the processes of narrative speculation and imaginative identification these fictions introduced provided a means of designating the acceptable parameters of difference within the body politic. Chapter 2 examines the role of narrative reconstruction in Edgar Allan Poe's "The Man That Was Used Up" (1839) and Nathaniel Hawthorne's "Mr. Higginbotham's Catastrophe" (1834). As the protagonists of these stories forge plausible accounts of cause and effect from narrative fragments, the perfect suturing they seek is stonewalled by galling eruptions of dissent. An inexorable breakdown in the system is not simply a secondary effect of an economy that relies on piecework or the ever-mounting apportionment of manufacturing tasks in commodity production. Instead, it signals irrepressible discord within the new republic and a market economy rife with internal conflict. Chapter 3 follows the painstaking ciphering, tactics of concealment, and acts of imaginative identification at the center of Edgar Allan Poe's treasure-hunting tale "The Gold Bug" (1843) and Robert Montgomery Bird's *Sheppard Lee: Written by Himself* (1836), a novel whose protagonist uses metempsychosis (the transmigration of the soul) to take up temporary residence in the bodies of a dandified city-dweller, a naive Quaker philanthropist, and a black slave, among others. In their movement between detached speculation and imaginative identification, between metonymy and metaphor, these texts contemplate the nature of interracial economic dependency as they eke out the fraught territory between enslavement and self-possession.

Moving to the late nineteenth century, Chapter 4 explores how authors continued to use elements of detective fiction to navigate possibilities for interracial sociability in a post-Reconstruction society confronting new forms of industrialization and racial competition. At the turn of the century, peripheral and provisional detective fictions emerged alongside new forms of economic geography fraught with racial tension: a South where the black legislative gains and white economic losses of Reconstruction were substantially rescinded; a fantasy postscript of rugged country called the American West; an urban landscape crowded with immigrants and by the new pandemonium of industrial life; and new regions abroad, as the Spanish-American War provided an opportunity for those who subscribed to the ideology of the "Lost Cause" to vindicate southern manhood by deploying their martial strength in service of the nation.

Chapter 4 examines narrative contiguity and temporal reconstruction in two texts that enter into "whoizzit" mode—scenarios in which individuals who claim distinct identities are revealed to be a single person whose criminal actions "hang together" "to constitute parts of the whole, which is the totality of a character's being-and-doing over time (synecdoche)" (Thompson and Thompson 55). The racial "passing" plots in Pauline Hopkins's serialized mystery *Hagar's Daughter: A Story of Southern Caste Prejudice* (1901–2) and William H. Holcombe's little-known *A Mystery of New Orleans: Solved by New Methods* (1890) advance forensic skepticism to contest a popular "romance of reunion" culture and the impermeable racial caste system that sustains it. *Hagar's Daughter* also amends detective fiction's standard task of backward construction through its conspicuous use of ellipsis; the narrative's hidden temporal center is the "absent but real" story of crime, which Hopkins uses to elucidate legislative fraud and fiscal hypocrisy and to discredit the acquisitive stance that drives the romantic reconciliation of the North and South.

The fifth chapter of this study turns to the golden era of detective fiction (1920s–1930s) and an unusual text: At once a work of black modernism created at the onset of the Great Depression and an exemplary work of classical detective fiction, Dr. Rudolph Fisher's *The Conjure-Man Dies: A Mystery Tale of Dark Harlem* (1932) is situated simultaneously at the center and the margins of the detective genre, as it synthesizes concerns explored on the genre's peripheries while consolidating a set of generic elements in a recognizable "genre text." At a moment when white-authored American detective fiction expressed broad interest in foreign persons and "exotic" accents, Fisher's delineation of the economic stakes of community formation is continuous with American authors' earlier use of detection's conventions to offer a sociology of race and labor. I argue that Fisher's classical detective novel doubles as sociological theory, bringing the effects of the Great Migration, efforts at urban uplift, and questions of economic empowerment for diverse black constituencies to the fore, but also anticipates the author's shift toward hard-boiled detective fiction in his final detective story, "John Archer's Nose."

In the conclusion to *Dreams for Dead Bodies*, I return to work of Chester Himes to address the advent of hard-boiled detective fiction, and to discuss the extent to which detective fiction's subgenres are resigned to the failed promise of an interracial industrial democracy. I close by considering the conceptual value of contemporary categories such as "ethnic detective fiction," given detective fiction's early investment in interrogating the limits of interracial sociability and economic interdependence.

The remainder of the introduction sketches the coordinates of this project, and elaborates on its arguments about the origins, history and cultural function of detective fiction in the United States. Taking as its counterintuitive starting point Arthur Conan Doyle's celebrated detective story "The Musgrave Ritual," whose origins I trace to Edgar Allan Poe's "The Gold Bug," the remainder of this introduction reframes the history of detective fiction to emphasize its early investment in questions of interracial sociability and to indicate how we might detect generic concerns by way of a "crooked" genealogy. I summarize the methodological approach that enables this interpretive shift from the center to the periphery to perform a sociology of genre. Finally, I continue to stress the significance of the puzzle element in detective fiction, as well as the collusion of the "rational" and the "fantastic" in the genre's narrative logic—an appraisal that not only emphasizes the importance of detective fiction for American literature, but also underscores the centrality of detective fiction to an American literary modernism.

"YOUR BUTLER APPEARS TO HAVE BEEN A VERY CLEVER MAN"

According to Dennis Porter, the genre of detective fiction comprises "deep ideological constants" and "surface ideological variables" (*Pursuit* 124–27), but detective fiction is exactly where superficialities and sureties are inter-reliant. In certain instances, some small feature of a text doubles as an abbreviation or model for the whole. The seemingly unassailable fourth-story apartment in Poe's "The Murders in the Rue Morgue" (1841), for example, with its windows nailed shut, its doors fastened securely, and every chimney "too narrow to admit the passage of a human being" (104), may be said to represent "in one simple architectural paradigm all of the insoluble conundrums and ingenious solutions of detective fiction" (Sweeney 1). That the Mmes. L'Espanaye should be slaughtered in such a place is inconceivable yet true; this law- and logic-defying paradox, this first among "locked room" puzzles, supplies a perfect metaphor for the genre's innate self-reflexivity and narrative closure (2). However, some imprecise impression, some small flaw might turn that reflection askew. For example, the gruesome decapitation of Madame L'Espanaye, who is found with "her throat so entirely cut that, upon an attempt to raise her, the head fell off" (Poe 100), finds its uncanny echo in the nail that ought to have secured her apartment window, only that the amateur sleuth Auguste Dupin finds "the head, with about a quarter of an inch of the shank, came off in my fingers" (111). And yet, when Dupin disparages the wisdom of the police prefect at the very end of the story, finding in it "no *stamen*": "It is all head and no body, like the pictures of the Goddess Laverna,—or, at best, all head and shoulders, like a codfish" (122), the stakes of the monstrous homicide and its elucidation are conspicuously altered. This insistent split in anatomy—what we might call Dupin's decapitation fixation—conjures a revolutionary violence, redirecting our attention to a critical subtext for the tale: those toppled by France's "National Razor."[9]

Another well-known argument of a narrative building block that functions as a small-scale edition of the whole can be found in Arthur Conan Doyle's "The Musgrave Ritual," a story in which Sherlock Holmes recollects his first major success as a consulting detective, and which is also the subject of a celebrated analysis by the literary critic Peter Brooks. In this story, Reginald Musgrave engages his old schoolmate to investigate the sudden disappearance of his butler, a wise guy and ladies' man named Brunton who possessed an unusual interest in the Musgrave family papers. Rachel Howells, the tempestuous Welsh maid and Brunton's spurned fiancée, has also bolted the Manor after the disappearance of her onetime suitor. To locate these suspicious characters, Holmes first devotes his attentions to the written record Brunton pocketed before he vanished. It is the Musgrave ritual, a transcript of a sort of call-and-response ceremony that has been recited as a perfunctory rite of passage for generations, in spite of the fact that it includes such suggestive topographical markers as the following:

"Where was the sun?"
"Over the oak."
"Where was the shadow?"
"Under the elm." (Doyle 614)

By charting the coordinates of this "catechism" on the Musgrave estate, Holmes deduces that the formula of this ritual script and its "absurd business," which, as Brooks points out, was "seen by the Musgraves simply to stand for the antiquity of their house and the continuity of their line," has an entirely different meaning (24). It comprises lines related to another long-forgotten plot: a scheme to safeguard the Stuarts' crown while Charles II remained in exile, and to restore it once the Stuarts again assumed the throne. And so the directives in "The Musgrave Ritual" guide Holmes to the spot on the estate where these temporary expatriates had been compelled to leave "many of their most precious possessions buried behind them," not the least of which were the crown jewels (Doyle 622). What is more, Holmes unearths the corpse of the missing Brunton, who, having grasped the design of this curious document, pilfered its contents and would have preceded Holmes in seizing the goods but for his asphyxiation in the remote cellar where the treasure was concealed. In his remarkable analysis of the case, Brooks explains that by taking "the apparently meaningless metaphor of the ritual" and "unpacking it as metonymy," Holmes not only solves the case but also mimics the activities of the mystery-reader (24). As Charles Rzepka summarizes, "Holmes physically re-enacts the process of mental re-enactment in which a reader gradually knits together into a coherent series an otherwise ambiguously related succession of narrated events" (*Detective Fiction* 24).

Brooks has designated this particular detective story an "allegory of plot" (26), a matter that is further emphasized, it is worth adding, by the fact that the story assumes the name of "The Musgrave Ritual," without recourse to the usual prefix "The adventure of"—a formal courtesy that Holmes, incidentally, affixes to *his* account of this affair when he recounts it *in* the story. The detective's delineations of the ritual on the Musgrave estate—what Brooks calls Holmes's "trigonometry in action" (24)—is a process that, on the one hand, recapitulates the movements of the obsequious and conniving Brunton and, before him, the "original plotmaker" who stashed the crown. On the other hand, Holmes's work is recapitulated in the practice of "plotting" that is often taken as the cardinal enterprise of classical detective fiction. In "The Musgrave Ritual," Holmes makes meaning and sense of a crime by telling its story, establishing a string of linked and temporally ordered signifiers from scraps of evidence (Hühn 454). What is remarkable about this particular story, however, is how plainly the record of the Musgrave ritual functions as a manual or a "collapsed metaphor" for the detective fiction formula (Brooks 27). But if this quantity is the genre in miniature, what precisely is the mechanism that connects the part to the whole? In an instance of self-similarity, it is not so simple to say which is the subsidiary and which is the principal, and if some small feature can be called self-reflexive because it replicates its frame of reference, it is no less true that the shape of the syntax can be swayed by the smallest unit of speech.

When Arthur Conan Doyle published "The Musgrave Ritual" in 1893, he was still basking in the phenomenal success of *The Adventures of Sher-*

lock Holmes (1892), a collection of twelve detective stories that had first appeared in serialized form in *The Strand* magazine. These works succeeded in establishing a detective fiction dominated by its puzzle element, and set a standard for detection stories that would follow it (Rzepka 119). The Scottish-born physician had, by this point, permanently abandoned the tedious routine of his not very successful medical practice for a literary career. His celebrity sleuth, who first appeared in *A Study in Scarlet* and *The Sign of the Four*, had graced the pages of *The Strand*; *Adventures* would sell over a quarter of a million copies in its first three years of publication; and Doyle was determined to devote himself to more serious-minded endeavors: his meticulously researched historical novels. Meanwhile, *The Strand*'s literary editor, Greenhough Smith, petitioned Doyle for another dozen tales. "The Musgrave Ritual" was one of this second series, which Doyle had only reluctantly agreed to produce. Feeling that Holmes impinged upon more important literary pursuits, the author first demanded the unheard of sum of £1,000 for the stories—and was only half-pleased when Smith took the bait (Miller 145). Doyle penned these quickly (rarely spending more than a week on any given Holmes story) and regarded revisions as "gratuitous and a waste of time" (qtd. in Miller 146).

But, like the crown of the Stuarts, the celebrated adventure of "The Musgrave Ritual" is itself a "relic which is of great intrinsic value" and one that turns out to be "of even greater importance as a historical curiosity" (Doyle 622), since Doyle's detective story retains certain traces of *its* historical precedent. Consider, for instance, that "The Musgrave Ritual" is unmistakably a variation on "The Gold Bug" (1843), a treasure-hunting tale by the American author Edgar Allan Poe. Orphaned in New England and reared by foster parents in the slaveholding South, Poe barely eked out a living from his inconstant employment as a writer and editor, though he adopted the persona of southern aristocrat and intellectual. Poe initially submitted the whole of "The Gold Bug," which he composed in 1842, for publication in *Graham's Magazine* for the sum of $52 (Mabbott in Poe, *Tales and Sketches* 803). The intermittently indigent author changed his mind, however, and requested its remittance from the magazine's editor, conspiring instead with Thomas Cottrell Clarke to print the tale as a two-part serial, complete with woodcut illustrations by Felix O. C. Darley, in an original enterprise, *The Stylus* (804). But when the April 5 issue of the *Dollar Newspaper* posted a story contest, the fate of "The Gold Bug" changed again. Poe's tale took first prize and was printed three times all told, each under the title, "The Gold-Bug. A Prize

Story. Written expressly for 'The Dollar Newspaper,' by Edgar A. Poe, Esq.; *And for which the First Premium of One Hundred Dollars was paid*": the first part was published in the paper's June 21 issue; the second part appeared in the June 28 issue alongside a reprint of the first; and both halves appeared again in the July 12 supplement (804, 806).[10] Though "The Gold Bug" appeared in the midst of Poe's three tales of ratiocination, "The Murders in the Rue Morgue" (1841), "The Mystery of Marie Rogêt" (1842), and "The Purloined Letter" (1844), this text is not typically designated detective fiction. Nevertheless, it is occasionally cited as its close kin.[11] Like "The Musgrave Ritual," Poe's story recounts a quest for stashed treasure with a genius at the helm and an uncommon map, and yet their ends (and even their beginnings) are distressingly at odds.

The great mistake of the Musgraves is to take a historic document for a "text with no meaning other than its consecration as ritual," or as a signifier without a signified, never imagining its place in some larger design (Brooks 24). By contrast, the act of ascribing some literal value to the bit of "dirty foolscap" and a "gold bug" Poe's eccentric protagonist William Legrand and his steward, the manumitted slave Jupiter, discover on the South Carolina beach is, to be frank, a question of making something out of nothing (Poe 200). Legrand feverishly pursues a pirate's plunder in a rough, contested wilderness that may be said to reflect his particular madness. Rumors of Captain Kidd's buried hoard and the prospect of it "still *remaining* entombed" prompt him to search for a cipher: "the body to my imagined instrument," Legrand explains (221, 220). His search for the "letter between the stamp and the signature" (Poe 220)—or what we might call the "lexicon" and the "grammar" of the story that unfolds—entails code cracking, treasure hunting, and some dodgy traffic with the dead. He also make inquiries of an anonymous, elderly Negro woman, one of the island's ancient inhabitants, which brings to mind Toni Morrison's observation that "through the use of Africanism, Poe meditates on place as a means of containing the fear of borderlessness and trespass, but also as a means of releasing and exploring the desire for a limitless empty frontier" (51). Furthermore, Legrand browbeats Jupiter to do much of the legwork to bring off his treasure hunt. After Legrand locates a skull (likely furnished by a member of Kidd's retinue) affixed upon the seventh limb of an enormous tulip tree, he turns over the thankless task of tree climbing to Jupiter, whom he has mercilessly tyrannized and thoroughly rattled. Still, the venture temporarily collapses because Jupiter drops the gold bug through the right eye of the "death's-head," rather than the left eye as Legrand instructs him. Only after Legrand hauls Jupiter over the coals and transposes his fifty-foot "bee line" from the tree to account for the servant's uncoordinated act do they uncover a treasure (226).

To reprise, "The Musgrave Ritual" has been taken for an "allegory of plot" and a "guide to plotting" (Brooks 26), but it also has a key: Reginald Musgrave himself, who is acquainted with the stature of every ancestral tree on the estate—only he lacks the spark of acuity necessary to decipher the remarkable document at his disposal. And yet his forename reeks of nobility; he is "a scion of one of the very oldest families in the kingdom" (Doyle 607). Indeed, Musgrave even resembles the family's land in western Sussex—or at least Holmes reports that "something of his birth-place seemed to cling to the man" and inevitably associates his former schoolmate with "gray archways and mullioned windows and all the venerable wreckage of a feudal keep" (607). Holmes's adventure never takes him beyond the long-fixed boundaries of the Musgrave estate—and what he retrieves for the Musgraves is something already in their own possession. By contrast, Poe's fallen aristocrat Legrand is a tenderfoot on South Carolina's Sullivan Island, having made his home there only after his fortunes plummeted. This terrestrial penitentiary off the coast of Charleston once served as a pesthouse for newly arrived slaves in the eighteenth century—it has been called the "Ellis Island of Black Americans" (Peter Wood, qtd. in Peeples 36). The Seminole leader Osceola was incarcerated there at the end of his life, and Poe himself spent a year stationed at its chief citadel, Fort Moultrie. Since neither the annals nor the terrain of this island prison is at his easy disposal, Legrand must coax forth intelligence and forge misleading compacts across race lines to gain possession of a prize to which he has no prior claim. And whereas "The Musgrave Ritual" deftly separates the prerogatives of the staff from the gentry, in "The Gold Bug," the task of treasure hunting is distinguished by an uneasy sociability between the manumitted man and his one-time master. In this case, the conditions of interracial dependency produce a debilitating "species of temporary paralysis" before its dividends become apparent (Poe 217).

Two points of comparison are especially worthy of note. First, Brunton, the servant and interloper who got hold of the Musgrave ritual and "tore its secret out of it and lost his life in the venture" (623) has, as his counterpart in "The Gold Bug," the manumitted slave Jupiter, whom we might speculate Doyle perceived as a threatening intelligence. "Your butler appears to me to have been a very clever man, and to have had a clearer insight than ten generations of his masters," Holmes remarks to Reginald Musgrave (614).

Jupiter, too, might be said to attempt to conceal a resolution of his own. How else are we to explain the servant's "dogged air of deliberation" when he muzzles Wolf—whose nervous yelps might be ascribed to the several skeletons in near vicinity (212)?[12] What of the "grave chuckle" the manumitted man admits while undertaking that first entirely ineffectual excavation? or of his "desperate pertinacity" when he inquires, "Aint dis here my left eye for sartain?" while deliberately singling out his right eye (211–12)?

Second, while "The Musgrave Ritual" concludes on a mostly reverential note, with little concern squandered on the grisly death of the manservant Brunton, the end to "The Gold Bug" has a more sinister timbre. Waylaid maid aside, Brooks writes that Holmes's decoding of the Musgrave ritual illuminates "a vast temporal, historical recess, another story, the history of regicide and restoration" that can, at last, be laid to rest (26). By contrast, Legrand imagines that human carcasses in the pit are proof enough that the pirate "may have thought it expedient to remove all participants in his secret," and is content to leave the matter open-ended. "Perhaps a couple of blows with a mattock were sufficient, while his coadjutors were busy in the pit," Legrand speculates, or "perhaps it required a dozen," but neither an account of the victims of Captain Kidd's "dreadful atrocity" nor an account of the origins of Kidd's fortune will be anything but unfinished business: "Who shall tell?" (229). As for the blurred lines between the dead and the living, the subject of Daniel Hoffman's uneasy deliberations on "The Gold Bug" ("By how thin a thread hang the lives of the Doctor and old Jup?" [128]), these are the source of a narrative that is ill at ease, its level edges sanded uneven. If the word and the world can be placed in perfect symmetry, it is more perfect still, it seems, to introduce a margin of error; we might say this is the difference between a Rubik's Cube and one of Escher's impossible objects.

If we cross the Atlantic again and return to "The Musgrave Ritual," though, it is precisely the story of the waylaid maid that does not permit itself to be told. Everything in "The Gold Bug" that might be construed as irrational, everything out of the ordinary, everything "outré" is compressed in the character of Rachel Howells: The "excitable Welsh temperament" and "sharp touch of brain-fever" tally, perhaps, with Legrand's "aberration of mind" (206), that "madness" in which Poe's narrator only later perceives "certain indications of method" (213); like the Negro Jupiter, who stalks Legrand, she wanders about fitfully "like a black-eyed shadow of her former self" (609); and it is also briefly hinted that Brunton has wronged her, "wronged her, perhaps far more than we suspected," possibly rousing a "smouldering fire of vengeance" that led the forsaken woman to make that concealed cellar in the Musgrave estate her former lover's "sepulchre" (623).[13] By contrast, Poe lays out stakes that signal the sources of a distinctly American detective story: the fraught territory between enslavement and self-possession, between a black servant (a manumitted man) and a white man (his former master)— the historical ground in which such plots could, and would, be plotted.

"A RELIC WHICH IS OF GREAT INTRINSIC VALUE, BUT OF EVEN GREATER IMPORTANCE AS A HISTORICAL CURIOSITY"

Reviewing Holmes's triumph in "The Musgrave Ritual" in light of "The Gold Bug" opens up possibilities for identifying the ancestry of detective fiction's devices and obtaining a sociology of the genre, though, admittedly, we are looking awry.[14] To regard "The Musgrave Ritual" in light of "The Gold Bug," we must adopt an analytical parallax and then reverse it, first taking Poe's tale as the textual echo rather than its antecedent, then re-inspecting Doyle's story with an appreciation that this unlikely successor from across the Pond is patterned after Poe's tale. For this awkward posture we are rewarded, however, since we both secure the perhaps unexpected association of "The Gold Bug" with the detective tale *and* underscore the neglected contents of Doyle's text—that is, its sacrificial scapegoat(s).[15] "The Musgrave Ritual" is, of course, simply one instance of the literary larceny at which Doyle exhibited such talent: "A Scandal in Bohemia" relies on an ingenious theft and creative reprisal of the intersubjective triad from Poe's "The Purloined Letter," for example; and Tonga, the "blood-thirsty imp" from the Andaman Isles in *The Sign of Four* echoes aspects of the culprit of "The Murders in the Rue Morgue" (234). In the particular case of "The Musgrave Ritual," where Doyle poaches a prototype from "the original plot-maker" and re-presents the recovery of plundered treasure in what is often regarded a detective text par excellence, he is, to borrow a phrase from Barbara Johnson, committing a "precise repetition of the act of robbery he is undoing" (189). The interpretive utility of acknowledging a kinship, however anomalous, between the two stories, is that it highlights the relevance of Poe's antebellum story to what was then the just emergent genre of detective fiction, a genre whose margins "The Gold Bug" might be said to occupy. What would it mean to take this alleged lineage (Doyle's implicit designation of Poe as the "original plotmaker") not as petty larceny, but as instructions for an analysis that can apprehend the historical phenomena that engendered detective fiction's devices?

As much as a cluster of attributes or a literary blueprint, genre consists of prearranged configurations of looking. If we train habituated eyes on "The Gold Bug," we find something like the circumstances under which the genre's mechanisms materialized, and the psychosocial landscape of its primal catechism. Here, a collapsed essay on imaginative identification and the manipulation of codes and clues (exercises in metaphor and metonymy, two mechanisms that would together come to constitute the core of classical detective fiction's clue-puzzle) appear as if they were devised to capture and cross-examine a precise reality: an asymmetrical, precarious and sometimes violent allocation of agency between a former slave and his former master, each of whom sees his solvency and self-possession hang upon a shaky promise of sociability between them. In his lunacy (albeit an invented one— and then again, perhaps it is not), Legrand lashes out at the ex-slave to perch closer to a death's-head, instructs him to decode it, and does not exactly disavow the deadly logic of production entailed in this suspended skull. It is in this face-off between the two men, and in Jupiter's and Legrand's adversarial interpretations of Captain Kidd's directives, that we discover the economic and interracial overtones of those narrative devices that would find their way into detective stories like "The Musgrave Ritual."

Of course, to maintain that literary genres are saturated with sociological facts is not a simple task; these sorts of assertions say little about how the former imbibed the latter (Bennett 90). Certainly what is historical is something more than the expressed content of the text, but even should certain features of the text smack of some historical circumstance, we are pressed to explain the "micro connections between sociological speculations and literary structural realignments" (Davis 6). As Franco Moretti insists, "An extra-literary phenomenon is never more or less important as a possible 'object' or 'content' of a text, but because of its impact on systems of evaluation and, therewith, on rhetorical strategies" (*Signs* 20). Poe's cultivation of the detective fiction's narrative-analytical tools in a text such as "The Gold Bug" roots the genre in an antebellum literary culture engrossed by slavery's fiscal operations. And to the extent that a story like "The Gold Bug" makes from detection's devices an aperture to anatomize both the provenance and the effects of racial knowledge in the antebellum economy, it belongs to the historiography of its own time. Poe's tale is, like the Musgrave ritual—a "crumpled piece of paper" that Holmes tenderly exhumes from his "curious collection" of odds and artifacts—one of these "relics" that have a history "so much so that they are history" (Doyle 622).

"THE BODY TO MY IMAGINED INSTRUMENT"

Dreams for Dead Bodies contends that there is a meaningful dialogue between literary works at the far reaches of the detective fiction genre and those at its center, a critical discursivity that we might compare to what Rita Felski dubs the "sociability" of a text: "its embedding in numerous networks and its reliance on multiple mediators," which "is not an attrition, diminution, or co-option of its agency, but the very precondition of it" ("Context" 589). In such cases as "The Gold Bug," the detective genre is, at best, an adjectival property of the text rather than substantive; the story has a detective "accent" and a syntax that is mutually intelligible, if not interchangeable, with "The Musgrave Ritual," its approximate heir. If, as Felski has suggested, "works of art can function as vehicles of knowing as well as objects to be known" (587), I contend that texts on the periphery (and the authors who create them) "know" something of the detective genre. Works on the margins that fruitfully incorporate detection's devices underscore the expediency of its mechanisms for illuminating patterns of interracial sociability and economic interdependencies. My interest in texts like "The Gold Bug," then, is not to confer upon them membership in the detective genre, but to emphasize that their value is located in their peripheral or provisional relation to a detective fiction canon. This relative distance facilitates an analytical approach by increments, one that takes as its starting point Dupin's proviso in "Rue Morgue": "To look at a star by glances—to view it in a sidelong way" permits us "to behold the star distinctly" (105). The effort of indirection produces a "more refined capacity for comprehension," explains Dupin, than what we might reap from a "scrutiny too sustained, too concentrated, or too direct" (105–6).

Accordingly, this study relies on a distinct methodology that emphasizes the heuristic value of examining "proto-," "peripheral," or "marginal" genre texts beside detective fictions' more celebrated catalog. I am interested in contemplating how *both* standard catalogs and shifting criteria for "legitimate" genre membership function as conceptual blocks to thinking about the social of occasion of genre. I return to the idea of an anomalous kinship—not simply an alternative to, antidote for, or respite from the detective genre's settled genealogy, nor a restoration of its "illegitimate" offspring and disowned brats, which anyhow seem to be slogging back to the fold and begging for attention. Instead, an anomalous association (signaled by some similarity in the armature of the text) supplies rather different conditions for reading than detective fictions long set up in polite society.[16] Such texts enable interpretive movement from center to margin and back again: from "popular" to "literary" texts, and from the peripheries to the core of generic discourse.

Works at the limits of the detective genre, ones that lack the refuge of its systemization and the urgency of its narrative aims (to crack a homicide, for example, or recover a lost object), shed light on the social stakes of particular generic mechanisms. They are in an unusual position to elucidate concerns of the genre that might be obscured or repressed in key genre texts. "The Gold Bug" is exactly this type of peripheral or proto-detective text, by which I mean it rehearses certain tactics that would become regularly associated with classical detective fiction, and it does so to address the psychodynamics of interracial dependency in the antebellum nation. The persistence of peripheral texts as generic expectations took more definite shape and, even after the genre established a more fixed range of conventions in the last decade of nineteenth century, indicates that detective fiction remained a significant source of narrative tactics for authors like Mark Twain and Pauline Hopkins, who were interested in exploring structures of interracial dependency and the potential for interracial sociability.

The sideways methodology I have suggested might seem at odds with the clear-cut rules and ideological intransigency we often associate with formula fiction. Franco Moretti, detective fiction's keenest and most cynical (not to say fanatical) detractor, classifies the genre according to the "perennial fixity of the [its] syntax," designating its framework "a cultural—not a syntactic—fact," a mechanism of indoctrination and an ideological assembly line (141). Moretti consigns mass culture to a category of ideological apparatus that, as Louis Althusser puts it, creates "a subjected being, one who submits to a higher authority, and is therefore stripped of all freedom except that of freely accepting his submission" (169). In detective fiction, therefore, "what one 'is' is completely irrelevant, because the only thing that counts is what the social syntax compels one to do" (Moretti 141). Focusing on the detective figure as arbiter of the law, many critics concur that detective fiction is a genre of "conformism" (Porter 220) consisting of discursive practices that affirm the power of the state to engage in targeted surveillance, naturalize disciplinary tactics, and internalize the law in the consciousness of its audience-subjects. In the figure of the detective, we find an individual whose "moral legitimacy" is never open to question (Porter 125). Holmes's investigations simply "blind readers" to perforations in what Foucault calls the "carceral texture of society" (Kayman 240, Foucault 304). Moretti, too, locates the detective in a bourgeois milieu, calling him "the figure of the state in the guise of 'night watchman'" who intervenes to transform "a situation of semantic ambiguity" created by a criminal into a narratable event (146). The detective's "single intelligence" and "scientific system" are exercised only to ward off any challenge to the system and not used in service of that system's advancement (155).

Is this case so easily made? The "syntactic" analysis to which Moretti refers deals with constitutive relations in a set of texts and apparently transfers from text to social terrain intact; "semantic" approaches to genre, by contrast, group texts according to their common traits (or building blocks), and neither of these categories functions independently (Altman 95–99). On the contrary, semantic signals set the stage for syntactic expectations, and any individual utterance, as I have suggested above, has the potential to rewrite the rules of the "grammatical" game (Altman 95–99, Schatz 20). Even if we were to restrict a genre whose chief operation is "deautomatizing signification and making things 'strange'" (Hühn 455) to some set of inflexible rules specially designed to conciliate and compel the reader "to conceive or imagine his or her lived relationship to transpersonal realities such as the social structure or the collective logic of History" (Jameson, *Political* 30), we might occasionally admit regions of textual unease; places where the narrative is fractured, labored, or overwrought; and plotlines whose resolution is egregiously implausible and artificial. In this way, the narrative parts and configuration of each detective text can be said to paraphrase or parse its cognition of the social, the structure and style together indicating *something more complex* than the "imaginary relationship of individuals to their real conditions of existence" the text proposes through its final elucidation of the puzzle element (Althusser 162).[17]

My emphasis throughout is that the genre's mechanisms do not easily and never necessarily resolve into the thrill-producing machine that regales its passive spectator. Charles Rzepka's distinction between detec*tive* fiction and the subgenre of detec*tion* is especially helpful in this regard: while the former merely features a detective among its characters, the latter is less invested in majestic displays of inductive prowess and stresses instead "the incitement and prolonging of inductive activity in the reader" (17). The formal apparatus of this last class of texts, which cultivate engagement in the reader, is the focus of this study. Detection invites its audience to construct speculative accounts to clear up the crime; it expects its reader will trace the parameters of plausible fact before capitulating in the last part to some far-fetched solution or likely card it has long kept up its sleeve. The point worth pressing is that if detectives are not merely heroic protagonists or model readers but the reader's intellectual adversaries, each instance of detective fiction enacts its proper theory of ideology, not by way of a staunch interpellation but by recruiting its reader to a delicate process of negotiations, coaxing them to concur with its particular image of reality. Rather than representing an exemplary exercise in "lowbrow" literary diversion, the techniques mobilized to dismantle the enigma within the detective text constitute a correspondence course in social logic. Accordingly, the reader's pleasure is precisely her appreciation of the formal means by which the social ends are achieved, at least "when the genre's literary self-awareness forms the starting point of analysis" (Pyrhönen, "Criticism" 45).

Additionally, while I am particularly attuned to the inventory of detection's narrative tools I describe in the first part of the introduction, in this study, I also attempt to honor recent developments in the study of the detective genre that have resuscitated critical attention to the infusion of gothic, supernatural, pseudoscientific, and surreal elements in detective fictions, despite the genre's long-standing associations with Enlightenment rationalism and scientific inquiry.[18] Indeed, spiritualisms and pseudoscientific epistemologies turn up continually in detective fictions of the nineteenth century, where they regularly facilitate criminal investigations in conjunction with forensic technologies. Dime-novels embroidered the larger-than-life adventures and shape-shifting talents of detectives rather than their intellectual rigor, and though the sleuths in detective fictions like Metta Fulla Victor's *The Dead Letter* (1866) and Anna Katherine Green's *The Leavenworth Case* (1878) valiantly stalked their culprits, their authors' formulated a set of competencies for the detective that included, in addition to intermittent bouts of inference and deduction, surveillance, psychic intuition, eavesdropping, hypnotism, chirography, and pure luck. Ron Thomas points out, furthermore, that those detective stories that fantasized new mechanisms of social control and dreamed up a formidable forensic science occasionally predicted methods that the police would come to adopt long before the technology necessary to implement those methods existed (4). In some of the stories I examine, the fantastic and forensic fuse in the production of racial knowledge and the ratiocinative mixes with the "irrational" in depictions of production. From the transmigration of the soul in Robert M. Bird's *Sheppard Lee, Written by Himself* to invisible strikebreakers in Mark Twain's *No. 44, The Mysterious Stranger*; from hypnosis, mesmerism, and psychic intelligence in William H. Holcombe's *A Mystery of New Orleans* to Frimbo, the Ivy League graduate who proposes he can change patterns of cause and effect in Rudolph Fisher's *The Conjure-Man Dies*, magical and pseudoscientific elements raise questions about individual will and autonomy, blurring boundaries between self and other, and so play a vital role in scripting interracial sociability and dependency in peripheral detective fictions. Rather than portray these magical phenomena as antagonistic to the genre's inner workings, I explicate whether and how these eccentric modes of detection furnish complementary varieties of analytical engagement.

The prolonged development of detective fiction, whose first appearances most critics date to the 1840s but whose golden era appeared nearly a century later, can also help to clarify how we might productively relate this analysis of the detective genre to the cultural strands of an American modernity, whose most celebrated literary products appeared in the first few decades of the twentieth century. Whether we describe literary modernism as the "aesthetic articulation" of the peculiar and ethnically individuated experience of modernity (characterized especially by the unprecedented scale of industrialization and the advent of technologies that agitated experiences of sound, space, and time) (Scandura and Thurston 11); as a stylistic engagement with anxieties about governance, mass democratization, and the drama of modern political consent (Chu 28–29); or as an art that reflects the "historically original problem" of the metropolis that cannot sustain self-sufficiency, which struggles to imagine a "self-subsisting totality" but remains nevertheless "radically incomplete" (Jameson, "Modernism" 58), it is certainly the case that peripheral detective fictions, as I have presented them here, engage with modernist aesthetics.[19]

The genre's modernist impulse becomes even clearer, however, if we reframe our inventory of genre elements to emphasize detection fiction's attention to failures of ocular omniscience and articulations of temporal displacement, the volatility of identity, the partial or limited efficacy of contiguity and metonymy as instruments of perception, and the elision of analeptic and proleptic possibilities that the narrative has itself generated. Its range of formal devices is as attuned to the discontinuities and degradations of modernity as the prospects for psychic coherence and political recognition it offers. In examining peripheral and "canonical" detection fictions in this way, as "self-reflexive textual enigma[s]," literary works "about readability and intelligibility" (Pyrhönen, "Criticism" 54), rather than as quasi-realist depictions of a rational, mechanistic world, *Dreams for Dead Bodies* demonstrates that American authors crafted and exploited detection's devices to map configurations of interracial sociability. Accordingly, I argue not only that the emergence of detective fiction is entangled with the inception of a cultural modernity in the United States, but also that this cultural modernity was grounded in an antebellum configuration of social and economic forces whose psychodynamic terms persisted long afterward. In other words, detection texts take us to an American modernity that corresponds to the long nineteenth century.

Undertaking any critical project about detective fiction no doubt brings to mind the work of the detective himself. As Felski and others have noted, the critic and the detective share the impulse to "track down and bring to light obscured patterns of causality" by way of an investigation designed to reconstruct past events ("Suspicious" 225). More than simply identifying the genius of literary texts, or highlighting the structural faults and superficial imperfections of each in its own right, the critic longs to ascertain how historical forces find their way into the literary text, whether texts battle contexts, or give birth to them (225). My own part in this project is, admittedly, not so different from the literary sleuth, though I might add that most of the works I investigate demand close scrutiny and, given their use of self-referential discourse, continually reflect on the engagement cultivated by the reading process and the ideological force of writing itself—which is to say, they are interested in the kind of detecting that texts and their readers can do together.

CHAPTER I

Reverse Type

The plots of God are perfect. The Universe is a plot of God.

—EDGAR ALLAN POE, *EUREKA*

In the "Murders in the Rue Morgue," for instance, where is the ingenuity of unraveling a web which you (the author) have woven for the express purpose of unraveling?

—EDGAR ALLAN POE, AUGUST 9, 1846,
LETTER TO PHILIP PENDLETON COOKE

Mark Twain's *Mysterious Stranger* manuscripts are a set of three distinct, unfinished novels Twain composed between 1897 and 1908.[1] The third text in this series of anarchic partial fictions on moral responsibility is *No. 44, The Mysterious Stranger* (1902–8). With its references to the growth of the industrial workplace and a burgeoning labor movement that would attempt to sever workers' "workaday selves" from those selves who must be afforded time for "what we will," the third of the *Mysterious Stranger* manuscripts takes modernity as its subject. It does not flinch from awful spectacles of human oppression and violence, some of them in a workplace Twain ought to have known well: a printer's shop. For many critics, *No. 44*'s printer's shop and its troublesome crew evoke Twain's well-known financial debacle as a "venture capitalist" for the failed Paige Compositor. Coupled with the Panic of 1893, this ill-fated investment would surely have ruined Twain, had not Standard Oil president H. H. Rogers bailed him out with financial advice. Twain's dream compositor was to have eliminated many of the most difficult jobs of the printer's shop, along with the labor force that performed those jobs. Little wonder, then, that one critic has called the novel Twain's "wish-dream of a supernatural shop" as well as a thesis on "threatened disintegration of personality" in the industrial age (Michelson, *Printer's Devil* 210, 220). Following Forrest Robinson's unelaborated but nevertheless intriguing claim that we can describe the *Mysterious Stranger* manuscripts as "a succession of approaches to the question of human enslavement that are no sooner tried than they are found to be unworkable" (*Bad Faith* 233), this chapter treats *No. 44, The Mysterious Stranger* as an exploration of historical contingency and free will. More specifically, this chapter argues that Twain's manuscript experiments with the conventions of adventure detective stories to contend with interracial tensions and anxieties about governance and consent in an industrial age.

By the early twentieth century, Twain had already tinkered with the popular detective novel in its various nineteenth-century incarnations. Michael Denning has observed that "almost uniquely, Twain bridged the gap between the audiences of the cultivated novel and the dime novel" (208). In works such as "The Stolen White Elephant" (1882, written in 1878) and the unfinished "Simon Wheeler, Detective" (written in 1877) there are the bizarre disguises, fiendish villains, and improbable settings that regularly appeared in adventure detective stories. According to Grant Underwood, Twain recognized that in acceptable reproductions of the genre "disbelief [must] not merely be suspended: it had to be forcibly wrenched from one's consciousness" (61). By the late nineteenth century, however, as the author increasingly abandoned realistic fiction for a blend of pessimistic parable and fantasy that was cynical when it was not utterly dystopic, Twain's attitude toward detective fiction changed drastically. For Twain, whose later writings fixated on "God and the devil, time and space, the origins and status of knowledge, free will, determinism, and what he took to be the inherent perversity of human nature," human history remained a major puzzle (Robinson, "Dreams" 454). In this period of his life, argues Underwood, Twain became "a structuralist in his relationship to the detective story," inventing narratives "in which the mystery is the condition of man and the detective is a god" (210). In *No. 44, The Mysterious Stranger* Twain turned to detective fiction to decipher the cosmos.

The magnificent ambitions of *No. 44, The Mysterious Stranger* make way for Twain's reckless expedition into the American racial imaginary and the irregular tempo of industrial life in the nineteenth century. For this reason, it supplies an expedient point of entry into the ways that texts on the margins of the genre cultivated detective fiction's devices for their own purposes. Twain's "cosmic" detection could not resemble the concise puzzle mystery that advances "the myth of the necessary chain," taking as its only proper solution a single, unassailable "step-by-step path of logico-temporal reconstruction" (Porter 41). If we were to situate *No. 44, The Mysterious Stranger* within a linear genealogy of the detective genre, we might suspend it loosely between an Edgar Allan Poe and an Agatha Christie. But Twain's is a text that brooks no literary lineage in linear terms. It is anything but automated. In this way, *No. 44, The Mysterious Stranger* resembles dime novel detective fiction of the late nineteenth and early twentieth centuries, as ideologically ambivalent a form as the proto-puzzle mystery, with its narrative intemperance and extravagant digressions. With a sprawling chronology, supernatural spectacles, and dramatic shifts in narrative scale and speed, Twain's manuscript wrestles to capture confrontations between labor and industry at the turn of the twentieth century—confrontations whose stakes were further complicated, it must be noted, by racial and ethnic tensions, as corporate bosses calculatingly recruited and manipulated immigrants, all-black convict labor, and African American "scabs" to undermine fragile forms of interracial cooperation and to quash possibilities for collective action. Twain's narrative strains to accommodate the multiple illogics of the shop. Taking the detective genre's tools as its own, it dramatizes how labor impinges on textuality while precipitating racial difference. It struggles to articulate individual and corporate resistance to a new ideology of industrial democracy, which would empower the working classes to think of themselves as consensual participants in a democratized realm of production.

Additionally, in *No. 44, The Mysterious Stranger*, Twain produces a character well suited to negotiate the commotions of an industrial age. While this third *Mysterious Stranger* manuscript shares a desultory outlook with its two predecessors, the "strangers" of the first two manuscripts, Bruce Michelson argues, were "not sufficiently strange, not temperamentally free enough for the task of ultimate escape, from death, mutability, nature, cultural oppression, human stupidity—*and* from confinements of an individual self trying to figure all this out" (*Printer's Devil* 219). By contrast, the mysterious figure in the third manuscript is so strange as to almost defy definition.[2] Twain's formidable rogue, who can crack labor conspiracies, sweet-talk shop bosses, and sometimes act as informant, is charged, in *No. 44, The Mysterious Stranger*, with the task of navigating industrial life.

"No. 44," the mysterious stranger of Twain's third manuscript, bears a strong resemblance to the dime-novel detective. A sharp wit, a physical powerhouse, and a master at disguise, the dime-novel detective is indeed an invention of the industrial world and among the chief personae in many popular literary depictions of American labor disputes. He is not merely the well-known Pinkerton agent who infiltrates the working classes on the company's payroll, but also appears as a superhuman being whose materializations in the midst of workingmen radically reconfigures conflict and reshuffles every piece of plot. An imposter given over to serial charades, Twain's No. 44 belongs to this breed of "avenger detectives" that populated dime novels. Most strikingly, No. 44's antics in the industrial shop bring into view the infrastructure of racial competition that fractures collective action and paralyzes workers. No. 44 is an escape artist, a whiz at impersonation, a master of disguise and doublespeak, and thus of what Henry Louis Gates calls "signifyin(g)": a "shadowing" or "(re)naming" of (white) terms, since signifyin(g) is a critique of "(white) meaning" or even the "meaning of meaning" (47). Twain uses No. 44 for illustration and exegesis and as a creature of extravagant antics, not the least of which include a vexatious, interminable recital on the Jew's harp, a minstrel routine as "Mr. Bones," and a syrupy Stephen Foster medley. No. 44 also makes direct textual interventions with an extraordinary typesetter's joke and a "Procession of the Dead" that is the manuscript's finale.

Importantly, dime novels supplied an alternative to nineteenth-century realism or the quasi-realist prose of the evolving "clue-puzzle" mystery. They invited allegorical readings insofar as they relied on "magical transformations to compensate for the impossibility of imagining 'realistic' actions by powerful agents" (Denning 74). In *No. 44, The Mysterious Stranger*, however, Twain amplifies and intensifies the allegorical dimensions of the dime novel to access affective and textual realms that constitute another order of prose fiction: an "expressive" realism. The dime novel's digressive, roundabout plot is externalized in Twain's impossible chronology of nested chronotopes, which leaps forward in time to register the degradations of the industrial workplace and to dramatize the dilemma of modern political consent. Besides these textual cogitations, Twain mobilizes No. 44's symptoms of "strangeness" to elucidate the obstacles to interracial sociability in the shop: racial and ethnic antagonisms fostered by industrial life. Finally, No. 44's assorted escapades end by denaturing narrative itself and, in doing so, demolish the industrial landscape that narrative buttresses. In Twain's manuscript, this textual rebuttal to the crises of industrialism and modern political consent involves nothing less than the annihilation of whiteness.

"WRITTEN RECORDS CAN LIE"

No. 44, The Mysterious Stranger approaches the dislocations of industrial modernity and the problem of modern political consent from the distant past. Twain dramatizes the pull of modernity through the temporal-spatial arrangements of his text, which takes literary history as a portable scaffold, and shifts with increasing velocity through various chronotopic registers to alight temporarily on the bildungsroman. But modernity is a centripetal force, and the narrative lurches ever forward, in search of a form befitting the scale and speed of the observable world. There is an industrial landscape at the center of the manuscript, and Twain turns to the dime novel and its remarkable adventurer detective in search of coordinates for social cohesion that have nowhere to emerge but from this world of work.

The novel's mise-en-scène is a heterochrony, countryside irregularly punctuated by temporal gradations and moving, like a set of nested, open-ended parentheses or an inverted telescope, from the "Dark Ages" to the turn of the twentieth century. The opening date is 1490, some years shy of the Reformation. "Some even set it away back centuries upon centuries and said that by the mental and spiritual clock it was still the Age of Faith in Austria," the narrator remarks, and the evolutionary line is held fast by the devout and dim-witted, so that it "promised to remain so forever" (221). There is no world, it seems, beyond Austria. What lies outside is an extraterrestrial abyss. Inland, however, in the midst of this comatose countryside, is "our village" Eseldorf, mired "in the middle of that sleep, being in the middle of Austria. It drowsed in peace in the deep privacy of a hilly and woodsy solitude where news from the world hardly ever came to disturb its dreams, and was infinitely content" (221).

Just past this pastoral haven for spiritual imbeciles and intellectual buffoons (saddled with a village name that is at best impolitic) there is a "mouldering castle" where the primary action takes place (229). Here the medieval scenery deteriorates and the Middle Ages fall from view. To be sure there is a magician, a real snake-oil salesman who commands awe from all corners of the crumbling castle, but the business of the castle lies elsewhere, in the operation of a printer's shop managed by a master craftsman (Master Stein) and staffed by various journeymen and apprentices. We have already leaped into the modern era, yet the inner workings of the shop turn on another anachronism: the very latest developments in movable type. And in addition to an up-to-date printing apparatus, there is what would have been for Mark Twain a fundamental shift in nineteenth-century corporate arrangements: the labor union. Into the midst of this industrialized workplace riddled with labor altercations and union disputes the Mysterious Stranger descends. He deals in the "goods" of the future: frilled collars and tobacco, cornpone and "coon" shows, not to mention news of Christian Science and the Russo-Japanese War—as if the unforeseen (and unpremeditated?) fruits of Western civilization were unsystematically distilled onto a pallet of break bulk cargo, or as Twain subtitled his manuscript, "Being an Ancient Tale found in a jug and freely translated from the jug."

But we are getting ahead of ourselves. In *No. 44, The Mysterious Stranger* "our village" Eseldorf is a setting the narrator August quickly abandons in favor of the castle, with its vocational promise, even though the publishing industry is censured by a Church dead set against the effects of mass production, which lead to "the cheapening of books and the indiscriminate dissemination of knowledge" (230). In spite of the Church, the printer's shop goes about its business unobstructed. What's more, its separate jurisdiction is also a temporal distinction, and its shifting coordinates in time and space are essentially a chronotopical shift. The chronotope, as described by Mikhail Bakhtin, is a temporal-spatial frame that delimits narrative genre and whose partial purpose is to parse the development of the novel as an apparatus of an expanding human cognizance of time (Tihanov 157). A chronotope is not to be differentiated from the human dispositions it informs, nor do subjects exist independent of its temporal-spatial arrangements. Life in Eseldorf, with its "mental and spiritual clock" stopped, is a bit like what Bakhtin designates "adventure time," a genre in which time never enters as a dimension of human life or is suppressed entirely (157). No part of the world is jeopardized by the prospect of annihilation by time; then too, there is no chance the universe will be "remade, changed or created anew" (Bakhtin, *Dialogic Imagination*,110). This seems right, and yet if we enter the drowsy village, with its "little homesteads nested among orchards and shade-trees," there are signs of something closer to Bakhtin's "folkloric chronotope": a world that takes its tempos from the seasons; harmonious, cohesive; a place where private duties have not yet been ripped from public life (Tihanov 160).

Of course, the very idea of the "folkloric" drips with sentiment, and pastoral Eseldorf could scarcely emerge from Twain's gauntlet of irony intact. Twain's stance is most evident in the depiction of Father Adolf, the self-aggrandizing Aesop who throttles any folk contrariness with his insidious susurrations and violent threats. August, Twain's narrator and clearly some kind of dupe, remembers with pleasure that holy man about his seasonal duties: the funerals, where Father Adolf lost no opportunity to bestow "a staggering whack in the face" upon any disrespectful "oaf"; various suicides, over which Father Adolf officiated with morbid efficiency to ensure "for himself, that the stake was driven through the body in a right and permanent and workmanlike way"; and that familiar "procession through the village in plague-time" when Father Adolf traded blessings for cash (225). The politicking of this tyrant alone punctures the pastoral idyll. Nevertheless, it is not obvious why Twain would see fit to bludgeon his readers (or, if he never intended to publish the work, the paper it was written on) with yet another uninspired essay in human hypocrisy, religious or otherwise. Could it be he means to show us Austria and the Dark Ages as something other than a blackboard for his arithmetic on the moral frailty of the human race? August's nostalgic reminiscences about the annual festivities of terror are simply naive or, if we admit him capable of sarcasm, are of a piece with Adolf's contention that in Eseldorf, "when you are in politics you are in the wasp's nest with a short shirt-tail, as the saying is" (223). If it is naïveté plain and simple, Twain is doling out what Frederic Jameson calls the "irony of the intellectual," which profits from the "incongruities of a peasant language and a peasant ignorance" (*Seeds of Time* 113). Otherwise we are anchored in a different kind of irony, irony as "some ultimate life stance and moral and political metaphysic" that orders reality (115).

But consider that Adolf's routine brutality is the work of a bureaucrat, that his power pales before the influence of the briefly mentioned prince Rosenfeld, who owns the land to whom the livelihood of each villager is ultimately mortgaged, and whose occasional visits dazzle the townspeople "as if the lord of the world had arrived, and had brought all the glories of its kingdoms along" (222). After their quick stopovers in Eseldorf, this local deity and his retinue leave "a calm behind which was like the deep sleep which follows an orgy" (222), perhaps because the event necessitated some frantic bacchanalia orchestrated to entertain the prince. Is this uncontested service and submission the actual target of Twain's derision? And, if so, is Father Adolf the inconsequential straw man for a duplicitous irony? Then we are dealing with Twain the vindictive exhibitionist, cutting up on every side with his "burlesque circus of authority's violence" (Lewis 69), the Twain whose narrator (August) stakes his memoirs on a familiar paradox: "Written records can lie"—though Twain gives that screw a third turn—"unless they are set down by a priest" (227). So Father Adolf supervises the villagers' dream life, and if the villagers accept his demands, it is permission issued in the dark and mediated by blind irony, permeated with a "forbidden laughter" that repudiates all. But Prince Rosenfeld, the master of their wakeful state, cannot be deposed by the "no" of "yes and no." To overthrow the despotism of the "folkloric," Twain must provide a total shift in narrative habits: a crescendo of human consciousness that reaches its height in the castle perched on a precipice just opposite the outskirts of the village.

"The chronotope is the place where the knots of narrative are tied and untied," writes Bakhtin, and in the castle the dullness and duration of the folkloric dissolves into a makeshift modernity. It is crude space initially, but one that pushes forward with a technological enthusiasm that culminates in the printer's shop, where men rapidly assembly plates of movable type. Later, the machinery runs with dizzying precision of its own accord. These technological developments are not simply the materials of modernity (and even industrial life, as I have suggested above). The mechanized industry, mass production, and alienated labor force are accompanied by temporal changes that irretrievably alter human experience. This experience, especially as it is narrated by August (lately of Eseldorf and still the lowest lackey in the print shop), also belongs to a chronotope, the bildungsroman. The task of the bildungsroman is to reconcile the buoyant, unfixable dynamism of modernity with modernity's representation; as a result, this chronotope is precisely a formal contradiction (Moretti, *Bildungsroman* 6). Its subject is youth, the "specific material sign" of modernity's energetic turmoil (6). But the force of youth must be checked, bracketed, abbreviated in the bildungsroman, since "only by curbing its intrinsically boundless dynamism, only by agreeing to betray to a certain extent its very essence, only thus, it seems, can modernity be *represented*" (6). Its objective, then, is the "interiorization of contradiction" (10), an enactment of social compromise and the truncation of the subject in its definitive sense. Franco Moretti asks,

How is it possible to convince the modern—"free"—individual to willingly limit his freedom? Precisely, first of all, through marriage—*in* marriage: when two people ascribe to one another such value as to accept being "bound" by it. It has been observed that from the late eighteenth century on, marriage becomes the model for a new type of *social contract*: one no longer sealed by forces located outside of the individual (such as status), but founded on a sense of "individual obligation." (22)

In *No. 44, The Mysterious Stranger* it is August who inhabits the newly unruly space of modern life and struggles to interiorize its anarchic course. As Schiller wrote to Goethe of Wilhelm Meister, "Everything takes place around him, but not *because of him*" (qtd. in Moretti 20). Like Elizabeth Bennett, August must refit himself to the world and apprehend it anew, and each act of conversation becomes an effort to absorb the world's activity (Moretti 50). Like both, August has the fortune to be "polyparadigmatic": each event of the novel takes its sense (should it have sense) from the "the internal harmony that it helps to bind or crack" when it crosses the threshold of his existence (42). But the bildungsroman requires contractual consent as its final stabilizing force. This union between the individual and the social order is a "reciprocal 'consent' which finds in the double 'I do' of the wedding ritual an unsurpassed symbolic condensation" (22).

Given the centrality of this "pact" between the individual and the social order, and the wedding vows that serve as its narrative emblem, August's fanciful betrothal to Marget Regen (the niece of Master Stein) toward the end of the manuscript is not out of place. It is neither a saccharine, sigh-inducing interlude nor evidence of an old man's self-indulgent digressions, as some critics have contended. Instead, it is a narrative checkpoint whose presence registers a genuine concern about modernity and the prospect of its representation. And in this intuitive litmus test, Twain's gauge of the odds for reciprocal consent in the midst of magic technology, modernity fails miserably. Marget is dreaming when she bestows her affections on August, a youth who never charmed her in her waking moments. Meanwhile August plays the Svengali with Marget's sleepwalking self, a dream creature who goes by the name "Lisbet von Armin." August is, in essence, a paramour whose object of affection is an insensible puppet, hardly capable in her dream state of accepting his proposal—and yet Marget swoons before his miasmic enticement "in obedience to suggestion" and recites her wedding vows (349). Theirs is a shotgun wedding, for when August discovers Marget in a dream state, he begins "to volley the necessary 'suggestions' into her head as fast as I could load and fire" until at last she makes "obeisance to imaginary altar and priest" and recites the marriage oath (349).

The problem of consent is at the center of the text: here, it is consent coaxed from an insensate; in Eseldorf, it is the villagers' blithe assent to the will of a commonplace tyrant, and so on. Consent in its uglier arrangements comes up again and again in Twain's *Mysterious Stranger* manuscripts. It is perhaps best embodied by the narrator of *The Chronicles of Satan*, who joins in the merciless stoning of an innocent—as if his willingness to join the slaughter is the only measure of his inclusion in the race. This capitulation to another's bidding illustrates Twain's dark proposition in *What is Man?* that humans are "moved, directed, commanded, by *exterior* influences—*solely*," a remark that implies, according to Forrest Robinson, "that humans are exempt, as machines are, from moral responsibility" ("Dreams" 455). Indeed, as Robinson points out, Twain is quick to exonerate any affiliate of the species, which "*originates* nothing, himself—not even an opinion, not even a thought" (qtd. in Robinson 455). And yet in Twain's writings, the least of these creatures, however morally inept, is not exempt from shame. Twain's young narrator, for instance, purports to have acted against his will: "All were throwing stones and each was watching his neighbor, and if I had not done as the others did it would have been noticed and spoken of" (150). Or there is the case of Twain's well-known tongue-tied introduction to President Grant, after which ensued "an awkward pause, a dreary pause, a horrible pause," during which Twain "merely wanted to resign," and then, extraordinarily, voiced the single thought that came to mind: "Mr. President, I—I am embarrassed. Are you?" (*Following the Equator* pt. 2, 16).

If man is, in Twain's appraisal, the fall guy, the easy mark who stoops to take direction, shame is the complement to his pathetic show of acquiescence or habitual deference to the mob. For the individual easily swayed, however, shame seems also to be the outward show of some invariable nature, the means by which one takes exception to one's own deference, or rather one's own failure to resign, one's failure to *not* consent. To put this more briefly, shame signals the self obliterated by consent, a consent that pollutes like vile slopped onto a canvas—though (as we shall see) there is in Twain's writings also the faint suggestion that some other part, like the person of Dorian Gray, escapes undisfigured.

And truly the business of consent annihilates the subject. Classical bildungsroman is predicated upon digesting social contradictions. It requires incorporating every subjective or partial view of events (*sjuzhet*) into a totalizing, unassailable narrative system (*fabula*) (Moretti 70). Narrative restructuration brings with it the end of subjectivity, is even synonymous with the deterioration of the individual. Still the bildungsroman, which is, like classical detective fiction, "always and intimately linked to the solution of a mystery" (70), achieves its ends by regulating the narrative's historic-diachronic dimension: "Not only are there no 'meaningless' events; there can now be meaning only *through* events" (6). *No. 44, The Mysterious Stranger*, as I have indicated above, gestures at this obligatory order but is plagued by temporal seizures, and the fits and starts in its historic-diachronic dimensions suggest why *sjuzhet* and *fabula* are perpetually misaligned. Twain draws on the parameters of the bildungsroman to give reality order and modernity an image of itself, but *No. 44, The Mysterious Stranger* is finally bereft of the act of genuine consent, that signature on the social contract embodied by the wedding oath.

In fact, Twain's subjects of modern life are no less spellbound than their chronotopical predecessors. But what is the thing that obstructs the possibility of narrative order, leaving subjectivity intact but listless, lumbering forth like the living dead, embarrassed? What spoils consent, averting the marriage of *sjuzhet* and *fabula*, and thus turns time out of joint? Moretti warns us that "capitalist rationality cannot generate *Bildung*," and in *No. 44, The Mysterious Stranger* an industrial order ushers in its own obligatory propositions: bodies mechanized in the mirror image of machines; labor and capital divided by their interests; capitalist acquisition, that never-exhausted engine, ubiquitous. This world of work, foreign to Elizabeth Bennett and Wilhelm Meister but wholly defining August's existence, baffles time.[3]

Having steered the text through heterogeneous configurations of landscape that arise in the Middle Ages and wind up in the twentieth century, Twain finds fiction no longer has a form to fit to, or at least the bildungsroman will not do. But *No. 44, The Mysterious Stranger* proceeds as capitalism wrenches interiority from its ordinary forms. The bildungsroman, that thing which adapts *sjuzhet* to *fabula*, which quashes everything that is irregular, perverse, and indigestible in narrative to its guileless contours, which diminishes mystery to the mundane, is superseded at last by its lowbrow kin: the dime novel. And it is in this world of permanent disorientation and temporal bedlam, a sort of hinterlands where the past "cannot stop having been and returns in the future as it has been transformed by the future itself" (Torlasco 62), that a stranger arrives.

"WHAT A DEVIL TO WORK THE BOY WAS!"

The trickster figure "No. 44" parades through Twain's novel as a far-fetched crossbreed engendered by the industrial age. He is a monstrous jumble of man, machine, slave, dog, and witch; Katzeyammer remarks, "Every time a person puts his finger on you you're not there" (Twain 39). But what is to be made of the fact that No. 44, whose supernatural alterity allows him to view the sum of human history and to sample the spoils of empire, bears the markers of a distinctly African American brand of servitude and, later, African American strategies of cultural resistance? With his serial charades, mercurial moods, and inexplicable talents, No. 44 is an unknown quantity. First tractable then tyrannical, humble then brazen, he raises the hackles of the workingmen and wins over Master Stein. Working in castle and then the print shop, No. 44 mediates the regimes of sociability and the fragile alliances among workers as well as the ethics of management. Codified in misgivings, suspicions, and outright hostilities, moreover, No. 44's "strangeness" elucidates an infrastructure of racial competition nurtured in industrial life. His ambivalent entrenchment in the manuscript is instrumental, in other words, since Twain uses No. 44 to decipher and then detonate the industrial landscape.

First, there is No. 44's numeric brand—a stamp of industrial make— the sort of designation that treats factory men as indistinguishable from the machinery they operate. What is of additional interest, however, is the conjecture in Twain's text that the number signifies he is a convict of some kind. This rumor immediately surfaces, and when he does not "seize the opportunity to testify for himself," kicks off "a low buzz [that] skimmed along down the table, whose burden was, 'That silence was a confession—the chap's a Jail-Bird'" (Twain 239). These suspicions of incarceration, given the presence of a "jail-number," speak to another industrial enterprise that Douglas Blackmon has incisively called "slavery by another name." The criminalization of black life in the South, beginning with Reconstruction and continuing far into the next century, supplied corporations with a workforce that had been captured and sold into involuntary and uncompensated servitude. In short, there is an articulation of the black subject through the consolidation of factory and penal signifiers.

Second, the rapport this pariah cultivates with the master of the shop adheres very distinctly to a model encouraged by the then prominent Booker T. Washington, who admonished black workers not to exert themselves seeking union membership. Washington insisted instead that blacks could surmount trade unions by appealing to employers and personalizing associations with management rather than struggling for union affiliation. Washington also attempted to persuade management of the black worker's superiority, noting that he was "not inclined to trade unionism" and "almost a stranger to strife, lock-outs and labor wars; [he is] labor that is law-abiding, peaceable, teachable . . . labor that has never been tempted to follow the red flag of anarchy" (qtd. in Foner, *Black Worker* 79). This brand of servile quietism characterizes No. 44's filial engagement with Heinrich Stein, who generously exploits the stranger while the other workers call for his eviction from the premises. No. 44 fends for himself, endures the merciless bullying of the other men, and doggedly completes demanding menial tasks, exhibiting the kind of excessive investment in his work that matches Washington's depictions of his own labor in the best-selling 1901 memoir *Up from Slavery*. Just as Washington diligently sweeps the recitation room at the Hampton Institute—the de facto entrance exam that will take him "up from slavery" and into economic solvency, No. 44 dutifully, almost farcically, applies himself to the tasks at hand.[4]

The protagonist August observes, "What a devil to work the boy was! The earliest person up found him at it by lantern-light, the latest person up found him still at it long past midnight. It was the heaviest manual labor, but if he was ever tired it was not perceptible. He always moved with energy, and seemed to find a high joy in putting forth his strange and enduring strength" (245). August's appreciation of No. 44's robotic, incessant labor dehumanizes the new arrival: No. 44 is taken for a workhorse and an unceasing mechanized apparatus. To the extent that his exertions have a diabolical cast, he is the sorcerer's apprentice (and actually the magician Balthasar takes credit for his superhuman achievements); he is an apparition of what Freud calls the uncanny, when "a symbol takes over the full functions of the things it symbolizes" ("Uncanny" 244); and he is sometimes forced to eat out of the dog's bowl. Again, we have the substance of neoslavery and all its degradations couched beneath pretensions to patriarchal benevolence, only here No. 44 faces added indignities from the other workers, who are vastly insulted at the prospect of taking him as their fellow. In fact, they decide to go on strike when the master elevates No. 44 to apprenticeship, a position he is accorded based on merit.

This brings us to a third example of the way that No. 44's labor doubles as an indicator of race: he is designated a "scab," or strikebreaker, at a historical moment when the terms "scab" and "Negro"—or more likely "nigger"— were used virtually synonymously (Foner, *Black Worker* 74). The rhetoric that annexed the stigma of the strikebreaker to the racial identity of African Americans was widespread, and efficiently circulated in the case of the American Federation of Labor (AFL). Facing reports of discrimination in 1897, the AFL reaffirmed its nondiscrimination policies, insisting that "it welcomes to its ranks all labor, without regard to creed, color, sex, race, or nationality," yet in practice the organization not only fully supported Jim Crow policies, but also strategized to build unions that served the purposes of white skilled craft workers and were unresponsive to semiskilled workers, immigrants, women, and blacks (qtd. in Foner, *Labor Movement* 347). Ultimately, in 1901, the Federation's executive council issued a statement exculpating itself for the dearth of black union members, claiming that "the colored workers have allowed themselves to be used with too frequent telling effect by their employers as to injure the cause and interests of themselves, as well as of white workers" (qtd. in Foner 352). Unions represented blacks and immigrants as "natural" strikebreakers, even though there was substantial evidence that the blacks and immigrants white employers imported to break strikes were rarely aware they were being used for such purposes, and generally sided with the strikers when they discovered the existence of a labor dispute (352). Moreover, unions kept membership out of the reach of black workers, systematically excluding them from craft unions by charging exorbitant initiation fees, requiring licenses they were not in a position to obtain, refusing them apprenticeships, and so on (349). Crucially, their methods (which supplemented other strategies designed to prevent black males from enjoying the benefits of full citizenship, such as the poll tax and grandfather clause) carefully elided accusations of discrimination, submerging racial hostilities in bureaucratic technicalities that effectively consigned African Americans to poverty wages in most industries.

Shunned, delinquent, sycophant, scab: these are the symptoms of "strangeness" with which Twain sketches interracial sociability in the shop. I am not suggesting that in *No. 44, The Mysterious Stranger* race is depicted as a proxy for class—or even that Twain's character *is* black, but that race is configured, or made implicit, in aspects of economic life—something like Toni Morrison's idea of a "a subtext" that is not part of "the surface text's expressed intentions" but "still attempts to register" it (Morrison 66). Here, race is an economic expression, a set of signifiers that coalesce around an identity, and an unspoken condition that brings meaning and sense to the labor crisis at hand. When his companionship with No. 44 is exposed, August is laid bare by the disgust of his colleagues, who address him with "the most capable and eloquent expression of derision that human beings have ever invented" (263). The highest insult in the printer's shop is the elusive expression "B-A": "bottle-assed," or in the Oxford English Dictionary "bottled-arsed," printer's slang that refers to type that is "wider at one end than the other." August is dismayed by the slur, at least enough to corroborate this particular smear on his character: "I was girl-boy enough to cry about it, which delighted the men beyond belief, and they rubbed their hands and shrieked with delight" (263). His sissified bawling over this "unprintable name" and its anatomical implications seems extravagant for a son of Eseldorf, whose residents are perpetually the butt of a joke, yet August finds it a tremendous humiliation, confessing it "shamed me as few things have done since" (263). To affix the dishonor of association with No. 44 to August's body is to liken the "girl-boy" to the denigrated subject of neoslavery, forging a link where, as Kathryn Stockton puts it, "the sign of anality flashes along the track of blacks' economic burdens" (32).

Organizing these racial signifiers around the entity No. 44, Twain uncovers the interlocking illogics of the shop that cultivate discord and mortgage individual interests in the process. The workers "insulted and afflicted him [No. 44] in every way they could think of—and did it far more for the master's sake than for his own. It was their purpose to provoke a retort out of 44, then they would thrash him. But they failed, and considered the day lost" (Twain 264). Their attempt to induce an angry reply from No. 44 is not something to marvel at; clearly it approximates those racist encounters in which the victim is compelled to insult his oppressor, thereby legitimating his or her own violent repression. What is of interest is the men's sense that this ruse is an offering to Stein, performed "for the master's sake." According to August, the worker's revenge reverses the stranglehold; he observes that Stein "was privately boiling over them; but he had to swallow his wrath" (265). The implication seems to be that in order to keep his men from striking, the master is himself struck dumb: "He must see nothing, hear nothing, of these wickednesses" or his ruin is imminent, but is it not the case that his failure to object to this hazing is the mark of a mercenary complicity? Or that the workers' efforts to lead No. 44 "a dog's life all the forenoon" (264) exemplify their own dogged devotion to the master, and a supplement to Stein's guise of liberality that would prove No. 44 unworthy of it?

In the print shop, August makes the much-badgered No. 44 his pet, wordlessly commanding the new drudge to perform unfamiliar tasks with perfect composure and, to the trained eye, without direction. August authors each telepathic memorandum that instructs 44 to handle printer's type; nevertheless, it is with some awe that August observes the novice "did it like an old hand!" (256). August is the operating manual from which 44 obtains his instructions, but the precision with which the apprentice executes each command is a wonder to behold. And No. 44's imitative faculty overshoots the mark, easily outstripping August at his own game and the rest of the workers as well when they take him for an "old apprentice, a refugee flying from a hard master" (257). In a predictably medieval approach to resolving their differences, the men in the print shop elect Adam Binks the shop's "inquisitor" and authorize him to administer a test to 44. Binks bombards 44 with difficult questions, but to no avail: "He wasn't competent to examine 44; 44 took him out of his depth on every language and art and science, and if erudition had been water he would have drowned" (258). August is first delighted by the mechanical skill of his human instrument; then the instrument outdoes its artist, and it becomes clear that August's assistance was merely lip service. No. 44 takes on the role of the inquisitor, becomes the protagonist of the print shop and transforms the plot and, in doing so, assumes the place of the dime-novel detective.

"PRINTER'S-DEVIL"

In the puzzle mystery, what the detective discerns strips the world of artifice, and offers an unornamented image in its place. From among the bits and pieces of evidence before him the detective finds the fixtures of a false scenario and, pursuing this false front to its inventor, uncovers a criminal and the details of a crime. Deceit is abolished, and "the story of the crime" is delivered in this second "story of the investigation," while the first story (which tells "what really happened") replaces the sham world the criminal concocted with a world that is cogent and perfectly intelligible (Todorov 45–46). There is no such "double inscription" in the dime novel. Here, no feat of mental prestidigitation or cognitive flourish transfigures reality, turning it honest. Instead, *in the very act of emerging from the fray*, the dime-novel detective denatures the landscape the text has set before us and reports the truth. But are these not both, to borrow the terms of the printer, forms of narrative "retraction"? The clue-puzzle and dime-novel detective fiction reel in the world to cast it out it again; both guarantee that the proverbial low tide will show us who has been swimming naked. What must be emphasized about dime-novel detective fiction, however, is that the plot need not turn on the evidence but, on the contrary, may be transformed by the person of the detective who is hidden in the text: "He can be anyone; anyone can turn out to be the detective in disguise" (Denning 147). The individual whom

Denning calls the "proletarian" detective is not up to his elbows in locked rooms and ratiocination (148). This detective deals instead in disguise; his disguise and its revelation are forces that drive the plot.

Dime novels were a form of inexpensive mass-audience entertainment pioneered by the Beadle and Adams Company in the 1860s. While early dime novels, like *Malaeska, the Indian Wife of the White Hunter* (1860), featured romantic frontier stories, by the 1880s and 1890s their subject matter gravitated toward crime and detectives, and they frequently incorporated class narratives and industrial settings. Dime novels quickly cooked up a hero distinct from the classical detective and his less cerebral twentieth-century successors (the hard-boiled sleuth, who very infrequently cracks a case with a burst of ingenuity, more often elbowing his way through the muck of a city stinking with corruption; and the procedural detective, up to his elbows in forensic data). This new hero of the dime novel was the avenger detective, an archetype of detective fiction distinguished by his penchant for vigilante justice, his totally implausible talent with disguises—some would call him an "American Vicdoq"—and his "uncanny method" with its near "extrasensory perception" (Hoppenstand 3, Cox 2). The classical detective and the avenger detective are men of very different species; to tell one from the other is no more difficult, Gary Hoppenstand notes, than discerning "the difference between the pathfinder, who picked and selected his clues, and the steamroller, which, like a juggernaut, propelled over clues and criminal alike" (136).

The adventures of the avenger detective are characterized by supernatural contact, narrow escapes, and protracted chases, all moderated by his moral purity. Typically the sleuth plays cat-and-mouse with the criminal and his or her equally felonious associates. For instance, the dime-novel detective King Brady (1882–98), who had not yet attained all those traits associated with the avenger detective, nevertheless belonged to a fictional cosmos that held the detective hero in high regard, as a *"superior* person" and spotless character (Hoppenstand 5). He bumps into supernatural beings in books like *The Haunted Churchyard*, where Brady, who "to a certain extent believed in ghosts" (10), is tugged by a gliding apparition with a "small, white and shapely hand" that leads him to a killer (32). In another series, the renowned Old Sleuth (1885–1905)—expertly assisted by Badger the Wall Street detective and the lady detective Maggie Everett—lures criminals to their doom. His successes are rather surprising, given his nearly monosyllabic exchanges with suspects and witnesses, and his utterly mystifying series of undercover getups. These include apparently foolproof disguises as criminals; the crooks themselves are often in disguise as well, or, by a stroke of ineffectual brilliance, they try to bluff Old Sleuth, costuming themselves as undercover police agents who have infiltrated their own gang! Sleuth's fellow detectives wonder at his prowess, speculating that he possesses "supernatural powers," or, in more extreme expressions of awe, that he "may be in league with the devil" (140). And Mr. Burton, the freelance detective of Metta Fuller Victor's popular detective fiction *The Dead Letter* (1867), must be classed with the avenger detectives: he is a master of chirography, a man of infinite patience, and the father of the child clairvoyant Lenore, who conveniently supplies new leads should Burton be temporarily flummoxed as to the villain's whereabouts. He humbly explains,

> Malice and revenge have followed me in a hundred disguises—six times I have escaped poisoned food prepared for me; several times, infernal machines, packed to resemble elegant presents, have been sent to me; thrice I have turned upon the assassin, whose arm was raised to strike— but I have come unscathed out of all danger, to quietly pursue the path to which a vivid sense of duty calls me. (Victor 250)

Dime novel avengers included the likes of *Manfred, the Ventriloquist Detective, Gypsy Frank, the Long Trail Detective,* and *Monte-Cristo Ben, the Every-Ready Detective.* Mark Twain's No. 44 belongs in the company of these indestructible bodies, with their superhuman strength, aptitude for disguise, and skill at impersonation.

The exploits of No. 44 are indeed a magic show in print. He is an escape artist of the highest caliber, repeatedly breaking free from fetters and cells (326). He chats with cats and other animals, "each in his own tongue, and 44 answering in the language of each" (312). This regular Agaton Sax even fakes his own death—a sort of spontaneous combustion with a "core of dazzling white fire" (309) and a pile of ashes, such that all believe he is consumed by "supernatural flames summoned unlawfully from hell" (311). And certainly he is fluent in the condition of man. He takes almost every opportunity to harangue upon the incompetence and hypocrisy of mankind, indelicately taking August as his audience. But it is his superb imitation of a printer's devil that is most remarkable, because No. 44 employs his genius at disguise to gain access to the shop and the activities of Stein's employees.

In this way, Twain casts No. 44 in a part frequently played by dime-novel and professional detectives alike: the undercover agent whose subterfuge supplies entry to a world of industrial intrigue. In fiction and in life, detectives were thoroughly embroiled in the turn-of-the-century struggles between workers and capital. Men affiliated with the Pinkerton Detective Agency infiltrated the workforce on behalf of industrialists or the state, and received plenty of bad publicity for their involvement in strikebreaking and union-busting, not to mention their alleged accountability for the bloodshed at the Homestead steel plant. Members of Pinkerton's staff were widely perceived (and in some cases represented themselves as) proxies of the industrial capitalist system who ensured production would proceed without delay (Reilly 159). While they were certainly not "neutral observers," Pinkerton's agents and the employees of other private detective agencies were, however, embedded among the labor force. They "smoked, drank, and chatted" with other workers and had opportunities to witness and report on their grievances (Lichtenstein 67). Similarly, in Master Stein's print shop, sociability is forged and alliances take shape when Twain's No. 44 poses first as a novice, then as an "old hand." When No. 44 plays telepathist, August's introspections are involuntarily broadcast and the grievances of the miners made transparent. His intimate access to the shop floor and its denizens exposes every workingman's quarrel with management, even as he inserts himself among their ranks.

The private detective's ambivalent entrenchment was explicitly treated in the dime novel, whose detective often infiltrated the working classes. This was habitually true in novelistic accounts of the sensational case of the clandestine and purportedly criminal organization the Molly Maguires, which had ended with the execution of nineteen men in 1878 and 1879. Early fictional accounts sidelined the Molly Maguires, treating them as mere foils to the honest, law-abiding mechanics from the Pennsylvania coalfields that faced undeserved harassment. Soon afterward, however, popular serials set their sights on an antagonist for the Molly Maguires. The detective, an expert at dissimulation whose false front might mask a mechanic hero or a corporate spy, could play that role (Denning 122). Detectives in these novels took their cues from the real-life Pinkerton agent named James McParland (alias James McKenna), who wormed his way into the confidence of Pennsylvanian coal miners in order to procure sufficient evidence to sentence the nineteen men to their deaths. This use of the detective radically rearranged fictionalized accounts of encounters with the Molly Maguires. The dime-novel detective needed to be as talented at subterfuge as his shape-shifting adversaries, the Molly Maguires, who were variously depicted as monopolist patsies, a gang of criminal thugs, or the "vengeful arm of the miners" (138).

In serials and dime novels, the Molly Maguires constitute a "multi-accentual sign": a capacious signifier whose bearing is ever indeterminate (Denning 138). This was also true in life, since it was an all-purpose label for any organization capitalists like coal magnate Franklin B. Gowen found unpalatable. Pinkerton's *The Molly Maguires and the Detectives* (1877), which was published months before McParland's exploits were made public, already describes the Molly Maguires as a "dark-lantern, murderous-minded fraternity" whose reign of terror and murderous schemes are the equal of "those performed by the KuKlux and similar political combinations in the Southern states" (15–16). Of course, Gowen's interests in regulating his employees extended beyond policing the Molly Maguires. In fact, he more or less invited McParland to instigate the kind of uprising that would justify a crackdown on all the miners, not just the Molly Maguires. These all-purpose villains provided opportunities for the detective to exercise his talents at disguise. McParland, however, was of an equally dubious disposition; he was an emissary of an outside agency and a de facto employee of Franklin Gowen. In his case, the man who embodied the "lineaments of a mechanic hero" was for all practical purposes also an undercover agent and a strikebreaker (Denning 122). By the same token, the disposition of the undercover fictional detective could turn on a dime. No less than the Molly Maguires, he constituted a multiaccentual sign. The detective hero of dime novels inevitably walked a tightrope between unions and bosses, which explains how the protagonist of Burt L. Standish's *Dick Merriwell, Mediator; or, The Strike at the Plum Valley Mine* (1911) could identify men at work in the mines as "the meshing cogs of the human machine," challenge company policies about wages and work, hide in the shadows to "obtain any information whatever about the strikers' plans," and finally discover that the men on strike are the honest dupes of the disguised villain George Clafin, whose "name was execrated throughout the labor world of the West as a traitor to the cause," all within the span of a few pages (8, 9, 12).

Whereas dime novels once dramatized the daily hardships of ordinary coalminers, they shifted the spotlight to the undercover detective among them—and to the success of his successive disguises, as he insinuated his way into the shop. This fixation with the extraordinary masks and super-human talents of an avenger detective invited allegorical readings of dime novels, insofar as they relied on "magical transformations to compensate the impossibility of imagining 'realistic' actions by powerful agents" (Denning 74). Still, to depoliticize this turn to fantasy simplifies the work of dime-novel detection, which imbues the everyday degradations of the workplace with a magical potential that lurks just below the surface of things. Merging a quasi-realist mode with fantasy and revelation, dime-novel detection retroactively casts its quasi-realist contents into question. Given the detective's genius at disguise, we are often far from a final disambiguation, and all the while guaranteed that a gauntlet will replace an impasse; only then will social cohesion prevail. If the dime-novel detective "can be anyone; anyone can turn out to be the detective in disguise" (Denning 147), what is first recognizable is temporarily out of joint. The world of production is warped because our hero inhabits it, defamiliarized because he is an unseen stranger in our midst. In this way, the mundane becomes part of an allegory-in-waiting. It demands scrutiny and foreshadows its own disfiguration.

In this same vein, Twain's prevaricating narrative calls for a strategy of second-guessing. What are the motives, means, and makeup of his mysterious stranger? Skulking in that indeterminate terrain that splits insiders from outsiders and union allies from corporate goons, No. 44 radiates contrariety. More than mediating between the gripes and grumbles of the workingmen and the soft coercions of the boss, No. 44 becomes a textual device, a wrench in the engine of narrative that promises to disrupt it. By swapping alliances in the midst of shop conflict, moreover, this multiaccented figure can recriminate collective action and then support it. He is fluent in every form of shoptalk and loyal to none. What was in Twain hesitation and ambivalence about the effects of industry on the condition of man is in No. 44 wholesome duplicity, for his supernatural exploits, like those of the dime-novel detective, will certainly rewrite the stakes of the standoff between labor and capital and introduce forms of conciliations unimaginable from the shop floor.

Before No. 44 subjects the workers in Master Stein's shop to the most terrible of his awesome talents, he appears to be a mere strikebreaker, and one whom the men can crack:

> They knew the master couldn't send the lad away. It would break his sword and degrade him from his guild, for he could prove no offence against the apprentice. If he did not send 44 away work would stand still, he would fail to complete his costly printing-contract and be ruined.

So the men were happy; the master was their meat, as they expressed it, no matter which move he made, and he had but the two. (Twain 266)

One of the many ironies lost on August is that the workers' chauvinisms do not operate in their own economic interests. The effect of his comic ignorance is that he paints the master, Heinrich Stein, as the victim of the workers' folly, a man with integrity destined for financial ruin. August's image of the heroic, magnanimous shop boss plagued by his workers' buffoonery doesn't ring true, however, if we consider the political content of the strike: the worker's spontaneous outrage at the prospect that their manhood, indeed, their conception of themselves as laborers will be violated by the tyrannical "liberalism" of the boss. When No. 44 is admitted to the castle, they rise up, determined "to protest against this outrage, this admission of a pauper and tramp without name or family to the gate leading to the proud privileges and distinctions and immunities of their great order" (252). But the boss issues a gag order, threatening to "turn adrift any man that opened his mouth"—an injunction that leaves the men "grumbling, and pretty nearly strangled with wrath" (252). It is Stein who has launched an attack on the social element of producer republicanism, slighting a nineteenth-century brand of labor radicalism that demanded the free contract of a man's labor, imagining that political equality could surmount economic hierarchy (Camfield 104). Stein's affront to union hegemony exposes his indifference to the will of the workers and ignites their worst suspicions of impotence in the face of management, even in spite of their vociferous exhibitions of dissent. Meanwhile, No. 44's maneuvers, indeed, his very presence, draw out competing interpretations of industrial relations, each edged by irony or undercut by indecision, so that we encounter something like an affective historiography of the industrial age in Master Stein's print shop.

"HOW UNDIGNIFIED IT WAS, AND HOW DEGRADING"

In *No. 44, The Mysterious Stranger*, the psychic cost of accepting Stein's decision to initiate No. 44 into the printers' league is unbearable and, indeed, Stein's manifestation of liberalism seems to cost the union men everything. "Their order, the apple of their eye, their pride, the darling of their hearts, their dearest possession, their nobility—as they ranked it and regarded it" have been devastatingly assailed by the master's decision to allow No. 44 to enter the craft (253). The workers' antagonisms and their efforts to exclude him from the guild harken back to an artisan age, even as the technology of the shop announces its modernity and the men attempt to strike. However, No. 44's subsequent magical interventions in the printer's shop align the coordinates of the conflict with the evolving creeds of industrial democracy.

At the turn of the century, arguments in favor of industrial democracy relied on egalitarian ideals derived from the American political creed, the Social Gospelers' vision of the Kingdom of God on earth, and one other modern proposition: a shift from a "state centered" to a "society centered" realization of democratic civic values (the democratization of the corporation) at a moment when workers increasingly perceived corporations and the corporate order as potential obstacles to individual autonomy in an arena that had eclipsed the terrain of civil and political rights (Harris 49). In *Race, Nationalism, and the State in British and American Modernism*, Patricia Chu argues that modern(ist) uncertainty was not, significantly, confined to an effect of the worker's estrangement from the means of production at the turn of the century (28). Rather, citizens feared that aspirations to mass democratization had been irretrievably botched and that the coercive tactics of the modern state were only adroitly presented as "derived from the will of the governed" (Chu 29). Under such circumstances, industrial life became a locus of consensual and nonconsensual relations.

Industrial democracy proposed that the working classes could identify industrial life as a litmus test for the exercise of individual agency, regardless of race. Nevertheless, its criterion was particularly important to black Americans in the South, for whom the experience of mass democratization depended primarily on one's relation to the program of state-sponsored peonage that revoked the civil rights instituted by the Fourteenth and Fifteenth amendments. The uncertainty of the freed slave's (and his or her descendant's) access to free and consensual labor was an ever present menace in face of social mechanisms such as "the Lease," the system commandeering black bodies and selling them as convict labor (Blackmon 121). Insofar as the self-organization of (mostly) white workers into unions made use of representative-democratic standards and allowed them to participate in collective bargaining with employers, however, the trade union could function as a unit of industrial democracy. This "constitutionalizing of American industry" imported governance into the economic system (Harris 52): "In short, through unions they could act like citizens in industrial life" (Mont-

gomery 25). Liberal reformers, who had wielded metaphors of feudal strati-
fication to condemn the corporatist industry, approved of the trade union
as a safe alternative to both statism and socialism. In their eyes, industrial
democracy was the antidote to social unrest and, more importantly, could be
administered in concert with their programs for social reform (Harris 48).[5]

Still, skepticism about the union as a venue for voluntary action surfaced
when workers impinged on the claims of capital, for instance during the
1880s, when strikes were timed to coincide with periods of high demand to
capitalize on the vulnerability of employers. This is the case in Master Stein's
shop, since the workers, enthusiastically led by Katzenyammer, propose to
abandon their posts as a lucrative deadline approaches. August's reluctant
acquiescence with the strike, by contrast, suggests the union is a force of
coercion. At the turn of the century, any suggestion of "draconian" disciplinary tactics on the part of the unions paradoxically characterized employers
as the defenders of workers' individual liberties (Montgomery 27). Along
these lines, August presents the union as a stumbling block to the exercise of
independent agency, and as a heavy-handed, nonparticipatory organization
that bullies its members. In doing so, he shows his secret sympathies with
No. 44 and canonizes Stein as his protector.

But Katzenyammer's impression that 44 is a rogue determined to em-
bezzle their birthright is confirmed when the men go on strike. First, No.
44 produces invisible figures or ghosts who complete the work they have
abandoned. Next, No. 44 supplies "the duplicates": exact reproductions and
specular doubles of the entire crew—for which Katzenyammer, the fore-
man, calls him a "bastard of black magic" (306)—to take over the work when
the men go on strike. The response to these scabs is, unsurprisingly, belliger-
ence. Katzenyammer demands of his ghostly double, "Do you belong to the
union?" and, calling upon his associates when the duplicate answers in the
negative, cries, "Then you're a scab. Boys, up and at him!" (306). But their
terror and fury at the apparition of these lookalikes soon turns into a pite-
ous recognition: "If the Duplicates remained, the Originals were without a
living" (306), and the life does seem to have been sapped from their bodies as
they come to terms with these "very grave and serious facts, cold and clammy
ones; and the deeper they sank down into the consciousness of the ousted
men the colder and clammier they became" (307). The relation of the Duplicates to the Originals is, moreover, graphically parasitic and one-sided. August agonizes, "It was all so unjust, so unfair; for in the talk it came out that

the Duplicates did not need to eat or drink or sleep, so long as the Originals did those thing" (307) and adds to this unsanctimonious theft his counterin-tuitive grievance that "the Originals were out of work and wageless, yet they would be supporting these intruding scabs, out of *their* food and drink, and by gracious not even a thank-you for it!" (307). The boss gracefully leaves the workers to their own devices, meanwhile reaping the material benefits of his supernatural crew.

No. 44 is quick to affirm that a human is an automaton, and in this he echoes Twain in *What Is Man?*: "His mind is merely a machine, that is all—an *automatic* one, and he has no control over it; it cannot conceive of a *new* thing, an original thing, it can only gather material from the outside and combine it into new *forms* and patterns" (333). Even so, when Twain's print-er's shop comes to be inhabited by a number of phantom workers, the union men who are flesh-and-blood counterparts to the phantoms are left miser-able. For the members of Master Stein's shop, there is no other interpreta-tion but that they have been wrenched from themselves. What remains of them is that part capable of consent. The rest, their doubles, know nothing of volition and work without relenting. These creatures, their second selves, are undeniably a physical threat, which is undoubtedly why Stein's employ-ees want to verify the substance of the merry usurpers (the "invisibles," the "Duplicates," and so on) by physical contests and other procedures.

This mechanization of production, experienced as a disconcerting mis-management of one's own body, perfectly coincides with Chu's description of a modernity characterized by "the fear of becoming nothing but a body endlessly consenting to its own lack of autonomy"(29). Chu uses *White Zombie*, a 1932 Hollywood film directed by Victor Halperin, as an example of artistic production that captures modern anxieties about the tenuousness of consensual governance. In this film, a sugar mill operated by zombies at the direction of their "Zombie Master" (a typically menacing Bela Lugosi) exemplifies the dreadfulness of government without consent, a dreadfulness to which Halperin gives full expression when the Zombie Master turns over the angelic Madeleine to a rich resident of the island, transforming her white body into an unfeeling, semimechanical object. In the film, the mechanized body of the "free" modern industrial worker and the commodified body of the Caribbean slave are simultaneously intelligible in the figure of the zom-bie, so that a historical anachronism is experienced as pure horror. Halperin's film "rests its case on the idea that a barbaric past practice has intruded into modernity," Chu explains, "while contradictorily asserting that the modern laborer (automaton) and the slave may come from the same moment" (25).

The twice-allusive image of Halperin's zombies necessitates an inconceivable periodization, a history that refutes the defeat of slavery, not to mention the legislative events that were to inter it for good. Thus the film is disrupted by a chronological conundrum, as with those late Victorian crime novels that presented some "monstrous" variety of criminality as foreign to modernity yet required, paradoxically, they be interpreted in the terms of "scientific or pseudoscientific rationalism" that undergirded modern life (Peach 7). In Twain's manuscript, too, the "Duplicates," the "invisibles," and No. 44 are atavistic monstrosities and technological marvels at once. More importantly, however, they are facets or facsimiles of the workingmen they mirror, never entirely "Other" and yet thoroughly strange.

The semblance of themselves the workingmen find in their identical "scabs" signals their recognition of something like interracial affinity, albeit tinged with terror and counteracted only by a desperate appeal to a "natural" hierarchy: "Originals" versus "Duplicates." That the Originals aim to measure the exact extent of the Duplicates' estrangement directs us to Chu's most subtle point: The zombie does not just function as a negative example, whose lack of agency reassures us of our own civic brawn such that we might, without regard for our neurasthenic bodies and monotonous jobs, pronounce, Thank heavens we are not zombies! On the contrary, in the presence of the zombie we cannot announce with any certainty that "the living dead act without being overtly coerced but are not acting of their own volition" (Chu 27). Yet if the zombie evokes the slave, still we must recall, especially when the venue of our thought-experiment is Haiti (as it is in *White Zombie*), that "slave labor implies the capacity for revolt" (27). Twain's puzzling parleys between "Originals" and "Duplicates"; his invention of "invisibles" who accommodate the market's every ultimatum; and finally his masterwork, No. 44, who puppeteers each unusual event, suggest a deep ambivalence about any human capacity for consent or resistance in the face of an industrial modernity.

Thus it seems that the arrival of No. 44 at the castle is something like the earliest iteration of *Guess Who's Coming to Dinner?*—by which I mean the presence of the guest demands every man take his stance with respect to this convenient placeholder, thus dramatizing the incipient tensions that structure material relations. His presence is the proxy by which the workers and the boss express their own doubleness. In the case of the workers, this is a nascent conception of themselves as wage slaves alongside their ostensible identity as citizens of an industrial democracy—not as a code word for collective ownership, but as consensual participants structuring the world they live in. In the case of Heinrich Stein, his status as heroic defender of individual liberties against the draconian coercion of the union is juxtaposed with the temperament of an unfeeling capitalist whose absolute dependence on the new order of industrial unions can only be sorted out by availing himself of strikebreakers.

This reading of the strike is an alternative to the reading Bruce Michelson offers in his book *Printer's Devil*, where he contends that Twain indulges in a succession of fantasies about printing in *No. 44, The Mysterious Stranger*: first, the apprentice par excellence in the figure of No. 44, who learns the rounds immediately; after that, the arrival of Doangivadam, "friend of oppressed proprietors, foe of shop stewards and thugs," to negotiate the terms between labor and management (218); next, Michelson calls the ghostly presences who take over the shop operations "ghosts of machines that never became what Mark Twain wanted—mechanical supermen to do the hardest, slowest work of the jour printers"; and finally the Duplicates, who work without pay and seemingly subsist on air (Michelson 217–18).

Michelson's reading, I think, belies Twain's careful attention to the emotional score of the labor conflict, as well as the unresolved tonalities in the text, which echo Twain's own troubled relation to printer's unions. We can see this confusion in his "The New Dynasty" essay from 1886, when he supported the Knights of Labor and, in Green Camfield's words, "personified the labor union as the world's king, the real nation that kings are supposed to embody" (98)—though the speech was in fact printed on the Paige Compositor, the "labor-supplanting" machine Twain hoped would revolutionize the industry. In this speech, Twain supported unions for the part they played in guarding against the tyranny of capital, but also as a moderate alternative to radical reform (Barrow 13). Twain's ambivalence about labor is more strikingly documented in an address to the New York Typothetae, the association of employer printers, in January of that year. Twain decided not to use a speech he had drafted that forecasted monumental change for the industry with the introduction of his automatic typesetter and a depleted workforce; he abandoned this tactless oration in favor of a nostalgic portrait of his own experiences as a printer in the traditional apprentice system. The point worth pressing is that Twain could neither devise a way to synthesize these incongruous sentiments about the industry, nor feel comfortable with the effects of industrialization and mechanical invention more generally—David Barrow has gone so far as to suggest that Twain "exiled the connection between violence and technology" to his novel *A Connecticut Yankee in King Arthur's Court* as a way of alleviating his anxieties about the social consequences of his investment (20).

The concept of "industrial democracy," which invited the working classes to imagine themselves exemplary citizens in the realm of production, was alarming insofar as the "tyrannical" law of the shop might overthrow the capitalist. But in *No. 44, The Mysterious Stranger*, August explicitly reiterates his sense that the standoffs between labor and management are insurmountable. When the men demand "waiting wages" from the master for the time they spent on strike, August writes, "So there we were, you see—at a stand-still" (286). Neither master nor men are willing to submit to negotiations, even though the heroic itinerant printer Doangivadam has arrived, urging the men to resume their work. When the Duplicates arrive on the scene, August repeats, "So there it was—just a deadlock!" (306). Workers are stripped of the leverage necessary to move their employer, and the presses in the Master Stein's shop never cease. From this purgatory of interminable print, however, No. 44 affects yet another revolution in textual relations, one that will reverse type.

"THE BLACK FACES THAT HAD BEEN DEAR TO HIM"

I have argued above that the eponymous hero of *No. 44, The Mysterious Stranger* bears a striking resemblance to the dime-novel detective. It is for this reason that we can confidently differentiate this manuscript from a sort of proto-postmodernism that is spellbound by self-referentiality and blighted by that dismal solipsism that drives authors to badger us by making a point of being in the text, as if it could have been otherwise, or was anyhow of special interest to us. Twain is not the "invisible" protagonist of the text; in *No. 44, The Mysterious Stranger*, it is No. 44 who is given to immodesty and fanfare, and as the major operator in the text, he is also the one who counters a world of accelerated production with a series of "command performances" (i.e., the "invisibles," the "Duplicates") that alter the material world and, as a finale, unmake that world. This last undertaking, which abandons the world at its beginning, is quite different from the act of "undoing plot" as Catharine Gallagher describes it: "the unmooring of a seemingly fixed narrative moment, [which] activates 'counterfactual possibility and throws the previously accomplished present into an unrealized state'" (qtd. in Levine 242). Gallagher's variables are narrative acts and objects, and their conditional effects are scored on the human calendar, so her inquiry lies in the territory of the puzzle mystery where the pieces determine the picture. For No. 44, by contrast, the intricacy of this form of "undoing plot" is a diversion in and of itself. In *The Mysterious Stranger* manuscripts, Twain devotes attention to historical contingencies; however, it is the infrastructure of the *textual* world No. 44 is unmaking. It is no good, however, to plunge headfirst into an account of Twain's profoundly baffling "Procession of the Dead" by trying, for instance, to imagine a story that undid *itself*. We can best approach this event by continuous increments, as No. 44 does, beginning with a more familiar exercise from the turn of the century: blackface minstrelsy.

Blackface minstrelsy is a paradox. According to Michael Rogin, it was predicated upon withholding freedoms expressed in the Declaration of Independence from blacks in America, and yet "Blackface staged the return of what the document repressed—slavery—by displaying the racialized body whited out beneath the Declaration's universalist claims" (*Blackface* 17). A medium through which immigrants enunciated their "assimilatability"—as in Henry Ford's now-notorious larger-than-life-sized melting pot, where his employees ritualistically shed their ethnic garments and emerged flag in hand—blackface minstrelsy was a "Declaration of Whiteness." Its function was aspirational and imitative—an ingratiating striptease that surrendered through performance what could not conform to American(white)-ness, which is why "blackface was an alternative to interracial political solidarity, not the failed promise of it" (37). In *The Mysterious Stranger* this bit of legalese is conveyed in the language of the printer's shop. No. 44's first turn to minstrelsy marks his attainment of the post of "printer's devil"—an apprenticeship to the printer's office, so called because of the black ink stains the apprentice acquired in the course of his duties. No. 44's response is the first of his several variations on race performance. Just after the promotion, "He got a little steel thing out of his pocket and set it between his teeth, remarking 'it's a jew's-harp—the niggers use it'" (299). August is the lone audience to No. 44's "extravagant and stirring and heathen performance," but this cacophonous recital on the Jew's harp and frenzied acrobatics are hardly light entertainment. In consideration of 44's feelings, August endures the nerveracking act with its "violent springing and capering" and its "most urgent and strenuous and vibrant" melodies, and is utterly enervated: "He kept it up and kept it up until my heart was broken and all my body and spirit so worn and tired and desperate that I could not hold in any longer" (299–300). August is immobilized in the presence of this comic whirling dervish, dazed by its perverse exuberance, or we might say that the perversity lies with August, who remains politely in thrall to a performance that damages him and is too embarrassed to report "how undignified it was, and how degrading" (299).

No. 44 oversteps all the limits of taste as though he were a force of antigravity, or speaking in terms of blackface, a centrifuge that pares some stigma attached to the surface with a shower of white noise. His second act in this vein shifts from the aural to the visual. No. 44 decides "to flaunt in the faces of the comps the offensive fact that he was their social equal" by "doing a cake-walk," sporting a real mess of garments:"embroidered buskins, with red heels; pink silk tights; pale blue satin trunks; cloth of gold doublet; short satin cape, of a blinding red," and all this is topped off with a "lace collar fit for a queen; the cunningest little blue velvet cap, with a slender long feather standing up out of a fastening of clustered diamonds; dress sword in a gold sheath, jeweled hilt" (303). His outlandish Elizabethan garb critiques the honor bestowed on the craftsman whose professional privilege is to shoulder a sword. No. 44's finery is preposterously lavish and far beyond the means of his fellow workers, moreover, so it adds an additional dig, insinuating the guildsman's vulgar ambition is to belong to the tacky clan of the nouveaux riche. To summarize, as an insult to the institution he has entered, No. 44 amplifies the material privileges it awards so they cease to be emblems of respect and become emblems of idiocy. This deadpan double-speak chastens and demeans his supposed "fellows" by ridiculing the terms of their affiliation.[6]

In these cases, No. 44 avails himself of a kind of generic extravagance, a painful overstatement that alerts us to an excess, or glut in the performance that is its own metacritique or form of undoing. A third scene offers another example: Toward the end of the manuscript No. 44 tries to cheer a despondent August with an opening act as "Mr. Bones," complete with a "mouth [that] reached clear across his face and was unnaturally red, and had extraordinarily thick lips, and the teeth showed intensely white between them, and the face was as black as midnight" (354). The disembodied features that are not moved but move themselves, the artificial colors, everything surreal ("unnaturally red," "extraordinarily thick"), and this inhuman image signal Twain's impression that this particular installment of the "coon show"—and even those back issues for whom it is said Twain's affection never dwindled—are uncanny entities. In this menacing mask, No. 44 sings Stephen Foster's "Old Folks at Home" in what August calls a "bastard English"—as if the lyric was ugly, or supplied by some deformed, illegitimate offspring of King James—and yet No. 44's mawkish rendition of "verse after verse, sketching his humble lost home, and the joys of his childhood, and the black faces that had been dear to him" (356) draws tears to August's eyes. No. 44 is satisfied with his achievement, but confesses, "I could do it if they were knot-holes" (356). Does he claim to coax tears from a stone? Or boast that these "black faces" whom synecdoche has deprived of body and soul, "knot-holes" themselves, are stage effects, fixtures in the modern waterworks?

In *Playing the Races: Ethnic Caricature and American Literary Realism*, Henry Wonham suggests that Twain was convinced of the "radical authenticity" of the minstrel show, in spite of its demeaning burlesque; indeed, Wonham explains, "When reality is so extravagant that burlesque can do nothing to exaggerate its conditions, racial caricature becomes a type of realism" (132). This seems to be the case in the entertainments No. 44 offers August. Wonham explains that "caricature inscribes ethnic markers as inflexible features of identity, which only become more pronounced with every comical step the irreparable alien takes toward the fantasy of perfect assimilation" (38), but adds that the basic premise of caricature—that "the essence of identity can be gleaned through observation and interpretation of the exterior form" (13)—involuntarily concedes an argument against itself, that identity is an illusory "improvisational, fluid cosmopolitanism" that cannot be cemented (38). In short, by assigning "type" one dismantles the "typeface" for what it is: a signifier that repudiates its so-called signified to disassemble the codes of signification that produced it. As with dime-novel detection, the extravagance of the minstrel show calls upon its audience to disfigure its superficial contents. Paradoxically, its alternate realism is denoted by what resists caricature at the very moment that caricature is impressed upon us; the element of resistance lies in the excessive substance of the minstrel caricature. This is analogous to the subject of the unconscious that Lacan christens the "dit-que-non":

> An enunciation that denounces itself, a statement that renounces itself, ignorance that dissipates itself, an opportunity that loses itself, what remains here if not the trace of what *must* be in order to fall from being? (*Écrits* 300)

This subject withheld or, better yet, withdrawn by "nay-saying" is more brilliantly captured by the retroactive effect of the detective's eruption from among the dramatis personae set before us in the dime novel. The dime-novel detective is the impersonal force who "can read the riddle because he is never personally involved" (Cox 8), but while he is concealed there is (or at least he will have been, after his triumphant appearance) something of the text speaks against itself.

When the dime-novel detective is at last an articulated agent, however, the text comes into its own as allegory. One body is now possessed of the detective's keen eye and purposeful gait, and he is the relentless, superhuman person whose "chameleon-like ability" paradoxically implied "that with the proper moral determination . . . anyone could alter—for the better—their physical reality" (Hoppenstand 137). The narrative is reformed according to his whims and only by his hand, though, never by an ordinary agent. But typically, the detective's world-making resolves matters according to predictable patterns. His motives amount to what François Trouillot would call "more than blind arrogance," because, as with the discovery of the "New World," they institute "a predetermined lexical field of clichés and predictable categories that foreclose a redefinition of the political and intellectual stakes," and impose a center of gravity to which all parts of the narrative are indemnified (115).

No. 44 is that force in *No. 44, The Mysterious Stranger*, but he is scarcely interested in the world's remediation. Instead, Twain adopts the incredulous reading-paradigm dime-novel detective fiction encouraged and appropriates its avenger detective to decommission the print shop. No. 44 tears suddenly through the surface of the text, as he has through time and space, to obliterate the industrial order in its entirety. This repudiation of industrial modernity follows No. 44's abdication of race as an infrastructure of industrial relations. It is analogous to and an extension of the work of No. 44's minstrel performance that, by its exuberant caricature, forswears its own vernacular as well as the socioeconomic and political regimes upon which it is predicated. In other words, Twain enhances and elevates the work of the dime-novel detective to the realm of textual performance, so that his renovation (or rather annihilation) of the world applies not only to the reality that text has configured, but to the text itself. Moreover, the exemplary and familiar act with which he begins to annihilate the world is blackface minstrelsy—an extravagant burlesque to which, in keeping with Wonham, we might attribute the dismantling of whiteness.

No. 44, The Mysterious Stranger's telescopic chronology very pointedly connects the dots between the Reformation and the modern industrial society Twain confronted at the end of his lifetime, as if the United States were a direct descendant of the Bible Master Stein and his workers send to press, as if Gutenberg invented America. The key insight to be had here, though, is not that Twain charts a continuous lineage from Gutenberg to the current state of affairs, but that for Twain, the bookend to America, or the ultimate end of Protestant individualism that is its source, is industrial crisis—a calamity the dime-novel detective was designed to solve.

Twain's "rejected" Typothetae speech reports,

[We] have seen methods of printing so changed that a press of today will turn off a job in a year which a customer of Gutenberg's would have had to wait nearly five centuries for—and then get it, perhaps, when interest in that publication had pretty much died out, and he would wish he hadn't ordered it. (Qtd. in Barrow 14)

Twain refers to the days of Gutenberg and Faust, rather than Gutenberg and (the more traditional spelling) Fust, for the moneylender who financed Gutenberg—perhaps a slip of the pen that indicates Twain's perception of print as a pact with the devil and a script with which the human race has been saddled. *No. 44, The Mysterious Stranger* is Twain's rebuttal to Gutenberg, his attempt to take the history it produced and "return to sender." Accordingly, Joe Fulton describes No. 44's final performance as "the aesthetic representation of what is in essence an ethical point" (186). No. 44's coup de grace is the reversal of time itself, which Twain's configures as a "tactile" joke, printer's type set backward to indicate the counterclockwise turn of events. The prank begins when the sun rises in the southwest and the clock turns counterclockwise, and then every act of the previous day is repealed as the day runs in the wrong direction. No. 44 promises, "It will be the only perfectly authenticated event in all human history," for no human is exempt from this "dizzying" torment of reversed speech and movement. Even this is only a narrative of time's reversal, but the text takes itself seriously: to represent the reversal of time, the text we have already read returns, only now each word and each sentence is rendered in reverse order. This unreadable incantation is a real narrative retraction; this is as close as a text could get to swallowing itself up. No. 44 tells August that the effect is "patented. There aren't going to be any encores" (396), though of course this strategy of retraction is also the premise of No. 44's last act, the "Assembly" and procession of the dead, which begins after a complete descent into the "blackest darkness," during which "all visible things gloomed down gradually, losing their outlines little by little, then disappeared utterly," and then a "silence which was so still it was as if the world was holding its breath" (401).

The Procession of the Dead is a parade of skeletons, both the unknown and the known figures of history, coming finally even to "Adam's predecessors" among whom there is one that No. 44 identifies as the "Missing Link." The effect of these two displays is a complete retreat from the printed word, first of all, then a regression to a moment before the appearance of the species, at which point "44 waved his hand and we stood in an empty and soundless world" (403). This annihilation of time and space is followed by 44's revelation to August: "You are not you—you have no body, no blood, no bones, you are but a *thought*" (404), and then, one more remove: "The dream-marks are all present—you should have recognized them earlier" (404). It is, finally, the enactment of the "Pudd'nhead Wilson's Calendar" fantasy about the "discovery" of the Americas: "It would have been more wonderful to miss it."

In *No. 44, The Mysterious Stranger*, Twain forfeits bildungsroman for the sprawling, quixotic contours of dime-novel detective fiction and its remarkable adventurer detective. Twain employs the narrative-analytical tools of this subgenre (its detective's preternatural expertise at disguise; its habits of narrative retraction; and its excursions into allegory) to gauge the degradations of the industrial workplace and to dramatize a crisis of modern political consent. Twain foregrounds the contamination of industrial relations by ethnic and racial competition with the ever-indeterminate figure of No. 44—a character's whose faculties at disguise and supernatural exploits bring to mind the dime-novel detective, who often appeared among the dramatis personae in fictionalized accounts of nineteenth-century labor disputes. Crucially, Twain critiques regimes of sociality cultivated in the world of production without relinquishing or resolving his doubts about an "industrial democracy" that would take collective bargaining as the cornerstone of representative-democratic standards and individual agency. Nevertheless, *No. 44, The Mysterious Stranger* embellishes and externalizes the mechanisms of the dime novel to access another order of prose fiction precisely suited to these equivocations. It is an "expressive" realism whose terrain is metatextuality, such that social knowledge becomes accessible in the cadence of the plot: its chronotopic shifts; its narrative dislocations; and the retroactive revisions made possible by the dime novel's tractable type and its supernatural sleuth. Mired in a cosmic "dead-lock" precipitated by industrial life, this last of the *Mysterious Stranger* manuscripts mines the tactics of dime-novel detective fiction to enact its own undoing. Finally, it is well worth noting that while *No. 44*'s prescription of "reverse type" eradicates all of time and space, his program of annihilation begins with the abolition of whiteness.

CHAPTER 2

The Art of Framing Lies

> Of all existing novel types none provides an example of such perfect closure
> as the detective novel. Like a sentence, it is a hierarchical verbal structure that
> binds a subject to a predicate and ends with a highly visible period.

—DENNIS PORTER, *THE PURSUIT OF CRIME*

The America that Edgar Allan Poe and Nathaniel Hawthorne inhabited
was on the move, deeply enmeshed in a process of self-creation and expansion restricted only by the plasticity of its populace. At the heart of this venture was the cultivation of republican virtue, an ambition succinctly outlined
by the American Enlightenment thinker Dr. Benjamin Rush in his 1798 essay, "Of the Mode of Education Proper in a Republic." Rush proposed to
"convert men into republican machines," an essential measure "if we expect
them to perform their parts properly, in the great machine of the government of the state" (qtd. in Nelson 13). Rush's aim, to forge a "manly civic ideal" from the rude material of the American man, demanded that the white
male citizen "equalize the contradictory demands of self, family, market, and
national interests *in his own person*" (Nelson 12). Pointing to the discipline
and individualism of the agrarian, Thomas Jefferson promoted the yeoman
farmer as the exemplary self-governing body (Rogin, *Fathers* 79). By the
early nineteenth century, however, the contours of American society were
already shifting. An industrial-corporate economy all but effaced farmer and
artisan from the center of commerce, and the brutal evacuation of Native
Americans from territories in the East made way for the expansion of black
slave labor and the growth of the cotton export sector (Takaki 78–79). Marrying an industrial-corporate economy, bound labor, and Indian removal to
liberal ideals of independence, civic equity, and hard work, however, entailed
pragmatic acts of self-deception.

Both Edgar Allan Poe's "The Man That Was Used Up" (1839) and Nathaniel Hawthorne's "Mr. Higginbotham's Catastrophe" (1834) negotiate these grave inconsistencies at the core of the national ethos. This chapter explores how Poe and Hawthorne develop narrative strategies to navigate economic and discursive conventions related to the exigencies of "black" chattel slavery (and contentious efforts to extend slavery into commandeered Indian lands), as well as the simultaneous advent of a "free" and "white" workforce resisting subjugation by an industrially oriented market economy. While these stories fall outside the designation of detective fiction, we might think of them as proto- or possibly metadetective fictions. They are texts that use the activity and the idea of narrative retroversion (the chronological sequencing of narrative fragments to reconstruct the past, also known as backward construction) to capture and theorize complex socioeconomic arrangements in the antebellum nation. In his essay "The Nineteenth Century as Chronotope," Hayden White differentiates between analytic approaches that merely anatomize the logical inconsistencies in the social fabric, presenting history as the sum of a "set of contradictions," and approaches that same history as paradox, seeking to determine "the *modalities* of the peculiar forms of *illogic* by which a society, an age, or a whole culture negotiates the distance between its *manifest practices* and *self-representations* and its systematically *hidden*, because psycho-dynamically *repressed*, thoughts, perceptions, and affects" (244). Along these lines, in representing present and past, Poe and Hawthorne do not merely unpack and parade the internal contradictions of antebellum society. Instead, they fashion narrative equipment that helps illuminate those modalities of illogic that sustained an economy struggling to manage internal discord and to regulate varieties of interracial sociability. In doing so, they formulate and explore the limits and possibilities of a narrative device, backward construction, that would routinely appear in classical detective fictions by the early twentieth century.

The narrator of Poe's "The Man That Was Used Up" is a sort of flaneur who mingles with high society, soliciting a full account of the exploits of the celebrated and extraordinarily handsome war hero General John A. B. C. Smith, only to find Smith's valet, Pompey, reconstructing the gentleman of mechanical bits and prosthetic pieces when he visits Smith's apartment. By contrast, Hawthorne's "Mr. Higginbotham's Catastrophe" follows tobacco peddler and pathological gossip Dominicus Pike as he struggles to make sense of misleading and irreconcilable tales of the murder of one Squire Higginbotham. Confounded by testimonies that call into question whether Higginbotham is dead at all, Pike makes his way to the squire's Kimballton estate and interrupts the man in Higginbotham's employ (an "Irishman of doubtful character") who is in the very process of perpetrating the assassination (87)! While the investigation in "The Man That Was Used Up" (subtitled "A Tale of the Late Bugaboo and Kickapoo Campaign") is propelled by the alluring vitality of the enigmatic General John A. B. C. Smith, "Mr. Higginbotham's Catastrophe" is powered by the kind of morbid curiosity about murder that would animate Poe's tales of ratiocination. Still, the principal activity of both tales is coordinating narrative fragments such that they coalesce into plausible historical accounts. What is more, these works generate discursive logics that grapple with interracial sociability. Managing narrative fragments doubles as racial management, since race differentiation forged in and fortified by the antebellum industrial order is *formalized*, coalescing in the activity of narrative retroversion. With a climactic illustrated act of assembly orchestrated by the Smith's black valet Pompey, "The Man That Was Used Up" supplies fleeting *images* of interracial class consciousness and social upheaval that are subsequently eclipsed by the radiant, undifferentiated figure of General John A. B. C. Smith, an ideal of Jacksonian manhood that gentrifies the violent discord and multiple clashing forces in the body politic. "Mr. Higginbotham's Catastrophe," on the other hand, is punctuated by multiple distinct, if understated, signposts of interracial working-class collectivity. Yet its central riddle summons ideas of interracial solidarity and sociability simply to stratify them; the conditions for economic revolt the story documents, and the cooperative ventures it apparently conceives, are eroded by the ratiocinative acts it requires. As both stories play with backward construction to forge plausible accounts of causes and effects from narrative fragments, they call attention to the cultural function of a narrative device: parsing the social effects of racial differentiation that were part and parcel of an industrially oriented market economy.

"A PERFECT UNDERSTANDING OF THE STATE OF AFFAIRS"

The unnamed narrator of "The Man That Was Used Up" is in search of a complete report of the past of the celebrated Brevet Brigadier General John A. B. C. Smith, hero of the Bugaboo and Kickapoo Indian campaigns. Though this protagonist's ambulatory investigation into the past of the national hero is limited to a single city's most prestigious cultural precincts: the opera, the salon, and so on, "The Man That Was Used Up" authorizes several antebellum propositions rooted in the remote material base of these cultural fronts. Among these are the degraded status of bound labor enforced by the discursive operations of "Sambo-making" in the South; the unconditional differentiation between black and white labor in the North; and the violent requisition of Native Americans lands in service of King Cotton. Robert Beuka emphasizes that this work lampoons Jacksonian manhood, exposing a "body politic" dismembered rather than unified by its politics of race: "Poe quite literally deconstructs his hero, in the process figuratively deconstructing the mystique of rugged individualism central to the Jacksonian vision of the American citizenry" (32). But beyond dismantling the mystique of manly perfection that the general is thought to personify, Poe's story employs narrative retroversion to dramatize the ideological process that sutures incommensurate parts of a political and socioeconomic landscape in the body and biography of General Smith.

In the person of Poe's narrator, we find the pure passion of the detective. First, there is his phobia for the unexplained—he observes, for example, that "the slightest appearance of mystery—of any point I cannot exactly comprehend—puts me at once into a pitiable state of agitation," a morbid, unremitting curiosity that informs the biographical inquiry he undertakes (Poe 66). His dismal methods, however, only confound the investigation. The narrator yearns for a complete report of the "tremendous events" of the Bugaboo and Kickapoo Indian campaign, but his single strategy is to extract it from various interlocutors; he expects others to supply what he is unwilling to find by indirection (67). An irremediably dense socialite, he initiates interrogations at injudicious moments (whispering from the pew while the minister delivers his sermon, interrupting a tense game of whist at a soirée, and so on) only to meet each time with a familiar spiel: "Great wretches, those Bugaboos—savage and so on—but we live in a wonderfully inventive age!—Smith!—O yes! great man!—perfect desperado—immortal renown—prodigies of valor!" (68). This vague but suggestive patina of social chatter enshrouds General Smith, rendering the man's exploits an enigma, though Smith's magnificent body remains a spectacular marvel that invites further inquiry.

Both in the repetition of an irregular biographical spiel and in the narrator's quest for a fully articulated account, Poe rehearses a method of assembling narrative that would become customary to classical detective fiction. Poe's narrator must pluck details from a rhetorical composite before him to build a historical account that fuses past events into a causal-chronological ordering bereft of snags or perforations. In detection fictions, such activity elucidates what was previously beyond the reader's grasp, coordinating disparate events into something linear, sequential, and coherent. The detective's process of reconstruction recuperates narrative fragments, including seemingly arbitrary and violent events, by incorporating them into a "meaning-conferring system," a seamless and intelligible story of a crime (Porter 219). However, in detective fiction narrative assembly is typically obstructed by what Dorothy Sayers calls the art "of framing lies *in the right ways*": detection texts can be labyrinthine, saturated with "collateral material" designed to confound readers or lead them astray ("Aristotle on Detective Fiction" 31).[1] Poe's narrator, by contrast, has almost all the critical details within his grasp, and what he repeatedly confronts is *already* a provisional ordering of events. Nevertheless, the discursive rehearsal of the general's exploits remains unintelligible, just so many rhetorical fragments resisting resolution. Though he gapes at "*the remarkable* something" and the "odd air of *Je ne sais quoi*" that envelop General Smith, he cannot seem to get at that glue of causation which would lend something like narrative integrity to the general's punctured past—and indeed, his efforts to eke out intelligence are inevitably indelicate (66).

Confronted with a syntactic imbroglio, the narrator is at wits' end. His fellow socialites speak in a fragmented idiom that discretely invites the kind of collating that would register, for instance, that the general was assailed by "savage" Indians, his body salvaged only by the march of technological invention. The narrator is anything but inventive, however. He becomes an increasingly tactless raconteur, oblivious to the social niceties that check any explicit, exhaustive account of the general's affairs. He fails entirely to fulfill the duties that would be assigned to a detective: to establish a "sequence and causality" from a jumbled chronology, to make meaning of the "effects without apparent causes" that envelope the unknown (Porter 29–30). For this reason, the narrator has no recourse but to descend upon the general himself, in order to "demand, in explicit terms, a solution of this abominable piece of mystery" (Poe 69).

Upon his arrival at the general's apartment, the narrator is horrified to hear a squeak emerge from a "large and exceedingly odd-looking bundle of something" lying on the floor, which he has just kicked out of the way. Whistling, "Ahem! rather civil that, I should observe!," the bundle demands, "I really believe you don't know me at all" (69). The narrator, aghast, retreats from the bundle and turns to confront Pompey, the "old negro valet" who has admitted him into the house:

> "No—no—no!" said I, getting as close to the wall as possible, and hold-ing up both hands in the way of expostulation; "don't know you—know you—know you—don't know you at all! Where's your master?" here [*sic*] I gave an impatient squint towards the negro, still keeping a tight eye upon the bundle.
>
> "He! he! he! he-aw! he-aw!" cachinnated that delectable specimen of the human family, with his mouth fairly extended from ear to ear, and with his forefinger held up close to his face, and levelled at the object of my apprehension, as if he was taking aim at it with a pistol. "He! he! he! he-aw! he-aw! he-aw!—what? you want Mass Smif? Why, dar's him!" (Poe 69).

Though Pompey attaches various prosthetic devices to the "odd-looking bundle" to resurrect the recognizable figure of John A. B. C. Smith, the ser-vant's initial derisive gesture would seem to irreparably damage the general's clout. The valet's motion is mimed violence, insubordination hardly hidden in plain sight. Accordingly, the dynamic between the two men tilts in the di-rection of what James C. Scott calls an "infrapolitics of the powerless," appar-ently dismantling a regime of domination that would "deny subordinates the ordinary luxury of negative reciprocity: trading a slap for a slap, an insult for an insult" (23). Beyond the narrator's discomfiting discovery that the pub-lic image of the general is an exquisite "prosthetic construct" that requires "the repression of its organic basis" (Rosenheim 103), then, we are dealing with a scene that not only discloses the *utter dependence* of the master upon his "old negro servant," without whom he is only an "odd-looking bundle of something" (Poe 69), but also effectively intimates the prospect of his violent dismantling by Pompey, who exposes the general's broken-down bits with fingers forcefully poised, "as if taking aim at it with a pistol" (69).

But the idea that the narrative treats the parasitic dependence of whites on blacks as knowledge that must at any cost remain suppressed—what Richard Godden in his work on Faulkner has fittingly described as the gen-erative "labor trauma" of the antebellum South—should be discounted in this case. Poe openly burlesques this degenerative state of dependence in "The Man That Was Used Up." In his toilette, General Smith's soliloquizing sounds somewhere "between a squeak and a whistle" and is peppered with intermittent volleys to his servant: "Pompey, bring me that leg!" and "Now, you nigger, my teeth!"—shrill decrees that hardly convey the impression of actual, enforceable power (69–70). Though Poe's depiction of Pompey is all stock parts, grotesque enlarged features and mulish "cachinnations," it is the servant who, as he assembles his caviling master, has "the knowing air of a horse-jockey" (70). Moreover, the general, who curtly captions his battle wounds and cites the shops where he purchases artificial parts, only attains "that rich melody and strength" in his voice for which he is renowned after his valet inserts a "somewhat singular-looking machine" into his mouth (70).

The *manual* task of attaching prosthetic contraptions to produce a republican gentleman is thus aligned with the *narrative* task of coordinating and uniting distinct events into a coherent biography of that gentleman. Pompey is the extraordinary mechanic-cosmetician who binds the general's war-ravaged bits and artificial parts into that "singularly commanding" and much-revered personage, and as each injury is attached to an historical episode, his retrofitting the body participates in a process of narrativization that fuses discrete parts into a single, systematic chronicle (66). Moreover, the coordinates of this grisly tableaux vivant capture an odd predicament of interracial dependency, one that, moreover, recruits the specter of the *invented* Bugaboo and *actual* Kickapoo Indians to illuminate the carnage inflicted upon the general's person—even while showcasing the artificial anatomy engineered to replace those sundered bits.

The servant's curt declamation ("Why, dar's him!") anticipates the grisly climax of Poe's 1844 story, "Thou Art the Man," a satirical rehash of Poe's earlier detective tales in which the narrator rigs up a murdered body with a whalebone contraption so that the corpse, jolted out of its wooden coffin, can gaze into the eyes of its assassin and proclaim: "Thou art the man!" (306). The talented ventriloquist of that tale achieves the ultimate payoff by compressing the evidentiary or explanatory narrative of the crime into an iconic moment when the corpse identifies the perpetrator. Accordingly, what we get with "Thou Art the Man" is a structural analogy by which a detailed account of a crime is, by mechanical mastery, compressed into shocking talk from a rotting carcass. Similarly, Pompey's exposé incontrovertibly signals the general's debility, and in piecing together the general he meticulously parades the man's corporeal defeat in the Indian wars. Pompey's gesticulations penetrate the primary reality of Poe's short story, surmounting Smith's euphemistic chatter, and goading the reader to entertain a historical drama in two acts: the demolition of Brevet Brigadier General John A. B. C. Smith's body in the Bugaboo and Kickapoo Indian campaigns, and his subsequent restoration as synthetic subject when mechanics swapped machines for his damaged parts.

By prolonging our attention to the program of deception that disguises the disfigured body, and by participating in the particulars of its reassembly, Pompey helps supply a historical context for that magnificent "text" which heretofore has awed and stupefied Poe's narrator. This scene does not merely locate the specific causes that yielded the general in his mostly prosthetic form. Rather, Pompey foregrounds the spectacular violence, the systems of production, and the regimes of sociality that bring this remarkable individual into being. While the general's shrill directives emanate from the "bundle of something" on the floor, Pompey tethers together a *material* and *discursive* explication of the "abominable piece of mystery" before us.

For instance, Pompey's activities direct our attention to how, as a preternatural industrial collaboration, the general *literalizes* the discourse antebellum labor activists adopted to deconstruct embodied capital. In an 1835 article printed in the *Workingman's Advocate*, for instance, Theophilus Fisk called capital a desiccated carcass, dead flesh incarnate and ineffective unless buoyed by manual workers (1). While the politicos of the "slave school"—a cadre that included John C. Calhoun and Geo McDuffie—also maintained that the laborer "cannot be an active member of the body politic" (qtd. in Foner and Shapiro 72), workers insisted the mechanic was "the bone and sinew of this proud country" who created wealth by the toil of his hands ("Important Decision" 6). "If we could sit in our seats like dried mummys [*sic*], and by a single scratch of a pen could construct canals, bridges, and railroads," Fisk remonstrated, "we might then talk about equality of rights and privileges with some degree of propriety" (1). Fisk dismissed the metaleptic logic that granted businessmen title to the products of workingmen's labor. Lamenting workers consigned to civil insignificance and destitution in the newly industrialized trades—the "thousands living and dying mere cogs in the social machine" (1)—Fisk exalted the distinct productivity of the working classes, especially in the face of what the working-class leader Thomas Devyr described as "the overwhelming competition of this occult power": the technology of the machine (qtd. in Foner, *History* 167). More machine than man, General Smith sops up this novel equipment with each genuine "cog" called to recoup his damaged body, the artisan or mechanic that made it vaporized by some variation on that oft-repeated expression: "We live in a wonderfully inventive age" (68). But the architects behind this anatomical catechism rematerialize in Pompey's pantomime, whose maimed "Mass Smif" is the product of an assembly line and a prop of the settler state.

Moreover, this episode controversially conflates white and black work by way of a racial cross-(ad)dress that recruits Pompey, "that delectable specimen of the human family," as understudy for the industrial workforce that keeps the general intact. Pointedly, it does so at a moment when labor called into question an individualistic work ethic that guaranteed remuneration to the hardworking and promised to penalize the idle. Though northern slavery had been extinguished in order to "reconcile workers, and bend the state to market ends by idealizing competition among free and juridically equal individuals," by the 1830s and 1840s, urban craftsmen struggled to become independent in the new economy while visible profits accrued to idle capital and impersonal merchant managers (Sellers 126). As workers unionized to fight for a ten-hour working day, opportunities for self-education, and political rights, they distanced themselves from the plight of black slaves in the South, whose liberation they feared could only impinge on their opportunities for economic independence. "What they failed to comprehend," as W. E. B. DuBois would point out in *Black Reconstruction*, "was that the black man enslaved was an even more formidable and fatal competitor than the black man free" (20). In the face of the market economy's invariable "depreciation" of what the Mechanics' Union of Trade Association called "the intrinsic value of human labor" (qtd. in Foner 102), however, some northern workers articulated the grievances of white wage labor by comparing its fate to that of bound labor. An 1836 article in the *National Laborer* explained: "He may change his master; but he is condemned to perpetual servitude; and his reward is the reward of every other slave—*subsistence*" (qtd. in Foner and Shapiro 34).

In "The Man That Was Used Up," the reader's flickering apprehension of Pompey's affiliation with white northern industrial labor makes clear the fitful nature of the comparison, given that for white labor, "it was difficult not to compare themselves to slaves, almost unbearable to make such a comparison, and impossible to sustain the metaphor" (Roediger 55). Though protestations against *white slavery* took the harrowing example of chattel slavery as a crystallization of white northern workers' worst anxieties regarding the excesses of industrial capitalism, the validity of this analogy remained suspect (86).[2] In 1837, one northern worker leveled an attack at this rhetorical trend, emphatically cataloging the insurmountable "Difference Between a Free Laborer and a Slave" in *The Liberator*. In this article, the subject of free labor is enunciated in opposition to the "perfect merchandise" that is the slave, who is "like a man dead and buried," "a fixture of the soil" in the fixed economy of the South, and "a lump of clay" destined only to contribute "to the wants of 'another race of beings'" (75). This white workingman's insistence on the black slave's autochthonous, agrarian disposition and on his status as a capricious article of commerce distinguishes the particular horror of slavery, to which free labor need never be subjected.[3] Of course, black mechanics and industrial workers abounded in the southern states, since southern industries were almost wholly reliant on bonded labor to continue their operations. Yet severe discrimination essentially prohibited blacks who made their way north from exercising their industrial skills. While it was simply profitable to recruit slave labor for industrial schemes in the South—"one of the great advantages of black labour is, that you can attach it permanently to the establishment by purchase," Charles Fisher reported in *The American Farmer* in 1828—the amicable coexistence of the races in the North depended on stratified occupational arrangements, with free blacks restricted to menial, low-paying, and sometimes dangerous work (qtd. in Foner and Lewis 85, 2). To the extent that white workers vehemently protested what they perceived as insidious subjugation and the requisition of their bodies, racial consciousness and republican pride intervened to curtail identification with black labor (Weinstein 21, Roediger 86). Nevertheless, Pompey, with his distinctly mechanical faculties, becomes visible as one of their own—and yet he also resembles that "formidable and fatal competitor" from the South whose bonded status presaged the bleakest prospects for white workingmen.

Though Poe's story signals its recognition of the industrial nature of Pompey's work, and intimates a certain sociability between a class of black "servants" and their counterparts, "free white labor," this knowledge quickly capsizes, overshadowed by the attention bestowed on the imminent body of General A. B. C. Smith, whose stature has been salvaged by increments. What Peter Coviello has identified as Poe's style of "phenomenological hypotaxis," the practice of syntactical subordination that allows Poe to record the event of corporeal disintegration in miniscule steps, "anatomized down to its least tremors and tiniest operations" in tales like "The Premature Burial"—in short, his capacity to document death as an activity *as it unfolds* (881–84)—is here executed precisely in reverse, so that Pompey's incorporation of the general's various bits and pieces is tantamount to an act of human animation. The general closely captions this event, delineating the sequence of man-made contraptions that constitute his body, and closing the logico-temporal gap created by the occluded record of the Bugaboo and Kickapoo Indian campaign. Crucially, the narrator's peripheral attentions to "the manipulations of Pompey" and the "very dexterous manner" in which the servant assembles the general's body parts—those details that evince Pompey's mechanical bent—cease at the moment of Pompey's final "alteration," when the "whole expression of the countenance of the General was instantaneous and striking," resembling again that figure that so impressed the narrator at the moment of their "original introduction" (Poe 70).

The materialization of General John A. B. C. Smith does not merely absorb the array of manufacturers who have supplied his corporeal parts. His incorporated presence eclipses these as he resumes his role as spokesman and representative for the new technologies, commenting, as is his wont, "upon the rapid march of mechanical invention" (67). That is to say, Poe's delineation of the microprocesses that sustain the general and occlude the fissures and flaws in his physique parallels the processes by which the bloodshed and territorial acquisitions of the Bugaboo and Kickapoo campaigns and the toil of the mechanic are finally vanquished from the social psyche. This exorcism includes Pompey, whose narrative presence recedes in the wake of the general's incorporation. What remains is an impeccable composite of a man, from "the handsomest pair of whiskers under the sun" to a very "properly proportioned calf" (66)—a continuous array of eye-catching features for which the general is celebrated.[4]

In this way, we can begin to see General Smith's repair as a general smoothing over that retroactively lays to rest the antagonisms in the ideological edifice, something like the Lacanian *point de capiton* (or quilting point) that totalizes the field of ideological meaning and for whom "the immanence of its own process of enunciation is experienced as a kind of transcendent Guarantee" (Žižek, *Sublime* 99). Or the "instantaneous and striking" reappearance of that distinguished countenance (Poe 70) signals a perverse variety of what Louis Mink terms *configurational comprehension*: what takes incongruent things for "elements in a single complex of concrete relationships" all fitted together in a "nice balance" (Mink 551). In other words, the narrativization of General Smith (the material and discursive restoration that takes place before the narrator eyes), and Poe's use of narrative retroversion specifically, illustrate a style of ideological interpellation that suppresses a concatenation of human carnage and mechanical toil, and the racial differentiation that both produce.

"THERE IS REALLY NO END TO THE MARCH OF INVENTION"

But let us return again to the brief prospect of intimate violence that is conveyed by Poe's positioning of the "negro servant" in relation to the general, fingers positioned as if "taking aim" with a pistol and preparing to execute the man. It is not simply that Pompey's identification of the general (the disconcerting exclamation "Why, dar's him!") doubles as a proposition of assassination and exposure, thereby functioning as a kind of blackmail that draws attention to the convertibility of master-slave relations. Instead, Pompey's rejoinder to the narrator, who turns an "impatient squint toward the negro" while maintaining "a tight eye upon the bundle" (Poe 69), initiates a moment of specular triangulation, an aggressive *disinterpellative* demand that forces the narrator to confront the disturbing, scattered parts and, most strikingly, that repulsive thing at the center of it all: an "exceedingly odd bundle," a disgusting object that pipes up with "one of the smallest, weakest, and altogether funniest little voices" and performs, "upon the floor, some inexplicable evolution, very analogous to the drawing on of a stocking" (Poe 69). This nauseating protrusion, a "single leg" performing a reverse striptease, is the general dishabille—the emperor without clothes, so to speak, which induces a repellent recognition. But Pompey's traumatic pedagogy is diverted to preserve the consistency of the social order, whose ideological threads are resecured by the general's materialization and the piecing together of his history in its familiar, enigmatic form.

Previously, when the narrator sought knowledge of the general at the theater, an acquaintance responded with a wholly deficient series of ostensibly unrelated fragments, utterances that nevertheless resembled a smooth chain, visually threaded together by Poe's dramatic use of dashes:

Horrid affair that, wasn't it?—great wretches, those Bugaboos—savage and so on—but we live in a wonderfully inventive age!—Smith?—O yes! great man!—perfect desperado—immortal renown—prodigies of valor! *Never heard!!* (This was given in a scream.) Bless my soul!—why he's the man. (68)

Here the final phrase is interrupted by the performance of the "fine tragedian, Climax" (68). To conclude that for the narrator to utter the "up," to fill in the blank at the end of the sentence that has been heretofore excluded, to say in so many words that the general is "The Man That Was Used Up," is a way of registering that the general is merely, as Jonathan Elmer suggests, "a string of consumer secrets," whose aura relies on the smooth, incessant circulation of signifiers (55). But this conclusion misses the point by taking these signifiers as *already sewn together*, rather than fastidiously fused to flatten what is "up" of the general: a terrifying living member, the disturbing extremity that becomes invisible adhesive. Smith's hideous erection is absorbed as a private secret, flattened into the kind of "smooth surface of euphemized power" by which the practice of ruling groups is homogenized (Scott 56). It is precisely through his utterance of the story's title, by which the axiom of identity is secured and the general established as "The Man That Was Used Up," that the narrator manages to repress knowledge of the irremediable excess of that shrill voice and protruding limb, and to leave "with a perfect understanding of the state of affairs" (70). In delivering the title's sentence, the narrator responds to the call of that reagent that joins the antimonies of Jacksonian democracy at their joints. Indeed, with this totalizing rejoinder he finally speaks the lingua franca of his fellow socialites.

So the title of the story is reiterated as its final line, but what again of the "old negro valet, who remained in attendance during my visit" (Poe 69), whose intimate knowledge of the general's fragmentation is a distasteful reminder of that glutinous mass whose shrill squeaks disrupted the "smooth surface of euphemism"? If the narrator's tendencies to repress trauma are implicit in his distressed narrator's chiasmic stammer, "don't know you—know you—know you—don't know you at all!," Pompey's performative exegesis unlocks the "abominable piece of mystery" regarding the renowned military hero, Brevet Brigadier Gen. John A. B. C. Smith. Nevertheless, the servant's eye-opening announcement leads away from rather than toward the "perfect closure" that would become the hallmark of the detective genre.[5] That Pompey's voyeuristic disclosures and menacing gestures presented something of a stumbling block is sufficiently indicated by Poe's decision to expurgate the three paragraphs in question from the story prior to its 1843 publication in his *Prose Romances*, even though they had already appeared in *Tales of the Grotesque and Arabesque* (1840), and had been previously published in *Burton's Gentleman's Magazine* (1839) and *Phantasy-Pieces* (1842) (Poe, *Tales* 377). Poe's bowdlerization of his own story returned the servant to the text's periphery, summoned only by the general's commands. In the tale's earlier appearance, however, Pompey's interpretative acts calls into question the stable social order retroactively instituted by the general's erection. In this way, the disinterpellative demand instigated by a black servant is itself the climactic moment of a story whose subtitle proposes it is "A Tale of the Late Bugaboo and Kickapoo Campaign." Then the function of the title "The Man That Was Used Up" is to occlude the subtitle that props *it* up and makes it possible: the violent contests between white settlers and American Indians. Moreover, this knowledge comes into view by way of a structural analogy, where the violent resistance of the "Bugaboo and Kickapoo Indians" finds its point of entry as much in the threatening person of Pompey as the general's bits and pieces.

Poe conjures a stark image of frontier violence in his choice of the quasi-sedentary Kickapoo, who among the Algonquian confederacy most emphatically eschewed acculturation over the course of several centuries. Having successfully resisted French, British and U.S. efforts at assimilation, during the War of 1812, the Kickapoo joined forces with the British to rout U.S. troops in battle. The Kickapoo became legend as premier "marauders" along the northwestern frontier and particularly in the Illinois Territory, where their extraordinary and "inventive brutality" was corroborated by reports of the O'Neal Massacre near Peoria, where Kickapoo looting and scalping of a settler homestead left ten persons "shockingly mangled," according to congressional documents (qtd. in Gibson 64). Shortly afterward, the 1812 Pigeon Roost Massacre occurred: twenty-one scalps were taken, a relief column of militia found homes looted and burned, and the entire village presented "a mournful scene of desolation, carnage, and death" (Wallace Brice [1868] qtd. in Gibson 69). Echoes of this 1812 terror surface in the general's abbreviated account of his much-butchered body.

At the moment Poe composed this tale, however, the Kickapoo were engaged in the Florida Indian wars, where the U.S. Army had enlisted about one hundred Kickapoo to fight the Seminole (White, *Kickapoo* xvi). Poe's own recruitment of the Kickapoo is an ironic reminder of the perpetually unfinished work of war and the anarchic, side-shifting economy of mercenaries (in the Missouri River region, Kickapoo had also guarded Spanish settlements against encroachment from the Chickasaws and the Osages). Pairing this tribe with the fictitious Bugaboo in the title of his tale, Poe makes a jest of the bogeyman Kickapoo, who lurked in the social imaginary of Indian "savagery," but more even than these discrete instances of carnage from the past, or the uneasy sociability of the present, the Kickapoo threat was that they frequently refused to entertain the Indian removal policies the U.S. government designed. Even though the 1819 Treaty of Edwardsville with the Illinois Kickapoo and the Treaty of Fort Harrison with the Wabash Kickapoo contracted an exchange of tribal lands in Indiana and Illinois for territory on the Osage River in Missouri, "renegade bands" repudiated these treaties outright (Gibson 80). After 1835, many of these retired to the West, but others remained; Chief Mecina, who led one of these bands, "denied that his tribe or any other could unilaterally sign away tribal lands and the resting place of 'the bones of their ancestors'" (78). Not to be reconciled to the prerogatives of the settler state, the Kickapoo persistently aspired to an overthrow of American rule and rejected the agrarian ethos paternalists like Governor Harrison tendered. Into the mid-nineteenth century they retained some ambition to overthrow the U.S. government. In "The Man That Was Used Up," the general's recollection of old Kickapoo-inflicted battle wounds opens up incongruities between the past and the moment of production of Poe's tale: that Indian removal policies designed to end frontier violence by sequestering Indians elsewhere and insulating settlers from contact occluded the *historically specific* and *perpetual* violent process of Indian removal, not to mention ongoing, troubled alliances with Indians required to sustain the "march" of settlement and make the general whole.

Additionally, as Pompey's threat mimes the attack of the absent (Bugaboo and) Kickapoo Indians, the text avails itself of a cultural logic that associates Native American revolt with black revolt. This logic was clearly at work, for instance, in the wake of the "Cataclysm" of August 21, 1831, when Nat Turner, joined by five other slaves, killed at least fifty-seven of the white residents of South Hampton, Virginia (Aptheker 298). Almost immediately after Nat Turner's South Hampton revolt, the *Richmond Enquirer* stressed the "horrible ferocity" of "the banditti," reconfiguring the shocking acts of intimate violence as administered from without by a troupe of marauding interlopers: on August 30, 1831, the *Enquirer* stated, "They remind one of a parcel of blood-thirsty wolves rushing down from the Alps; or rather like a former incursion of the Indians upon the white settlements" (Tragle 43). By equating the way the two groups impinged on the interests and viability of white settlers, the *Enquirer* legitimizes the violent suppression of "foreign" elements. On the other hand, the peculiar effect of aligning the struggles of Indian "intruders" and Turner's gang—at a moment when confusion reigned over Turner's motivation and intent and the possibility of legitimate retaliatory violence was not yet dismissed—has the effect of retroactively undermining the strategy of Indian killing at the core of Manifest Destiny, and shedding light on its "single dark premise" of settler culture: "that American culture is a successor culture that founds itself by extinguishing the culture already in place" (Fisher 30). Pompey's mimed threat of violence reiterates the bloody genesis of the disintegrated general in the hands of the Bugaboo and Kickapoo Indians, who, as we shortly discover, not only scalped and butchered the man but were also the damned "vagabonds" who "took the trouble to cut off at least seven-eighths of my tongue" (Poe 70). The general's epithet—disgorged, no doubt, with the surviving bit of tongue as well as a "singular-looking machine" (70)—works to bind the Indians to disreputable itinerancy, erasing the possibility that their encounter took the form of a dispute over property rights, just as Turner's revolt incited all manner of explanations but those that would acknowledge emancipation as the goal of his revolt.

Lesley Ginsberg has suggested that Turner's motive, like Poe's purloined letter, suffered from "the paradoxical invisibility of the obvious" (102), and indeed, many of the newspapers that described the carnage were strikingly oblivious to the demands for emancipation explicit in the revolt.[6] This propensity to conceive of the black slave population as anything *but* a violent threat to the existing social order belies the private terror of a society perpetually troubled by the prospect of slave rebellions in the wake of the gory slave revolts in the West Indies, Denmark Vesey's barely suppressed conspiracy in 1822, and Nat Turner's revolt less than a decade later (Takaki 121). Nevertheless, while the breathtaking scheme of slave management that Ronald Takaki has called the "Sambo-making machine" defended against the planter class's anxieties about deceit and "savage" retribution at the hands of their slaves, the image of the Sambo (with happy, lazy, immature, and childlike qualities) and the broader image of the black "child/savage" served another important purpose in a slaveholding society (116). It allowed white southerners to conceive of their system of subordination as vastly preferable to the free-labor society in the North, where the political rights of exploited white workers could lead only to clashes. By contrast, slaves' lack of legal rights enabled slave masters to exercise complete control in curbing their workforce, even as the slaves' status as "capital" necessitated that slaveholders be concerned about their well-being (124).

That Poe took the trouble to cut out Pompey's gesture of insubordination indicates an interest in restricting the servant's role, rather than allowing various sociopolitical resonances to proliferate in his performance. Or perhaps Pompey's shocking pedagogy was simply not subtle enough for polite company. Yet Poe's initial positioning of Pompey's threat—directly prior to the general's degrading harassment of his servant, when Pompey performs as a grumbling but obedient Sambo—makes it seem as if Poe had extorted from that character a sufficient excuse for the general's subsequent rhetorical policing and degrading harassment. Poe's expulsion of that portion of the text in which Pompey appeared as an overly proximate, voluminous, threatening racial Other suppresses the full horror of the narrator's traumatic confrontation with the gentleman stiff whose dissolution jeopardizes the social order, leaving a crude stereotype whose function is to immobilize any threat of black revolutionary violence.

To sum up, there are several cultural propositions that Poe's story sets before us. First, the discursive and material operations that consolidate multiple strands of Jacksonian political culture under a single figurehead (or general icon, John A. B. C. Smith) entail an obscene surplus (the "exceedingly odd-looking bundle of something" with its high-pitched squeal) that must be repressed. That Poe's story sufficiently executes the cover-up is suggested by the critical work on "The Man That Was Used Up," which tends to locate the central premise of the tale in the general's *exposure* as "empty signifier," "a string of consumer secrets," or in the man's persistent acts of misrecognition: "he perceives no discrepancy between his continual description in society and the 'nondescript' bundle of flesh he has become," rather than the narrator's *interpellation* in the face of this secret (Elmer 53, 55, Rosenheim 103). Though Poe uses Pompey to deconstruct the fantasy that suspends the entrancing body of the general between the narrator and a traumatic confrontation (with the horrifying shrill squeak that emanates from the glutinous bundle and Pompey's "cachinnating" voice), the black servant becomes that never-exhausted quantity through which we access both the possibilities for interracial sociability and revolutionary violence, at least until they are gentrified by the sight of the general, in all its blinding incandescence. The partial experience of Pompey's rebellion (foreclosed by Poe's expurgation of an image of black violence), his faint resemblance to northern industrial labor, and his structural affinity with the Bugaboo and Kickapoo Indians (both positioned as the fantasmatic support for Jacksonian political culture) are subjects for knowledge that are simultaneously extruded and suppressed.[7] Moreover, Poe's revisions intimate that the resemblance of white industrial labor to black slave labor must be warded off—not only in order to elide those degradations northern white workers associated with blackness, but also so that southern planters could insist that their "capital" investments (in contrast to the producers of "capital" parts that outfitted the general) were outfitted with a servile, Sambo-like nature that would preclude insurrection.

In the face of urban industrial transformation, expanding investments in land and slaves, and Andrew Jackson's bellicose Indian removal policy, General A. B. C. Smith is made the explicit "representative" of democracy, the kind of "citizen *qua* individual" on whom "anxieties about political division and social disorder, along with counterphobic imperatives for 'wholeness' and 'unity' were transferred" (Nelson 182). Poe's narrator, moreover, is an anonymous actor who enters into a fraternal contract with the general and other agents of white male hegemony, anticipating John Cawelti's definition of the "detective-individual" as one devoted to "*restoring the serenity of the middle-class social order*" rather than "laying bare the hidden guilt of bourgeois society" (*Adventure, Mystery, Romance* 96). "The Man That Was Used Up" foregrounds the device of narrative reconstruction that would be central to Poe's version of the detective story, but to the extent that Poe's story tenders a critique of republican ideology through Pompey's inspection and assembly of the general, this critique is retarded and Pompey's inquiry is foiled by the peripatetic protraction of the investigation, the vacuity of the narrator's various interlocutors, and the general's unwillingness to acknowledge his fragmentation. Nevertheless, the narrator's final affirmation and the effect of the tale seem to part ways. If the narrator manages to swallow his revulsion and to depart (albeit somewhat dazed by the encounter), returning his disquieting discovery to the realm of the unthinkable, the climactic horror of the dismembered body shakes the reader out of the imaginative interpellation associated with what Dennis Porter calls the "perfect closure" of the detective novel (Porter 219). Pompey, the agent capable of revelation, must be edited out of the text in order to secure the narrator's ascendancy and cultural secret keeping.

"NO, I CANNOT PRONOUNCE IT"

One of the sources for Nathaniel Hawthorne's story "Mr. Higginbotham's Catastrophe" might have been "Mr. Mark Higginbotham's Case of Real Distress," which first appeared in the London publication *New Monthly Magazine and Literary Journal* in 1825. This anonymous but certainly fictional anecdote was reprinted that same year in the *Salem Gazette*, which Hawthorne, now returned to Salem from college, undoubtedly had opportunity to read. The substance of this short piece is the bellyaching of a man named Mark Somers, who has inherited the estate of a well-to-do brickmaker named Timothy Higginbotham (his wife's uncle) on the condition that he adopt the surname of the deceased as his own. Somers, who fancies himself debonair, revolts at becoming "the nominal representative of a vile Hodton dealer in argillaceous parallelograms," even when a fortune hangs in the balance (290). Having ever been "squeamish, fastidious, fantastical about names" (290), Somers cannot bear to dispose of his own and be branded a Higginbotham:

> Give a dog an ill name, says the proverb, and hang him. Never dog had a worse than mine, and I feel already as if I were hung up aloft for the finger of score to be wagged at, and condemned to stand in the pillory of my own appellation as the wretch Hig—No, I cannot pronounce it. (291)

Somers likens the burden of this "degrading *sobriquet*" to a public execution and cannot even complete the sentence—yet his wife has coaxed him into compliance, and the "hideous appendage" becomes his own (290). His name swallowed by his wife's unpolished ancestor's, the narrator struggles to extricate himself from this difficulty while upholding his end of the bargain. That is, like General Smith, this gentleman of fashion tries to resurrect the old self used up by this least welcome of inheritances, to rescue "Somers" from the hangman that is "Higginbotham." He begins "writing letters and describing myself to tradesmen and others as the late Mark Somers" (291), but is the dupe of this new debacle, since undertakers, clergy, and sexton descend upon his home, jockeying for command of the funeral arrangements, "and were not to be persuaded, without considerable difficulty, that I was still alive as Mr. Higginbotham, though unfortunately extinct as Mr. Mark Somers" (291).

The "real distress" of this tale is class anxiety, since Mark Somers's many professions of gentility are endangered by his new, unsavory association with a mere merchant and maker of bricks, whose name incidentally is branded upon him. Though it entails death in name only, Mark Somers's predicament might have prompted Hawthorne to compose "Mr. Higginbotham's Catastrophe," a tale that also speculates about what it might mean for a man to be made of some other person's money. But Hawthorne's story, an American production, connects the fates of merchants and manufacturers, a man of industry and a common peddler, and a bunch of working stiffs who very briefly forge a murderous alliance. Tying together the vagaries of class and nerve-racking industrial developments in his presentation of the many men and women who populate a regional economy, Hawthorne mobilizes narrative retroversion to tell a story about race relations and economic mobility.

Eventually one of Hawthorne's *Twice Told Tales* (1837), "Mr. Higginbotham's Catastrophe" first appeared in the December 1834 issue of *The New-England Magazine*, neatly framed by "The Storyteller. No. II. The Village Theatre," the second (and, as it turned out, final) installment in what Hawthorne had hoped would be a serialized adventures of a tale-telling vagabond. Having been reared by one Parson Thumpcushion, who resolves to make the young man adopt some profession, and finding the entirety of New England loathe to admit "that any good thing may consist with what they call idleness" (353), Hawthorne's narrator resolves in the first episode of the series to take up the itinerant life of a teller of tales. In "The Village Theatre," he has his first professional engagement in a country-town tavern, and "Mr. Higginbotham's Catastrophe" constitutes the whole of his shtick, though he professes to have "manufactured a great variety of plots and skeletons of tales, and kept them ready for use" (358).

The tale in question features the tobacco peddler Dominicus Pike, who hears a piece of news there is no accounting for: Mr. Higginbotham, the Kimballton merchant, was murdered in cold blood only the previous night!—and yet somehow this news has reached Pike, who happens to be more than a day's travel away from the scene of the crime. Accordingly, the story turns on the presentation of an "achrony": what Mieke Bal defines as "a deviation of time that can't be analysed any further," for instance, when "an event which has yet to take place chronologically has already been presented" (96). But Pike, a storyteller himself, is obliged to resolve the narratological conundrum he confronts; not only does his reputation hinge on its unraveling, the life (or death) of a Mr. Higginbotham apparently depends on it. In divining that fine line between life and death, Pike tries his hand at the kind of temporal reconstruction that would be at the center of the puzzle mystery. In doing so, he sheds light on the potential for working-class alliances that cut across race, though these possibilities are suppressed in the interest of preserving Mr. Higginbotham.

Like "The Man That Was Used Up" and "Mr. Mark Higginbotham's Case of Real Distress," "Mr. Higginbotham's Catastrophe" is about the unlikely resurrection of an individual who commands a certain influence, but Hawthorne's story pursues something less than a fatality; for almost the entire story, it isn't clear whether Mr. Higginbotham has *actually* died. And if the protagonist of "The Man That Was Used Up" departs relieved by his "perfect understanding of the state of affairs" once General Smith again stands before him, synthetic bits sutured into "that truly fine-looking fellow" (70, 66), Dominus Pike is of two minds as far the Kimballton merchant's murder is concerned. A consummate salesman and storyteller, Pike turns a profit by chronicling the ghastly details of Higginbotham's assassination while he peddles his wares. Nevertheless, he rushes to Higginbotham's aid when he finally perceives the merchant in danger—and is well rewarded, even if he cannot "account for his valor on this awful emergency" (166). Finally, where Pompey's pantomime provides a point of entry into the complex entanglements in the antebellum republic, Hawthorne's storyteller fashions Higginbotham's "Catastrophe" as a composite narrative, repeatedly reworked as Pike, a purveyor of gossip, consolidates intelligence gathered along the road to understand this unfortunate event.

The process of properly situating events in time and space is one Hawthorne places front and center, since between Morristown, where Dominicus Pike begins his journey, and Kimballton, where Mr. Higginbotham apparently met his "doleful fate," any "little trifle of news" travels at an astonishing rate: "Kimballton was nearly sixty miles distant in a straight line; the murder had been perpetrated only at eight o'clock the preceding night; yet Dominicus had heard of it at seven in the morning, when, in all probability, poor Mr. Higginbotham's own family had but just discovered his corpse, hanging on the St. Michael's pear tree" (151–52). Pike, who broadcasts the news without the slightest reserve, accounts for the physical implausibility of this intelligence by "supposing that the narrator had made a mistake of one day in the date of the occurrence"—further revising the historical record by setting an event that has not (yet), it turns out, transpired in the more distant, rather than immediate, past (152). By contrast, the "ill-looking" traveler who has likely "footed it all night" and introduces Pike to this "horrible intelligence" in the morning does "hesitate a little, as if he were either searching his memory for news or weighing the expediency of telling it" (151).

Hawthorne's storyteller attributes the impulse to hold back to two possible causes: on the one hand, the itinerant may be rummaging through his full stock of "intelligence" to locate that which might still constitute news, or, on the other hand, he is considering what might be the advantage (or "expediency") of making his knowledge known. He weighs haste against delay, and in hindsight, we might conclude that the wanderer sees no better way of distancing himself from the assassination of Squire Higginbotham than by putting himself at geographical and temporal remove. Consequently, he attempts to side-step self-incrimination by offering a full chronology that identifies victim and villain, time, place, and manner of death:

> Old Mr. Higginbotham, of Kimballton, was murdered in his orchard at eight o'clock last night, by an Irishman and a nigger. They strung him up to the branch of a St. Michael's pear tree, where nobody would find him till the morning. (151)

This calculated alibi profits from Pike's conviction in the velocity of news (that it would outstrip the traveler who delivered it—"ill news flies fast," the peddler observes [152]) and second, the peddler's bearing of that news: ideally, Pike's bulletins will distance themselves from the suspect, returning to their perceived point of origin (Kimballton), rather than tailing him as he hastens away from the scene of the supposed crime. Finally, with all his rumor-mongering and business-bartering, Dominicus Pike is considerably slower than the unrelenting traveler, so that the tale's homecoming is much delayed with respect to its abrupt departure. But there is, all the same, a fatality that pursues Pike—or rather, that Pike pursues, since his arrival in Kimballton is synchronized with the crime in progress.

So this story is always at its (wit's) end, its final event (save denouement) almost the sole subject of the text, and yet murder is never an event that is anticipated; on the contrary, what will take place in the narrative future seems from the outset to have taken place in the near past. In this way, the formal arrangement of "Mr. Higginbotham's Catastrophe" bears some relation to Tzvetan Todorov's 1966 account of the detective story: it comprises two stories, "of which one is absent but real, the other present but insignificant" (46). And for Todorov, each of these stories has its particular utility; "The first—the story of the crime—tells 'what really happened,'" Todorov explains, "whereas the second—the story of the investigation—explains 'how the reader (or the narrator) has come to know about it'" (45). Moreover, their occurrence is temporally distinct, since "the first story, that of the crime, ends before the second one begins" (44). Certainly, "Mr. Higginbotham's Catastrophe" proposes a different configuration for these stories. In this case, what we might call the story of the crime is handed over, intact, like an affidavit or theorem that we might dispute, but we soon discover the activity is meaningless, since it is a "tall tale"—a shadow that has yet to give rise to substance, a text that lacks context. To state this rather differently: to hem and haw over the particular details surrounding Mr. Higginbotham's assassination, to amend what might be considered, under other circumstances, a complete account of textual events or a *master array* (Charles Rzepka's term for that set of occurrences which the reader "imaginatively constructed and reconstructed" until he or she arrives at something akin to a master narrative, a "single, coherent sequence in the projected time-frame of the world the story represents" [*Detective Fiction* 19]) is hardly worth the effort, since we are finally informed that Mr. Higginbotham is alive and well!

But if the story or stories of the crime are not the concern of this riddle, what does concern us is how not one, but two men come to deliver misleading reports to Dominicus Pike, and how it is their reports so closely resemble a crime that will *not quite* come to pass. To borrow Todorov's terms, it is not the story of the crime but *the story of* the story of the crime that is "absent but real," and the investigation of this matter is what brings Dominicus, at last, to Higginbotham's orchard, where the crime itself (that is, the specific circumstances of the ongoing attack against Higginbotham) becomes "present but insignificant." After Higginbotham is safe and sound, the enigma is unraveled:

> If the riddle be not already guessed, a few words will explain the simple machinery, by which this "coming event" was made to "cast its shadow before." Three men had plotted the robbery and murder of Mr. Higginbotham; two of them, successively, lost courage and flew, each delaying the crime one night by their disappearance; the third was in the act of perpetration, when a champion, blindly obeying the call of fate, like the heroes of old romance, appeared in the person of Dominicus Pike. (166–67)

But like "The Man That Was Used Up," this story is about an industry of storytelling, a point the narrator promises to show and not simply tell when he notes that, "as will be seen in the course of my story, the pedler [*sic*] was inquisitive, and something of a tattler, always itching to hear the news, and anxious to tell it again" (150). Pike is a habitual tale-bearer, afflicted by an irresistible urge to spout gossip and regurgitate rumors, yet he sees his social function in rather a different light: "He found himself invariably the first bearer of the intelligence"—never mind that the news is already at one remove, the audience at every tavern is fresh—"and was so pestered with questions that he could not avoid filling up the outline, till it became quite a respectable narrative" (152). In his loquacity, Pike resembles a nineteenth-century archetype. Itinerant peddlers who traveled from village to village were known for their sharp tongues and sharper trading, and considered something of a prototype for the New England Yankee: "not speechless but voluble, not despairing but ambitious" (Perry 174, 183). With a quick tongue, fashionable merchandise, and a "neat little cart, painted green," Pike is primed to make a respectable living on the road. Still, Hawthorne's reference to a painting of "an Indian chief, holding a pipe and a golden tobacco stalk, on the rear" invites us to consider the colonial project that delivered this product to the world; to understand, indeed, that Pike has superseded indigenous peoples on a trade route that likely long preceded his particular expeditions (450). And though he is an audacious colorist, Dominicus is relieved of the full burden of fibbing when he hears "one piece of corroborative evidence" from a former clerk who "manifested but little grief at Mr. Higginbotham's catastrophe": the gentleman in question did in fact frequent the locale where he is said to have met his end (152).

In fact, Pike continues to take liberties with the tale until a disagreeable interlocutor casts doubt upon his report. The peddler is content to freely dispense his report until he encounters a neighbor to Squire Higginbotham some miles short of Parker's Falls, an old farmer who spoils his fun by insisting he had a drink that very morning with the man in question, during which Higginbotham "didn't seem to know any more about his own murder than I did" (154). "I tell the story as I hear it, mister" Dominicus admits to his cross-examiner: "I don't say that I saw the thing done" (153), which is to say that the facticity of the peddler's account is dashed by direct evidence. The farmer's testimony, spewed forth with the "vilest tobacco smoke the peddler [sic] had ever smelt," trumps hearsay, annihilating the sanctity of whatever "gospel" Dominicus hoped to deliver to his eager audience—not to mention the perfume of the peddler's sweet tobacco, since Dominicus discards "his half-burnt cigar" in the face of the farmer's foul smoke and is left "quite down in the mouth" (153–54). This "sad resurrection" of the corpse leaves Pike irritable—"he so detested" the gall of this unfortunate witness "that his suspension would have pleased him better than Mr. Higginbotham's" (154)—but also despondent to the extent that the peddler is plagued with dreams of hanging from that pear tree himself.

Pike's utter deflation lays bare his business model: storytelling is essential to the peddler's enterprise, and narrative has its value in ready money. And when, the early following day, Dominicus cross-examines a stranger with "a deep tinge of negro blood," just come from Kimballton, and discovers that, according to this rather startled stranger, "There was no colored man! It wan Irishman that hanged him last night, at eight o'clock," the peddler throws himself back into the spirit of the thing, and proceeds to Parker's Falls with the news ready on his tongue (155). Rather than "think of raising a hue and cry after him, as an accomplice in the murder," though, Dominicus resolves to give his reluctant herald leave, since "I don't want his black blood on my head; and hanging the nigger would'nt unhang Mr. Higginbotham"—and having Mr. Higginbotham unhanged is hardly in Pike's interest, insofar as the story of Higginbotham's death makes for stimulating conversation and stellar sales (156). This is the principal lesson, Thomas H. Pauly suggests, of a plot that is "neither complex nor profound" (171). Pike is "hawking local gossip to increase sales," Pauly explains, and, upon hearing of Higginbotham's gruesome death, assembles a full-blown narrative from this trifle of news—and profits from it (171).

If Pike cultivates his tales from the most rudimentary truths to promote sales, there is nevertheless something more to the equation here, where Pike leaves the dark-skinned stranger, very likely a would-be assassin, at liberty. The peddler's level-headed notion, that "hanging the nigger would'nt unhang Mr. Higginbotham," mixes run-of-the-mill racism with an appreciation of their interracial mutuality and interdependent mobility too, since Pike has found a coconspirator to resuscitate that thrilling chronicle of Higginbotham's murder, and lay low the squire once again. The news of Higginbotham's death offers unparalleled prospects for the tobacco salesman, so Pike takes the stranger for his Scheherazade, an anonymous source stool pigeon or no, for the fellow has traded him a toothsome tale for undisturbed flight—a real bargain where Pike is concerned. In this way, at least, his business ethic contrasts with that of the storyteller who invented him. After his first public exhibition before "an audience of nine persons, seven of whom hissed me in a very disagreeable manner" the storyteller owns up to shortcomings as a performer (358). He admits that "it would have been mere swindling to retain the money which had been paid, on my implied contract to give its value of amusement; so I called in the door-keeper, bade him refund the whole receipts, a mighty sum, and was gratified with a round of applause, by way of offset to the hisses" (358). Pike, by contrast, disposes of "a whole bunch of Spanish wrappers among at least twenty horrified audiences" circulating hair-raising yarns about the destruction of one of the hoary pillars of New England business, not as entertainment but as truth (152). Once he gets the ball rolling, his profit promises to expand exponentially, if each in his audience is an envoy, and every telling of the tale is a new occasion for a smoke. But since Pike's literary speculations lead him to witness a bona fide attempted murder and become Mr. Higginbotham's rescuer and heir, his homicidal brainstorming is vindicated: "Fiction now becomes fact," and his fortune is made (Pauly 172).

But the correlation between the peddler's contrivances and cash in hand isn't by any means fixed. Pike's storytelling habits are a source of market fluctuations in each town he visits, and not merely because he interrupts the daily business to conduct his own. In stark contrast to the discrete chatter of socialites in "The Man That Was Used Up," the peddler of "Mr. Higginbotham's Catastrophe" preys upon the grisly sensibilities of villagers so starved for entertainment they long to hear every violent detail and anatomical particular of the Higginbotham's homicide, laying into Pike's supply of tobacco all the while. There are great upheavals after Pike issues his reports and upheavals again when they are rescinded, particularly in Parker's Falls, where Higginbotham is "part owner of the slitting mill and a considerable stockholder in the cotton factories," sufficiently invested in the region that "the inhabitants felt their own prosperity interested in his fate" (157). We learn quick enough that the dead man's repute extends about as far as his money does—that is, the purported execution of Squire Higginbotham is not incidentally a pecuniary drama. A special edition of the *Parker's Falls Gazette* commemorates the occasion, and memorializes crimes against the squire. Under the immense headline "HORRID MURDER OF MR. HIGGINBOTHAM!" the report tells the story of Higginbotham's death, and also announces "the number of thousand dollars of which he had been robbed" (157). The hysterics of Higginbotham's niece are enthusiastically reiterated in the newspaper, which explains how the lady "had gone from one fainting fit to another, ever since her uncle was found hanging on the St. Michael's pear tree, with his pockets inside out" (83)—her fits presumably but not necessarily attributed to the assassination of her closest kin and not only the discovery that he has been relieved of his fortune. And when Higginbotham's lawyer arrives in Parker's Falls, he sternly proposes that the false reports of his client's end are "a willful falsehood, maliciously contrived to injure Mr. Higginbotham's credit" (159).

"HE COULD NOT AVOID FILLING UP THE OUTLINE, TILL IT BECAME QUITE A RESPECTABLE NARRATIVE"

What I am trying to stress is that while it would be imprecise to call this tale a work of detection, "Mr. Higginbotham's Catastrophe" is a metafiscal narrative. The narratological conundrum whose unraveling it pursues is set against a landscape of financial and industrial cataclysm, and its chronological puzzle takes intelligible shape only when this plot and its industrial subtext collide, and when a purported past event enters the present tense of the tale. In this moment, the "riddle" of the text turns into a theory of interracial sociability in an industrially oriented market economy, and the solution to "the story of the story" of the crime comes into relief only if this context sets the terms for the text.

In an antebellum economy beleaguered by unexpected downturns or "panics," the news of Mr. Higginbotham's death is a commercial event, a tremor in a series of bewildering market seizures that were variously construed as lawless attacks on clean-living peoples or chance shocks that escaped explanation (Larson 10). At the same time, the bewildering proliferation of money-issuing institutions was considered tantamount to a "free-for-all" (59). And after 1832, a multitude of banknotes, "originated with often distant corporations, entered into the streams of commerce, and floated far away from the legal abstractions that had issued them," while their worth rose and fell "at a value relative to the perception that the bank could redeem its [paper] promises" with specie stored in its coffers (Mihm 12, 9). What is more, differentiating between notes issued by legitimate banks or state-chartered corporations and those generated by "wildcat" banks and counterfeiters was no easy task. To the layman's eye, these may as well have been cut from the same cloth. Along similar lines, Pike's dreadful intelligence gains currency though his claim is unsubstantiated. Like counterfeit currency, or like a note that circulates "below par," it cannot meet its obligations, and yet his word passes for a genuine thing. Though he is not exactly crying wolf, on each occasion his tale is appraised, it is discounted, and yet no effort will suppress it; it is never entirely recanted. Indeed, even after the incensed citizens of Parker's Falls oust Pike from the premises, pelting the peddler with clay munitions, he is amused to think "the paragraph in the Parker's Falls *Gazette* would be reprinted from Maine to Florida, and perhaps form an item in the London newspapers," with predictable effects: "Many a miser would trouble for his money-bags and life" (Hawthorne 162). To say that Higginbotham's condition is analogous to the solvency of some institution is not extravagance, then, and who would disallow that Hawthorne's equal concern with "accounts" and the "teller" belongs to a system of elaborate puns?

But why is it a question of putting stock in Higginbotham's death? That the picture of the murder is not susceptible to adjustment, such that another man might substitute himself for the squire, leads me to propose that in Hawthorne's tale, the structuring absence (the subtext for the false text that lacks context) is a particular motive for the crime. Why, indeed, must Higginbotham be the casualty of this conspiracy in life and in yarn? Why is he, rather than any other man, the proprietor of this catastrophe? The explanation is to be found, I would argue, in the economic particulars of the narrative that Hawthorne advances. As Pike approaches Kimballton, all evidence conspires to show that Higginbotham belongs to an economy that has outpaced him. His estate once "stood beside the old highway," but now it has "been left in the background by the Kimballton turnpike," Pike discovers (165). The squire's health is so poor he seems in person to substantiate reports of his "horrid murder," or if not, Higginbotham is perhaps a picture of his pecuniary health. The toll gatherer confides to Pike that the squire is deathly "yellow and thin"; he is "more like a ghost or an old mummy than good flesh and blood" (164), and Dominicus follows not a man but a "grey old shadow" onto Higginbotham's premises (165).

And what has transpired to make Higginbotham such an antiquated fixture of the economy? Higginbotham is part proprietor of the mill at Parker's Falls, which seems to be one of those picturesque and semirural outfits that simply spun yarn by water power, according to an model of textile production pioneered by Samuel Slater at the end of the nineteenth century (Larson 72). Parker's Falls comprises "shopkeepers, mistresses of boarding houses, factory girls, millmen, and schoolboys" (Hawthorne 157)—whose sheer presence is proof of how Slater-style operations frequently entangled entire districts in the business of textile production (Larson 33). And yet Hawthorne's evasive observation that the town is, "as every body knows, as thriving as three cotton factories and a slitting mill can make it" is little proof of the residents' prosperity, especially since "the machinery was not in motion, and but a few of the shop doors unbarred" when Pike drives into town in the early morning (156). By the 1820s or 1830s this kind of manufactory was strictly modest compared to the massive water-power facility, heaps of textile machinery, and legions of unmarried women operatives that Francis

Cabot Lowell installed along the Merrimack River in Massachusetts. Mammoth factories like Lowell's brought economies of scale as well as integrated production to bear on the textile industry and all its lesser producers. Consequently, by the mid-1830s, market forces trimmed local profits to a narrow margin, and the expense of new technology ensured that any would-be industrialists had already divested themselves of any genuine concern for the worker's welfare (Larson 73–74, 138).

In the case of "Mr. Higginbotham's Catastrophe," we might say that the "simple machinery" of the plot that allows a "coming event" to "cast its shadow before" is *actual* machinery: the apparatus of an early textile industry whose spinning mills were cushioned from British competition by the 1807 Embargo Act and the War of 1812 and whose market share was suddenly eclipsed by the expensive machine technology of a massive enterprise like Lowell's (Sellers 28). Hawthorne's Higginbotham seems to have plunged full tilt into the modern capitalist economy, managing somehow to keep himself afloat—very possibly by accommodating the markets at the expense of labor. A former clerk, who "manifested but little grief at Mr. Higginbotham's catastrophe," insinuates that the man is a "crusty old fellow, as close as a vise" (Hawthorne 152–53). The businessman's passion for economizing is corroborated, moreover, by Pike's discovery that the squire "had in his service an Irishman of doubtful character, whom he had hired without a recommendation, on the score of economy" (87). Hawthorne insinuates that Higginbotham belongs to those small-scale manufacturers who sought out immigrant workers at low wages with little concern for the welfare of those local inhabitants they replaced. What bitterness the residents of Parker's Falls reserved for the squire is only half-hinted at, however, when the storyteller poses it as a counterfactual. "So excessive was the wrath of the inhabitants" on discovering Dominicus Pike's intelligence is faulty, the storyteller observes, "a stranger would have supposed that Mr. Higginbotham was an object of abhorrence at Parker's Falls and that a thanksgiving had been proclaimed for his murder" (85)—not quite implying that the opposite is false (that is, that Mr. Higginbotham is an object of adoration, and that his unexpected restoration would provide occasion to celebrate), but not *not* implying it either.

And what of those would-be assassins who might be held liable for this ascendency of misinformation, the men who "successively, lost courage and fled" from Kimballton, abandoning the orchard where Higginbotham was to meet his maker(s) and leaving an apparently unsavory Irishman alone to eliminate the boss (167)? Teresa Goddu proposes that Hawthorne painstakingly depicted these marauders as racially Other. In saddling the first "ill looking" traveler Pike encounters with a bundle on a stick, Goddu points out, Hawthorne "deploys the conventional printer's image of the slave used in runaway slave advertisements" ("Hawthorne" 134). Having "blackened" this villain and his coconspirators, Hawthorne swaps class hostilities for racial conflict (134). Goddu maintains, moreover, that the near-assassination Hawthorne depicts is based on an *actual* homicide: the 1830 murder of the East India merchant Captain Joseph White, whose contract killing was ultimately pinned on Richard and George Crowninshield, both constituents of Salem's merchant class, and apparently commissioned by businessmen Joe and Frank Knapp, brothers who thought themselves likely to inherit a fortune if Captain White died without a will (134). The "real rivalry" of the event is displaced not once, but twice, Goddu argues, so that in "Mr. Higginbotham's Catastrophe" the internal antagonisms and aggressions of the merchant class are recast as a working-class menace, one that can be "blackened" and finally "contained" (134).[8] By contrast, in "Nathaniel Hawthorne, *The Concord Freeman*, and the Irish 'Other,'" Monica Elbert alerts us to the "rampant xenophobia" manifest in the tale's distinctly anti-Irish attitudes (63), an added insult to the story's "average racism."[9]

But this troupe of would-be assassins is not *uniformly* "blackened," even if Hawthorne likens their civic status to the slave's, nor is the Irishman alone sullied by the scheme to hang Higginbotham. Instead their racial heterogeneity is critical. Of the first, we have not got much in the way of description, though the "ill-looking fellow" speaks "rather sullenly" and pulls "the broad brim of a gray hat over his eyes" (150); the second, by contrast, is distinguished by his "deep tinge of negro blood" (155); and these two accessories to the crime abandon their Irish coconspirator to undertake the deed himself. Pike's individuated encounters with this trio and Hawthorne's attention to racial and ethnic distinctions indirectly reflect an interracial sociability most likely cultivated in Mr. Higginbotham's employ. The three men (the first "unvarnished," presumably white, the second black, the third Irish) in sequence might correspond to consecutive waves of labor in the market revolution (each man having been crowded out of a job by his successor).[10] That these racially and ethnically differentiated parties banded together against a common enemy only to disperse, leaving each man to fend for himself, hints at the way that conflict related to ethnic and racial differences might crush the very possibilities for class solidarities that industrialization put in place. More importantly, Hawthorne leads us to understand that Mr. Higginbotham prevails because the racial divisions that prevented his unhappy workforce from uniting against him.

These signposts of an interracial working-class history are indisputably present, and yet so understated as to make a martyr of Higginbotham and sweep aside the question of motive. It might be said, however, that as laborer's associations federated in the New England Associations of Farmers, Mechanics, and Other Workingmen in the 1830s, conducting as many as 172 successful strikes between 1833 and 1836 in the Northeast alone (Sellers 338), Hawthorne's proposition that three workingmen united in opposition to Mr. Higginbotham is as likely as its conclusion is not. A. H. Wood, who piloted the strike for the ten-hour day in Boston, called the struggle "neither more nor less than a contest between *Money* and labor," and admitted to "arraying the poor against the *principles* of the rich, and if this be arraying the poor against the rich, I say go on with tenfold fury" (qtd. in Sellers 338). Hawthorne's workingmen amount to only three, but they are criminal conspirators and they have cold feet besides. Consequently, the "singular combination of incidents" (163) by which the announcements of Higginbotham's death precede his attempted murder coalesce in something other than a cautionary tale. The "catastrophe" in question, that "sudden and violent change in the physical order of things" (OED) which places the "old, identical Higginbotham" in the orchard, "not indeed hanging on the St. Michael's pear-tree, but trembling beneath it" with a "sturdy Irishman" looming above him (166), is a temporary disruption of the social order, nothing more; Hawthorne makes a puzzle of proprietricidal fantasy and a plaything of cause and effect.

Along these lines, it is worth pointing out that Hawthorne's storyteller indulges a rather trivial anachronism in relating the heroic rescue of Higginbotham by that peddler Dominicus Pike. The story of Pike's ascendency to Higginbotham's estate is not just that of a peddler rising to join the bourgeois elite. It is also a story in which tobacco production usurps the hold of textiles on the New England economy. And yet cotton superseded tobacco, not the other way around. It was cotton in the South, after all, that paired with the mechanical inventions in the North to produce a textile industry of international significance—and one that would neither have been launched nor sustained without the labor of slaves and the growth of that peculiar institution. In fact, the depressed market for tobacco in the 1780s and 1790s led planters in the Chesapeake to issue manumissions (Howe 53); and if the market for cotton was largely indigenous in the late eighteenth century, industrial textile production in Britain ensured that by 1820, cotton would replace tobacco as the nation's preeminent export and remain in demand at home (Howe 132, 158). Why, then, in the story's denouement do we discover that, having married the squire's niece and inherited Higginbotham's property, Dominicus Pike has now ceased to reside in Kimballton and has "established a large tobacco manufactory" in the storyteller's "native village"? (167). Hawthorne has imagined a world without that "simple machinery" which made slavery once again profitable: Eli Whitney's cotton gin.

And why, moreover, is Dominicus Pike's tobacco manufactory set before us in the very first issue of "The Story Teller" as an enterprise that, with the exception of its "splendid image of an Indian chief in front," appears to the narrator in the early morning fog as "an affair of smoke" (354)? Pike's success in "Mr. Higginbotham's Catastrophe" (which we might call an extension of Hawthorne's storyteller's "pipedream") is overdetermined or at least resolved in advance, by the frame of Hawthorne's "The Story Teller," which makes a fossil and a trophy of the "splendid image" of an American Indian and a prosperous merchant of the itinerant peddler. If a program of backward construction in the detective-story plot leads inexorably to an absolute narrative coherence, encouraging "anticipation of retrospection" in its readers, who might "continually project a diagram of the totality it [the story of the crime] will eventually constitute" (Brooks qtd. in Pyrhönen, *Mayhem* 10, Pyrhönen 10), the bit of underhanded prolepsis that propels Hawthorne's story goes one better. It cues the reader of the discontinued serial "The Story Teller," in which the tale "Mr. Higginbotham's Catastrophe" initially appeared, to the ultimate end and effects that that tale contrives: to achieve an upward mobility for that wandering salesman and teller of tales, Dominicus Pike, albeit at the expense of the three men who contrived to murder Mr. Higginbotham. Indeed, this preemptive finale implies by example that the itinerant storyteller will make good on his project of bartering tales for a livelihood as well—an outcome that no doubt appealed to the young and not-yet-successful author of "The Story Teller," Nathaniel Hawthorne. The riddle "Mr. Higginbotham's Catastrophe" purports to unravel leverages another end: a perfectly lucrative resolution for Dominicus Pike.

To ascribe genius to the perfect resolution of a mystery was misguided, Poe pointed out in an August 9, 1846, letter to Philip Pendleton Cooke. After all, "Where is the ingenuity of unraveling a web that you yourself (the author) have woven for the express purpose of unraveling?" (328). Poe likely viewed the ratiocinative tale as a "program of deception that is eventually explained" rather than an act of "imaginative expression" or even "genuine analysis," Stephan Rachman asserts, pointing out that "the moral activity which disentangles" in "Murders in the Rue Morgue" (1841) suggests Poe was at least as interested in the act of unraveling narrative as in the agent who could accomplish it (Rachman 18, 21). "The Man That Was Used Up" and "Mr. Higginbotham's Catastrophe" use narrative retroversion to disentangle a "program of deception" that configure the social experience of an industrial-oriented economy and the frontier violence that both complements and sustains it. It is by this use of narrative retroversion, moreover, Poe and Hawthorne entertain processes of racial formation in the world of production, as well as prospects for interracial sociability and collectivity in the realm of work. Their self-reflexive use of backward construction foregrounds its ideological power, its assimilatory and exclusionary effects—though Poe more than Hawthorne seems to have been alarmed by the gentrifying potential of this narrative device. In Poe's grotesque general we have a picture of a puzzle form that turns a problem into a pastime and, in its resolution, suggests a system for "restoring rational order to a psyche threatened with disruption" (Cawelti 101). Yet interventions on the part of the black servant Pompey briefly unsettle the cultural intervention that coordinates the antimonies of Jacksonian America. And in "Mr. Higginbotham's Catastrophe," Dominicus Pike, like Pompey, offers access to an image of interracial sociability, showing potential for a reversal in the order of things—even if Pike's melodramatic rescue of the squire, who escapes certain death by a hair's breadth, proves instrumental to the peddler's enrichment. In these texts, narrative retroversion systematizes and rationalizes practices of racial differentiation and frontier violence that support an industrially oriented market economy. In doing so, they signpost the early cultural functions of a narrative device whose work is far from simple: to affix prepositions to propositions, like sinew to bone, and reconstruct the past.

CHAPTER 3

To Have Been Possessed

We know that a capitalist society more willingly pardons rape, murder, or
kidnapping than a bounced check, which is its only theological crime, the crime
against spirit.

—GILLES DELEUZE, "THE PHILOSOPHY OF CRIME NOVELS"

He has made a slave of me with his looks. He has forced me to understand him,
without his saying a word; and he has forced me to keep silence, without his
uttering a threat.

—CHARLES DICKENS, *THE MYSTERY OF EDWIN DROOD*

"You will say that man cannot hold property in man," James Henry Hammond argued in his 1845 "Letter to an English Abolitionist," then pointed
out that quite the opposite was true: "The answer is, that he can and actually
does hold property in his fellow all the world over, in a variety of forms, and
has always done so" (104). According to American advocates for the "peculiar institution," slaves were indispensable acquisitions, assets that could not
be properly relinquished. More importantly, if the slave might be read as a
"sign and surrogate" of his or her proprietor, explains historian and literary
critic Saidiya Hartman (120), in manumission the captive did not exchange
slavery for self-possession. Manumission could not resurrect the slave from
a state of social death, only submit him to an arithmetic of double negatives,
enacting "the negation of the negation of social life" (Patterson 211). The
manumitted man was, in a word, an unthinkable entity. For one, the Janus-
faced picture that proslavery propagandists had so carefully formulated—
one part simpleton and Sambo, another part savage—would grip him long
after emancipation (Frederickson 53). Nevertheless, as the proslavery apologist Professor Thomas Roderick Dew explained, in the wake of that "inhuman massacre" in Haiti and, more recently, in Southhampton, and given
the ferocity of that "fanatical negro preacher" Nat Turner, "the imagination

was suffered to conjure up the most appalling phantoms" of slave insurrection (290). A niece of George Washington referred to Turner's rebellion, or perhaps to Turner himself, as "a smothered volcano—we know not when, or where, the flame will burst forth, but we know that death in the most repulsive forms awaits us" (qtd. in McDougall 64). Neither the collapse of slaveholding in the South nor the "universal ruin and desolation" of its white citizens could be avoided in the face of any abolition scheme (Dew 290).

Every free Negro in the antebellum South was, therefore, as W. E. B. DuBois would reflect in *Black Reconstruction*, "a contradiction, a threat and a menace" (7). Villain or vagrant, tradesman or hired hand, he jeopardized the tenure of King Cotton and "must not be. He must be suppressed, enslaved, colonized" (7). Hammond, who served variously as congressman, governor, and senator from South Carolina in the decades before the Civil War, insisted that southerners "cannot be flattered, duped, nor bullied out of their rights or their propriety" (151). They were as little likely to surrender their human property as their New England adversaries were to turn over their estates to "the descendants of the slaughtered red men" who first possessed them (103). And yet the proprietary rights Hammond revered might engender a distressing reliance, a dependent state. There was no guarantee that slavery as an economic and social enterprise could be prolonged either peacefully or indefinitely, since the slaveholder's economic and social existence was in every respect contingent upon his human "property."

These psychodynamics of property and possession are the subject of Edgar Allan Poe's short story "The Gold Bug" (1843) and Robert M. Bird's two-volume novel *Sheppard Lee: Written by Himself* (1836). This chapter argues that "The Gold Bug" and *Sheppard Lee* reside at the periphery of the detective genre, as they make use of metonymy and metaphor, two of the principal mechanisms we associate with detection fiction, to survey antebellum interracial sociabilities. In other words, they avail themselves of detection's devices to contend with the lopsided, indefinite, and sometimes brutal allocation of agency between former slaves and former masters, for whom solvency and self-possession hang upon an unsteady compact. Metonymy is the rhetorical device enlisted in our interpretations of a "clue," and foregrounds contiguity and direct relations by substituting a trace or part for its whole, or an effect for a cause. Metaphor, by contrast, is a species of analogy that links *distinct* domains of meaning; Kenneth Burke calls it "a device for seeing something in terms of something else" (qtd. in Ritchie 6). In detection texts, metaphor typically emerges in acts of "imaginative identification" between doubled, oppositional figures (detective and criminal, for example), as the former strives to access the sensibilities of the latter. Both the forensic utility of metonymic traces (as chains or collections of partial objects that lead the detective to the criminal agent) and the "bilateral asymmetry" that typifies imaginative identification, situating the detective as the criminal's "*antithetical* double" (Pyrhönen, *Mayhem* 31) are explicated at length in Poe's tales of ratiocination, especially "The Murders in the Rue Morgue" (1841). As "The Gold Bug" and *Sheppard Lee* move between speculative lines and imaginative leaps, between metonymy and metaphor in an antebellum terrain, however, they supply historiographies of interracial sociability, limning the fraught territory between enslavement and self-possession in a slave-holding society.

"The Gold Bug" is a tale of treasure hunting whose protagonist, William Legrand, recoups his fallen fortunes after he discovers a coded message and treasure map on a bit of "dirty foolscap" (Poe 200). By pretending violent lunacy, Legrand cajoles his uneasy physician-friend (the narrator) and his steward Jupiter, a manumitted slave, to assist him in the enterprise; at the end of the story, the three men find themselves in possession of Captain Kidd's buried plunder. Though the title of Poe's story references an unfamiliar species of scarabaeus Legrand and Jupiter discover on the South Carolina beach, it also alludes to a crisis of monetary policy during the Jackson and Van Buren administrations, particularly the quarrel between the "paper money" men and the "gold bugs" who despaired of "the tendency of paper money to distort our 'natural' understanding of the relationship between symbols and things" (Shell 18). Along these lines, when Legrand struggles to manufacture meaning of the gold-colored insect, scribbles on parchment, hieroglyphic puns, and coded messages, he appears to be making something of nothing. Meanwhile, the physician-narrator aches to diagnose Legrand's idiotic follies and prescribe treatment suited to his conduct, which seems to him to indicate some form of madness.

Receiving a bit of correspondence conspicuously changed from Legrand's ordinary style, the narrator muses, "What new crotchet possessed his excitable brain?" (204). That Legrand is seemingly crazed by some "crotchet" ("a perverse conceit" or "peculiar notion"), that he poses a threat as an *apparently deranged individual*, is sufficient incentive for the steward Jupiter and the physician to placate him (OED). Consequently, Legrand's performance economizes on actual displays of violence when he enlists their assistance in his hunt for Captain Kidd's buried treasure. Yet Poe also supplies an additional dose of duplicity in the comings and goings of the manumitted slave Jupiter, whose acute solicitude for his former master approximates surveillance, and whose "sabage kind ob style" is a source of semantic digressions that subtly chip away at the unified effect of Legrand's performance (214). This critical appearance of something other than a "public transcript" (a realm of discourse that undercuts the "hegemonic aspirations" that regulate public contact) is a "hidden transcript," a clandestine dissent cultivated by a superficially subordinated individual, and it invites us to inspect Legrand's *and* Jupiter's deceptions more closely—and their habits of detection as well.[1]

By contrast, the eponymous, first-person protagonist of Robert Bird's text tours the antebellum landscape by means of metempsychosis (a transmigration of the soul akin to mesmerism), which allows the untethered spirit of the protagonist to take temporary residence in a variety of recently deceased bodies. Over the course of the novel, Lee peripatetically takes on and closely scrutinizes the identities of an affluent squire, a dandified city-dweller, a despised Jewish shaver, a naive Quaker philanthropist, a black slave, and a dyspeptic plantation owner—in short, an abbreviated lineup of the antebellum classes and social strata—before he finally recovers his body and sets about a career of honest labor. Bird's representations of psychosocial phenomena in *Sheppard Lee* delve into not only the civic presence and personality of Sheppard Lee's subjects, but also delineate the constitution and "innate" characteristics of each body the protagonist inhabits. Joseph Buchanan compared the mesmerist's long-distance "power of diagnosis or detection of character, of disease, and of thoughts" to a process of "mental sympathy" in *Neurological Systems of Anthropology* (1854) (qtd. in Fuller 44); by contrast, *Sheppard Lee's* spirit sightseeing is both analytical and sympathetic, and habitually blurs the boundaries between the personalities of the protagonist and the bodies he inhabits. Lee swings between metonymic and metaphoric talk in his diagnostic tourism, or as Poe complains in his review of Bird's text, "The hero, very awkwardly, partially loses, and partially does not lose, his identity, at each transmigration" (137).

To access and represent a sociology of racialized labor, "The Gold Bug" and *Sheppard Lee: Written by Himself* develop and draw upon an anatomy of genre conventions that would be associated with the clue-puzzle mystery. Poe and Bird avail themselves of detection's devices to schematize the interracial sociabilities at stake in the total conscription of a subordinate's body, and also to imagine the end(s) of such conscription: the capacity of such bodies to *have been* possessed. In the dynamic interplay of imaginative identification and metonymic inquiry, these works explore whether men might swap captivity for self-possession, and plot the economic interdependencies at the core of antebellum interracial sociability. We can gain some insight into the social uses of the rhetorical devices these works employ, and their particular value for exploring interracial sociability in the antebellum period, by examining Poe's first tale of ratiocination, "The Murders in the Rue Morgue."

A GRAVE HOAX?

A striking aspect of "The Murders in the Rue Morgue" (1841), in which Poe's detective C. Auguste Dupin tracks down the creature that brutally assassinated Madame L'Espanaye and her daughter, is its fixation on that curious word *possession*, which takes both transitive and intransitive forms. Of the analytical faculties, Dupin's companion (the narrator) explains, "They are always to their possessor, when inordinately possessed, a source of the liveliest enjoyment" (92); indeed, at a game like Whist, the intellect will find himself "in full possession of the contents of each hand," though he has not laid a hand upon them (94). Poe's detective "designates" a sailor of a Maltese vessel "the possessor of the beast" that carved Madame L'Espanaye with a razor, ventriloquizing, "Should I avoid claiming a property of so great value, which it is known that I possess, I will render the animal at least, liable to suspicion" (118). Soon afterward, Dupin will coax a confession from the sailor, to whom he remarks, "I almost envy you the possession of him" (118). When the sailor arrives at their doorstep, his complexion is sunburned and "half hidden" by hair, and he bears a "dare-devil expression of countenance," comportment that the narrator painstakingly characterizes as "*not altogether unprepossessing*" (118, my italics)—this last pair of negatives or semantic "double take" a triumph of idiomatic prestidigitation that dislodges the very notion of self-possession—though after Dupin resolves the affair of the Rue Morgue he finds the police prefect is "fain to indulge in a sarcasm or two, about the propriety of every person minding his own business" (122).

What I am getting at is, of course, a provocation roused by the uneasy traction of self-possession in Poe's earlier detective story: that quite apart from the question of the orangutan who was supposedly in the sailor's custody and apparently the perpetrator of these gruesome murders, the story only just hints Poe's sailor is a escaped captive, perhaps a black one, and in disguise. We might consider, however preposterously, that Poe's tale takes its cues from certain tantalizing biographical details attributed to Toussaint-Louverture, whom the French government deported from Saint Domingue in 1802. Poe's sailor's "Neufchatel-ish" accent situates him somewhere near the Jura Mountains, where Toussaint was imprisoned in a secure cell of the Fort de Joux and allowed only the courtesy of a cursory daily shave (Girard 268). James Stephen's *The History of Toussaint Louverture* (1814) describes Toussaint's detention sympathetically, lamenting that the hero was deprived of all company and conversation "with the exception only of a single Negro attendant, who was as closely confined as his master" (88), though Citizen Baille, commandant of Fort Jura, wrote to naval officer Denis Decrès on October 30, 1802, that Toussaint "can shave himself only before me, who give him his razor, and take it back when he has finished" (qtd. in Adams 154). While Toussaint was reported to have died in France in 1803, Stephen's *History* nevertheless observes, "Some people entertain a notion that this great man is still living" (92).

Straight razors, silent attendants, and shades of Haiti aside, it is Poe's production of a spectacularly violent if extradiegetic animal assassin and *not* a Maltese sailor that has purchased the attention of literary critics interested in Poe's representations of blackness and of slavery. Elise Lemire rigorously argues that Poe's inclusion of a "barbering primate" reflects the commonplace Cuvier-styled racism of the day and replicates the precise logic of a taxidermy exhibition at Philadelphia's Peale Museum "whereby [the stuffed] monkeys are black barbers and thus barbering blacks are bestial" (188)[2]—though Charles Rzepka locates an important tension in Dupin's discovery that the fugitive ape went through the motions of shaving himself as well as Madame L'Espanaye, one of the women whom he murdered.[3] "If any symbolic meaning can be attached to this bizarre gesture," Rzepka argues, "it must be that the orangutan is trying to bestow the only sign it understands of the freedom and authority culturally reserved for those who make second-class creatures of both slaves and women" (*Detective Fiction* 86). Along these lines, we might place Poe's text at odds with the unfinished business of the Déclaration des droits de l'homme et du citoyen (1789), particularly the "imprescriptible" right to "la liberté, la propriété, la sûreté et la résistance à l'oppression" it describes in its second article. Rzepka tops this talk of self-possession, however, by observing that "Rue Morgue" finesses the *Memoirs* of Eugène François Vidocq, that notorious thief turned celebrated thief-taker and finally director of the Sûreté Nationale, with which Poe was undoubtedly familiar. Vidocq spent part of his youth with a traveling circus, where he was made to grow his hair wild and turn naked and "savage," taking "for your model the ourang-otang who is in cage number 1" (qtd. in Rzepka 88).

We might contrast such accounts with Richard Kopley's astonishing excavation of the *Philadelphia Saturday News*, which locates the "raw" materials for "Rue Morgue" in this newspaper's pages. Kopley directs us to an article titled "Deliberate Murder in Broadway, at Midday" (August 4, 1838), a report of the "atrocious murder" perpetrated by one Edward Coleman, a black man who, suspecting his wife Ann of infidelity, slit her throat, "nearly severing her head from her body with a razor," and afterward adopted insanity as his defense (qtd. 33). Many other items from the *Philadelphia Saturday News* were enlisted in creation of Poe's tale, proposes Kopley: one of its articles details the escapes of an "Orang Outang" from the London Zoo (May 26, 1838); it recounted how "A Mischievous Ape" escaped from a livery stable and nearly tore the hair off of a boy (September 22, 1838); and "Deaths in New York" describes how two black women suffocated from a charcoal furnace (January 12, 1839). Kopley's reading of "Rue Morgue" fixates on Poe's compositional activity, interpreting the tale as issue of its journalistic contexts, whose inherited properties (or trace) Poe acknowledges by his deliberate inclusion of contrived newspaper articles as a principal source of information for Dupin's investigation—a strategy the author would employ again in "The Mystery of Marie Roget." Along these lines, the most arcane riddle in "Rue Morgue" is a superficial one. It asks to be decoded at the narrative surface where metonymy achieves its aims, rather than prying beneath it for the sort of allegorical dimensions that Rzepka pursues (Martin Priestman qtd. in Pyrhönen, *Mayhem* 38).[4]

The interpretive approaches these literary critics employ are easily as intriguing as the human and literary relations in Poe's short story. Lemire's associative inquiry takes the Philadelphia Peale Museum exhibit as the secret of the text (her metonymic interpretive act opens up an allegorical interpretation). Rzepka sees metaphor as the explicit activity of "Rue Morgue," even as Poe apes Vidocq, a literary rival and antecedent. Kopley is content to discover the tale's print relations through textual fragments.[5] Jeanine Marie DeLombard has recently cautioned against discerning any "imaginative identification" between man and orangutan that presumes "access to the ape's presumed criminal intent" (199). If we accept it, we are too easily seduced into the habit of "assigning personhood to just any perpetrator of a violent act," she insists (204)—a slippery slope that Dupin does not himself pursue, even if the Maltese sailor makes such conjectures in the story, at least according to the narrator's synopsis of the sailor's account of the crime. Instead, Dupin's solution to the mystery relies precisely on his "discerning appreciation for 'that startling absence of motive' that has, from the beginning, constituted the mystery" (204). DeLombard's apodictic warning against imaginative identification underscores the role that Dupin's reading habits *might* play in instructing our own. As readers of Poe's "tales of ratiocination," what amount of "deep reading" are we invited to pursue? How should we engage with metonymy and metaphor as interpretive methodologies, and what sorts of instructions for reading do these critical approaches supply?

As "the basic figure governing the creation and interpretation of clues," metonymy plays on direct relations of close association (Rzepka 18). It operates according to contiguity rather than similarity, but lingers in a single conceptual domain, so the knowledge it yields is circumstantial: effect stands for cause, part for whole, and so on. A variety of associative thought, metonymy frequently incites inductive activity that leads the detective to the culprit. Its methods are not fail-safe, however. Dupin, for one, finds them of limited value. Certainly, his preliminary solution to the crime in "Rue Morgue" is built from bits of circumstantial evidence: tresses of tawny hair at the crime scene; a small bit of greasy ribbon knotted in a manner "peculiar to the Maltese"; the astonishing bruises on Mademoiselle L'Espanaye's throat and other signs of a "prodigious strength" and "wild ferocity" that Cuvier attributes to the orangutan; the exclamation "Mon Dieu!"; and so on (117, 116). This bit of abduction concluded, Dupin surmises, "A Frenchman was cognizant of the murder" (117); still, he demurs:

> I will not pursue these guesses—for I have no right to call them more—since the shades of reflection upon which they are based are scarcely of sufficient depth to be appreciated by my own intellect, and since I could not pretend to make them intelligible to the understanding of another. (117)

Even Dupin's inspired account of the *hypothetical* sailor's calculations stresses the flimsiness of metonymic relations in establishing a person's guilt: "It would be impossible to prove me cognizant of the murder, or to implicate me in guilt on account of that cognizance," and when the sailor arrives Dupin assures him that there is "nothing, certainly, which *renders* you culpable" (117, 119, my italics). Dupin's conjectures, based on "shades of reflection," are traces twice over, scarcely to be "appreciated."

While metonymy yields only circumstantial evidence and is an odious if indispensable tactic in Dupin's repertoire, metaphor emphasizes a distinct agency of perception in the person who attempts it. Dupin boasts in "Rue Morgue" that "most men, in respect to himself, wore windows in their bosoms," a phrase that, by its orientation ("in respect to himself"), merges a geography of metonymy with the epistemological audacity of *imaginative identification*. His is an act of aggressive insight by which the detective "throws himself into the spirit of his opponent" and "identifies himself therewith," seducing his adversary into error (Poe 96, 93). The narrator of "Rue Morgue" fancies this talent is connected to the Orphic philosophy of the "Bi-Part Soul," whereby the conscious soul is a mere sliver of the Oversoul (an unconscious intelligence that animates the universe and makes transmigration possible) (Rzepka 87). And yet imaginative identification must also account for a "structural antagonism" central to that "positional constellation" which situates the detective and criminal as inverted doubles (Pyrhönen, *Mayhem* 31–32). Such antagonism is certainly crucial to Poe's third tale of ratiocination, "The Purloined Letter," where Dupin matches wits with the seditious Minister D——. Lindon Barrett has brilliantly observed, however, that Dupin's accessory is the anarchy of the street: a "pretended lunatic" and "man in my own pay" whose musket disrupts their tête-à-tête, drawing Minister D—— to the window of the apartment, so that Dupin might seize the queen's stolen missive and replace it with his own vicious and vengeful memorandum (Barrett 192). A "report" from the street is the belligerent codicil that turns the tables to Dupin's advantage, but is violence integral to such schemes of mental sympathy?

Appraising René Girard's theory of mimetic desire, Pierre Saint-Amand concedes that

> the concept of imitation can be considered only through its principle of ambivalence; it operates fundamentally as a double bind. . . . Reciprocity's sudden crazes, the way it brings mimetic interferences to a head, lead to processes of undifferentiation, to a collapse of hierarchies, to forms of social desymbolization. The silence maintained around the antagonistic dimension of imitation represents a scandal that Girard's theory relentlessly attempts to denounce. (8)

In "Rue Morgue," there is an uncanny reciprocity implicit in the sailor's fantasy of the terror he inspires in his prized possession: he imagines he is the "the dreaded whip" whose flourish converts "fury" into "fear," rendering the razor-wielding orangutan suddenly "conscious of having deserved punishment" (121). Dupin intuits this strange brew of malice and civility engendered by the sailor's association with the orangutan in his "exclusive possession" when he (Dupin) finds evidence of the two interlopers in the L'Espanaye apartment—and one of these conceivably "innocent of all participation in the bloody transactions which took place" (116). In doing so, Dupin joins the associative work of metonymy with imaginative identification and fathoms, more than the mind of an adversary, the stakes of an *interpersonal* enmity. Dupin's apprehension of a hostile reciprocity between two others (their subservient order violently skewed by insubordination) belongs to a different register of perception. As with that "inordinate possession" of the analytical faculties, Dupin fully appreciates, at one remove, the back-and-forth between them, taking in tandem the metonymical and metaphorical relations at hand. His talent is to puzzle out the hostile reciprocity that engendered the "bloody transaction" on Rue Morgue, and to make the terms of an equivocal possession *his* business.

This theme of possession in "Rue Morgue" takes immediate terms in "The Gold Bug." The bug is to "to reinstate me in my family possessions," Legrand vows as he embarks on his treasure hunt, coaxing his browbeaten valet and the befuddled narrator to assist him in a series of eccentric directives that are, unbeknownst to the narrator, taken from Captain Kidd's coded commands on a scrap of foolscap (205). Legrand's succession of strange behaviors is finally redacted by a meticulous cryptography lesson at the end of the tale. His conspiracy of misrepresentation, or "sober mystification," was a deliberate guise of madness, it turns out: a strategic deception aimed at punishing the bewildered narrator for his "evident suspicions touching my sanity" (229). And yet what first gave the physician pause was another strange bit of correspondence, which Jupiter hand-delivers. "There was something in the tone of this note which gave me great uneasiness," the narrator explains. "Its whole style differed materially from that of Legrand. What could he be dreaming of?" (204). A distinction between Legrand's odd letter, his "sober mystification" and actual derangement, however, is not easily resolved. Instead, the story ends at the moment Legrand suggests an sinister addendum to the order he has just offered: that the death of Kidd's minions was the indispensable coda to Kidd's work, so that the secret of the treasure could remain concealed: "Perhaps a couple of blows with a mattock were sufficient, while his coadjutors were busy in the pit; perhaps it required a dozen—who shall tell?" (229). "By how thin a thread hang the lives of the Doctor and old Jup?" speculates Daniel Hoffman, gauging the effect of this macabre postscript on the reader (128).

Intimations of lunacy in this alarming denouement leave the reader reeling at the prospect, or even recursive inevitability, of additional deaths— what we might call a narrative-contract killing. However, Poe's uneasy ending does more than reorient the explanatory narrative within a framework of new criminal possibilities. Instead, the structure of the story says something: events come to meaning and to sense only when we retrace our steps, relieved of whatever stupefaction the tale initially afforded. Add to this, moreover, that it was not merely Legrand's plotting that determined the precise site of their excavation, nor yet the bit of subterfuge or "sober mystification" that drafted his steward, his dog Wolf, and the narrator to his errand, but the coordinates supplied by Jupiter, who shouldered all the "*risk* of the achievement," scrambling up the tulip tree and onto a nearly dead limb to establish the location of the buried hoard (208). Still, Jupiter mistakes right for left, which wrecks all of Legrand's delicate measurements and nearly turns the grueling enterprise into a fruitless expedition. As they dig in the wrong spot (wide of the mark), however, the enterprise elicits a "grave chuckle" from the valet. Proceeding from a pit, a makeshift mausoleum, this "chuckle"—which the OED defines as "a laugh of triumph and exultation: formerly applied to a loud laugh, but now chiefly to a suppressed and inarticulate sound by which exultation is shown"—calls into question the subjugation Jupiter has tolerated, however uneasily, throughout the story. Does Jupiter play the confidante or adversary in the grave hoax Legrand has concocted?[6] Is the ex-slave, like the narrator, another stooge of Legrand's pretend psychosis, or does he calculatingly sabotage Legrand's directives, determined to possess the treasure himself?

Jupiter's relationship with Legrand remains inscrutable—the narrator, at least, hardly interrogates the odd relations between them. Though Legrand routinely berates the former slave, Jupiter remains alert to Legrand's stratagems, reporting that he (Jupiter) "Hab for to keep mighty tight eye pon him [Legrand's] noovers" (Poe 202). This intent surveillance apparently extends to eavesdropping on Legrand's dreams to learn about his former master's search for gold: "why cause he talk about it in he sleep—dat's how I nose" (203). Jupiter's monitoring talk and its dividends (or lack thereof) have garnered much critical attention. In his well-known essay "Gold in the Bug,"

Jean Ricardou issued the following declaration: "Legrand est seul capable de dechiffrage; Jupiter et la narrateur, en revanche, sont en mauvais termes avec le langage" (36), though Daniel Kempton points out that it is the critic who, "through the mediation of his [Legrand's] authoritative voice," reasserts Legrand's linguistic authority, "evidently encouraged to legitimize and duplicate an obliteration in the text" (2). Decrying Legrand's ruthless and punitive approach to the other characters' linguistic practices, Kempton sees in Jupiter a "valuable, if unorthodox, model of literary interpretation" (3), while Richard Hull observes that Jupiter's semantic slipups and "silly words, about the bug being of solid gold," are what lead Legrand to the treasure in the first place: Jupiter's "doubling of meaning lets a truth happen" (2).[7] Jupiter's presence and utterances in "The Gold Bug" reconfigure our understanding of the tale no less than Legrand's put-up job; then, Legrand's act of "sober mystification" theorizes a structure of deception, rather than a single instance of deceit.

In "The Gold Bug," as in "Rue Morgue," to parse the "hostile reciprocity" that characterizes an implausible affiliation between two individuals, we wade into the thick of an interdependency that registers in curious instances of metonymic slippage and metaphoric leaps. Poe mobilizes metaphor and metonymy—devices that, respectively, model the figure of the "clue" and the acts of "imaginative identification" at the core of classical detective fiction—not solely in pursuit of Kidd's gold, but also to conceptualize an elaborate structure of possession. "The Gold Bug" deliberates the implications of conscripting bodies and imagines prospects for interracial sociability and competition in the antebellum period. What is more, Jupiter's manumitted state and the absent physical record of his manumission are central subtexts of the story because they pull together questions of metonymic kinship and metaphoric relation, signaling what, in a slavery economy, it might mean "to have been possessed."

A NERVOUS POSSESSIVENESS

> Value, therefore, does not stalk about with a label describing what it is. It is value, rather, that converts every product into a social hieroglyphic. Later on, we try to decipher the hieroglyphic, to get behind the secret of our own social products; for to stamp an object of utility as a value, is just as much a social product as language.
>
> —KARL MARX, *CAPITAL*

Jupiter's manumission certifies that this man has ceased to be another man's commodity, even if its possession is no guarantee he acts according to his free will. In a slavery economy, this document divests Legrand of capital; it is the antithesis of Kidd's treasure map, which restitutes the fallen fortunes of Legrand's ancient Huguenot family. Poe writes that Jupiter was manumitted prior "to the reverses of the family," an unpropitious act, it seems, given their impending descent into penury (199). Nevertheless, Jupiter has not deserted his charge, even in the face of "threats" and "promises"; Kempton wryly observes that an official release from bondage "has brought no palpable relief from the rigors of domestic servitude" (10). Jupiter has refused to take his manumission, a discharge from the hand of the master, at its letter. At the same time, however, the circumstances surrounding his service are suspect, given that Legrand's family has "contrived to instill this obstinacy into Jupiter," or somehow conspired to sustain this dogged devotion (Poe 199). Thus with Jupiter's manumission we see something like the familiar figure from Poe's story "The Purloined Letter," of which Lacan writes, "We are quite simply dealing with a letter which has been diverted from its path; one whose course has been *prolonged* (etymologically, the word of the title), or, to revert to the language of the post office, a *letter in sufferance*" ("Purloined" 43). In the case of "The Gold Bug," *mettre à gauche* the manumission of Jupiter is to ensure his "right of attendance upon the footsteps of his young 'Massa Will'" (199).

Yet Jupiter's entitled presence—a sort of absence in turn because there is no proper title with which to address him, and he generally retains the old mark of slavery in the text—is now charged with the character of pursuit. Jupiter's "attendance" suggests acts of reading or detection as he follows the traces left by William Legrand. He has become the former master's shadow, tracking his footsteps, though perhaps inadvertently according to the wishes of Legrand's family, who have encouraged in Jupiter the "supervision and guardianship of the wanderer" (199). Jupiter's function is authoritative, protective, and at the service of Legrand's clan. His vision sticks to Legrand's movements, a policy that reveals some foresight since Legrand will finally uncover the treasure necessary to overturn the "misfortune" of his wealth. Meanwhile, Legrand's "misfortune" is a legacy of missed fortune for Jupiter, who apparently holds his manumission in reserve, who inhabits a position in an order of things that has been evacuated. His presence is sanctioned by a past servitude from which he was dismissed; the manumission testifies to this earlier relation. A loss of the document, on the other hand, would signify an equally precarious set of relations, which would in antebellum America be quickly shored up via the reinstatement of Jupiter's slave status. Consequently, his condition is noted with fluctuating terms—his value as commodity can neither be pinned down nor negated.

Orlando Patterson has noted that insofar as manumission resuscitated slaves from a state of social death, it entered into an arithmetic of double negatives, enacting "the negation of the negation of social life" (211). This peculiar transaction, configured, as it seems to be in the case of Jupiter, to relieve Legrand of the responsibility for his slave in light of his own fiscal "mortification," implies that Jupiter's manumission is less an effect of revolutionary idealism than evidence of a recession in his master's power. That Jupiter should profit from Legrand's loss of fortune, though, is an unexpected contingency. Patterson contends that manumission is "an act of creation brought about by an act of double negation initiated by the freely given decision on the part of the master to part with something—his power—for nothing" (211). But has Legrand parted with power if Jupiter has not parted with Legrand? By 1841, manumission throughout the South was no longer simply a prerogative of the master, as it had been in the wake of independence. Instead, from the 1820s on, manumission required sanction from legislative and judicial bodies and generally carried with it stipulations that the freed bondsman depart immediately the state in which he had been enslaved (Berlin 28–29). To ensure the freed bondsman's departure, legislation permitted emancipated slaves to be seized as payment for debts held by their former masters (138). Though he is newly established on Sullivan Island—a port of entry where slaves were once quarantined in anticipation of induction to that "peculiar" institution—Jupiter's unremitting proximity to his former master suggests that, the manumission notwithstanding, his place is of a handy retainer. Their continued association, a metonymic link never entirely severed, lends Jupiter the air of bound labor.

Thus the missing manumission might function as a map of the meaning of Jupiter's body, a map of floating signifiers and prevaricating signs, since the document that manumits reveals both a history of servitude and its subsequent termination, all present evidence to the contrary. His black skin, for instance, is no longer an indicator of servitude. And the manumission takes up the position of the fetish, since it simultaneously acknowledges and disavows the dehumanizing circumstances of master-slave relations. Still, it also points to an ironic mimicry of those relations, since the rendering of his own value to Jupiter gives way to a comedic upheaval of fates, with Jupiter acting as Legrand's warden. Having been sent, he now tails after his former master, a piece of circular logic that evokes a relationship of debt in which Jupiter, though no longer technically compelled to extend his services, does so compulsively and of his own inclination. Poe's ex-slave who remains a slave is evidence of the repressed returned, anticipating a cycle of indebtedness that would characterize the relations of blacks and whites in America following emancipation, where "the very bestowal of freedom established the indebtedness of the freed through a calculus of blame and responsibility that mandated that the formerly enslaved both repay this investment of faith and prove their worthiness" (Hartman 131). Unspoken stipulations of debt suspended the subject in a state where his or her freedom was necessarily affixed to a moment of futurity. Along these lines, Jupiter's manumission is unwieldy currency at best.

The failure (or the success) of writing to confer value upon the reader and writer alike is clearly one of the concerns of "The Gold Bug," and it is an interest that links the terms of aesthetics to the terms of production. The perception that paper and coined money could be an insubstantial or "shadow" stand-in for gold (rendered thus purely by an act of Congress in the early Republic) corresponded to a view of aesthetics that allowed a voluntary suspension of disbelief to convert the written word into "the real thing" (Shell 18). From 1825 to 1845, however, the proliferation of "ghost notes" from "phantom banks" that masqueraded as legitimate tender did little to enhance the case for paper. Notes that "passed" destabilized economies *and* aesthetics, drawing attention to the uneasy relations between symbols and the things to which they referred, and engendering public wariness toward an unsound system of signs. Marc Shell comments, "The sign of the monetary diabolus, which many Americans insisted was like the one that God impressed in Cain's forehead, condemns men to misunderstand the world of symbols and things in which they live" (18–19). This mark of Cain— which was also, incidentally, employed unfailingly as a justification for the differentiation and enforced labor of blacks in antebellum America—was evidence of a distortion or failure of natural relations between the sign and its substance, leading to a postlapsarian state of commodity, and linguistic, slippage.

Jupiter's presence as shadow in "The Gold Bug," and the slippage that results, is perhaps best revealed by a vaudevillian encounter in which Jupiter makes a report of Legrand's activities to the narrator.[8] A "dispirited" Jupiter recounts, "Todder day he gib me slip fore de sun up and was gone de whole ob de blessed day" (202). Legrand had shrewdly discovered the means to detach himself from his shadow (by departing before sunrise) in consequence of which Jupiter had prepared "a big stick ready cut for to gib him d——d good beating when he did come" (202). Moments later, the narrator reads this letter from Legrand that Jupiter has conveyed to the mainland: "Would you believe it?—he had prepared a huge stick, the other day, with which to chastise me for giving him the slip, and spending the day, *solus*, among the hills on the main land" (203). Jupiter's words dovetail neatly with Legrand's report, a reverberation of an identical tale heard in advance, or conversely, Legrand's letter substantiates the claims Jupiter has already made. In this scene, Jupiter, the narrator, and the letter are a threesome; the letter makes Legrand an absent presence, though his stand-in, his "shadow" is there already. Does that make Jupiter the shadow to a dispatch? He is at the same time an echo and an emissary (making the encounter merely a twosome—or perhaps a foursome): he is a doubled shadow. Jupiter and the letter he carries jointly describe the giving of "the slip" on Legrand's part, an activity that (like the manumission) associatively combines a scrap of paper with the termination of contact and contractual relations. In addition, both point to the stick that Jupiter had proposed to use to discipline the subject who eluded his pursuit, who did not "stick" to him, though Legrand's letter tenders another moment of slippage by construing Jupiter's brutal intent, a "d——d good beating" as a rhetorical gesture, chastisement. Whatever the intended punishment, it ultimately went undelivered on account of Legrand's manner; he notes, "I verily believe that my ill looks alone saved me a flogging" (203). This hint at a reversal of master-slave relations and Jupiter's potential to inflict damage on his former master is curtailed by Legrand's "ill looks alone," a phrase that may describe the decline of his health as a result of "spending the day, *solus*," without his shadow—or possibly the malevolent glance of Legrand is sufficient to regulate Jupiter's own arm, turning it to his wishes.

Legrand's capacity to regulate Jupiter, to exploit him as both follower and field guide, is essential to his treasure-hunting project. It is no wonder that Kempton identifies Jupiter as the "slave at hand" and "prosthetic extension" Legrand requires to succeed with his project (10). Since Jupiter is not a slave, however, Legrand's achievement is to make Jupiter revert to his former status, which he manages to do through rhetorical and monetary inducements. And to the extent that Jupiter offers a sort of amplified dexterity to Legrand's pursuit of treasure, he comes to exemplify the function of the slave-commodity. He embodies Legrand's aims by becoming emptied of his own. Saidiya Hartman explains,

The fungibility of the commodity makes the captive body an abstract and empty vessel vulnerable to the projection of others' feelings, ideas, desires, and values; and, as property, the dispossessed body of the enslaved is the surrogate for the master's body since it guarantees his disembodied universality and acts as the sign of his power and domination. (21)

Already at one remove from his own will through his status as prosthesis (the greenback to Legrand's specie), but no longer a slave, Jupiter is and is not what he is not (a slave, a sign of the master's power); he fills the space of the sign that technically does not exist because the manumission signifies its erasure.

To the extent that Jupiter is depicted as under the sway of Legrand, the two replicate the parts of Hegel's master-slave dialectic, where the lord or master is posited as "a pure self-consciousness," while the bondsman or slave is the "dependent consciousness whose essential nature is simply to live or to be for another" (115). What is of particular interest in Hegel's conceptualization of lordship and bondage, however, is the unsatisfactory stalemate precipitated by the master's discovery that he is handcuffed to that being whom he dominates—insofar as the lord's evidence of "being-for-self" is mediated through the bondsman, one for whom "thinghood is the essential characteristic," there can exist between the two only "a recognition that is one-sided and unequal" (116).[9] Given that the "servile consciousness" of the slave cannot supply the recognition he desires, and seeing as he is, nevertheless, *utterly dependent* on the bondsman, the master finds himself restricted to the parasitic enjoyment of the products of slave labor (Bull 227). This is "the unthinkable and productive episode during which the master both recognizes and represses the fact that his mastery is slave-made, he and his are blacks in whiteface," which Richard Godden points to in his writing on slavery in Faulkner (3–4), or what Alexandre Kojève has described as "an existential impasse" experienced by the master (9).[10]

The relationship between Jupiter and Legrand is not so easily grasped, however, especially as Jupiter plays both the domestic and an antagonistic quest-companion to Legrand in the eyes of a narrator whose scopic insight is highly suggestible. That "thinghood" Hegel ascribes to the slave, his existence as sign and surrogate (the substance of some other self), hardly gets at the precariousness of the antebellum economy Jupiter inhabits or the inconsistencies of perception and attribution in the eyes of every party. Consider, for instance, that the American enthusiasm for racial slavery required slaves embody the incongruous aspirations at the core of a capitalist ethos: they must be of "fixed character" *and* flexible worth, yielding to market volatility (O'Malley, *Face Value* 15). Moreover, the structure of interracial socialization that restricted the social existence of enslaved persons was not buttressed by a homogenous regime of disciplinary tactics; on the contrary, spectacular physical penalties and panoptic surveillance colluded to govern the status of the slave (Wiegman 39). But social regulation was always uneven, piecemeal, the antebellum world a social text characterized precisely by lapses, overlaps and perforations in the administration of racial hierarchies, including manumission. Robert Olwell points out that even in pre-Revolutionary South Carolina, "Low Country Slaves were regarded as property, first, last, and always"; the Negro Act of that state designated slaves "subjects of property, in the hands of particular persons"—and yet slaves could, in various ways, bend market laws to their own interests by acquiring property, the first step necessary for "transcending, or at least disguising, their legal condition as property" (145). Under these conditions, the slaveholder (a disciple of "possessive individualism" whose station was conferred in part or in sum by ancillary possessions) might suffer from what historian Ronald Takaki calls a "nervous possessiveness" (74).[11] Accordingly, a manumitted man or, for that matter, any variety of free labor was a distressing sign of his dissolution, or a dispersal of his interests. One defense against this irritation, however, was to forcibly reincorporate free(d) men into the antebellum economy, subjecting them to new forms of bonded labor—forms that often anticipated the fate of the emancipated slaves at the end of the Civil War, when, "reduced to the machinery of bodily physical labor, black people *learned to appear* before whites as though they were zombies" (bell hooks qtd. in Holland 15, my italics). To put this slightly differently, a mutual duplicity born of hostile reciprocity superficially preserved preexisting relations (and for the emancipated slave, a pretense of "thinghood" safeguarded its opposite).

In the same way that Jupiter wraps the gold bug in a covering of invisible text in order to incapacitate it, Legrand's manumission paralyzes rather than emancipates the former slave—or at least it appears to. Jupiter leaves traces of Legrand's authority at every turn. As Legrand's shadow and prosthesis, Jupiter is, like the gold bug, a metonymic curiosity, but he is also something like the "unknown bivalve" that Legrand claims to have discovered in conjunction with the gold bug at the opening of the tale. We first discover Jupiter as a benign stereotype "grinning from ear to ear," mimicking, perhaps, the appearance of the hinged shell the mollusk sports (199). Like the coin-shaped shells, restricted to the enormous bank of Sullivan Island that stretches "about three miles long" (198), Jupiter is consigned to a liminal space, neither strictly commodity nor strictly free. And if Legrand has discovered in the bivalve a "new genus," Jupiter is no less a new species of bivalue, whose worth has been both distorted and prolonged by the manumission. He is, like the joined shell of the mollusk, intrinsically a doubled figure.

What can be said finally about Jupiter's manumission? The most grotesque implication is the possibility that the restitution of Legrand's fortune would return Jupiter to slavery, facilitating a perverse chiasmus whereby the rise of one reverses the fortune of the other. A more elusive proposition takes Jupiter's subservience for the guise of hostile reciprocity. Then his manumission is currency held in reserve and waiting only to be redeemed.

MORE THAN KIN

> One morning, very early, before the sun was up,
>   I rose and found the shining dew on every buttercup;
>   But my lazy little shadow, like an arrant sleepy-head,
> Had stayed at home behind me and was fast asleep in bed.
>
> —ROBERT LOUIS STEVENSON, "MY SHADOW"

"The Gold Bug" performs a sleight of hand by which, as I have suggested, Jupiter appears in the part of the slave rather than the independent agent. Yet Legrand depends on Jupiter to track down the landmarks that lead to Kidd's treasure. Though Jupiter may seem a vestigial appendage to his former master, the treasure hunt sheds light on the precise nature of their relationship. It spurs them to consider the management and manipulation of a man's body according to another man's whims.

When Legrand instructs Jupiter to crawl out on the near-rotten bough of the tulip tree with the gold bug in tow—a service for which he will be compensated with a silver dollar—Jupiter complies, and discovers, with the series of exclamations "o-o-o-o-oh!" that there is "noffin but a skull" attached to the branch (209–10). Jupiter's observation that "somebody bin lef him head up de tree" suggests two competing insights in one: first, there is a voluntary act of disembodiment (some body, a subject, has left its head), and second, an act of abandonment (somebody, an object, has "bin lef") (210). Critically, the skull located on the tulip tree is affixed to what Jupiter and Legrand determine is a "*dead* limb," and the use of catachresis here foreshadows the discovery of the bones of Captain Kidd's murdered associates, meanwhile suggesting the assembly of an untidy and very compressed skeleton (209). The skull corresponds to the image of the death's-head on Legrand's treasure map. On the mainland, however, an actual skull cannot function exclusively as a signpost for the treasure. It divulges its own chronology, and the tree branch it is fixed to involuntarily re-members its living antecedent, as the limb that keeps it in its place. When Legrand demands, "How is it fastened to the limb?—what holds it on?"—a question that is perhaps immaterial to a treasure hunter, but indispensable to another kind of code-cracker—Jupiter answers, "Dare's a great big nail in de skull, what fastens ob it on to de tree" (210). Jupiter had remarked of the rotten branch that "him dead as de door-nail"; in this case the nail on the disintegrated limb suspends, or rather clinches, the death's-head (209).

According to Legrand's treasure map, the skull establishes one of the coordinates required to locate the treasure. The map instructs him to "shoot from the left eye of the death's-head" (228). In order to plot the point, however, it is necessary for Jupiter to do the legwork by shadowing the laborer who deposited the skull there in the first place at the behest of Captain Kidd. Legrand instructs him:

> "Pay attention, then!—find the left eye of the skull."
> "Hum! hoo! dat's good! why dar aint no eye lef at all." (210)

Jupiter's ironic comment implies that the absent eye, an organ apparently gouged long ago by scavenging birds, empties the skull of its subjectivity (its "I"), stressing its indexical and cautionary functions. Jupiter associates the "eye" with the "I": whereas "somebody bin lef him head," a mere figure or unit, there was "no eye lef at all." Legrand insists, on the other hand, that the left eye can be discovered.

> "Curse your stupidity! do you know your right hand from your left?"
> "Yes, I nose dat—nose all bout dat—tis my left hand what I chops de wood wid."
> "To be sure! you are left-handed; and your left eye is on the same side as your left hand." (210)

Terms of servitude are most literally (if not unambiguously) figured in the guidelines Jupiter uses to locate the correct eye. This technique for distinguishing right from left requires a laboring subjectivity; an "I" can be seen only in relation to the hand with which Jupiter chops wood. Additionally, that Legrand's initial demand, "Do you hear?" is followed by Jupiter's unwitting enumeration of other sensory organs (the "nose" and "eye") suggests that the matter at hand is dismemberment or deprivation, the severing of body parts and their dissection from the world—the "division" of a laborer. It is also in this sense that the topic that Jupiter knows "all about" (seemingly skirts) is the slip that allows a nose to transform into a noose. Interestingly, Jupiter employs both the terms "left" and "lef" but not according to some pattern of semantic differentiation; instead the term that suffers from dismemberment ("lef") is used to single out the disembodied skull. Kempton remarks, "The 'left' eye of the skull is the portal to gold, for it is through this eye that the shot must be dropped; but because no eye is 'lef,' the 'left' eye, which is a hole (or cipher), is also associated with emptiness and loss: discovery is linked to deprivation, the golden plentitude to the absent eye, via the nexus 'left'/'lef'" (12). In this case the "o-o-o-o-oh!" becomes the series of bullets Jupiter expels when he confronts the skull, a string of missing "eyes," or, like a noose, the articulation of the loss the "o-o-o-o-oh" embodies.

The conundrum Jupiter faces is that insofar as the skull is construed as pure sign, it ceases to have a correspondence with the body. Should he lower his gaze to locate its absent arm, no hand is in sight. The struggle to locate the left eye of the skull produces "a long pause," following which he demands of Legrand, "Is de lef eye of de skull pon de same side as de lef hand of de skull too?—cause de skull aint got not a bit ob a hand at all—nebber mind!" (210). Later, Legrand will speculate that "the mind struggles to establish a connexion—a sequence of cause and effect—and being unable to do so, suffers a species of temporary paralysis" (217). At this moment in the tale Jupiter's hesitation marks an attempt to reconstruct the conditions of servitude, to make the connection between the anatomical cavity of the "lef eye" in the human carcass that makes the skull valuable to Legrand, and the missing "I" to which it refers, the ghastly act of invisible labor that generated the skull (its morbid production). Paradoxically, the laboring body must momentarily materialize for the sign to function, which in turn requires an imaginary repetition of the act of violent dismemberment; the imaginary restitution of the labor behind the commodity is the flip side to this act of erasure. The distinction here is between metonymy and metaphor. To read the skull as sign, as Legrand does, is to locate the treasure (using what is "left"), but Jupiter imaginatively retrieves that skull's lost limb—a bit of wordplay that hoists the eyes again upward (a measure of the physical interval between the homographs "limb" and "limb") and suggests the contours of another paralyzing circuit: a perpetual recollection of the terms by which the skull came to be fixed to the tree.

And what of the distinction between right and left that Kidd's map requires of the treasure hunters? Some clue to the meaning of this directive may be found in Poe's 1836 essay "Maelzel's Chess Player." In this work, Poe investigates an exhibition piece that he calls the Automaton Chess-Player, an apparatus invented in 1769 by one Baron Kempelen and subsequently taken possession of by Maelzel. This device, worthy of mention in M. Brewster's *Letters on Natural Magic*, takes the form of an oversized "Turk" seated cross-legged on a maple box or cabinet, and typically engages a member of the audience in a game of chess. Poe's essay is devoted to challenging the supposition that the automaton is "unconnected with human agency in its movements" (138). One anonymous author, Poe's speaker reports, concluded that the human who controls the "automaton" conceals his operations by shifting from one end of the cabinet to another, so that the doors of the cabinet, opened in turn, expose only machinery and never a human agent. The man peers out at the chess game in progress through a curtain of gauze in the chest of the cabinet, but scutters from any opening that would disclose his position. Accordingly, his presence remains veiled to the senses. As a result, the true operations of the automaton are impossible, on the one hand, to arrive at "by any inductive reasoning" and, on the other, superfluous to demonstrate: "It was altogether unnecessary to devote seven or eight pages for the purpose of proving what no one in his sense would deny—viz.: that the wonderful mechanical genius of Baron Kempelen could invent the necessary means for shutting a door or slipping aside a panel, with a human agent too at his service in actual contact with the panel or the door" (155–56). Thus one object of fascination is exchanged for another. The "wonderful mechanical genius" who pretends to have engineered a mechanical "Turk" has concocted something altogether more wonderful: an apparently mechanized device that actually operates by the effect of an invisible human hand, a puppeteer all "entirely out of the reach of the observation of the spectators" (156).

Poe's speaker goes on to detail seventeen particulars that substantiate his claim that the device functions through human intervention, but it is the last of these that is of interest for our purposes. If the arrangement were purely mechanical, he asserts, if it were merely a contraption set into motion by Baron Kempelen, the use of its machine arms should be arbitrary. It ought to be equally capable of handling the chess pieces with its left or right appendage. This is in stark contrast to the principles that govern the human body, "wherein there is a marked and radical difference in the construction, and, at all events, in the powers, of the right and left arms" (173). Poe concludes that because the automaton's dexterity is confined to its *left* arm, however, it implies the presence of a man inside the maple box comfortably controlling the mechanism with his *right* arm: "The Automaton plays with his left arm, because under no other circumstances could the man within play with his right—a *desideratum* of course" (173). The absence of an ulterior, or rather interior, hand would secure the automaton's emergence as a thing, while its "preference" for the left hand, a gesture distinctly alien to the human body, finally proclaims the presence of a right-handed individual in the cabinet. In "The Gold Bug" Jupiter intimates his own left-handedness, but he also seems to recognize his arms indifferently, given that for some reason he shoots the gold bug through the wrong eye of the skull, the right rather than the left. Is this due to a misapprehension that the orientation of the skull on the branch is identical to his own, rather than its mirror image? Is it that Legrand presumes Jupiter's left-handedness, though Jupiter is actually right-handed? For Poe, it is this problem of mirroring—"We must imagine some *reversion*—for the Chess-Player plays precisely as a man *would not*"—that ultimately exposes a concealed human presence (173). John Irwin comments that

> whether Jupiter is actually left handed, as his master suggests, is not clear from the story, but what *is* clear is that the difference between master and slave, between the mind that gives the orders and the physical mechanism (the body) that carries them out, is associated here with the difference between right and left, a knowledge that "Massa Will" (as Jupiter calls him) possesses and that his body servant does not. (*Mystery to a Solution* 107)

If Legrand only imagines that Jupiter is left-handed, then he (Legrand) asserts that *his* is the hand that maneuvers Jupiter, the "head" that props up Jupiter's arm. What then of the tree limb Jupiter has attained; whose is the head that propped up that arm which props up the head somebody "bin lef"?

At this point, the point worth pressing is the degree to which Poe's tale and its critics (including myself) are preoccupied with veering to the left, when such an examination obviously comes at the expense of contemplating Jupiter's rights. The difference between left and right seems critical in a situation where confusion apparently prevails over where and even what Jupiter's rights might be and actually are. His impulse to choose the right eye rather than the left results in violent threats—though Legrand can rectify the "error" through computation—while Jupiter's supposed preference for his left hand implies some hidden management. So far we have accounted for the story's play on the terms "right" and "left" and its insistence on confusing one with the other: the right to have left, the right of attendance, the right to wait, the right to "be lef." Kidd's message, too, colludes in a disciplinary act that reproduces the laboring "I" slaughtered to safeguard treasure. The line of reasoning that has yet to be examined is whether the right is a line that can be pursued. Is it possible, for instance, that Jupiter has calculatingly dropped the bug through the right eye to deliberately misdirect (i.e., double-cross) Legrand so that he can later assert proprietary rights, returning to drop the gold bug through the left eye and dig up the treasure for himself?

And yet the conscription of his body as commodity and currency surfaces again. After Kidd's hoard is unearthed, Jupiter submerges himself in the treasure chest. The narrator observes that "Jupiter's countenance wore, for some minutes, as deadly a pallor as it is possible, in the nature of things, for any negro's visage to assume," a physical transformation that suggests the golden coins have produced a vampiric effect and mesmerized the man—"He seemed stupefied—thunderstricken" (Poe 214). This fading in the face of gold also brings to mind the practice by which currency floats. Jupiter, whose labor had afforded him some value, now pales in comparison to the specie in the pit; his value is exhausted, or it has become invisible—or white? Shortly afterward, Jupiter tumbles into the chest, a posture that evokes as fellows the two laborers whose "complete skeletons" were discovered in the pit alongside the precious metals. Or perhaps Jupiter is himself a poor kind of coin—corroborating the narrator's deadpan observation about the contents of the treasure chest: "There was no American money" (215).

The narrator's assertion that Jupiter lounges in the treasure "as if enjoying the luxury of a bath" seems wide of the mark (214), as does Kempton's suggestion that he is "receiving baptism at the sacred font of the treasure chest" (13). Instead, this event is both an allegory for Jupiter's function as a commodity and a reenactment of the murders that Legrand will soon speculate may have occurred: Jupiter falls into the set of social relations according to which his value is established: the "stupefied" man plunges forward and onto his knees, "burying his naked arms" in the gold—almost as if he has received the "couple of blows with a mattock" that Legrand later intimates was the fate of Kidd's companions (214, 229). Moreover, this picture of Jupiter, dazed and prostrate, recalls earlier occasions in the tale when Jupiter risks defying Legrand's orders. When he resists climbing up the tree with the gold bug in tow, and again when he insinuates he might drop the thing, Legrand terrorizes him: "I shall be under the necessity of breaking your head with this shovel" (207). And when it occurs to Legrand that their failure to find the treasure might be due to errors on Jupiter's part, he seizes Jupiter by the collar, after which "The astonished negro opened his eyes and mouth to the fullest extent, let fall the spades, and fell upon his knees" (212). Violence, in Poe's story, finally intervenes to refute the question of the laborer's rights. This is a discipline that would reinstall subjugation. Under such circumstances, Jupiter seems to submit to Legrand's will, meekly responding, "Yes, massa, needn't hollo at poor nigger dat style" (209).

Let me attempt to sketch the structure of the proprietary relations I have related thus far. The central object in "The Gold Bug" is a fortune found by deciphering a map whose markers are made, in part, of a man's body. I have suggested that, when they confront the map, Legrand and Jupiter part interpretive ways: the former adopts metonymy, the latter metaphor as his modus operandi. Tied to a metonymic chain of circumstance, Legrand finds himself "under the necessity" of pursuing it to its end, even violently recruiting a manumitted man to stick to the chase. By contrast, Jupiter's imaginative identification with the bare bones of the treasure map moves him to mirror the person the skull summons to mind, and to picture this laborer's fate. And yet in the moment Legrand seizes Jupiter by the collar, a face-to-face exchange admits they too are doubles, joined perhaps by Legrand's desperate dependency or Jupiter's misgivings toward Legrand's master plan. If Legrand terrorizes the manumitted man into mimed or actual subservience, Jupiter is also both the profound and the obscure object of Legrand's desire, the target of a hostile reciprocity whose form is vitiating hailing ("hollo" words). At this point, Jupiter becomes the ever unattainable, phantasmatic individual (the "poor nigger") Legrand proposes to possess.

CRANIA AMERICANA

It may be asked, why I made no efforts to retrieve my fortunes? I answer to that, that I made many, but was so infatuated that I never once thought of resorting to the obvious, rational, and only means; that is to say, of cultivating with industry my forty acres, as my father had done before me.

—ROBERT M. BIRD, *SHEPPARD LEE: WRITTEN BY HIMSELF*

The interdependencies figured in "The Gold Bug" are central to another antebellum text preoccupied with treasure hunting: Robert M. Bird's *Sheppard Lee: Written by Himself* (1836). In this book, imaginative identification takes the form of metempsychosis (spirit possession), and "foreign" bodies become objects of knowledge the protagonist fathoms as their contours become his own. And yet the transitive and intransitive experiences of possession also give rise to metonymic relations, structures of associative thought that reframe metempsychosis as diagnostic tourism and make the protagonist a spectator before the "alien" bodies he inhabits. *Sheppard Lee* leverages this combination of detection's mechanisms to parse the hostile reciprocity between different classes of persons in the antebellum landscape, and to delineate a continuum of interracial sociabilities that extends from pure parasitism to strange forms of symbiosis.

Like Legrand in "The Gold Bug," the protagonist of *Sheppard Lee* initiates a search for treasure, though his quest in the New Jersey swamps is explicitly indebted to a slave. Sheppard Lee's familial inheritance includes one Jim Jumble, who, despite Lee's conscientious attempt to release him from bondage, emphatically refuses to comply with this design. Instead, "He burst into a passion, swore he would *not* be free, and told me flatly I was his master and I should take care of him" (1:23). In Bird's text, Lee lays the motives of the slave clear: Jim Jumble prefers a lackadaisical existence of permanent servitude (at the hands of a master whose indolence and incompetence matches his own) to "labouring hard to obtain a precarious subsistence as a free man" (1:23). Consequently, Lee's servant's devotion is figured as matter of debt, if not pure parasitism, since Jim Jumble is "determined to stick by me to the last, whether I would or not" (1:24). Sheppard Lee unembarrassedly disavows the economics by which slave owners profit from master-slave relations, even contending that the old slave has no value to speak of—though there is an evenhandedness to Lee's confession, which further unsettles proprietary relations: "I had but one friend, if I dare call him such; though I should have been glad half the time to be rid of him" (1:23). And Sheppard Lee's halfhearted proclamations of friendship still pale against Jumble Jim's enthusiastic legalisms: "The absurd old fool ended by declaring, if I made him a free man he would have the law of me, 'he would, by ge-hosh!'" (1:23). Jim invokes slavery as a restitution of his rights, rather than a deprivation of them, and yet he also implies that the upshot of freedom would be a reversal of master-slave relations, resulting in his control over and management of his former master. Significantly, Lee is depicted as at the mercy of Jumble

Jim so long as the slave remains in his possession. Jim had "the upper hand of me" (1:23), Lee explains, and Jumble Jim eventually comes to (mis)manage Lee's rapidly disappearing estate. Curiously, Lee resists holding Jim liable for the depreciation of his fortune. On the contrary, he naively insists that "Jim would never have cheated me, except on a small scale" (1:25).

Jim obstinately consigns himself to Lee's custody, despite the latter's efforts to invoke a more amicable than proprietary kinship. By maintaining this attachment, however, Jim obtains access to Lee's coffers and indefinite profits, so long as he does not fully squander the estate. By contrast, in "The Gold Bug" gestures at reversal are short-lived: they are curbed by "ill looks" and threats of violence, or taken for comedy, rather than assessed at face value. For instance, Jupiter's name follows "the condescending practice of giving slaves imposing names" (Weissberg 136). "Jumble Jim," by contrast, suggests something of the Saturnalia that is at work in Bird's tale, which has Sheppard Lee reject the proceeds of honest labor in favor of a run at treasure hunting.

Jumble Jim supplies the lore from which Sheppard Lee gleans his mystical directives. In stark contrast to Legrand's strict use of Kidd's memorandum, Lee sticks to the letter of Jim's legends and, according to Jim's counsel, consults his dreams for a spirit guide who will lead him to the treasure. Lee does not succeed in this adventure, however. After digging a hole of some depth in a swamp, the aggravated Lee drives his mattock into the ground with great force and accidentally plunges the tool into his own foot! A break in the narrative indicates that Lee briefly loses consciousness at this point, only to resume his account by remarking upon a marvelous turn of events: "*There* I lay on the ground, stiff and lifeless; and *here* I stood on my feet, alive, and surveying my own corpse, stretched before me" (Bird 1:61). The violent injury, albeit self-inflicted, has resulted in a mysterious doubling of the protagonist, a separation of his corpse from another "I" that surveys it, wandering aimlessly in the forest only to return to its duplicate.

The Lee that narrates becomes preoccupied with the fate of the Lee that lies lifeless, commenting, "I forgot my extraordinary duality in my concern for myself—that is to say, for that part of me, that *eidolon*, or representative, or duplicate of me, that was stretched on the grass" (1:61). Lee's conception of his physical self as phantom, substitute, and copy systematically enumerates the breadth of metonymic relations, and indeed, this preoccupation with the proliferation of half-lives seems to overshadow the mere fact of duplicity. But Lee is two selves, each autonomous of the other: a body and an "I" that ought to have that body in its possession, but does not. He bewails the state in which he is "*two persons*, one of which lives and observes, while the other is wholly defunct" (1:62).

His treasure hunt abandoned, the protagonist (or at least his untethered spirit) takes up temporary residence in a variety of recently deceased bodies, peripatetically taking on the identities of an affluent squire, a dandified city-dweller, a despised Jewish shaver, a naive Quaker philanthropist, a black slave, and a dyspeptic plantation owner, before he is finally reunited with his body and sets about a career of honest labor. Every step along the way, Sheppard Lee meets with disagreeable conditions: he is driven to suicide by the indignities the wealthy Squire Higginson endures at the hands of his insufferable wife and from a painful case of the gout; he despairs in the body of the duplicitous fop Dulmer Dawkins, who has incurred unimaginable debts for his frivolities, and so on. However, it is frequently difficult to distinguish the possessor (Lee) from the subject whose body he possesses. This complex affiliation between Lee and his bodily subjects suggests Lee's metempsychosis is something like mesmerism: under the influence of the mesmerist, the somnambulist "becomes, as it were *one body* with himself—the *egoism* or self-consciousness of the one being blended with the *egoism* or self-consciousness of the other" (Haddock 69). In each instance, however, Lee's enmity toward his corporeal host is attended by a gradual undifferentiation between the body and its ungrateful tenant, underscoring a hostile reciprocity that builds between the protagonist's "I" and the "other" he inhabits.

This is a variety of "nervous possessiveness." Finding his social existence fundamentally intertwined with another body's yet unable to secure that body as his property, Lee makes that body a criminal object whose rude gestures and ill deeds he anatomizes with uncanny fluency. As the phrenologist traces emotional temperament and cognitive aptitude to the bulges on the subject's skull (Rzepka 41), Lee takes every suspect act for a defect of an entire race. Moreover, through its proliferation of ethnic slurs and stereotypes, *Sheppard Lee* foregrounds how metempsychosis and mesmerism pretend to investigate human bodies as objects of knowledge. In practice, however, mesmerism also entailed the mesmerist's exercise of influence upon "the somnambulist," depicting it as a kind of (potentially adversarial) possession. As Chauncy Hare Townshend would attest in his widely circulated textbook *Facts in Mesmerism, with Reasons for a Dispassionate Inquiry into It* (1841), "*Man can act upon man*, at all times and almost at will, by striking the imagination."; "Signs and gestures the most simple may produce the most powerful effects," namely hypnotic inducements to act on the desires of the mesmerist (60). This account of mesmerized subjects as mere marionettes evokes a dynamic of subordination that was distinctly reproduced in the relationships between masters and slaves in the antebellum period. Still, in magnetic sleep, "The intuitive and the ratiocinative meet in the borderland between wakeful and ecstatic states," and the somnambulist, though subordinate to the mesmerist, partakes in the universal while retaining her own consciousness (Mills 56). As a result, the complex rapport between the mesmerist and his patient offered a model of domination and subordination distinct from master-slave relations.[12]

But what we see in *Sheppard Lee* is the apparent incompatibility of one soul with another, since Lee and the various individuals whose bodies he appropriates are depicted as wrestling tenants—even as Lee is nearly subsumed by the personality associated with the other's form. The regularity with which Lee's personality is eclipsed and partially subsumed by the entity he hopes to displace does not merely call into question the duality of the soul of the Jew, the Quaker, the slave, and so on. It also registers each of these personalities as a single-mindedness anchored in the body, whose domination of the protagonist is anathema, and, as such, an obstruction to the observance of republican ideals. In this case, Lee's acts of imaginative identification (which paradoxically double as attempts to exonerate his own choices by indicting his proximate hosts) are predicated on pure projection, an effect of aggressive insight that willfully misses its mark. To imagine the "other" one inhabits as burlesque comes perilously close to divesting oneself of the obligations of possessive individualism. It divulges a masochistic longing to have one's "I" swallowed up by a caricature.

Poe's review of *Sheppard Lee* also scrutinizes this "conception of the metempsychosis which is the basis of the narrative": the protagonist's habitation of various bodies once released from his own corpse (137). It is this shared property that is the pretext for abandoning self-propriety. When out of necessity, for instance, Sheppard Lee's spirit plunges into the dead body of the Jewish shaver Abram Skinner—the "old Goldfist," as he has called him in a previous incarnation—the protagonist is immediately seized by a single-minded aim: "The only idea that possessed me was, 'What am I worth? how much more can I make myself worth?'" (Bird 1:258). At the first opportunity, the sickly Skinner (now inhabited by the spirit of Sheppard Lee) unearths his book of accounts "over which I gloated with the mingled anxiety and delight that had doubtless distinguished the studies of the true Goldfist," and proceeds to engage in dubious financial dealings designed to swindle his clients (1:258). Poe calls Lee's "adventures" by proxy in the world of Abram Skinner "full of interest," applauding the "racy details of stock-jobbing and usury" with an unpleasant vigor, though Bird's poorly elaborated notions of metempsychosis are also most evident here ("Sheppard Lee" 134).[13]

In depicting the transmigration of his protagonist's spirit from one body to the next, Bird clumsily lodges two consciousnesses in one body, but never manages to definitively designate which part controls its other. The result is, in the person of Abram Skinner, a kind of stuttering anti-Semitism. For instance, while Lee volubly protests against "the love of money" that "was the ruling passion" of Abram Skinner when he describes the time spent in the man's body (1:260), Skinner is also his alibi, since Lee's activities energetically embody the forces of social antagonism he otherwise condemns. His careful attribution of his treacherous dealings to "I, or rather my prototype, Abram Skinner," implies that Skinner's body enjoins Lee to act the part of the avaricious "Jew"—as if the body's biology were the source of moral putrefaction or some other dark influence that would imprison the soul (1:259). Lee at least concedes that he is himself to blame for selecting so unpropitious a specimen as the chief residence for his soul, judiciously commenting, "He who rides with the devil must put up with his driving; and he who deals with his nephews must look for something warmer than burnt fingers" (1:268). The protagonist's internalization of the nefarious transactions of the "Jew" only multiplies the confusion. Is it the body that would fleece the soul who dares enter it? What are we to make of the exact equivalence between Lee's impersonation of Abram Skinner and his moral estimation of the Jew? Poe's critique of *Sheppard Lee*, which advises a strict ratio of one soul per body, is a call for a soul-segregation that would preclude such messy dealings. By contrast, *Sheppard Lee* suggests that the "other" is conjured by equal parts association *and* imaginative identification. In this way, a mix of metonymy and metaphor (a protective projection that allows Lee to profit while guarding against "contamination") transforms proprietary relations into hostile dependency and allows interpersonal affiliation to double as its opposite.

In *Sheppard Lee*, a complex interplay of interpersonal affiliation and forensic sightseeing produce anti-Semitic confusion and ontological seesawing. This disorder persists in the second volume of the novel, when Lee is obliged to escape the body of the Quaker philanthropist Zachariah Longstraw—who has been taken for an abolitionist, kidnapped, and "sent downriver" for a spectacle lynching—and plunges into the body of an injured slave known only as "Nigger Tom." At first, this turn of events affords

Bird the opportunity to paint a degrading racial caricature. After discovering upon his head a "mop of elastic wool, such as never grew upon the scalp of a white man" (2:158), Lee catches a glimpse of himself and is repulsed by his own appearance: "Miserable me! my *face* was as black as my arms—and, indeed, somewhat more so—presenting a sable globe, broken only by two red lips of immense magnitude, and a brace of eyes as white and as wide as plain China saucers, or peeled turnips" (2:158). As his spirit "settles in" and assumes the disposition of "Nigger Tom," however, Lee's memoir of plantation life turns Edenic. When the other slaves dance and sing, Tom is "seized with an unaccountable desire to join them" (2:168). Intuiting Tom's view, Lee is vastly pleased by this reversal of fortune; he ceases to consider "my own bitter state of servitude" and instead declares, "I was filled with a foolish glee" (2:168). The droll slave happily submits to being made use of as child's toy by his master's son Tommy: "Down I dropped on my hands and knees, and taking him on my back, began to trot, and gallop, and rear, and curvet over the lawn, to the infinite gratification of himself" (168).

Lee repeatedly describes his satisfaction with his life as a slave, emphasizing that "I sought no opportunity to give my master the slip, and make a bold push for freedom." Instead he is "content, or very nearly so, with my condition, free from cares, far removed from disquiet, and, if not actually in love with my lot, so far from being dissatisfied, that I had not the least desire to exchange it for another" (2:170–71). Should this statement strain all credulity, Lee protests that a "defect of memory will account for my being satisfied with my new condition": "I forgot that I once had been a freeman, or, to speak more strictly, I did not remember it, the act of remembering involving an effort of mind which it did not comport with my new habits of laziness and indifference to make, though perhaps I *might* have done so, had I chosen" (2:171). Tom's conquest of this habitual spirit traveler—even to the point of depriving Lee of the faculty of memory—is, paradoxically, the sign of the slave's malfunctioning intellectual engine. And despite Lee-as-Tom's professed contentment, the text undermines the protagonist's reconciliation with bondage, since in this part of the text slave's vernacular is firmly distinguished from the narration, which retains the character of Sheppard Lee's original voice. (By comparison, when Lee impersonated the Quaker Zachariah Longstraw, the narration gave itself over to a profusion of "thee" and "verily" that peppered the man's speech.) Here, Lee's narration is impervious to the dialect spoken by "Nigger Tom." This failure of affect unsettles Bird's enterprise, since Lee never ventriloquizes Tom's predilection for the institution of slavery except in his (Lee's) private, noncolloquial ruminations on the subject.

This episode in *Sheppard Lee* is more properly a cautionary tale on the effects of incendiary literature, namely, the dangers of abolitionist pamphlets that might incite slaves to revolt. Yet the text also seems to argue against this alarmist position, given its portrayal of slaves as both illiterate and congenial beings, taken with "mimicry and merriment" when they come across some woodcuts that show "negroes in chains, under the lash, exposed in the market for sale" and so on (2:182). So far are these images from the purview of the southern slave's experience, Sheppard Lee insists, that their conception of slavery is completely inconsistent with its reality. The slaves initially respond by cursing the pamphlet and abolition more generally, crying out, "Little book big lie!" (184) when Tom (who for reasons unexplained has inherited Lee's literacy or has been literate all along) reads the pamphlet aloud to them. In fact, the slaves object to representations in the pamphlet, since "the chain and scourge appeared no longer as the punishment of an individual; they were to be regarded as the doom of the race" (2:183–84).

Thus an argument chastising the slaveholder elicits a revolutionary impulse among the slaves, whom the pamphlet informs that "the horrors of Hayti would be enacted a second time, and within our own borders" and teaches "to look on themselves as the victims of avarice, the play-things of cruelty, the foot-balls of oppression, the most injured people in the world" (2:191). This "fatal book," Lee reports, "infected my own spirit," delivering him over to "sentimental notions about liberty and equality, the dignity of man, the nobleness of freedom, and so forth" (2:193)—notions that were presumably organic to his personality as a white man, if rendered foreign by his habitation of a black body. Significantly, these reading habits (and not self-realization through labor) incite the slaves to emancipate themselves. Moreover, the uprising Bird invents depends on Lee's assertion that slaves do not work. In fact, Lee never extorts labor from the indolent, lounging, and unproductive "Nigger Tom." Consequently, it is Bird's exaggerated depiction of a self not fit to govern itself that comes closest to his original image of the protagonist Sheppard Lee, who is a foe of honest labor.

But if Bird's defense of slavery is his picture of Negro ungovernability and imminent rebellion, what are we to make of the slaves' collective refusal to observe a protocol of subservience, or their becoming an organized force prepared to revolt against the master and to battle to their deaths? When the mesmerist takes control of the somnambulist, Hegel explains, "There is only one subjectivity of consciousness: the patient has a sort of individuality, but it is empty, not on the spot, not actual" (qtd. in Bull 238). This is not the case with Sheppard Lee, however. In contrast to his other "in-body" experiences, where time induces an exculpatory sympathy between Lee's spirit and the alien body he inhabits, the revolutionary cause jolts Lee and Tom from their easy rapport and pits each against the other. Sheppard Lee stops Tom dead in his tracks when the slaves, initiating plans for revolt, prematurely install themselves in the positions of future king, emperor, president, and so forth, and proceed to divvy up the master's daughters as their prospective brides. Aghast, Lee (Tom) sounds the alarm at the suggestion of contact between black men and white women, a contact so depraved it would surpass "the horrors of Hayti."[14] He attempts to expose the planned insurrection but has no opportunity to do so; his fellows have placed him under surveillance. "I conceited that they were watching me, dogging my every step, prepared to kill me the moment I attempted to play them false" (2:200–201), Lee explains, until finally "My disorder of mind became so great, that I was in a species of stupid distraction when the moment for action arrived" (2:201). Lee sees himself always under the eye of the slaves; his "second sight," which is broadened to include the gaze of all the slaves on the plantation, patrols the first and keeps it from betraying the rebellion or disowning the cause. Tom seizes the upper hand in this clash of incompatible ideals, however, and Lee must accompany him to the gallows. There is no chance of transmigration; even should Lee enter the dead body of one of his accomplices and bring him again to life, there is no doubt that "my fate must be equally certain to be hanged" (211). The slave revolt is subdued and its chief perpetrators, including Tom, are executed; the soul of Sheppard Lee quickly locates a new domicile, this time the body of the dyspeptic, dissipated southern aristocrat Arthur Megrim.[15]

This episode in *Sheppard Lee* seems intent on unpacking (or at the very least imagining) the explanatory narrative that would satisfactorily elucidate another violent rebellion in "Old Vawginnee." (Nat Turner's initials are eerily echoed in the debased moniker "Nigger Tom," and the moral of Bird's account corroborates the positions of proslavery alarmists like Thomas Dew, whose 1832 "Abolition of Negro Slavery" emphasized the danger of elevating ignorant slaves to "the condition of free men," and pumping them full of "dangerous notions of liberty and idleness," and denounced emancipation as a "chimerical scheme" [qtd. in Faust 45].) Lee chalks up his calamitous sojourn in the body of "Nigger Tom" and the "stupid distractions" that plagued him to a "disorder of the mind," yet he does not establish *whose* mind was so grievously disordered, nor is the rehearsal of his experiences as "Nigger Tom" anything more than a "confused recollection" (2:201). All the same, his relations with the revolting slave equivocate between metaphor and metonymy, sometimes allowing for a convergence of mind through imaginative identification, sometimes taking that convergence as an effect of association.

Once restored to his body at the end of the novel, Lee marvels at the strange powers of the mesmerized slumberer "who reads a sealed letter laid on his epigastrium, sees through millstones and men's bodies, and renders oraculous responses to any question that may be proposed him," and, in fact, each of the bodies he possesses exerts an irresistible influence over him (2:274). But Sheppard Lee finally imagines *himself* the slumberer in question, and one whose mummified body has all along been in the possession of the eccentric, nefarious corpse-robber Dr. Feuerteufel, who exhibited it for profit—some small comfort for a creature whose experiments in treasure hunting and spirit possession resulted in death. And even this model of spirit possession is too terrifying to contemplate at length, for Bird ends his novel by sequestering Lee's adventures in the realm of dreams.[16]

A FRETFUL SELF-REFECTION

What *is* of special interest to us in Poe's analysis is the notion that the difference between mind and machine, between a human and nonhuman organization, is that a human organization possesses, or is capable of producing, "a marked and radical difference" *within* itself, a difference that creates the possibility of" parts" in the self, the possibility of physically representing the self's relatedness to itself.

—JOHN IRWIN, *THE MYSTERY TO A SOLUTION*

When Poe's treasure hunters depart the mainland to return to Sullivan Island with sack loads of gold, they leave two gaping holes, like enormous eyes, in the landscape. Shortly afterward, Legrand confesses that a proliferation of "money-seekers" and a dearth of "money-finders" informed him of the existence of Kidd's treasure. He reasons, "It seemed to me that some accident—say the loss of a memorandum indicating its locality—had deprived him of the means of recovering it, and that this accident had become known to his followers, who otherwise might never have heard that treasure had been concealed at all" (221). It is paradoxically this absence of evidence that confirms the presence of buried treasure. Rumors are launched, put in circulation; they are "given first birth," Legrand explains, "and then universal currency" (221). But this chain of association turns to imaginative identification in the final moments of the tale when Legrand reflects upon Kidd's homicidal predilections and its human cost.

By contrast, Jupiter's last words in "The Gold Bug" are spoken, it seems, to himself:

> And dis all cum ob de goole-bug! de putty goole-bug! de poor little goole-bug, what I boosed in dat sabage kind ob style! Aint you shamed ob yourself, nigger?—answer me dat! (214)

Jupiter appears to relinquish metaphor for metonymy, conceding that the gold bug guided the men to treasure—though Poe finally discloses that the bug's association with Kidd's horde is pure invention, a piece of Legrand's "sober mystification" (229). Yet Jupiter takes the bug for substance and shadow: It is handsome and supple ("putty"), unpolluted and penniless ("poor"), both phantom and plunder ("ghoul"). And his crooning apostrophe calls a double into being. This is a self that must account for the abuse of the bug, a self that relinquishes possession of an imagined other, a self of whom the manumitted slave demands, "Aint you shamed ob yourself, nigger?—answer me dat!" (214). His fretful self-reflection (an internal doubling) corresponds with Sheppard Lee's concerns about his own doubleness: his "anxiety in relation to my poor body,—or *myself*, as I could not help regarding my body" (Bird 1:64).

No less than his tales of ratiocination, Poe's "The Gold Bug" negotiates the interplay of metonymy and metaphor in Legrand's and Jupiter's acquisition of clues and their exploration of the (criminal) "Other"—in this case a pirate, Captain Kidd, and the men he made dig their grave. Poe's text theorizes a hostile reciprocity that orbits a missing document (Jupiter's manumission) and, in doing so, delineates an interracial sociability situated between metaphor and metonymy. In Robert M. Bird's *Sheppard Lee*, transmigration of the soul provides a template for exploring the mix of imaginative identification and association that would be central to classical detective fiction. Though they are not detection tales per se, "The Gold Bug" and *Sheppard Lee* reside at the periphery of the genre as repositories of "generic intelligence" *avant la lettre*. That their respective authors used detection's tools to examine the nature of possession in the antebellum economy indicates that the social function of these literary devices was to embody and interrogate the psychodynamics of interracial dependency. In this way, Poe and Bird provide glimpses of the persistent, inescapable hostilities and exceptional sociabilities that might surmount what DuBois called the "more complex form of misrecognition" that followed emancipation (qtd. in Bull 247).

CHAPTER 4

The Great Work Remaining before Us

No one learns to be a connoisseur or diagnostician by restricting himself to practicing only preexistent rules.

—CARLO GINZBURG, "CLUES: ROOTS OF AN EVIDENTIAL PARADIGM"

This chapter explores narrative contiguity and temporal reconstruction in two texts on the periphery of the detective genre. Both of these novels enter into "whoizzit" mode—narrative situations in which characters who appear to be distinct persons are suddenly identified as a single individual, whose crimes comprise a continuous, coherent set of acts, a "totality of a character's being-and-doing over time" (Thompson and Thompson 55). The racial "passing" plots in Pauline Hopkins's serialized mystery *Hagar's Daughter: A Story of Southern Caste Prejudice* (1901–2) and William H. Holcombe's little-known *A Mystery of New Orleans: Solved by New Methods* (1890) advance modes of forensic skepticism that contest a popular "romance of reunion" culture and the impermeable racial caste system that sustains it. *Hagar's Daughter* also amends detective fiction's standard task of backward construction through its conspicuous use of ellipsis. The narrative's hidden temporal center is the "absent but real" story of crime, which Hopkins uses to elucidate legislative fraud and fiscal hypocrisy, and to discredit the acquisitive stance that drives the romantic reconciliation of the North and the South.

Hopkins scrutinizes the reunion between North and South in the late nineteenth century, using detection's devices to critique "reconciliatory" politics that silenced calls for racial justice and restitution, and destroyed possibilities for a fruitful interracial sociability. *Hagar's Daughter* imagines a commingling of races not predicated on financial exploitation or social domination, but on a political and social civility that would engender union, ultimately calling into question the legitimacy of racial categories.

Hagar's Daughter follows the fortunes of the well-to-do and almost-only-ever-white Hagar Enson, whose inveterate gambler brother-in-law St. Clair Enson and a callous slave trader named Walker produce an ancient bill of sale that brands her a black slave. Her infant in tow, Hagar escapes the degradations of Washington's slave markets on the eve of the Civil War, only to appear again in the nation's capital after an ellipsis of twenty years. Now she is Estelle, the charming wife of the new western senator Zenas Bowen and mother of the enchanting ingénue Jewel, who is courted by General Benson's guileless aid Cuthbert Sumner. Their lot is threatened, however, by same villainous crew: the suave General Benson (Enson) and the shady, scheming Major Madison (Walker), now grafters who have infiltrated Washington's high society determined to pilfer the Senator's pockets any which way, even by kidnapping Jewel, whose racial birthright is finally uncovered. A novel in two acts, *Hagar's Daughter* brings together the puzzle of racial identity, which is neither manifest nor capable of being known; hidden genealogies of white theft; and the bewildering "temporal union" that joins the antebellum period to the post-Reconstruction era. Hopkins's emphasis on reconstructing the intermediate years, and her rewriting of the detective's roles and detection fiction's principles of temporal organization to do so, vitally depend on the narrative mechanisms we associate with detective fiction, though she cautiously modifies the genre to address the "problem of the color-line."

In Holcombe's *A Mystery of New Orleans*, the young Chicago architect Hugh Stanford is appointed to search for Gordon Clark, a prosperous businessman who left the country with his young daughter in the midst of the Civil War and has since disappeared. Scouring New Orleans for the slightest intimation of Clark's fate, Stanford falls in love with Ninette, the adopted child of the respected Colonel Du Valcourt. New Orleans's high society ostracizes Ninette when her jealous sister claims Ninette is of black ancestry, but Stanford does not suspend their engagement. Instead, he busies himself tracking paranormal phenomena and employing a local psychic, tactics that lead him to Clark's murderer and also reveal that Ninette is Clark's lost daughter. Significantly, Stanford dedicates himself to Ninette when she crosses the color line and, of course, when she doubles back. With this apparently resilient and briefly interracial couple, Holcombe explores the possibility of a sociable end to a Civil War and recoils at an aftermath in which slavery and race prejudice have not been eradicated but have assumed new forms. Like *Hagar's Daughter*, Holcombe's novel violates the conventions of late nineteenth-century popular culture by depicting the "romance of union" as an interracial plot. Additionally, Holcombe proposes an unorthodox forensics to mine an obscured past. And while both *Hagar's Daughter* and *A Mystery of New Orleans* propose that black Americans are vital sources of historical intelligence, Holcombe also imagines psychic phenomenon and supernatural forces that can link the present to the past, once and for all exhuming a candid historical record.

HISTORICAL RECORDS

> It may be inspiring, but it is certainly not the truth. And beyond this it is dangerous. It is not only part foundation of our present lawlessness and loss of democratic ideals; it has, more than that, led the world to embrace and worship the color bar as social salvation and it is helping to range mankind in ranks of mutual hatred and contempt, at the summons of a cheap and false myth.
>
> —W. E. B. DUBOIS, "THE PROPAGANDA OF HISTORY"

Hagar's Daughter: A Story of Southern Caste Prejudice briefly features an elderly black man named Mr. Henry, a veteran of the Fifty-Fourth Massachusetts Volunteer Infantry led by Colonel Robert Gould Shaw, half lame and, incidentally, an undercover detective. From his post at the general store near the old Enson estate in Maryland, Mr. Henry provides a firsthand account of the 1863 Battle of Fort Wagner, describing the advance of the fearless black troops who "kep' right on an' up de hill tel we war han' to han' wif de inimy" (230). Then, he explains, in the heat of battle, a remarkable event occurred:

> Fus' thing I 'member clearly after I got het up, was I seed a officer standin' wavin' his sword, an' I heard him holler, "Now, give 'em h—— boys, give 'em h——!" an then thar come a shot; it hit him—zee-rip—an' off went his head; but, gent'men, ef you'll b'lieve me, dat head rolled by me, down de hil sayin' as it went, "Give 'em h—-, boys, give 'em h—-!" until it landed in de ditch; an' all de time de mon's arms was a wavin' of his sword." (230–31)

Split into a head and horseman but unapprised of his injury, torn in two by the bullet that ripped through his neck but pressing ahead nevertheless, the officer tumbles down the hill. And this recipient of a grotesque decapitation rolls down like a gramophone, though his talking head simulates a skipping record that never advances. Mr. Henry maintains that the head did not cease to speak even when it arrived at the foot of the hill. Indeed, it happened "so suddint," and in that split second "he hadn't time to stop talkin'. Why de water in de dith mus' have got in his mouf fere *I seen him* when he spit it out" (232). While Mr. Henry briefly describes the storm of bullets and the retreat that followed, his account prolongs the regiment's courageous advance toward Charleston, the "cradle of succession," with their death-defying commander's last request to "Give 'em h——!" ringing in their ears.

Contemporary historical records attest that the troops at Fort Wagner encountered an onslaught of bullets two hundred yards before the ramparts. Colonel Robert Gould Shaw, the commanding officer of the Fifty-Fourth Massachusetts Volunteer Infantry, met his death almost immediately they ascended the hill, "pitching forward, sword upraised, a bullet through his heart," and a massacre ensued (Kirstein). However, the content and the context of Mr. Henry's account capture the major concerns of Hopkins's serialized mystery, as well as many of the ways the author's engagement with the detective genre are brought to bear in the prolonged chronology of *Hagar's Daughter*.

To begin with, Mr. Henry's Civil War story offers a staggering image of integrated union in a book whose central investigation is the available configurations for interracial sociability in a post–Civil War era. By the late nineteenth century, the sentimental reconciliation of North and South found its literary form in novels that featured an "intersectional wedding" between white northern men and white southern women, and these "staple[s] of popular culture . . . had no interracial counterpart in the popular imagination" (Blight 125). Yet Mr. Henry's yarn dramatizes how black perceptions of the past might unsettle reunion culture. In addition to picturing a white officer partnered with black troops, Henry describes a peculiar sociability in the midst of battle, where black soldiers found themselves "han' to han' wif de inimy," practically married to the Confederate soldiers at Fort Wagner, where black and white men died side by side. These are recovered images of interracial sociability, all but crushed in the popular imagination by plantation nostalgia and the rise of Jim Crow in late nineteenth century. Mr. Henry's record of an antagonistic but interracial commingling on the battlefield implicitly pulls both blacks and whites into the process of reunion.

Importantly, Mr. Henry's story signals Hopkins's departure from a standard detective formula; *Hagar's Daughter* is a work in which forensics and common notions of "history" ("reasoned reconstruction of the past rooted in research" [Blight 1]) will not suffice. Hopkins's literary politics push to resuscitate a lost history of interracial sociability and to understand its implications for the present. Along these lines, Mr. Henry's narrative work is clearly a project of historical recovery, though it is not something out of the history books. Instead, the split between "I seem him" and "ef you'll b'lieve me" is a paradox of the tall tale as truth-telling. Mr. Henry's "spitting image" of Colonel Shaw is a record rooted in what we might call an ethical archaeology, a testimony to the spirit if not the image of a historical event. With a mix of memory-work, commemoration, and mythmaking, Mr. Henry participates in the struggle for the meaning of the Civil War in the face of laissez-faire economics and Lost Cause ideology. His story is of necessity a polemic.

An advertisement for Hopkins's series "Famous Men of the Negro Race" in the September 1900 issue of *Colored American Magazine* exemplifies this politics, pointing to the suppression of a particular past:

> To the Negro is denied the stimulus of referring to the deeds of distinguished ancestors, to their valor and patriotism. He is distinguished only as the former slave of the country. Truth gives him the history of a patriot, a brave soldier, the defender of the country from foreign invaders, a "God-fearing producer of the nation's wealth." (*Colored American Magazine* qtd. in Pamplin 174)

Hopkins biographer Lois Brown argues that Hopkins's "narrative incursions into the past" were equally "political and sociocultural excavations" that could broadcast the distinguished deeds of African Americans, as Mr. Henry's tale-telling does (326). There are other means by which one might encounter the past, or even retrieve it—a feat made suddenly possible with the 1877 invention of the phonograph, with which Mr. Henry's tale fascinatingly aligns itself.[1]

Hagar's Daughter is, appropriately, an inspired meditation on the permeability and receptivity of the present, and detection is essential to its project. Detective fiction is structurally suited to this inquiry; the genre is compelled to perform "an act of recovery, moving forward in order to move back," and saddled with the task of distilling the past from the site of the present (Porter 29). Since the duty of detection fictions is to facilitate backward construction, reassembling what has gone before, the text must serve "as a mediator between the reader and the story of the crime" (Todorov 46). In *Hagar's Daughter*, Hopkins avails herself of temporal configurations built into the genre in order to register the past through its assaults on the present, though it imagines the use of literature as alternative to a "forensic" record.

Crucially, Hopkins's weathered tale-teller Mr. Henry is an undercover agent whose project of historical recollection doubles as detection. His story provides cover for Venus Johnson's excavation of an old slaveholding estate, Enson Hall, to retrieve two kidnapped women, both of them former slaves. In this case, historical recovery coincides with physical rescue; they are parallel narrative actions, or at least the latter passes as the former. And while Mr. Henry's long-winded narrative reenactment stresses the bravery and fortitude of African American soldiers during the war, it is also instrumental: his thrilling yarn reels in Isaac Johnson (Venus's father) away from Isaac's coconspirators in crime. Mr. Henry and Venus see through the assumed identities of two soon-to-be-exposed scoundrels: Colonel Benson and Major Henry Clay Madison (the former Isaac's master in antebellum days); these southern war-profiteers turned Washington crooks will pay for their crimes. Meanwhile, Isaac gravitates toward the storyteller, with whom he drinks immoderately, finally clearing the way for the intelligent no-frills maid Venus Johnson to retrieve two abducted women, Jewel Bowen and Aunt Henny Sargeant, from the depths of the old Enson estate. "It's as sure as preaching that somebody who knows something must take hold of Miss Jewel's case," Venus points out as she decides to take up the work of detection herself; "The police are slower 'n death" (221).

Spurred by necessity, this self-appointed sleuth shoulders the law and takes to the field, while Mr. Henry's wild yarn intimates storytelling is itself a guise of detection. As they collaborate in the field, their white associate, Detective Henson, is deskbound in his Washington office. But by uniting these three characters in a collective enterprise, *Hagar's Daughter* transforms and broadens conceptions of detection to admit interracial and intergenerational collaboration, and to draw special attention to the unique competencies of her African American detectives.[2] Though the government bureaucrat Detective Henson is a man with "vast experience," he is as a rule incapable of locating concrete proof to advance the case (222). This is anathema for "a legal machine" for whom "tangible evidence was the only convincing argument that he knew" (221). In this mystery, fraught with domestic intrigue and disguise, it is fair to say that Mr. Henry's and Venus's expertise supersedes Detective Henson's. But Henson is soon moved to rely on women's "intuitive deductions" and pursue the course indicated by his client's, Jewel Bowen's, "suspicions," which he can "trace in the tone" of her voice; he also expresses confidence in the insights of Venus Johnson (190, 189). The success of the three detectives depends on a broader, integrated vision of detection, one that is supple enough to accommodate methods other than deciphering the "clue."

As a result, *Hagar's Daughter* moves beyond the meaning-making capacity of forensic signifiers, suggesting that a quasi-empirical model of crime solving is not sufficient to penetrate "a passing plot" or unmask disguise, though intuition, grammatical lapses, or storytelling may well unveil a history of racial uplift and betray criminal tendencies. This is not to say that Hopkins discounts dactyloscopy (the talent of penetrating disguise). Instead, her detectives gravitate to methods besides the forensic: phonological blunders and historical echoes, intuitions and repetitions. These devices of detection, narrative half-rhymes and slipups, are the formal machinery of Hopkins's text.

Hagar's Daughter advances a theory of detection anchored in the shifting signifiers of respectability and uplift, villainy and vice rather than conventional forensics.[3] For instance, the irreproachable Senator Bowen is ethnically unidentifiable. He is "an elderly man of dark complexion," and though he has "the hair and skin of an Indian" we find that "his eyes were a shrewd and steely gray." Hopkins calls him "peculiar" but also finds in Bowen "the spirit of the man of the world" (76, 80). While this composite sketch of the senator calculatingly frustrates any attempt to assign race, the Washington neophyte is not wholly enigmatic. What he carries about him is "a decidedly Western air," and in his voice his origins are betrayed rather than effaced (76). Hopkins writes, "It was his habit to fall into the use of ungrammatical phrases, and, in this one might easily trace the rugged windings of a life of hardship among the great unwashed before success had crowned his labors and steered his bark into its present smooth harbor" (80). In Bowen's case, there is no chance of obtaining an incandescent biological record. However, the purposeful course of his life is evident. He is a man of the "self-made pattern" for whom the Civil War proved a mechanism of social advancement. He joined the northern army at the outset and "at its close was mustered out as 'Major Bowen'" (80). Hopkins concludes that the virtuous senator is "an example of the possibilities of individual expansion under the rule of popular government" (80). Along these lines, when the self-appointed sleuth Venus Johnson pleads her case to the government official, Detective Henson, her accent slips; she "forgot her education in her earnestness, and fell into the Negro vernacular, talking and crying at the same time" (224). An involuntary memory that suddenly surfaces, the grammatical relapse indicates Johnson's ascent to educated, middle-class respectability.

Hard work leaves an audible trace in *Hagar's Daughter*, and the author shows her hand here: insofar as Hopkins disavows the color line, she draws a line instead between those who strive for self-improvement through hard work, and those who reject honest labor (Pamplin 169). Claire Pamplin reflects that Hopkins borrows from a "rhetoric of gentility and Anglo-Saxon superiority" (176), and Augusta Rohrbach concludes that even if "what we see is not what we get" in *Hagar's Daughter*, Hopkins's essentialism here can be contrasted with the more "fluid notion of identity" that would characterize a later work like *Of One Blood* (484, 495). They are exactly right, I think, and yet what seems to be at issue here is less Hopkins's endorsement of uplift than the difference between what we get and what else we can and cannot see.

Without disregarding what other critics have designated as the text's posture, we might consider other interpretations that may have resonated with the novel's turn-of-the-century audience. The *Colored American Magazine*, which printed *Hagar's Daughter* in serial form from 1901 to 1902, could claim a nationwide subscription base of about fifteen thousand (Schneider 159), and to label the publication a homogeneous treatise for middle-class respectability would be an oversimplification. During most of its run and including Hopkins's tenure as a contributor and editor, the staff of the *Colored American* was "Pro-Civil Rights Bookerites." They approved "high minded self-improvement" but despised the government's failure to protect the franchise and stop lynching (160). They were first implicitly and later explicitly managed by Booker T. Washington, who paraded his accommodationist policies but fed the magazine out of his pocketbook. However, they also emulated "Boston Brahmins" intellectually and politically, at least partially because of their abolitionist and Republican roots. Given this extraordinarily awkward situation, it is surprising the editorial staff was not completely tongue-tied, or that they managed more than pseudonymous, middle-of-the-road editorials (162). These circumstances alone warrant close examination of the magazine's contents, which may have frequently toed the separatist-accommodationist party line, sometimes dispensed a straightforward discourse of uplift or advocated for race assimilation, and on occasion even included radical denouncements of government policies that sustained race prejudice—and let us not renounce the possibility that writers like Hopkins did not attempt to make all of these positions available simultaneously or at least side by side.

The work of a serialized novel such as *Hagar's Daughter* may be best illuminated by Michael Denning's reflections on the nineteenth-century dime novel. According to Denning, in such texts we find "the use of disguise as a narrative equivalent of metaphor rather than as the sign of an enigma to be solved" (153). The narratives themselves "are the dream-work of the social, condensing (compressing a number of dream-thoughts into one image) and displacing (transferring energies invested in one image to another) the wishes, anxieties, and intractable antinomies of social life in a class society" (81).

The sweeping allegorical dimension of *Hagar's Daughter* takes the Civil War's unfinished business as its subject, and so traces of the past return in the guise of the present, at the level of Senator Bowen's or Venus Johnson's speech, or in the farcical reappearance of nearly all the dramatis personae from the first part of the novel in its second act. Then too, there is the resurrection of antebellum slavery in the postbellum world through the story of Aunt Henny Sargeant, a former slave whom the villains General Benson, Major Madison, and Isaac Johnson kidnap and haul bodily to the crumbling Enson estate, the site of antebellum servitude.

These veiled continuities between the antebellum and post-Reconstruction nation are both "metaphor" and "an enigma to be solved," and Hopkins's indictment of broad social and economic tendencies that span these eras push the boundaries of another of the genre's characteristics: its tendency from the turn of the century on to externalize guilt by depicting crime as the act of an individual, an aberration, rather than an intrinsic property of the social order (Cawelti, *Adventure* 104).

At the end of the novel when Cuthbert Sumner acknowledges his share of responsibility for the death of the spouse, Jewel Bowen, that he abandoned, he has the following insight: "Then it was borne in upon him: the sin is the nation's. It must be washed out. The plans of the Father are not changed in the nineteenth century; they are shown us in different forms" (283–84). Though it seems Sumner's epiphany is cultivated for his own solicitude, it also annexes his transgressions to a broader historical context. If, in gorgeous hindsight, Sumner discerns the "lesson of the degradation of slavery" and finally perceives the crimes of the nation and his own unfeeling youth, he also sees that expiation does not end with his own (284). Hopkins refuses to conceptualize crime as the mere act of one person; *Hagar's Daughter* is a far more sweeping meditation on blame. As a result, the novel defies the conventions of a genre devoted to restoring social order by evicting aberration in the form of a single criminal entity, and breaks with detective fiction's custom of assigning blame to specific individuals, whose arrest apparently repairs the "integrity" of the bourgeois social order.

Though Hopkins's novel does not painstakingly implement detective fiction's conventions, *Hagar's Daughter*'s significant engagement with the genre classifies the work as a peripheral genre text. The author reenvisions the work of detective figures, the dimensions of detection, and the scope of the crimes and the nature of the perpetrators her detectives confront. Finally, *Hagar's Daughter* reimagines the process of assembling the past and present upon which the detective genre depends. It is worth dwelling on this last narrative mechanism, since Hopkins's narrative experiments with reconstructing the past help clarify the powerful political and economic arguments that *Hagar's Daughter* advances as it explores configurations of interracial sociability over time.

RECONSTRUCTION IN TIME

> Yet in this sweeping mechanistic interpretation, there is no room for the real plot of the story, for the clear mistake and guilt of rebuilding a new slavery of the working class in the midst of a fateful experiment in democracy; for the triumph of sheer moral courage and sacrifice in the abolition crusade; and for the hurt and struggle of degraded black millions in their fight for freedom and their attempt to enter democracy. Can all this be omitted or half suppressed in a treatise that calls itself scientific?
>
> —W. E. B. DUBOIS, "THE PROPAGANDA OF HISTORY"

Apart from its plots of disguise and mistaken identity, its melodramatic courtroom scenes bloated with the requisite exposés, and the various sensationalized snapshots of political debauchery and corrupt scheming as sordid as any in *The Quaker City*, *Hagar's Daughter* is principally a story about the unexpected disclosure of black blood, which has tragic consequences for both of the novel's heroines. The first part of the book is devoted to the plight of Hagar Enson, who falls victim to the machinations of her unscrupulous brother-in-law, the inveterate gambler St. Clair Enson. An obsequious, scheming slave-trader who goes by the name of Walker is Hagar's supposed owner, privy to Hagar's black ancestry—the knowledge of which she is herself unaware. Walker demands payment from Hagar's husband. Recognizing that the law of the land "forbids me to acknowledge as my wife a woman in whose veins courses a drop of the accursed blood of the Negro slave" (59), Ellis Enson resolves to abandon their Baltimore estate and travel abroad with his wife and their newborn child. These plans go awry, however, when Ellis disappears and St. Clair is made heir to the estate. Hagar and her child are swiftly conducted to a slave block in the nation's capital, and she escapes the fate that awaits her by flinging herself off the Long Bridge, her infant daughter in her arms.

The focus of these early episodes is Hagar's astonishing transformation in the wake of Walker's shocking disclosure. Hopkins succinctly conveys this shift in the thoughts of her protagonist: "Only this morning she was his wife, the honored mistress of his home; tonight what? His slave, his concubine!" (58). In an essay on Hopkins's magazine fiction, Rohrbach points out that a linguistic shift further demarcates the conversion of Hagar and her child into human chattel. The infant, once the "heiress of the hall," is called a "pickaninny" and "brat," while the pure and spiritual Hagar becomes a "handsome polished wench" (Hopkins 39, 55, 72, Rohrbach 487). In *Hagar's Daughter*, race is idiom and not color; racial identity, in turn, rewrites Hagar's station, seizing her property and possessions as it consigns her to bondage.

Hopkins's unmistakable critique of this arrangement lies in her depiction of slavery (rather than racial identity) as a "contaminated" institution strutting about in the trappings of legitimacy. Walker, who regards Hagar as his property and prey, pulls his bill of sale from a "large sheepskin pocketbook" (52), for instance, and when Ellis Enson repudiates the "God-given principle" that would condemn his wife and child to servitude, he sees slavery disrobed, as an "idol, stripped of its gilded trappings, in all its filthiness" (59). The text also emphasizes that slaves are not merely a source of labor but also what Nell Painter terms "embodied currency" (398). Stripped of rank and birthright, Hagar and her daughter generate wealth. Walker returns Ellis Enson's family to him at the "bargain rate" of six thousand dollars. Since "the child follows the condition of the mother," the slave trader gloats, "I scoop the pile" (Hopkins 56). And when, following the apparent suicide of his older brother, the disreputable St. Clair Enson inherits the family property, he liquidates the estate, escorting his slaves—including his newest assets, Hagar and her daughter—to private pens in the nation's capital, where "they would be assured of quick sales and large profits" (72). Between them, Walker and Enson devise a scheme that can "compass the impossible": creating capital where once there was none (29).

This pecuniary farce hints at the unexpectedly comic or absurdist aspects of Hopkins's mystery, where depictions of senseless speculation (what we now call the irrational exuberance of the markets) are part of the substructure of an otherwise gloomy story, and one that shifts the text to the periphery of the detective genre. Moreover, the profound irony that attends race speculation paired with the burlesque of other attempted disguises in the aftermath of the Civil War (St. Clair Enson becomes General Benson; his brother Ellis Enson passes as Detective Henson, and so on) generates a twisted structure of black humor. To clarify the arithmetic of this dark comedy, I will briefly turn to the follies of Petroleum Vesuvius Nasby, the comic alter ego created by Ohioan journalist David R. Locke during the post–Civil War era.

As with Hopkins's *Hagar's Daughter*, an "impossible" economy—one generated from within the family—is an explicit focus of one of journalist and humorist David Locke's "Petroleum V. Nasby" satires. Nasby, Locke's coarse southern protagonist, is assembling the curriculum for his "Southern Classikle, Theologikle, and Military Institoot uv Confedrit X Roads"; "Joe Bigler, the drunken Confedrit soljer" furnishes the following contribution to the college exams (Locke 397):

> A high toned, shivilrous Virginian, twenty years ago, hed a female slave which wuz ez black ez a crow, and worth only $800. Her progeny wuz only half ez black ez a crow, and her female grandchildren wuz sufficiently bleached to sell in Noo Orleans for $2500 per female offspring. Required. 1st. The length of time necessary to pay off the Nashnel debt by this means. 2nd. The length of time required to bleach the cuss of color out of niggers of the United States. (398)

An internal contradiction emerges from Locke's after-the-fact appraisal of southern monetary policy: on the one hand, interracial, coercive procreation that produced wealth was a source of revenue in the antebellum economy, while its indispensable corollary, that "race tended to disappear in commercial intercourse—the term being chosen deliberately" (O'Malley, "Specie and Species" 382), threatened a collapse of the market. Locke sneers at a people so preposterously thick they are unable to account for the unsustainable effects of "race-inflation" and an inevitable market crash. He also derides southern pretensions to "shivilrous" civilization, particularly any mythologizing of an "Old South" that proposed to heroically remedy the national debt and permanently resolve the "cuss of color."

Just as *Hagar's Daughter* underscores the depravity of southern enterprise, almost the entire Petroleum V. Nasby compendium plays up its un-relenting contempt for despicable transactions that were the mainstay of the antebellum slave economy. In "'Psalm of Sadness' for his friends South," for example, the ill-mannered Petroleum Nasby recollects the "normal results uv the conkunbinage I sold," which subsidized a sumptuous existence for the slave owner: "On the price thereof I played poker, and drank mint-juleps, and rode in gorgus chariots, and wore purple and fine linen every day" (Locke 194). The fixtures of this antebellum idyll, Nasby and his compatriots vary little from Hopkins's "high toned" card sharp St. Clair, who must liquidate human assets in order to pay his gambling debts. In the war's aftermath, how-ever, the fates of Nasby and St. Clair Enson part ways. His slaves now free laborers, his licentiousness curbed, and his dream "bustid," Nasby laments, "Now shel I hev to stain my hands with labor, or starve. In what am I better than a Northern mudsill?" (194). Locke implies that slavery alone hoisted the boorish southerner above his northern counterpart, but the terms of this analogy are evasive and suspect. If the end of slavery returned to the freed-man his labor value, though not the property owed him; if it made a "mudsill" of the white southerner, placing him on par with the wage laborer; if the status of this wage laborer—undergirded by principles of legal equality and free contract broadly endorsed in the North as the cornerstone of "free labor civilization" (Cohen 29)—was sufficiently degraded to be tainted with the stench of slavery and called by the name "mudsill," then the rewards guaran-teed by the North's free-labor ideology were at best dubious.

Not only does Nasby's "Psalm" insinuate that the spoils of war redound upon the northern capitalists, whose fiscal domain encompasses laborers in the North and the South, it also suggests one reason why the reach of Re-construction did not extend to the breach of property rights and the redistri-bution of wealth in the South: Northern capitalists could neither invent nor defend principles that distinguished their political economy from a southern aristocracy (Bensel 350). Thus, the South and the North shared an invest-ment in a "sufficiently" black subject: while antebellum southern wealth de-pended on the annexation of black bodies, northern Republicans—at least those who eschewed any radical extraction—would be joint parties to the separation anxiety precipitated by Reconstruction.

But both Hopkins's and Locke's treatments of antebellum slavery use the national government as a point of reference. Each scenario draws the fate of the entire nation into its orbit. A statist principle is wheedled into the first "Nasby" anecdote, since its comic object is the southerner's belief that coercive, incestuous intercourse could have wiped away that great "stain upon the nation." It is the tendency of "Joe Bigler, the drunken Confedrit soljer" to read black skin as a cosmetic setback that can be cleared, a "cuss" that the white man can expiate while remaining indifferent to the sexual violence upon which his racial arithmetic depends. Yet while it disregards the racism intrinsic to American slavery, Bigler's curiously literalist bent leans toward an antiessentialist ideology, absolutely contravening the "one-drop rule," which maintained a single drop of black blood could tarnish whiteness. What is more, Bigler characterizes interracial endogamy as fiscal patriotism (a practice of filial devotion used to settle up the "Nashnel" debt), thereby implicating federal trade policies alongside southern "industry" in an integrated economy. Hopkins's evocation of the national government takes a different form. Hagar's death scene very pointedly reproduces the substance of William Wells Brown's *Clotel; or The President's Daughter*, in which Thomas Jefferson's illegitimate mulatto progeny, the captured fugitive Clotel, finds the only way to evade her pursuers is to leap to her death: to crash into the "deep foamy waters of the Potomac" beneath that same Long Bridge, "within plain sight of the President's house and the capitol of the Union, which should be an evidence wherever it should be known, of the unconquerable love of liberty the heart may inherit; as well as a fresh admonition to the slave dealer, of the cruelty and enormity of his crimes" (Brown 217). Susan Hays Bussey points out that when she jumps over the bridge, "Hagar severs her generic ties to the passive white females of domestic fiction, and joins rank with literary African American mothers" (307). Moreover, Hopkins's use of the Capitol as the backdrop for Hagar's death reiterates Brown's indictment of American political culture for its callous failure to extend civil rights to every person in the nation.

Like Locke's "Instatoot uv Confedrit X Roads," *Hagar's Daughter* conceives interracial union as inevitably recursive. However, while "Joe Bigler, the drunken Confedrit soljer" locates these strictly fiscal affairs in a preempancipation era, Hopkins second picture of a truly affectionate and reciprocal interracial relation moves the controversial union from South to North, and her narrative hurdles twenty years ahead. In the second part of the novel, set twenty years later, Hopkins revisits Hagar's cataclysmic predicament. A Washington debutant and "petted darling of society" named Jewel appears with her mother (Hagar Enson, now Estelle Bowen), only to discover, as her mother once did, that she too is of African descent. In the postwar era, Jewel is not confronted with the prospect of slavery; nevertheless she imagines the "astonishment, disgust and contempt of her former associates when they learned her story" (280–81). Indeed, once their racial origins are made public, neither Jewel nor Hagar is received by Washington society. Jewel finds the heft of antebellum social prejudice intact, especially in the case of her husband Cuthbert Sumner. Sumner is appalled by Jewel's revelation, though after a day's length of "mental torture" he magnanimously declares that he will "overlook and forgive all" (282). Sumner's change of heart is disastrously belated, however; Jewel and her family have left for the Continent. When, at the end of a brooding year, Sumner travels to Enson Hall to be reunited with his wife, he discovers that Jewel died abroad of Roman fever.

Cuthbert's surname evidently alludes to the Massachusetts senator Charles Sumner, whose commitment to republican principles and racial equality entailed vehement opposition to state prohibitions against interracial marriage, which he helped to repeal in 1843. Cuthbert Sumner is a decaffeinated, half-rate version of his predecessor, however. Though a son of New England, his allegiance to race equality is purely vacuous, and, moreover, Cuthbert makes his living as a government clerk and aide to General Benson (the erstwhile St. Clair Enson), with whose prejudices Cuthbert is apparently reconciled. Cuthbert's attitudes make for a striking contrast with Charles Sumner's.[4] Sumner was mercilessly antagonized and insulted by the proslavery wing for his unyielding commitment to racial equality (not to mention his readiness to spout indelicacies rather than mince words). For instance, the South Carolina senator Andrew Pickens Butler confounded Sumner by enjoining the abolitionist to write a play about a "negro princess in search of a husband" and a white man's repulsion by "her white teeth . . . black skin and kinky hair" (qtd. in Sinha 242). Hopkins's character Cuthbert Sumner, by contrast, openly confesses his repulsion for a woman "contaminated" by a drop of Negro blood, observing that "the mere thought of the grinning, toothless black hag that was her foreparent would forever rise between us" (271). This ancestral, black-as-a-crow monstrosity is the scenery of his subconscious. Cuthbert Sumner's tremendous bias against interracial intercourse suggests that his historical equivalent is Hopkins's contemporary William Graham Sumner, a Harvard social Darwinist whose support for atomistic individualism and classical economics could be concisely summarized: "At bottom there are two chief things with which government has to deal. They are the property of men and the honor of women" (Sumner qtd. in Cohen 150).

In the second iteration of Hopkins's race drama, a Gilded Age so-called liberal who abandons his wife (Cuthbert Sumner) replaces the diabolical son of the South who sells his sister-in-law (St. Clair Enson), and so Jewel's story ends, as Hagar's did, unhappily. These distinctly unfortunate but remarkably similar developments are separated by an extraordinary ellipsis: the twenty-year gulf between the onset of the Civil War and 1882, five years after the Compromise of 1877 drew a curtain over Reconstruction efforts, revoking many of the legislative achievements of the Radical Republicans, and limiting reparations for freedmen to the Fourteenth and Fifteenth Amendments. Hopkins's explicit ellipsis here—a temporal leap forward to "a fine afternoon in the early winter of 1882" as her heroine Hagar has only just plunged off the Long Bridge into the Potomac—joins the antebellum world to its late nineteenth-century counterpart, pointedly overlooking the tumultuous decades in between (75).

What is to be inferred from this unexpected acceleration is not a vacancy in the intermittent years, nor even that sort of inquiry into historical possibilities which Gary Morson has called "sideshadowing"—the "appreciation of potentialities" or attention to alternative sequences by which a text makes clear that incontrovertibly real historical events "might just as well not have happened" (118–19)—but that the *continuity* of the antebellum and post-Reconstruction moments is itself the fatal transgression the text aspires to elucidate. The "absent but real" story of the crime can only be grasped retroactively; it is situated at the narrative's temporal center. Whereas the typical arrangement of the whodunit depends on the superimposition of only two temporal series (Todorov 45), the initial drama and the investigation that follows (which, in the detective novel's "purest" form remain temporally distinct), *Hagar's Daughter* supplements this formula with an additional quantity, a narrative antecedent that makes it possible to establish and then reconstruct the novel's temporal abyss. In fact, the work of the novel hinges on this narrative portion and the subsequent ellipsis, which foregrounds a crime that would otherwise come into view only as socioeconomic inertia: the antebellum status quo.

In this case, no ordinary analeptic strategy can secure the contents of the ellipsis. Instead, we can extrapolate the substance of this temporal elision only if we take notice of its sylleptic character. As a narrative "unit" it serves a double syntactic function (modifying two adjacent propositions or, for our purposes, narrative vectors) and must be reassembled vis-à-vis both of its temporal bookends. The appropriate parallel here is Slavoj Žižek's appraisal of the absent melodic line or "inner voice" ("*innere Stimme*") in Robert

Schumann's "Humoresque." In order to account for the relation between the right- and left-hand piano lines, Žižek contends

> one is thus compelled to (re)construct a third, "virtual" intermediate level, the melodic line, which for structural reasons, cannot be played. Its status is that of an impossible real which can exist only in the guise of the written. Its physical presence would annihilate the two melodic lines we effectively hear in reality. (*Violence* 169)

Žižek describes the absent melodic line as a constitutive lack that never materializes as such but, as in the "second phase" of fantasy in Freud's "A Child Is Being Beaten," exists out of necessity. Along similar lines, Hopkins withholds access to an intermediate and occluded phase of events that mediates the second and the first parts of the book; the ellipsis calls upon the reader to discern the meaning of the repeated motif. Some difference inhabits the sameness, and it is a difference that leads Hopkins's most thorough biographer to conclude that a novel that almost completely avoids reference to the failure of Reconstruction is nevertheless "a narrative account of a monumental battle to preserve and reinstitute bondage and chattel slavery, as well as of calculated and political efforts to taint and invalidate personal freedoms" (Lois Brown 329).

What differentiates the first and final scenarios, establishing that Hopkins has invented something other than a twice-told tale? We might take Hopkins's double take for an instance of what Malcolm Bull dubs "epistemic abjection," wherein the strange continuity of the two narrative lines in *Hagar's Daughter* denotes a paucity of knowledge to assist the knower, a dearth of the historical clues a detection text is duty-bound to provide. Yet the extraordinary puzzle posed by these historically distinct narrative consistencies could steer us toward the subtexts that give rise to each part of the text. In the brilliant essay "Ideology and Race in America" Barbara J. Fields notes that ideological shifts might "easily pass undetected," and that in the peculiar case of the late nineteenth century, while "it is easy enough to demonstrate a substantial continuity in racial 'attitudes,' this apparently uninterrupted set of attitudes in no way indicates that their ideological underpinnings have remained intact" (154–55). Fields's observation helps us to grasp the basic function of Hopkins's conspicuous ellipsis: to establish historicity in terms of the doctrinal body that inspires the narrative rather than the narrative itself, to chart tectonic activity along fault lines as opposed to visible seismic events.

ANTEBELLUM ECHOES

> The detective maps the labyrinth (the mystery, the murder) by trying to cut through the distorted view of the past available in the present (the mirror). As finders of solutions, detectives are "mapmakers" who grapple with the flow of the present, which, by moving farther away from the time of murder, changes and distorts the image of that past.
>
> —STEFANO TANI, *THE DOOMED DETECTIVE*

The first of these "fault" lines I have suggested above: the meaningful doubling-up of Charles Sumner with William Graham Sumner in the character Cuthbert Sumner, who serves as their common lodgings. What remains to be established is an articulatable switchpoint at which one is substituted for the other. Or, if not, surely the effect of Hopkins's signature pun is to inscribe its reader at the place of the switchpoint itself, as the experiential and cognitive witness to an anomalous, even paradoxical pairing (in this case, the union of democratic principles and laissez-faire corporate capitalism). But what is most common of these fault lines is a moment of an uncanny encounter with continuity: the present as the mirror image of the past. In this way, Hopkins's narrative design is an ingenious variant on the "whoizzit" mode that frequently appears in classical detective fiction. The "whoizzit" typically refers to narrative scenarios in which multiple persons with apparently distinct identities are exposed as a single individual whose criminal actions "hang together" over a period of time, which may span a distant past to the immediate present (Thompson and Thompson 55). Hopkins's uncanny ellipsis, however, applies the logic of the "whoizzit" to the identity of the nation as well as the novel's dramatis personae. She also engineers a temporal ellipsis that calls into question the "marriage" of past and present, ties it to questions of fiscal hypocrisy, and, as we will soon see, makes both attendants to the reunion between North and South.

A conversation between the couple Marthy and Isaac Johnson, two former slaves, provides another set coordinates with which to calibrate what "hangs together" over time, and the ideological shift that undergirds this temporal ellipsis. Working as an assistant to Colonel Benson, Isaac insists that his wages will be duly paid, and will uplift his family from their slave origins to the level of the "high-biggotty Wash'nt'n 'stockracy," an ambition conspicuously free from reference to compensation for slavery in the form of land, or in any other form, for that matter. Isaac's proposed route to affluence is compatible with the postpanic, anticaste liberalism adopted by late nineteenth-century Republicans, who did not concede that racial justice required renovations to the existing economy (Horton 22). But his expression of naive faith in a free-labor paradigm holds no weight with Marthy, who grumbles

> I don' trus' no' white man. 'Member all the money went up in the Freedman's bank, don' yer? I don' guess he'd be slow makin' a profit outen yer by keepin' yer wages. Plenty gentmen'd do it 'fore yer could bat yer eye. (177)

Marthy makes the case that in the post–Civil War era, white men have not ceased to profit from the labor of African Americans.

Hopkins uses Marthy's analysis of the Freedman's Savings and Trust Company as a case in point. A "benevolent" institution chartered by the federal government in 1865 and founded by the Congregational minister John Alvord, the Freedman's Savings and Trust Company was to provide black veterans with a place to deposit their back pay and to encourage thrift and industry in the freed population more generally. These principles were part of a broad platform endorsed by northern Gilded Age liberals who simultaneously venerated the invisible hand of the market, treated respect for production as a gauge of civic maturity, and used savings as a metric for uplift (Fabian 11). The political economist Amasa Walker, who championed this hard-nosed liberalism, declared, "The amount of deposits in savings banks, so far as made by the working classes, forms *the best index* of the real progress of those classes, in pecuniary independence and in social improvement" (qtd. in Cohen 38). Postwar-variety liberals explicitly connected the freedmen's capacity to act as economic men—to assume their proper place as market-oriented producers—with prospects for race equality and democratic citizenship (Cohen 66).[5] The former slave's induction to civil society would hang in the balance.

By contrast, postwar liberals associated gambling with the licentious habits of the freedmen and working classes. According to Gilded Age pedagogy, gambling constituted a means of seizing wealth against which all other forms of acquisition, including speculative profits in land and stock, were absolutely wholesome (Fabian 4–5), and an emerging social Darwinism justified northern financiers' uninhibited speculation with the capital invested in the Freedman's Bank. But Marthy insists that the responsibility for the market enterprise be pinned on this new class of pro-laissez-faire financiers: the "Wash'nt'n 'stockracy." After all, blacks who deposited their savings were prey to a "sinister paradox," as Ann Fabian has pointed out: while the Freedman's Bank promoted producerism, it did not offer its rewards. Though in sum black men and women stored some $3,684,739.97 in the bank, the investment would be sapped through mismanagement (132). Nevertheless, critics of the bank associated its failure with the moral fiber of its depositors, supplying Darwinian accounts of the freedman's economic shortfalls to replace outdated proslavery arguments (O'Malley 384, Cohen 80).

We can link Marthy's powerful indignation to the fact that by 1874, following rampant abuse and mismanagement of funds, the Freedman's Bank had defrauded many depositors of their savings, leading Frederick Douglass, who had been recently installed as president, to describe his appointment to the bank as "marriage to a corpse" (qtd. in Fabian 135). Yet her subsequent admonition slips into what seems like the idiom of the antebellum marketplace, with its expeditious method of converting a man into revenue. She warns Isaac that his employer is "makin' a profit outen yer" by withholding wages for services rendered. According to this logic, local instances of misappropriation and labor exploitation are the upshot of federal profiteering, of which the failure of the Freedman's Bank is a single illustration. This shift from individual instances of abuse to federal consensus—or rather their re-arrangement, since Marthy's chronicle of financial mistreatment seizes upon the mishandling of the Freedman's Bank as the precedent for other fiscal violations—adroitly and decisively reformulates observable configurations of cause and effect. She shrewdly points to Reconstruction's collapse (and the general mistrust of white men it inspired) as the prism through which she assesses black indigence and white exploitation. For this reason, the evaporation of black assets in the midst of Reconstruction and afterward is continuous with the nation's antebellum habits.

Significantly, Hopkins also grounds the fear that Isaac is yet a cash cow, a source of never-refunded revenue, in antebellum intelligence. Just before the Civil War, for instance, Isaac's master St. Clair Enson decided to ante up "the whole of this boy," valued at "eighteen hundred dollars any day on the

New Orleans market," in a high-stakes poker game—an entirely fraudulent wager since the inventory wagered was expected to steal away and return to his master's ancestral home (27, 26). Nevertheless, Ike (Isaac) is apparently content to see his fortunes rise and tumble with the "Wash'nt'n 'stockracy" in whose hands he has left his wages "fer 'ves'men,'" principally in Colorado gold mines (176). In private, Ike muses, "De major do be under some repetition as a bad character, but de Gin'ral's all right. Dar's heap o' his paw in 'im" (177). Ike's aside reveals that his current employer, the not especially artfully named General Benson, is in fact his former master, the "recreant Southern son" St. Clair Enson (22). Meanwhile the slave trader Walker, St. Clair's associate and a "man of unsavory reputation" (49), has rematerialized as the quasi-respectable Major Henry Clay Madison, though his slave trader self was wholly snubbed by southern aristocrats whose dealings in human chattel he had meticulously enumerated in his receipts.

That Ike, once a man's man, seems the sole possessor of Benson's and Madison's true identities (knowledge that will only be publicly uncovered in the novel's climactic courtroom scene) shows that he has peered beyond the facade of the newfangled configurations of rank and has found the old ones intact. Ike's divergent assessments of Benson and Madison—the former evaluated in terms of parentage, his reputation unsullied (even despite a "mix-up in the Lincoln assassination" to which Benson owns up [78]), the latter yet villainous, "under some repetition as a bad character" despite the military embellishment his name has recently acquired—underscores the preservation of class and birth markers after the Civil War (177).

Ike eulogizes St. Clair Enson in a peculiarly fraternal reminiscence:

Dar neber was a better man den ol' masa, an' I orter know. Law*se*, de times me an' young massa had t'gedder, bar hunts, an' gamblin''bouts, an' shootin' and ridin'. He goin' so fas' I skacely cud keep up tuh him. We bin like brudders. All his clo's fits me *puffick!* Our size is jes' de same as ever. En jurin de wah I jes' picked him twice outen de inimy's han's; my sakes dem was spurious times. (177–78)

While Ike's rote praise for St. Clair Enson borders on the comical, the bucolic era he describes doubles as Hopkins's ironic imagination: here slavery (all of its degrading paternalism intact) appears in hindsight as a sort of fraternal association. Of course, Hopkins writes early on in the text that "the only saving grace about the scion of aristocracy appeared in his [St. Clair's] treatment of Isaac," a slave who was "the lurking deviltry of a spirit kindred to his master," with whom he shared a reciprocal devotion. Ike's practice of misremembering sheds light on the sardonic cast of such commentary (22, 28). Officially designating St. Clair Enson his "brudder" in various scrapes, Ike edits the syntax of each antebellum scene to shift his own role, retro-actively, from object to subject: *now* he *was* an equal player in the "gambli' 'bouts" where once Enson played the stakes and Ike was the stakes; now he was one who dressed at Enson's wardrobe and not simply the onetime recipient of his discarded garments (or botched "'ves'men'"); now he was En-son's playfellow at tag and not required to play the stooge in hot pursuit of a wayward aristocrat.[6]

Ike's closing remarks in this parenthetical leak, though, are most in need of our attention, for here again his commentary sheds critical light on the ellipsis at the heart of Hopkins's text. Ike refers to the Civil War as "spurious times," as if in this era of general lawlessness and illegitimate dealings, Ike was finally furnished an equal place among Benson's other strange bedfel-lows, including the leechlike and conspiratorial Major Madison. It seems Ike occasionally held the upper hand, since he plucked Enson from the enemy's clutches according to his own prerogatives. On the other hand, Ike was born and trained as "dat lim' o' Satan" and supremely qualified to serve as life sup-port for St. Clair Enson, a Luciferian by all accounts (46). And insofar as Ike's allusion to "spurious" times evokes an irruption into the carnivalesque subversion of the law, it seems less a celebratory antiauthoritarianism than a breach of democratic principles that thrust the social order in the direc-tion of permanent lawlessness.[7] General Benson's ascension to the national Treasury exemplifies this new institutional criminality. Though he with-holds Ike's wages, he has all the "secret workings" of the nation's finances "under my eye" (79). So if indeed these tempestuous intervening years sus-pended social hierarchies, they also modified the nation's seats of power to accommodate the least law-abiding. Though Major Madison remarks to the profligate Benson, "My boy, you'll never fit into the dignified position of a fa-ther of this country," it appears he already has (77). Furthermore, northerner Cuthbert Sumner's current service to Benson foregrounds a calamitous alli-ance forged between whites in the North and the South during this period. In this context, the "spurious" bent of the era Ike describes reminds us how the suspension of the law might unleash all manner of civil violence. For Hopkins, these disquieting activities are family matters.

AN INTERRACIAL UNION

> Apart from such unusual instances as these, the less love in a detective-story, the
> better. . . . There is the whole difficulty about allowing real human beings into a
> detective-story.
>
> —DOROTHY SAYERS, "THE OMNIBUS OF CRIME"

Hagar's Daughter uses kinship arrangements to address the late nineteenth-century alliance between North and South. Rohrbach calls attention to the prevalence of incest in Hopkins's magazine fiction more generally, arguing that these narratives juxtapose the dreadfulness of endogamy to the virtuous exogamy of race-mixing; this "analogy of oppositions" punctures the so-called horror of miscegenation (484). Though Rohrbach suggests that we can gauge the integrity of the accidentally estranged interracial Enson household (comprising Ellis Enson [Detective Henson], Hagar [now Estelle Bowen], and their daughter [Jewel]) by the fact that their road to reunion is "never once threatened by incestuous desires" (488), this is not precisely the case. Jewel's unenviable role as (Uncle) Benson's romantic conquest is fraught with incestuous overtones, since the genealogical proximity (of which neither is aware) is a source of dramatic irony. At some point in their first tête-à-tête, in fact, Jewel addresses another form of kinship she shares with Benson: a familial bond brought about by the reconciliation between the North and South only a few decades after the end of the Civil War. This solidarity surfaces in the language of a new white supremacist ideology, one that is a by-product of the nation's reattachment. For instance, Jewel responds sympathetically to Benson's ingratiating report that the disastrous war led him abroad "until the pain of recollection should be somewhat dimmed":

> "Ah!" she said, with a gentle sigh of pity, "how dreadful that time must
> have been. Thank heaven, ours is a united country once more. And you
> are mistaken, too, in your judgment: we have no foreigners here. We have
> effaced the word by assimilation; so, too, we have no Southerners—we
> are Americans." (121)

Jewel's use of the term "assimilation" designates a strictly regional rather than racial amalgamation. To the attentive reader (or any other in hindsight), however, the context of her comments stirs up a number of other potentially disconcerting family ties. The specter of an unthinkable endogamy *and* socially proscribed interracial relations materialize in Benson's advances upon his niece, even as the pair discusses a different sort of union. Moreover, Jewel's mixed blood is, in this scene, only an elusive subtext, and the authoritative place from which she offers solace to the dejected southerner is as a daughter of the West, "with all the independence that the term implies" (118).

Along these lines, Hopkins's tongue-in-cheek take on turn-of-the-century political geography depicts the West of the middle to late nineteenth century nearly as the historian Frederick Jackson Turner described it in his 1893 essay, "The Significance of the Frontier in American History." In this seminal essay, Turner summarized the West's restorative features, both moral and material, "which could combat the debilitating influences of class and sectional division," unifying the nation around a set of exceptional traits—democracy, individualism, and so forth. Out West, where a distinctive set of American characteristics were on display, Turner wrote, "North and South met and mingled into a nation" (29). Hopkins presents Jewel as an exemplary western girl; her father, Zenas Bowen, too, is "an example of the possibilities of individual expansion under the rule of popular government" who embodies the strength of character and self-made quality associated with the frontier (80).

It is crucial to point out, moreover, that Jewel's image of sectional harmony summons up the words of Jefferson Davis in the very first installment of Hopkins's novel. Speaking for the first time as president of the Confederacy, Davis declares that "when our principles shall have been triumphantly established over the entire country—North, South, West—a long age of peace and prosperity will ensue for the entire country" (17). For Davis this national merger depends on the maintenance of slavery, which he describes as a fiscally and biologically "necessary" institution, and one superior to what northerners call "free labor": "What is it but a conglomeration of greasy mechanics, filthy operatives, small-fisted farmers, and moonstruck Abolitionists?" (17).[8]

Without adding to the confusion, let us consider what purpose Hopkins serves by crediting Jefferson Davis with this triumph of political vision. As I have suggested above, Jewel's multiple identities create an unexpected, new proximity between the West and the South. If we follow Davis's pledge to extend southern rule across the continent, what emerges is an analogy between the exploitation of nonwhite and near-white slaves in South and the anticipated extraction of wealth from western land. This conclusion seems exceedingly plausible, given that Zenas Bowen has the "hair and skin of an Indian" and sports a suggestively "dark complexion" (76). Hopkins adds to this the somewhat ambiguous observation that Bowen is "one of those genial men whom the West is constantly sending out to *enrich* society" (80, my italics). To corroborate this point, we only need return to the motives of General Benson and his associate, Major Henry Clay Madison (whose postwar alias is simultaneously indebted to the Father of the Constitution and that "Great Compromiser" whose most celebrated accomplishment was to temporarily postpone sectional crisis while strengthening the Fugitive Slave Act). These men treat Zenas, Estelle, and Jewel Bowen as cash cattle. They begin by slowly but resolutely siphoning Senator Bowen's investments into a fraudulent enterprise, the Arrow-Head Mining Company of Colorado. When the proceeds of this scheme fail to satisfy Benson's "financial dilemma," he applies for a direct line to the old man's bank account, announcing to his partner in crime, "I have taken a decided fancy to Miss Bowen," whom the two identify as "the key to the old man's cash-box" (94, 99, 203).

Hopkins's depiction of familial, racial, and sectional identities introduces a new dimension to the late nineteenth-century culture of sentimental reconciliation between the North and the South. This culture translated political matters into novelistic tropes of romantic union that generally paired a white northern male with a white southern woman (Silber 116). "Reunion discourse" depended on gender and power configurations that efficiently communicated the economic primacy of the North over the South through its romance plots, but often included the business ventures that joined men from the North and South, typically financed by northerners (107). This transfer of authority resembled the kind of gift giving that, in the blueprints of the sex-gender system Gayle Rubin supplies, "confers upon its participants a special relationship of trust, solidarity, and mutual aid" (778), and which, in its most typical manifestations, links the "men who give and take" women in valuable kinship structures (779). Eve Sedgwick's discussion of asymmetrical sex/gender arrangements in *Between Men* helps expand on this point. To borrow the language of this framework, reunion discourse enabled a pattern of passionate homosocial attachment that routed the affiliation of aggressively masculine white northern men with white southern men in erotic drag. This, of course, depended on a practical displacement: white men trafficking in the commodified bodies of erstwhile southern belles in order to sustain a partnership that financed capitalist patriarchal structures.

As the rights of freedman evaporated from the Republican agenda in the North, reunion culture's structure of sentimental attachment and plantation nostalgia increasingly disregard the injuries slavery had wrought. By the 1890s, affectionate representations of a romanticized South made the most lethal racisms suddenly digestible (Silber 125). *Hagar's Daughter* performs a critical reappraisal of reunion culture as its complicated maze of regional and interracial relations illuminates the racial and economic stakes that invalidate any imagined reconciliation between North and South. Hopkins grounds this fiasco in the homosocial partnership between General Benson and Cuthbert Sumner. Benson, a Lothario of the first order, is "voted" the most charming and the "most perfect lover imaginable" by the many women who have "sighed and wept at his defection" (93). Sumner has also played Casanova, having been "in love with the sex, more or less, since the day he left off knee-breeches" (84). Both Benson and Sumner romanced and discarded Aurelia Madison, the major's quadroon daughter, even before Sumner's industrialist father exercised influence to obtain for his son a position as Benson's private secretary (84). When Benson's assistant, Elise Bradford, is murdered at the end of a night spent at the office, it is not entirely surprising that the blame should be assigned to Cuthbert Sumner, with whom she has just shared an intimate conversation. Certainly Benson showered Bradford with promises of marriage—Aunt Henny bluntly explains that Benson "was jes' makin' dat po' gal b'lieve de moon was made o' green cheese an' he'd got the fus' slice" (254)—before he calculatingly poisoned her. But Sumner is also capable of such coldhearted cruelty. Bradford, a southern working-class woman of white descent, reproaches his rough treatment of Aurelia (Sumner recoils with disgust when he discovers he has almost been "betrayed" into marrying a quadroon), calling his prejudice "a relic of barbarism"; it is this prejudice that will also destroy his affections for Jewel Bowen (160).

For most of the second half of *Hagar's Daughter*, Benson and Cuthbert vie for Jewel's hand in marriage. Jewel, the erotic plaything they toss back and forth, licenses a rivalry that shapes their professional associations, and, as Sedgwick demonstrates in her critique of Rene Girard's *Deceit, Desire, and the Novel*, "the bond between rivals in an erotic triangles" is far stronger than "anything in the bond between either of the lovers and the beloved" (21). One of the chief functions of their homosocial affiliation is, apparently, a prophylactic against interracial marriage. In the first half of *Hagar's Daughter*, St. Clair Enson puts an end to his brother's marriage to Hagar; in the second half, it is Cuthbert who addresses Ellis Enson (Detective Henson), sputtering indignantly that the "wholesale union between whites and blacks" must be prevented at all costs (270). The miscegenation taboo (encapsulated by Cuthbert Sumner's rhetorical demand, "Ought we not, as Anglo-Saxons, keep the fountain head of our racial stream as unpolluted as possible?") prevails (271). The more subtle point to be made, however (and one that can be made only by reading Hopkins backward and then forward again), is that the fraternal pact and collusion between Benson and Sumner is a system of misuse that opens the West for plunder, principally by taking advantage of Jewel and Zenas Bowen. The civil and social oppression of African Americans and expansion west of the Mississippi are coterminal ventures. But why use a detective story to make this case?

Detective fiction begins, writes Dennis Porter, at "the deadest of dead ends"; immediately afterward, it enters into a process of retrieval that meticulously arranges fragments of evidence into a plausible account of events (16). John Cawelti calls this an ideologically conservative means of coping with modern complexities, since the abstract process of narrative reconstruction distances detection fictions from the social conflicts and forms of injustice that realistic works might address (*Adventure* 97). Indeed, in detection, the even tally between the evidence (the constituent parts) and a narrative whole (a puzzle pieced together from these constituent parts) ensures a perfect union of narrative materials. *Hagar's Daughter* proposes, however, that this novelistic machine designed to suture what is splintered is also predisposed to distort or even to annul the historical record as part of its program of reconstruction. Nevertheless, Hopkins draws on detective fiction's devices to open up a history of racial caste, fiscal hypocrisy, regional difference, and territorial conquest. In doing so, she points to the social functions of these particular conventions, possibilities that otherwise recede in the face of what seem to be the genre's depoliticized investments.

"BLOOD STICKS TO SUCH COIN"

> "If war among the whites brought peace and liberty to the blacks, *what will peace among the whites bring?*"
>
> —FREDERICK DOUGLASS, "THE COLOR QUESTION"

William H. Holcombe's *A Mystery of New Orleans: Solved by New Methods* (1890) mobilizes the same detective conventions Hopkins exploits (the "whoizzit," the problem of temporal reconstruction and forensic skepticism) to examine possibilities for interracial sociability in the post-Reconstruction era. Though *A Mystery of New Orleans* depicts the Civil War as an event that tore at the loyalties of white men, it takes for granted that emancipation was its chief accomplishment. Hopkins's bleak ending contrasts with Holcombe's more optimistic picture of reunion culture, which initially merges regional reconciliation and *interracial* union in its romance plot—though at the end of the day it can't quite stomach the latter. And while Holcombe's more "enlightened" characters initiate exhaustive dialogues about the problems of so-called racial degeneration and prospects for racial equality, these conversations and their verdicts are restricted to white men. Like *Hagar's Daughter*, *A Mystery of New Orleans* manifests forensic skepticism; the novel calls into question the ordinary evidence of the eyes and ears and recognizes black Americans as historical and genealogical authorities. Significantly, however, *A Mystery of New Orleans* substitutes another astonishing epistemology in place of forensics: a theory of metaphysical testimony that corroborates every crime and psychic specialists who exhume the past. Yet for Holcombe, even these psychic powers cannot contest new, paranormal forms of slavery. Nevertheless, *A Mystery of New Orleans* foregrounds the value of detection's devices for exploring familial, racial, and sectional identities in the post-Reconstruction era.

A Mystery of New Orleans is the story of a belated investigation into the fate of a man named Gordon Clarke, and like *Hagar's Daughter*, Holcombe's novel hinges on events that took place during the Civil War and in its wake. Torn between states' rights and national sovereignty, having been taught "the universal political creed of the South from Thomas Jefferson to Jefferson Davis" but nevertheless "devotedly attached" to the Union, Gordon Clarke split the difference and "expatriated" himself from the nation in a time of civil dispute (Holcombe 10). In spite of all his political dithering, however, this patriot's true fealty was to the markets. When, after the Battle of Gettysburg, the end of the war seemed inevitable and close, Clarke "began speculating on the differences between gold and greenbacks, and realized a large sum" (11)—having already made a fortune as a "successful speculator" in California when he turned abroad and began dabbling in mining ventures in Mexico and Costa Rica. Finally, his thirst for capital landed him in Havana, where his wife and eldest child were (heavy-handedly) stricken with yellow fever. When Clarke and his remaining two-year-old daughter Sarah disappeared in the vicinity of New Orleans, his brother Ephraim had to entertain the far-fetched proposition that Clark decided to "pocket his fortune and sail for Europe or the tropics, abandoning friends and country forever" (17).

A young architect from Chicago who goes by the name of Hugh Stanford is enlisted to track down Gordon Clarke and his daughter some twenty years after their disappearance, now that the money held in trust for Clarke's heir has blossomed from twenty thousand to a half million dollars. Stanford's expedition is barely under way when he becomes infatuated with the southern beauty Ninette Du Valcourt. A few chapters in it is evident to the reader that Ninette is none other than the mislaid Sarah Clarke, though it takes Stanford a couple hundred pages and the assistance of the city's eminent black medium Cora Morette to reach this fairly parsimonious solution. In the meantime, Stanford divides his time between romantic pursuits and psychical phenomena. Colonel Du Valcourt toasts Stanford's plans to wed his adopted daughter Ninette; to boot, "an additional bumper was consecrated to the perpetual Union of the States and of all true lovers, North and South" (120). However, the prospect of blissful North-South nuptials is foiled by a flurry of insinuations about the origins of Du Valcourt's handsome daughter. Stanford's proposed "romance of reunion" is most irregular, since it would join a white man with a woman suddenly suspected to be black, in a metropolis so baffled by the question of race that a tarnished bronze statue of the nation's "Great Compromiser" invites a little girl to inquire of her mother, "Was Henry Clay a black man?" (163).

It happens that old Caesar, an octogenarian and the last living descendent of the Du Valcourt slaves, is proprietor of the family's genealogy, and it is Caesar who corroborates Rose Villemaine's suspicions of the illegitimacy of her stepsister Ninette. Caesar insists that "dare ain't a spect of Valcourt blood in her veins, anyhow, sho'" (87). Even if Caesar maintains that Ninette is positively "some orphing or picked-up chile," however, Villemaine's only evidence that Ninette's ancestry is racially suspect is a printed remark in the confidential files of the orphanage where Ninette was deposited as a child. Nevertheless, and with no little assistance from Villemaine, rumors begin to fly, and soon Ninette's name is acquainted with those vulgarities that roll off the tongues of affluent clubmen. She is denigrated by their language and soiled by their looks. Though her name was never on any bill of sale, to them her person is, even in an age past slavery, for purchase. One of this scurrilous lot takes note that "when a woman falls a hair's-breadth below the white line, like Miss Du Valcourt, she becomes the legitimate prey of any clubman who can meet the expenses" (207). As was the case with Hopkins's Jewel, that "hair's breadth," or one drop—and in *this* case the faulty gossip of that one drop, since Ninette has the good fortune to be free of even a particle of black blood—turns New Orleans's elite against her.

While she is not exactly ousted from the family seat, Ninette obliges polite society and expels herself. Lethe Maxwell, the black woman who could
well be the girl's grandmother, consoles Ninette that, "although she could
not go to the opera at night in full-dress, she could attend all the *matinées*, to
which every one was admitted" (200). But Holcombe proposes that the ultimate dilemma of the color line can be summarized in a single "test-question":

> Shall we permit a beautiful, educated, refined, virtuous young woman,
> so far white as to be indistinguishable from ourselves in physical or men-
> tal qualities, to be stricken from our rank, which she has so charmingly
> adorned and can still adorn, and to be consigned irrevocably to the de-
> graded social conditions of the inferior race? (252)

The substance of racial difference, or rather the difficulty of substantiating it, is the crux of the matter, and if Holcombe repeatedly suggests that
race is no *observable* fact, he does not go so far as to suggest it is not a *genuine*
fact. For instance, he writes that "none but a connoisseur could have detected
the slightest trace of African descent" in the light-skinned Emily Gordon,
the bona fide black woman who is allegedly Ninette's birth mother (297). It
is worth noting, moreover, that a specialist of some skill is also required to
make sense of regional linguistic differences. Upon his arrival in New Orleans Stanford concludes that dialect in the novels of George Washington
Cable is artless and crude; indeed, English spoken by Creoles is so faultless
that "only the most attentive and cultivated ear could detect any deviation
from the standard" (58). The infinitesimal variations on standard English,
the subtleties of accent and intonation are merely "*nuances*," which is to say
that "they never could be transferred to paper, or represented by any possible
species of bad spelling" (58)—and to say otherwise is mere prejudice. More
chivalrous by far than the spineless Cuthbert Sumner, Stanford stands by
Ninette, albeit after he is assured by a medical professional that "children
of such marriages" do not "have a tendency to revert to the lower or darker
type" (193).

Strangely enough, this northerner who fervently defends the "spiritual
solidarity of the human race and in the final composite union of all the races"
is also the champion of a supernatural forensics that can verify racial pedigree and, in this case, avert interracial marriage. In Holcombe's own idea of a
happy ending Ninette is heir to the Clarke fortune and decidedly not "a ne-
gress" (198). But throughout the novel the question of racial "amalgamation"

poses a strange challenge to Stanford's "new metaphysics." As Stanford investigates Clarke's disappearance, he wholeheartedly contends that no past is past; he insists that every "antecedent phenomena" makes a permanent impression in the "psychic ether"; all "sights, sounds, thoughts, deeds" leave their marks, though these may not be perceived by the average man (24). But the mind of the true medium pierces time and can "just as readily see what happened a thousand years ago as it recognizes what is now transpiring" (38–39), especially if provided with some material object imprinted by the eye of the missing person.

For this reason Stanford remains confident that Clarke's murderer cannot escape detection. "Blood sticks to such coin," he remarks, and it "finally drives the unfortunate possessor into the depths of misery or into the hands of justice" (20). Unfortunately, this is not exactly true of Dr. Hypolite Meissonier, Magnétiseur, the villain with psychic powers who slaughtered Clarke for his money. We discover that the doctor's criminal tendencies "were nurtured and developed" in "the vivisection-rooms of Paris," where the cruelties of the medical profession—experiments in poison, the dissection of the living, and other unimaginable horrors—"became familiar to us, then excusable, then interesting, and finally, monstrous to relate, even amusing and fascinating!" (129). Little wonder that Meissonier is content to make humans the subjects of hypnotic suggestion and have them do his bidding. His assistant, Dr. Hilary Dupont, is putty in his hands, "a mere automaton" and slave who confesses that Meissonier's "voice strikes me with terror; I have no power to disobey" (74, 262). Dupont is only an operative in Meissonier's pay; nevertheless his actions are not his own. A "rascally mesmerizer" possesses his body, and bringing this "vampire" to justice proves exceedingly difficult, especially because Meissonier's coercions sap men and women of their wills without leaving a shred of evidence behind.

In *A Mystery of New Orleans*, Stanford's "new methods" uncover the past when forensics and the evidence of the senses cannot. In doing so he wards off interracial union, but is powerless against the new order of slavery Meissonier has invented. Holcombe splices quandaries of race and region together with the detective's case, regardless of Stanford's race politics. But these same dabblings in metaphysics cover Meissonier's tracks, since the doctor usurps the body of another and compels it to act as the "independent" agent of an unseen master. Holcombe's novel suggests that the "romance of reunion" is fraught with racial danger, and yet his northern protagonist is steadfast in the face of every southern devil's advocate who favors "voluntary" segregation between the so-called superior and inferior races. Even in the epilogue to the novel Stanford demands, "Is not this [segregation] the spirit of slavery with the institution left out? And would it not reproduce the institution if that were practicable?" (321). Stanford's faith in race equality and the "new metaphysics" notwithstanding, the powers of a mesmerist like Meissonier *are* likely to reproduce the spirit of slavery by suppressing the question of consent. That is, at "the deadest of dead ends" where a man is, contrary to all appearances, the mere mechanism of another's mind, it doesn't seem to matter much whether or not his working orders are written, as Stanford suggests of the past, in "invisible ink" (24).

CHAPTER 5

Prescription
Homicide?

No ordinary physician, Rudolph Fisher earned a medical degree from Howard University in 1924 and completed postgraduate research at Columbia University. A clergyman's son who received B.A. and M.A. degrees from Brown University, he toured the eastern seaboard accompanying Paul Robeson on the piano to raise funds for college. He was a roentgenologist who once held private practice on Long Island but had, since the onset of the Great Depression, worked as an X-ray technician at Harlem Hospital; he would die in 1934 at the age of thirty-seven from a stomach disorder caused by exposure to his own equipment. He was also a moderately acclaimed writer of the Harlem Renaissance who palled around with the likes of Alain Locke, and supposedly intimidated Langston Hughes with his sharp wit.[1] Still, only a few documents in the Rudolph Fisher Papers at the John Hay Library at Brown University are written entirely in the author's hand. In addition to drafts of a few stories ("The Lindy Hop" and "Skeeter"), scattered notes, and the beginnings of a clearly polemical essay titled "White Writers of Current Black Fiction," there is a sheet of paper titled only "The New Negro."[2] On this page, Fisher scrawled a free-form "medical" evaluation of a body of work that he dubbed "The novel of the life of the 'new negro.'"

In his brief report, Fisher delineates the peculiarities of "Negro Life as Literary Material" according to three classes of descriptive symptoms of the "Negro himself." He begins with a list of books that treat the subject of the negro "Physically," an inventory that contains Jessie Fauset's *Plum Bum*, Nella Larsen's *Passing*, and Wallace Thurman's *The Blacker the Berry*, plus many more. The next column lists books that portray the negro "Spiritually": Langston Hughes's *Not Without Laughter*, DuBose Heyward's *Porgy*, Fauset's *The Chinaberry Tree*, and so on. Finally there is his "Situation in

America," a catalog comprising W. E. B. DuBois's *Dark Princess*, George Schuyler's *Black No More*, Carl Van Vechten's *Nigger Heaven*, and Fisher's own *The Walls of Jericho*, among others. Fisher's diagnosis comes down to the "estimation of the condition of this body of literature," likely a comment on the perceived aesthetic "failure" of the "Negro Renaissance" of the 1920s by the early 1930s (Hutchinson 8).[3] But the doctor advises a regimen, beginning with "less of the poor little yaller gal, let's have a comedy. More of conflicts about internal diversity—this—hidden in varieties of hair, huckleberry to patent leather, and in degrees of pigmentation—chestnut, seal skin, brown . . . cream, light yellow, and pink." Fisher's literary prescription also includes additional emphasis on "resiliency" and calls for less stress on "situation," proposing a purposeful turn to what he calls "pigmentation of the brain, not skins." And with an ultimate, sweeping flourish, an arrow points to the title of Fisher's second and last book, a work of detective fiction titled *The Conjure-Man Dies: A Mystery Tale of Dark Harlem* (1932).

Does this grand gesture indicate that Fisher intended to treat some infirmity in a body of literary productions on the "The New Negro" with a text about the murder of one of its members? *The Conjure-Man Dies* is a "locked-room" (or rather "waiting-room") puzzle that follows police detective Perry Dart and the physician John Archer in their joint efforts to finger the client who murdered the enigmatic African soothsayer N'Gana Frimbo—and their perplexing discovery, halfway through the book, that Frimbo staged his own death in anticipation of the assassin's arrival. To date, critics have positioned Fisher's murder mystery as primarily a rejoinder to a white-authored tradition of detective fiction writing. Stephen Soitos treats *The Conjure-Man Dies* as an instance of black "blues" detection whose distinct lineage can be traced to Pauline Hopkins's serialized *Hagar's Daughter: A Story of Southern Caste Prejudice* and J. E. Bruce's *Black Sleuth*. According to Soitos, we can differentiate these works from white-authored detective fictions based on their use of distinctly "black" detective themes, including "altered detective personas, double-conscious detection, black vernaculars, and hoodoo" (93). Along these lines, Fisher's version of the whodunit incorporates aspects of urban African American culture into the classical detective formula to renovate the genre, and even implies that a "meld of Afro-centric and Euro-Americentric views might be possible" in the person of its conjure-man—a possibility that is, however, dashed by N'Gana Frimbo's *actual* assassination at the end of the book (116). Adrienne Gosselin offers the more provocative claim that the "Dusky Sherlock Holmes" in Fisher's text is neither Perry Dart, the Harlem police detective, nor his "Doctor Watson" John Archer, but the eponymous N'Gana Frimbo, whose soothsaying talents evoke the ratiocinative flair Arthur Conan Doyle assigns to Sherlock Holmes in his early novellas (610). Consequently, Frimbo's (second and real) death in the final pages of the text represents, among other things, Fisher's attempt to obliterate the kind of thinking pioneered by Sherlock Holmes as well as that sleuth's iconic status, "to reject the monolithic voice of Eurocentric classical detection by destroying the genre's most recognizable symbol" (617).

These interpretations of *The Conjure-Man Dies* are predicated upon the text's supposed antagonism with a genre whose most celebrated works extol the deductive prowess of white male detectives. Additionally, they imply that Fisher appreciated his status as a generic interloper and took detective fiction as the central object of his revisionary ambitions, helping to pioneer an alternate, oppositional tradition of black-authored detection texts. By contrast, this chapter foregrounds Fisher's symbiotic engagement with the mechanisms of detection fiction, proposing that the genre supplied an expedient wheel for spinning the literary material of Negro life. Unlike the works examined in other chapters of this study, *The Conjure-Man Dies* can be situated simultaneously at the center and the margins of the detective genre, as it synthesizes concerns about interracial sociability typically explored on the genre's peripheries while consolidating detective fiction's repertoire of generic elements in an exemplary "genre text."

This chapter argues that *The Conjure-Man Dies* is a work of black modernism whose exploration of interracial sociability takes place through its negotiation and use of a preexisting form. Not only does the text avail itself of detection's devices to negotiate the racialized regulation of bodies and economies, the author's deliberate engagement with its narrative-analytical tools (his detection "prescription") affirms the racial heterogeneity of the genre. Fisher exploits the sociopolitical subtexts of the "locked room" puzzle to generate a work of literary sociology that, in accordance with his recommendations for Negro literature, foregrounds the varieties of "blackness" in Depression-era Harlem, a setting the author once described as a "modern metropolis turned black" (*City of Refuge* 330). Moreover, while Fisher uses the rites of integration rooted in classical detective fiction to assemble a community of Harlemites, *The Conjure-Man Dies* remains highly conscious of that community's relationship to white-dominated institutions. Rather than attempting to annihilate a "monolithic" voice of white-authored detective fiction, Fisher's work is in conversation with contemporary detective fictions (as well other forms of popular culture) fixated on "foreign" persons and "exotic" accents. *The Conjure-Man Dies* certainly punctures or at least pokes fun at narrative "prejudice"—a faulty cultural logic that exists at the level of genre—as well as at any popular primitivism that would enlist Africa as source of "savage" ancestry or a place of primordial wholeness. But Fisher's classical detective novel doubles as a sociology of race and labor, confronting the effects of the Great Migration, efforts at urban uplift, and questions of economic empowerment for diverse black constituencies. His attempt to depict a "pigmentation of the brain, not skins" generates a complex account of black experience, but also foreshadows the author's shift toward hard-boiled detective fiction in his final published work, "John Archer's Nose."

A MODERN METROPOLIS TURNED BLACK

"You're an American, of course?"
"I is now. But I originally come from Savannah, Georgia."

RUDOLPH FISHER, *THE CONJURE-MAN DIES*

Fisher's ideas about black experience are partially elucidated by Norman Klein's July 27, 1932, article for the *New York Evening Post* whose headline, "Harlem Doctor Produces Dusky Sherlock Holmes," is accompanied by the somewhat lurid subtitle: "'I Was Once a White Man,' Author Explains, 'but My Brain Pigmentation Changed'—His Doctor Watson is Dark and Clever."[4] The "dusky" sleuth Klein refers to is one of the protagonists of Fisher's *The Conjure-Man Dies: A Mystery Tale of Dark Harlem*, police detective Perry Dart. In that same interview with the *New York Evening Post*, Fisher explains that police detective Dart was "drawn from a real Negro policeman. One night two men broke into my office on Seventh Avenue at 138th Street. That is how I met Detective Boyden of the 135th Street precinct station." In *The Conjure-Man Dies*, however, the "real Negro policeman" partners with an amateur investigator to solve the case: Dr. John Archer, a Harlem physician who, unsurprisingly, bears close resemblance to Dr. Fisher. The small matter of "brain pigmentation," however, is Fisher's invention alone. "When I became a physician and went back to practice in Harlem," the writer explains to Klein, "I acquired pigmentation. I change color in Harlem. Yes, a pigmentation of the brain. I saw black. I thought black. I have been through a most thrilling experience."

But how does this mental inclination translate into Fisher's bizarre tale of the murder of N'Gana Frimbo, the Harvard-educated king in absentia of the (invented) African nation of Buwongo, who makes a living as a sort of consulting psychic and soothsayer out of his Harlem brownstone? An appreciative review in *Time* counts "3 ½ corpses, 2 investigators, 7 suspects, 2 funny persons, 1 error by investigators, 2 errors by culprits" in the book, but points out that instead of supplying the requisite "new trick," Fisher's work of detective fiction relies on a "new combination of old ones" to keep readers on their toes.[5] These are "reanimation" (the sudden appearance of Frimbo, alive and well, halfway through the investigation) and the use of "double dual identity" that leads to the revelation that not one but multiple characters have disguised themselves over the course of the fiction. If it is so easily appraised according to the conventions of so-called white-authored detective fiction, what claim has this "Mystery Tale of Dark Harlem" to a patently black perspective, to the "pigmentation of the brain" Fisher describes?

Fisher's novel shows its color precisely by borrowing the blueprints of the genre. Certainly *The Conjure-Man Dies* entails recognizable revisions of the puzzle mystery's conventions: Soitos points out that Fisher substitutes the Harlem "cityscape" for a country estate, for instance, and swaps the English manor for a New York City brownstone (Soitos 107, 101). But this transformation isn't a revision of a blueprint so much as a well-trodden Americanization; from Anna Katherine Green's *The Leavenworth Case* (1878) to S. S. Van Dine's *The Benson Murder Case* (1926), the Manhattan residence had many times supplied a venue for homicide. Nevertheless, the clue-puzzle formula of classical detective fiction formula actually facilitates one of Fisher's strongest aspirations as an author: to present Harlem as a site of internal diversity. In "At Home in Harlem," the *New York Herald* 1928 review of Fisher's first book, *The Walls of Jericho*, Eric Walrond stresses that Fisher's work strives to presents Harlem in all its fiscal and social heterogeneity.[6] Walrond argues that while novels of the 1920s quite often border on formlessness and are perhaps best (or only) gauged by a "standard of bulk," in Fisher's work "the seeming lack of form does not signify meretriciousness of purpose," since *The Walls of Jericho* somehow succeeds at portraying no less than three tiers of Harlem society, and so "achieves a feat which has been the Waterloo of most Negro fiction writers." Whereas *The Walls of Jericho* is characterized by abrupt shifts between Harlem's social strata, with *The Conjure-Man Dies* Fisher's varied cast is tied together by shared circumstance: the seven suspects and their circles of close associates and adversaries, the team of policemen and their professional consultants are all involved in the investigation of an individual's death. By virtue of their presence in Frimbo's waiting room, seven members of the all-black cast might become immediate objects of interest. The opportunity to depict such a large cast of characters is also a challenge, however. As John Cawelti points out, "If the characters [in the puzzle mystery] are not interesting enough to involve us in their fates, the mystery structure will seem like a sterile and desiccated skeleton and to that extent fail to sustain our involvement" (*Adventure* 110). But Fisher rises to the challenge, using the puzzle mystery as impetus to chronicle the social experiences of diverse black Americans in Harlem. Not only does his adherence to the genre's conventions enable Fisher to pose his varied, all-black cast under an equal spotlight, the fact that each of his characters is conscripted to a play a role in a murder investigation calls attention to the reality that community membership is contingent upon—indeed, constituted by—a particular relationship to the state and its laws.

In one of his first published short stories, "The City of Refuge" (1925), Fisher problematizes the rapport between the individual and Harlem law enforcement. This story features King Solomon Gillis, a southern expatriate who, having escaped the "country" of his birth—and very likely a lynching, for he has shot a white man—arrives in New York City still wet behind the ears. While not serendipitous, Fisher writes, the shooting may be said to have "catalyzed whatever sluggish mental reaction had been already directing King Solomon's fortunes toward Harlem," where the "land of plenty" he had oft aspired to could double as the "city of refuge" (*City of Refuge* 36). Of the many marvels Gillis stumbles upon in the city, one stands out once he arrives: its "Cullud policemans!" whose presence directing traffic in the streets of Harlem is "too great to believe simply by seeing" and leaves Gillis awestruck with disbelief; "Black might be white, but it couldn't be that white!" (36). "Even got cullud policemans—even got cullud" becomes the soothing lullaby and strange refrain that Gillis croons to himself (36). He moons over this miracle of the metropolis, explaining to his new acquaintance Mouse Uggam, "Dass all I want to be, a policeman, so I kin police all the white folks right plumb in jail" (41). But the street-smart Uggam has other plans for King Solomon Gillis; he ropes guileless Gillis, whom he regards as "a baby jess in from the land o'cotton and so dumb he thinks ante bellum's an old woman," into a drug-distribution scheme. The countrified King Solomon is easy prey, and Uggam is not so upright he won't stoop to framing his innocent drug-runner. Uggam plants some of his stock of "valuable French medicine" on Gillis's person and hands him over to the police (37, 41). No stranger to the arm of the law, the burly Gillis knocks two white officers flat, then faces a third, black policeman, and is again starstruck: "Very slowly King Solomon's arms relaxed very slowly he stood erect, and the grin that came over his features had something exultant about it" (47).

Fisher's story, which ends with Gillis hauled away by the cops, still muttering his usual tribute to the "cullud policemans," is characterized by the light but penetrating satire that is typical of author's work. On the one hand, the "cullud policeman" King Solomon reveres unquestionably overhauls the order of things he had come to expect down south. He is a great symbol of a (partially) integrated and (somewhat) equitable system of law enforcement and a source of real pride and identification in Harlem. And yet King Solomon Gillis is mollified by his own peculiar incantation, as if he had submitted to a bit of self-subterfuge, made mesmerized and biddable by a man whose mission, in spite the face of things, is to incarcerate him for a crime he has not knowingly or intentionally committed. Fisher's tongue-in-cheek illustration of racial pride paradoxically figures urban assimilation as reflexive incarceration, without entirely dismissing the real meaningfulness of having African American representatives among New York City's law enforcement officers. In this way, Fisher's depictions of the residents of Harlem are neither sycophantic nor condescending, but laced with an irony that marvels with raised eyebrows. His writing tenders social critique without refuting the significance of a cultural imaginary as a form of psychic support. As a result, he achieves a satirical social realism that both delineates the conditions of community and defamiliarizes those conditions.

In *The Walls of Jericho*, too, Fisher approaches the boundaries of the "black metropolis" from an unlikely direction. He writes of a Fifth Avenue that abandons its "aristocracy" uptown, where, as it approaches Harlem, "You can see the Avenue change expression—blankness, horror, conviction" (4). He perceives its dismay at suddenly finding itself in "the dark kingdom's backwoods" crammed with "bargain-stores, babble, and kids, dinginess, odors, thick speech" (4, 3). If only, Fisher laments, it had pursued an alternate route!—escaped these horrors by making its way to the "Seventh Avenue of a Sunday afternoon," or "The Hill": the "so-called dickty sections" inhabited by the well-to-do black bourgeoisie. What are we to make of this city street's shame of association with its second self, or that the thoroughfare, a horrified Harlem gatecrasher, pits Patmore's Pool Parlor against Strivers' Row? Is Fisher's Fifth Avenue an interloper incarnate, like those "ofays" to whom, as Fisher wrote in his essay on the "Negro Metropolis," "Harlem falsely appears to be a curious carnival, dancing away its nights and sleeping away its days" (*City of Refuge* 330)? Does this crosstown passage turn up "dickty" disdain for Harlem's working-class "rats"? Or perhaps its address *is* the "backwoods": a sendup of "high-toned" ambitions to be "white" and well-heeled. The precise location of the narrative voice remains strange; its subject is indefinite. More baffling still is the book's subplot about the well-to-do, light-skinned lawyer Fred Merrit, who decides single-handedly to racially redistrict that "snob of a street" Court Avenue, and is firebombed for his troubles. But the firebug is not Court Avenue's high-strung spinster Alma Cramp, who longs to "uplift" her neighbor. Instead, it is Henry Patmore, who has long borne a grudge against the lawyer. Even Merrit is impressed by this plot twist: "Can you imagine it? A Negro—using white prejudice to cover what he wanted to do—putting the blame in the most likely spot—almost getting away with it, too—Can you beat that?" (279–80). In its opening sally and in certain contortions of its story line, *The Walls of Jericho* traverses narrative clichés to underscore a cacophony of conflict. Fisher offers an intricate if tendentious image of inter- and intraracial discord that vitalizes a Harlem whose residents are all too conversant (and perhaps disenchanted) with "respectable" plotting.

However, Fisher also offers us a more jovial image of Harlem that brings the denizens of Patmore's Pool Parlor into peaceful contact with the black middle classes. The "colony" convenes at the General Improvement Association's Annual Costume Ball: "This is the one occasion in Harlem when everybody is present and nobody minds," writes Fisher, and, "Out on the dance floor everyone, dicty and rat, rubbed joyously elbows, laughing, mingling, forgetting differences" (71, 74). In the "panorama" of Fisher's Harlem, literary critic John McCluskey Jr. construes this dance floor as a "metaphor of democratic participation," though one that is quickly ruptured by the author's razor-sharp irony, since the moment the music stops, each repairs to his or her own "level": a "tier of boxes that encircled the hall" for the "dicktys" and "ofays"; the round-top tables on the "terraces" for plain folks; and downstairs for the "rats" (*City of Refuge* 20, *Jericho* 72).[7] But if *The Walls of Jericho* fails to merge its many classes into a fully constituted group, the conditions of community become the subject of *The Conjure-Man Dies*. In this book, the "locked room" of classical detective fiction affords Fisher the means to articulate the strange stakes of community formation in black Harlem.

In her discussion of the premises of classical detective fiction, Joan

Copjec focuses on the act of suture that the introduction of the locked-room paradox facilitates. Copjec's starting point is a well-known essay by Jacques-Alain Miller, which defines suture by drawing on Frege's concept of the number "not identical with itself": it is "the excess which operates" in logical discourse; it is summoned only to be rejected by the discourse of logic "in order to constitute itself as that which it is" (Miller 32). Miller's claim is founded Frege's assertion, in *Grundlagen der Arithmetik* that a theory of natural numbers can be logically established *only* with the introduction of the number 0 (the number that belongs to the concept not identical with itself). Frege's logicist project proceeds from the belief that *numbers* are independent objects and not attributes, and that statements about *numbers* belong to substantival rather than adjectival constructions (Beaney 106). For Miller, by contrast, Frege's "impossible object" shows us the Lacanian subject in its relation to the signifying chain; it is that which must be introduced "in order for the logical dimension to gain its autonomy definitively, without any reference to the real" (29), and it is, more important yet, what the discourse of logic "summons and rejects *wanting to know nothing of it*" (32). Copjec applies this theory of suture to the locked-room paradox, describing the creation of the "locked room" as a nonempirical "obligatory addition" brought to "the series of signifiers in order to mark the *lack* of a signifier that could close the set" (176). Moreover, since Copjec links the birth of classical detective fiction with the appearance of modern statistics—a form of political science that deals "with the collection, classification, and discussion of facts (especially of a numerical kind) bearing on the condition of a state or community" (OED)—the implications of the locked-room paradox extend beyond the ousting of a criminal individual from a small circle of suspects. Indeed, the locked-room paradox poses "one of the most fundamental questions of political modernism." Copjec asks,

> How, after destroying the body of the king, which formerly defined the boundary of the nation and thus closed the set of subjects belonging to it, how then does one constitute a modern nation? What is it that allows the nation to collect a vast array of people, discount all their positive differences, and count them as citizens, as members of the same set, in logical terms as identical? This question poses itself within detective fiction which, classically, begins with an amorphous and diverse collection of characters and ends with a fully constituted group. (174)

On these terms, what is at stake in classical detective fiction is nothing less than the "legal-rational legitimacy" of the modern nation-state.

This analysis partially supports the widely held critical consensus that detective fiction momentarily calls into question the positive effects of individual freedom as espoused within the framework of classical liberalism, only to dispel the specter of chaos and anarchy embodied by the criminal hidden in our midst. The function of the detective, in this vein, is to banish a "regime of doubt and confusion" and to transfigure a cast of scheming, suspicious, and self-serving individuals whose presence marks the failure of "communal bonds" to materialize. To put it briefly, the detective's climactic elucidation of the crime gives us the switchpoint where civil society is cinched to the network of its own, disavowed "nightmarish inversion" (McCann 8). Copjec, however, goes a step beyond this typical claim that the detective's habitual rooting-out of the "bad apple" preserves peace of mind. Whereas Franco Moretti calls the detective "the figure of the state in the guise of 'night watchman'" whose "scientific system" is exercised only to ward off any challenge to the system and not used in service of that system's advancement (*Signs* 155), Copjec is subtler, I think, in her presentation of the detective as therapist and not thug. Most importantly, her essay presents the locked-room paradox as a syntax of semantic glitches whose unraveling has sociopolitical freight; it is a pretext that "allows the nation to collect" and collate its members.

This paradoxical production of the nation is famously constituted in the snowbound *Calais Coach* that is the setting for Agatha Christie's ingenious detection fiction *Murder on the Orient Express* (1934). In this celebrated text (which appeared just two years after the publication of *The Conjure-Man Dies*), an urgent telegraph to Istanbul summons Christie's sleuth Hercule Poirot to London by way of the Orient Express bound for England via Calais, France. Aboard the curiously crammed train, Poirot and his close acquaintance Monsieur Bouc, the director of Compagnie Internationale des Wagons-Lits, marvel at the kaleidoscopic assortment of passengers that hail from multiple nations, cultures, and classes: a Swedish missionary from Africa, a Russian princess, an Italian car salesman, and so on. Most visually striking among these is an American philanthropist named Ratchett, whose "strange malevolence" and "unnatural tensity in glance" so repulse Poirot that the detective spurns the philanthropist when he attempts to purchase Poirot's services, coldly remarking, "I do not like your face, M. Ratchett" (34). When the train runs into a snowdrift that night and Ratchett is found brutally stabbed to death the following morning, however, Poirot's callous stance is vindicated. The so-called American philanthropist, it turns out, was the notorious gangster Cassetti, who kidnapped and murdered the child Daisy Armstrong in America some years ago. But as the train is snowed in somewhere in Yugoslavia and the assassin deprived of the possibility of escape, Poirot concludes that the murderer *must have remained on the train,* so that each member of the international troupe of passengers becomes a suspect—and yet every one of them has a remarkably strong alibi provided by his or her fellow travelers. When M. Bouc, frantic with confusion, remarks, "How can he [the murderer] have vanished into thin air? My head, it whirls. Say something, then, my friend, I implore you. Show me how the impossible can be possible!" the sleuth counters: "'It is a good phrase that,' said Poirot. 'The impossible cannot have happened, therefore the impossible must be possible in spite of appearances'" (156). Ronald Thomas contends that Christie underscores Ratchett's criminality by employing "the language we have heard applied to the exotic criminal body in criminal anthropology and detective literature of the past": he is "a wild animal—an animal savage," like the throat-slitting orangutan of "The Murders in the Rue Morgue" (271). But while the "unequal voice" of Poe's orangutan in "Rue Morgue" denoted a creature without a nation, the expression that proceeded from the victim's locked cabin on the night of the murder was entirely intelligible. A peculiar voice—and not Ratchett's, because he did not speak French, as we are repeatedly reminded—announced "Je me suis trompée," which we might translate as "I was mistaken" or even "I misspoke." This impossible voice, which speaks only to nullify its utterance, is precisely that nonempirical "obligatory addition" that constitutes the locked-room paradox that Copjec describes. Meanwhile, the multiplicity of accents aboard the *Calais Coach* leads Poirot unexpectedly to infer that every one of them is connected: the passengers and crew are the self-appointed executioners of Cassetti. How could such an assortment constitute a unity? Poirot explains:

> The answer I made to myself was—only in America. In America there might be a household composed of just such varied nationalities—an Italian chauffeur, an English governess, a Swedish nurse, a French lady's maid and so on. That led me to my scheme of "guessing"—that is, casting each person for a certain part in the Armstrong drama much as a producer casts a play. Well that gave me an extremely interesting and satisfactory result. (243)[8]

Just as the ballroom in *The Walls of Jericho* enlists a balcony and stairs to separate the "dicktys" from the "rats," the first- and second-class accommodations aboard the Orient Express spatialize the upstairs-downstairs arrangements in the Armstrong household. Nevertheless, the classes crossed paths in the dining compartment and, more pertinently, in Cassetti's cabin, where, one by one, the self-selected jury of twelve plunged a knife into his back. For our purposes, though, it is worth observing that Christie's imagined America included neither black accents nor even a Jim Crow car.

To summarize, Copjec provides us with a description of classical detective fiction in which the (allegorical) articulation of the community or nation depends on a differentially determined identity (the not-identical-with-itself), here identified as a logical incongruity we call the locked-room paradox. This possibility of successfully enunciating community by way of the locked-room mystery sets the stakes for *The Conjure-Man Dies*. In "A Corpse and Hocus Pocus in Harlem," a review of Fisher's book for the *New York World News*, Harry Hansen conceded, "Everything in the tale is Harlem, and you'd be surprised to find how complete a world it is in its own way."[9] But the Harlem community that is the subject of Fisher's text is more ruptured than resolved, and this tension is underscored by Fisher's text.

A MYSTIC CHAMBER

Negro problems are problems of human beings . . . they cannot be explained away by fantastic theories, ungrounded assumptions or metaphysical subtleties.

—W. E. B. DU BOIS, *THE PHILADELPHIA NEGRO: A SOCIAL STUDY*

N'Gana Frimbo "put his people in that spotlight and he stayed in the dark," notes Detective Perry Dart when he scrutinizes the setup of the psychist's inner sanctum (45). Each customer seated in the reception room was ushered through by a turbaned assistant for a consultation, settled in an "uncomfortably illuminated chair," seeing nothing by the "blinding glare" of a hanging droplight aimed directly at his or her face (65, 66). Here the figure of the psychist appeared before them, but only as a "dark shadow," and one that, according to the testimony of Jinx Jenkins, "seemed to fade away altogether and blend with the enveloping blackness beyond" as he spoke (67). An unseen eye discerned its clients' troubles "in their faces" and reported them in a disembodied voice "so matter of fact and real" that it could "dispel doubt and inspire confidence" in its subsequent predictions, however trivial or fantastic (67). Frimbo's "mystic chamber," clad from top to bottom with black velvet drapery and adumbrated as if it were designed for an illusionist, is the "obligatory addition," the nonempirical something whose waiting room convenes a cross section of Harlem's residents at the moment when the conjure-man is apparently and inexplicably struck dead (66). And Frimbo's peculiar talent, as Dart discovers when he takes a seat at the psychist's desk and becomes "merely a deeper shadow in the surrounding dimness," was to irradiate the burdens of the past and present lurking in the darkest recesses of the mind, and to "change the course of a life" (45, 69).

While his acute powers of observation square with the bravura of a Sherlock Holmes, Frimbo is practitioner of an "applied determinism" whose ambitions lie beyond parlor tricks (226). He claims, "I can study a person's face and tell his past, present, and future"—and typically does, displaying a remarkable breadth of knowledge, his enviable powers of deduction given over to a narrativization of social data that gestures at a whole person (226). Apart from his far-fetched declarations of divinity, Frimbo's most astounding faculty is his sociological instinct. His thorough grasp of urban life and insight into its effects on black Americans adheres to the multifaceted model W. E. B. DuBois pioneered at the turn of the century. Making epistemological pillars of historicism and empiricist positivism, DuBois's groundbreaking *The Philadelphia Negro* (1899) had forged a sociology capable of "deconstructing the sacrosanct Anglo-American idea of a preestablished social order obeying immutable natural laws" to account for the sociopolitical and economic forces that influenced black Americans' lives (Saint-Arnaud 140). Chief among DuBois's insights was his recognition of continuity between the past, present, and future of black Americans, whose history of enslavement is not detached "heritage" but an ongoing influence (140). Frimbo's appreciation of a history of racial oppression as the intimate antecedent for contemporary black experience; his phenomenological grasp of urban conditions; and his inductive prognostications constitute a sociologist's credentials. Furthermore, his narrativization of urban experience and close attention to human feeling bear some resemblance to the work of the Chicago school of sociology.

In the first few decades of the twentieth century, the University of Chicago's sociologists attributed urban social problems—what they politely called "personal demoralization"—to demographic shifts in American cities due to the arrival of immigrants and rural migrants, namely, their transition from

"non-rational" and "primitive" social interactions that bound individuals together based on tradition or custom, also known as "primary group contacts"
(*gemeinschaft*), to what sociologists perceived were the pragmatic relations
associated with modern commercial societies and developed according to
market forces, called "secondary group contacts" (*gesellschaft*) (Reed 20–21).
Whereas primary social relations forfeited individuality and opportunity on
the altar of personal obligation to the whole, and secondary social relations
allowed individuals to profit from the many benefits of demographic and
economic heterogeneity, the intermediate phase was characterized by "the
collapse of institutional life" itself, not to mention the disintegration of morals and conduct that would make it increasingly difficult to maintain order.
Consequently, sociologist W. I. Thomas's social disorganization and reorganization theory proposed launching new social institutions that could allevi-
ate the malaise of disorganization, bridging the gulf between gemeinschaft
and gesellschaft. A cadre of "social technicians" (social workers) would
provide assistance to rural migrants or immigrants, helping them develop
voluntarist institutions like immigrant cooperatives, which could "mediate
tensions between the individual and the community" but ultimately achieve
the desired acculturation (21).

Variations and refinements on Thomas's social disorganization and reorganization theory included the ethnic cycle, an assimilationist model created
by sociologist Robert Park, who advocated for constant relations between
peoples to create "an organic cultural exchange that infused elements of each
culture into one" (22), and urban ecology (another of Park's inventions),
which presented urban space as "a functioning organism" and divided the
city according to economic processes and the distribution of populations
in various districts (23). Social disorganization and reorganization, ethnic
cycle, and urban ecology theory opposed scientific racism and nativist prejudice in their insistence that race and ethnicity were merely social constructs.
Nevertheless, the Chicago school's assumption that black and white eth-
nics would encounter identical challenges to assimilation, and its dark logic
that "crime and poverty were the consequences of institutional decay; ethnic
ghettos were simply part of a natural process of succession; and conflict between groups would whither on its own" limited the initiatives available to
the Urban League, which wholeheartedly swallowed the guidance Chicago's
social theorists had to offer and focused its programs on developing workplace competence and public manners (26). One study of African American families in Harlem indicated that median income plummeted almost

50% between 1929 and 1930, but in 1931 the New York Urban League offered limited industrial and domestic training as its only prescription for what it euphemistically referred to as "enforced leisure" (107, 76–77).

By contrast, in *The Conjure-Man Dies*, N'Gana Frimbo's is a "social-technician" of sorts; under the guise of his "conjuring," the psychist offers career coaching, marriage counseling, practical psychology, and medical advice to the individuals who assemble in his waiting room. Aramintha Snead, a onetime migrant from Savannah, arrives determined to put an end to the unremitting abuse of her husband, a shiftless drunk who "greets me at the door with a cuff side o' the head," she explains to the police, "jes' by way of interduction" (Fisher 81). Unsatisfied with the minister's unvarying counsel ("Daughter take it to the Lord in prayer" [81]) and with two years' perfect attendance at prayer meetings down the drain, Mrs. Snead repudiates religious instruction in favor of Frimbo's conjuring: "I been takin' it to the Lord in prayer long enough. Now I'm goin' take it to the devil" (81). Drug addict Doty Hicks entered the conjure-man's chamber convinced that Frimbo had cast an evil spell on his brother at the behest of the brother's show-gal wife, but Frimbo has clarified all: "He simply has pulmonary tuberculosis—in the third stage. He had had it for at least three months when your sister-in-law came to me for advice" (114). Numbers runner Spider Webb claims he was present to take Frimbo's bet and to take advantage of Frimbo's "system of playing the game that couldn't lose" (137), while Pullman porter Easley Jones came to consult the psychist on a matter of infidelity.

Bubber Brown, formerly of the DSC (Department of Street Cleaning), lost his municipal employment, but attempted a fresh start as a private detective, figuring that in Harlem, "The only business what was flourishin' was monkey-business" (49). Nevertheless, Bubber lacks vocational training—or shall we say, professional discretion—a sad deficiency that becomes impossible to ignore after he successfully conceals himself behind a trunk in a lady's boudoir to witness an illicit tryst, but then knocks over the trunk to surprise the lovers in flagrante delicto. "Only I thing I wanted to detect," he confesses, "was the quickest way out" (53). Accordingly, Bubber was on hand to ask Frimbo for professional advice. Meanwhile, Bubber's close friend Jinx Jenkins is really down and out, and did not even need to admit as much to Frimbo, who began their appointment with this "simple statement of fact, presented as a comprehensive résumé of a situation" (68). In his "mystic chamber," Frimbo recapitulated Jenkins's plight: weeks of unemployment, plummeting hope, the humiliating necessity of procuring "the financial aid of your friends" and even of borrowing money to pay Frimbo's fee (68). The psychist prophesized Jenkins would have "food and shelter in abundance," but little happiness, in the immediate future, a prediction that foreshadows Jenkins's stay in prison as the conjure-man's suspected killer. More "uncertain fortunes" would follow these, Frimbo observed, and presumably the conjure-man would have offered additional guidance on such matters had he not been unceremoniously assassinated.

By and large, the Harlem Fisher depicts lacks social institutions that can contend with the problems his characters face. Nevertheless, the community Fisher presents is characterized by a shared determination to surmount fiscal deprivation and physical abuse, constituted by its search for an end to the social "disorganization" and widespread economic malaise in Depression-era Harlem. Paradoxically, the constitution of the community via the detective fiction formula depends on the assassination of the conjure-man, who is apparently the sole provider or social worker with the wisdom necessary to prevail in these desperate circumstances. Ultimately, the materialization of Fisher's Harlem requires coming to terms with the absence of an omniscient and omnipotent "social technician," the community fixture or communal fantasy whose integrity, it turns out, was—like King Solomon Gillis's "cullud policemans"—compromised all along. "Killing" the conjure-man becomes an ambivalent compulsion of the text, and it is one that Fisher used the devices of detection to do.

The collective substance of Frimbo's sessions, which are folded into classical detective fiction's routine cross-examination of its witnesses, coalesces into a variegated sketch of city life—a collective ethnography, if you will, of Depression-era Harlem. Moreover, Fisher's narrator pencils in the sounds and sights of Harlem's streets when the police round up their suspects. In this way, too, the study that Fisher undertakes is something like the Chicago school sociology of his time. In *Sociology Noir: Studies at the University of Chicago in Loneliness, Marginality and Deviance, 1915–1935*, Roger Salerno explains that Chicago school sociologists used ethnography to investigate urban conditions, and regarded narrative as a suitable instrument for depicting metropolitan life (170). Their distinct and somewhat controversial "pedestrian research" of urban experience differed sharply from the theoretical work and anthropological studies of European sociologists (166). If elsewhere sociologists consolidated social survey data in mind-numbing tables and graphs, the monographs of the Chicago school were powered by *Verstehen*, a term Max Weber used to capture the "quest to understand human behavior in terms of feeling, motivation and spirit" (52). Salerno contends that these innovative studies comprised an art form equal to the finest literature of that period (152). Carla Cappetti's *Writing Chicago* goes so far as to suggest that novelistic and autobiographical studies of the city by the likes of Richard Wright, James T. Farrell, and Nelson Algren should be shelved alongside the theoretical and empirical writings produced by Chicago's urban sociologists (2).

In this same vein, we might label Fisher a literary sociologist for his thick descriptions of urban experience and distinctive characters, as well as for the blend of "artistic imagination and the scientific method" McCluskey perceives in *The Conjure-Man Dies* (*City of Refuge* 27). And if N'Gana Frimbo plays the social technician, fashioning theoretical and empirical accounts of life in Harlem, then astonishing his clientele by recounting their misfortunes, Fisher's foray into urban ethnography is more complex still. Since this detection fiction begins with the conjure-man's "death," police detective Perry Dart's interrogations must pry Frimbo's dealings and prognostications from the late conjure-man's clients. To speak of their encounters with the "departed" psychist requires they reproduce Frimbo's account of their troubles and also offset his account with their own. The result is a self-signifyin(g), as each suspect becomes the mouthpiece for his own exogenous ethnography, though adding an endogenous echo by way of critique. These dialogic descriptions of individual experience sometimes pitch science and superstition side by side and in unresolved tension. They are also intersubjective labyrinths that lure the language of one man out of the mouth of another. Fisher takes an unusual stab at reverse focalization in the case of Jinx Jenkins, who enters the mystic chamber with a defensive "mask of scowling ill-humor" and, when asked by Dart to identify himself, growls, "I mean I say I'm who I is. Who'd know better?" (65). Yet as he begins to describe his interlocutions with Frimbo, Fisher notes,

> His imperfections of speech became negligible and were quite ignored; indeed, the more tutored minds of his listeners filled in or substituted automatically, and both the detective and the physician, the latter perhaps more completely, were able to observe the reconstructed scene as if it were even now being played before their eyes. (66)

Jenkins idiosyncratic grammar and colloquialisms recede from the text, and we are apparently presented with a perfectly transparent account of a subjective experience, albeit paradoxically depersonalized. This bit of fine-tuning makes Jenkins, as he tells his own story, the mouthpiece and medium of *narrative itself*—though he is merely one of many men bringing his troubles to the office of the conjure-man. But this fantasy of access to the social margins and the textured variety of urban life through an intersubjective network of overlapping reports is precisely that: a fantasy. And the "mystic chamber" that amalgamates so many voices is also a crime scene—where a man who appeared to be N'Gana Frimbo was choked to death, a handkerchief stuffed into his larynx by a brilliant assassin, given that the assassin was, as John Archer marvels, "bright enough to think up a gag like this" (23).

RHAPSODY IN BLACK AND BLUE

> I cheerfully admit the "escape" motive in the crotchet that divides my interest
> with the detective story—books on strange and out-of-the-way corners of the
> world. Tibet, Greenland, the Australian wilds, desert China, the reaches of the
> Amazon—they and their denizens perennially fascinate me, and I know why. It
> is because they are the farthest extreme from the seemingly tame and ordered
> life that civilization has wished upon me. But the detective story doesn't interest
> me in that way at all.
>
> —HARRISON R. STEEVES, "A SOBER WORD ON THE DETECTIVE STORY"

An August 21, 1932, review of *The Conjure-Man Dies* in the *Long Island Daily Press* proposed that "here was another piece of lively art, a work bound up with racial feeling and as perfect as a dance intricacy by Bill Robinson, a rhythm by Cab Calloway or a spiritual by Paul Robeson."[10] The *Press's* citation of other black American cultural forms situates Fisher's book amid distinctly African American entertainments rather than in the realm of predominately white-authored detective fiction, but its associative connection with jazz, dance, and spirituals likely reflects Fisher's very conscious interpolation of a multitude of black cultural texts into his own. When, for instance, police officer Hanks and Bubber Brown make a stop at the Hip-Toe Club on Lenox Avenue to pick up dope dealer Doty Hicks for questioning, Bubber stops dead in his tracks, captivated by a shapely dancer who "was proving beyond question the error of reserving legs for mere locomotion" (Fisher 102). Later on, Bubber tries to dodge Tiger Shade, a flunky for numbers runner Spider Webb who "done agreed to lay for you and remove both yo' winnin's and yo' school gal complexion" (234) by slipping into Mr. Crouch's morgue and playing ghost beneath a sheet in the undertaker's parlor. An eerie chorus wafts through the wall from an adjacent Sunday church meeting, terrifying Bubber with its wistful query, "Lord, was I born to die— / To lay this body down?" (244). The juke joint is an interlude in the investigation, and the church and the crime scene are overlapping spaces. In other words, Fisher's crime novel is not standard literary refection with an ethnic "flavor"; instead, the detective formula has to contend with the milieu it depicts.

The *Daily Press* calls *The Conjure-Man Dies* "a mystery with a theme song," since the book first page gives way to "the frequent uplifting of merry voices in the moment's most popular song" (Fisher 3):

> I'll be glad when you're dead, you rascal you,
> I'll be glad when you're dead, you rascal you.
>> What is it that you've got
>> Makes my wife think you so hot?
> Oh you dog—I'll be glad when you're gone!

Just as the printed notes that begin every chapter of W. E. B. DuBois's *The Souls of Black Folk* evokes an "unarticulated text (the unprinted words)" for the reader conversant in musical notation (Sundquist 470), these lines supply a cue—that is, a clue—to the jazz literate. As a sort of musical overture, the lyrics of Samuel Allen Theard (Spo-De-Odee)'s smash hit "I'll Be Glad When You're Dead, You Rascal You" supply a narrative preview and synopsis to the initiated, who might make out the murderer's motive (adultery and revenge) and pinpoint the killer when he appears: Easly Jones, a man who claims to be a Pullman porter, and who explains to the police exactly why he sought the services of the conjure-man N'Gana Frimbo—"I was hyer to ask 'bout my wife—was she true *to* me or f'ru *with* me" (129). It seems worth emphasizing that this "theme song" is neither an epigraph, nor exactly a subtext, but a concomitant composition that takes the part of the murderer without giving him away. Its intermittent surfacing in the storyline implies a different sort of relationship than code and key. Is one *riffing* on the other? Or if Fisher lays out Theard's lyric in the first page of the text, is the investigation that follows an improvisation on this "establishing shot"?

Of course, it is very often the case in classical detective fiction that the corpse is particularly susceptible to murder. Franco Moretti points out that in many of Arthur Conan Doyle's stories, a prior transgression sets the stage for the murder plot. "The victim, that is, has *asked for it*," having committed some offense against the murderer (what we might call in Fisher's text a "rascal-ism") that compels retaliation (*Signs* 136)—though in the golden era what we typically find is that nearly all of the circle of suspects have perfectly legitimate objections to his remaining alive. Consequently, the investigators happen across any number of motives for bumping off the person in question; as Roger Caillois notes, "each enigma" in the puzzle mystery "is subject to as many solutions as the imagination can invent for it" ("Game" 3). In S. S. Van Dine's *The Benson Murder Case* (1926), for instance, aesthete and amateur detective Philo Vance lays out a solid circumstantial and material case against no less than six suspects for the murder of Wall Street broker Alvin Benson: Mrs. Anna Platz, the housekeeper, clearly disliked the man—and could have done it, too, as a "shrewd, determined German type" (141); Lothario loafer and big-game hunter Leander Pryce needed back some borrowed jewels he used for collateral to pay a debt to his father-in-law (and well deserved some sort of criminal sentence, "if only for the way he dresses," notes Vance [145]); Muriel St. Clair, ingénue and single singer Cinderella suspected Benson of toying with her money on the market and could have shot him cold when he got awfully close to toying with her; Captain Philip Leacock resolved to protect the reputation of his fiancé Miss St. Clair, and so on. The detective's intellectual calisthenics are sufficiently diverting to take the reader's mind off murder as moral transgression, or death as human tragedy, per se (and we are little concerned with the morality of the thing, Moretti points out: "Agatha Christie's first book is set at the same time as the massacres of the Great War, yet the only murder of interest occurs on the second floor of Styles Court" [*Signs* 135]). More to the point, the extraordinary calculus of motives and means ends by substantiating the murdered party's villainy, leaving little time to lament his death. This tendency seems to verify Caillois's observation that the puzzle mystery is "cold and sterile, perfectly cerebral" (11).

Proving the deceased was singularly predisposed to face unlawful death cannot be exactly what Fisher had in mind, though, since Frimbo is not, it turns out, the target of more than two or three homicidal imperatives, nor does he appear to be the "lady-killer" Theard's song depicts. Perusing Frimbo's "luxuriously appointed" apartment and finding neither "frills" nor a trace of perfume, Sergeant Dart goes so far as to conclude that Frimbo is a "woman hater," though Dr. Archer is mystified by this "over-absence of the feminine" and speculates the psychist might have been "a Lothario of the deepest dye" (23–25). Instead, Fisher's paraphrasings of the sexual tomfooleries in "You Rascal, You" materialize as several subplots in which N'Gana Frimbo is only peripherally involved.

As a self-minted street detective who specializes in "monkey-business. Cheatin'—backbitin', and all like that" (49) and whose card promises "evidence obtained in affairs of the heart" (48), Bubber Brown becomes well versed in infidelity. He takes two dollars from an evil-looking woman to discover whether her husband is consorting with an attractive woman in the ticket box at the theater. "Keepin' my eyes on her was the easiest work I ever did in my life," reports Brown (51). Meanwhile, hopped-up Doty Hicks holds Frimbo's conjuring responsible for the infirmity of his brother Spats, who grabbed his show-gal wife, "smacked her cross-eyed" for taking up with a sugar daddy, and soon afterward succumbed to pulmonary tuberculosis (112). These minor riffs on a major theme (the hard-boiled and social realist variations that are adjacent to the ratiocinative) change our perception of the detective genre and its narrative functions. The puzzle mystery, in this case, shifts its status from *langue* to *parole*; it is not a meaning-making device but a sound vernacular, whose capacity is entirely adjectival, and that modifies a substantive category that Theard titles "You Rascal, You" but Bubber Brown simply calls "monkey-business" (51).

If we take jazz as our metaphorical prompt, then in Fisher's text the detective fiction formula might cease to function as narrative syntax and start to serve as something like sonic material, a scat-styled rendering of pure narrative whose gist as detective fiction is shy of intelligible. But how does one use generic syllables to move beyond genre talk? Murder, motives, means, investigation, revelation—all the usual suspects of the mystery—might be detached from intelligible combinations, as they are, for instance, with Frimbo's uncanny reappearance midway through *The Conjure-Man Dies* as an ex-cadaver turned amateur detective who "walked in, sat down, and pronounced himself thoroughly alive" (172). Nothing has prepared Detective Perry Dart for the eventuality: "It swept the very foundation out from under the structure which his careful reasoning had erected and rendered it all utterly and absurdly useless" (172). On the other hand, Caillois declares that shuffling and inverting generic conventions is customary within the genre of detective fiction, since to restore novelty to the intellectual exercise, the author may be "forced into audacities that sometime seem excessive" (8). Any shock to the system, then, even one that swaps a corpse for a sleuth, is predictable and necessary, "commonplace" within *this* genre (8). Still, Fisher does his best to defamiliarize the logic, narrative and otherwise, that is the foundation of detection. Some way into the investigation, the reanimated N'Gana Frimbo diverts Dr. Archer with discourse on "diverse and curious topics," turning the amateur sleuth's attention from "the mystery of this assault" that he hoped to probe (228–29). Plying the doctor with bold metaphysical talk, Frimbo alludes to "an order in which a cause followed its effect instead of preceding it" and proclaims himself an inhabitant of that other, nondeterministic order (227). Scoffing at Archer's methods, Frimbo announces that "genuine mystery is incalculable" and cautions the doctor that "the profoundest mysteries are those things which we blandly accept without question" (230). Finally, the psychist disputes the utility of the investigation outright, demanding, "What on earth does it really matter who killed Frimbo—except to Frimbo?" (230). Frimbo's open critique of the concerns of detective fiction, added to Fisher's shifts in the usual narrative syntax and his juggling of generic elements—not the least of which is Frimbo's literal detachment from his role as corpse and his reappearance as a kind of metaphysical sleuth—dispel some of the order that genre fiction habitually imposes, without effacing its individual parts.

This synchronized semiconstitution and dissolution of detective fiction (an activity that is at least hinted at, or even partially encapsulated in the title *The Conjure-Man Dies*) yield a carefully articulated inarticulacy, whose methods bear comparison to scat singing in jazz. Scat singing is often portrayed as a form of vocal improvisation concerned with "dissociating the vocal line of verbal meaning" in order to approximate instrumentalist performance, which is uninhibited by "extra-musical associations" (the denotative sense of expressive speech), but this "crossover" characterization precludes understanding the practice as an "expressive medium in its own right" (Bauer, "Scat" 303–4). Take its apocryphal (indeed, entirely false) origins in Louis Armstrong's February 26, 1926, recording of "The Heebie Jeebie Dance" with his Hot Five, when Armstrong supposedly dropped the printed lyrics and commenced to scat rather than break up the recording session. Brent Hayes Edwards points out that reports of this "fortuitous fumble" postulate a perforation between written and oral to account for "the way that Armstrong's voice peels gradually away from the reiteration of the chorus, and from linguistic signification altogether," which, importantly, "happens as a kind of erosion or disarticulation, not a sudden loss: 'Say you don't know it, you don't dawduh, / Da w fee blue, come on we'll teach you'" (618–20). We might treat these quasi-verbal vocables, which land us somewhere between "absolute" music and intelligible syntax, as a distinct form, however; consider, for example, that the "subtle melodic inflections and timbral effects" of Armstrong's scat singing can't be recorded according to the parsimonious conventions of standard musical notation (Bauer, "Armstrong" 137), and are better deciphered by a linguist than a lyricist. As a consequence of both "dispossession and invention, perdition and predication, catastrophe and chance," scat seems to constitute an idiosyncratic idiom of its own (Edwards 620). Crucially, however, Edwards suggest that the distinctive sounds popularized by jazz artists like Cab Calloway and Louis Armstrong belong on a continuum with other cultural productions that deliberately mobilized "linguistic deformity" in ways that attached "illiteracy" and "inarticulacy" to nonwhites (627). Jazz songs from the early twentieth century regularly featured "alterity projected onto the level of linguistic impenetrability and absurdity," from the mock Chinese in Gene Green's "From Here to Shanghai" (1917) to the "equal opportunity scat reification" in Slim and Slam's counterfeit-Chinese "Chinatown, My Chinatown" (1938), ersatz-Yiddish "Matzoh Balls" (1939), and simulated-savage "African Jive" (1941) (627).

This broader category of racially tendentious (but also potentially ambivalent) modes of representation, to which the conventions of blackface minstrelsy and dialect fiction, with its eccentric, often demeaning orthography, are routinely assigned, might also include American detective fiction of the mid-1920s to the mid-1930s. Maureen Reddy proposes that the description of "blond Satan" Sam Spade that opens Dashiell Hammett's *The Maltese Falcon* is a "specifically racial code" and, pointing to dehumanizing stereotypes in hard-boiled detective stories like Hammett's "Dead Yellow Woman," concludes that racism "is in fact a cornerstone of that fiction's ideological orientation" (6, 27). By contrast, Thomas argues that Hammett presents "foreignness" as a more suggestive, amorphous quality and consequence of British and American imperialism: there is an "aura of unintelligible foreignness," Thomas contends, in the contents of Joel Cairo's wallet, which includes "a much-visaed Greek passport bearing Cairo's name portrait; five folded sheets of pinkish onion-skin paper covered with what seemed to be Arabic writing"; "a post-card photograph of a dusky woman with bold cruel eyes and a tender drooping mouth"; and a handful of United States, British, French, and Chinese coins" (Thomas 265, Hammett 47).

Representations of ethnic, racial, and national variety also appealed to American practitioners of the puzzle mystery, whose prodigious experiments in constructing foreignness belied one of Ronald A. Knox's commandments for detective fiction: "No Chinaman must figure in the story"

(195). Amateur sleuth Philo Vance's "omnivorous reading in languages other than English, coupled with his amazingly retentive memory, had a tendency to affect his own speech," S. S. Van Dine (Willard Wright) informs the reader, but it is the man's wealth of exaggerated Anglicisms ("The chap's dead, don't y' know," or "Most consid'rate ... eh, what, Markham?") that prove irksome and at times unbearable (14, 16, 17). One can't help but note, moreover, that "Vance's Manhattan appears not to extend beyond 125th Street" (Van Dover 90) and that the sleuth's adage "Culture is polyglot" applies principally to "the world's intellectual and aesthetic achievements" and not at all to its persons (Van Dine 14n). Vance does lend a sympathetic ear to Egyptian Anupu Hani's grievances against artifact-pilfering Westerners in *The Scarab Murder Case* (1930), and he talks Boxer Rebellion and ceramics with Liang Tsung Wei, an Imperial and Oxford University–educated activist (who is also, for reasons that are never explained or called into question, a white man's cook) in the blithely anachronistic *The Kennel Murder Case* (1933) (Van Dover 90–92). Ultimately, Philo Vance's cosmopolitan engagements are limited the foreigner willing to function as a mouthpiece for antiques.

By contrast, fantasy foreign accents were bread and butter for an author born and raised in Canton, Ohio, and educated at Harvard: Earl Derr Biggers, whose rotund Chinese police detective Charlie Chan is given over to "reckless wanderings among words of unlimitable English language" (qtd. in Huang 17). Chan's makeshift Confucianisms and subject-free aphorisms (e.g. "Murder like potato chip—cannot stop at just one" [300]) bear no resemblance to actual pidgin. In a 1929 letter to a friend, Biggers explained, "If he talked good English, as he naturally would, he would have no flavor, and if he talked pidgin, no mainland reader would tolerate him for one chapter" (qtd. in Van Dover 73). In the case of this ethnic detective, "Authenticity is a red herring," claims critic J. K. Van Dover (74); Chan's contrived and blunder-ridden English and his fat form (with cheeks "chubby as a baby" [37]) became his signature and calling card—and a far cry from the wiry lean strength of his whip-wielding, real-life counterpart, Hawaiian police detective Chang Apana, who was, incidentally, fluent in Chinese and Hawaiian and spoke pidgin English. In fact, in *The House without a Key* (1925), the first in the Charlie Chan series, Boston Brahmin John Quincy Winterslip is duped by a Honolulu crook impersonating Chan over the phone. "You savvy locality?" the voice demands, arranging a rendezvous in Honolulu's Chinatown (Biggers 120). This was, Winterslip later reflects, "a clumsy attempt at Chan's style, but Chan was a student of English; he dragged his words painfully from the poets; he was careful to use nothing that savored of 'pidgin'" (121). And Chan's speech acquires a new dimension of factitiousness in *The Chinese Parrot* (1926), when the detective disguises himself as house-boy Ah Kim to protect a $300,000 strand of pearls from foul play from the enemies of magnate P. J. Madden: "All my life," Chan grumbles to Bob Eden, the son of a prominent jeweler, "I study to speak fine English words. Now I must strangle all such in my throat, lest suspicion rouse up. Not a happy situation for me" (Biggers 184). Suffocated by this spurious tongue that simulates a racist stereotype of broken English, Biggers's undercover Chan (inadvertently?) signifies against his creator, who took his own ideas of "yellowface" as requisite for the detective's professional success.[11] These layers of linguistic irregularities and phony "foreign" talk approach absur-dity, but should also redirect our attention to epistemological pretexts as the most certain source of mystery: Ah Kim is no houseboy; nor is P. J. Madden. P. J. Madden, it turns out, is but a crook impersonating the multimillionaire. N'Gana Frimbo makes this point more explicitly in *The Conjure-Man Dies.* "You are almost white," Frimbo tells Dr. Archer. "I am almost black. Find out why, and you will have solved a mystery" (230).

By engaging the detective genre, Fisher deliberately enters into an "an enduring voyeuristic economy between whites and African Americans" that is central to the history of an American modernism (Borshuk 3). Rather than treating an African American aesthetic as extraneous or unconnected to the preoccupations of Anglo-American modernism, Fisher foregrounds his participation in an interracial modernism with a performance of genre conventions that veers between an absolute music and intelligible syntax. Significantly, white representations of black accents in the first few decades of the twentieth century frequently associated African Americans with a "savage" and "primitive" Africa. For example, white poet Vachel Lindsay in-discriminately collapsed impressions of linguistic deformity, drunken bar-barity, and Africa in his "own personal idea of jazz": the racist rhyme "The Congo," which portrayed "fat black bucks" pounding on wine barrels and warned, "Be careful what you do, / Or Mumbo-Jumbo, God of the Congo, / And all of the other / Gods of the Congo, / Mumbo-Jumbo will hoo-doo you" (qtd. in Anderson 27). However, at a moment when black dialect, "a resort freely open only to whites," was regarded as "linguistic slovenliness" but also a foil for unsullied and utterly illusory "pure" English (North 24), Fisher's multiple registers of "black" talk and intersubjective narrative style contest a simplistic, insidious "cult of primitivism." At the same time, his depiction of urban modernity escapes pressures to deliver "proper," respectable images of black life that were no less "consigned brutally to type" (Thaggert 8). Fisher pushes against what Miriam Thaggert calls "the chain of both stereotypical portrayals and mimetic, transparently 'positive' or literal representations" (8), facetiously foregrounding his own role as literary (and, to some extent, linguistic) sociologist whose principal narratological tool is a generic pretext that demands a hybrid enunciation of community. Capturing the feeling, motivation, and spirit (*Verstehen*) of black urban life entails a fantasy of sociolinguistic access that the detective genre, with the prestidigitation of its locked-room paradox, supplies. After all, "Our very faith in reason is a kind of mysticism," as Frimbo explains to Dr. Archer in *The Conjure-Man Dies* (214).

Fisher's enterprise can be clarified, perhaps, by exploring another version of the musical refrain that runs through the book. The Fleischman Brothers offered a provocative illustration of faux-foreign accents in their 1932 animated short *I'll Be Glad When You're Dead, You Rascal, You*, which features Louis Armstrong and the Hot Five in a rendition of Rudolph Fisher's "theme" song, alongside an extraordinarily tanned Betty Boop on jungle safari with Bimbo the Dog and Koko the Clown. In this short, Betty is abducted by androgynous, frond-clad cartoon cannibals, a turn of events that seems designed to corroborate centuries-old racialist fantasies (O'Meally 288). Moreover, as Koko and Bimbo rush to Betty's rescue, they are hounded by a single "savage" suddenly transfigured as an animated, disembodied head that dissolves into Armstrong's face as film image, gaily crooning and scat singing "You Rascal, You." At another moment, the film turns to Armstrong's drummer, Alfred "Tubby" Hall, whose film image temporarily dissolves into that of the animated cannibal cook, rhythmically stirring a stewpot.

Rather than simply cross-cutting between the captivity narrative and the Armstrong band, the cartoon casts Armstrong "as a primitive among primitives" (290), although its fusion of musical and visual forms lends itself to a kind of productive interaction between the artists and the stereotypes the film appears to foist upon him. The short is billed as a Betty Boop cartoon, and yet the animated adventure arbitrates its jazz "accompaniment," while the musical entertainment encroaches upon the animation. "Despite its 'fried chicken' lyrics and foolishness," Robert O'Meally writes, the Fleischman Brothers' short "is unmistakable in its aggressive declarations that its singer will be glad when 'you'—the 'whites' in the cartoon? Betty? The producers? The audience?—are all dead" (290). The soundtrack sandwiches

"You Rascal, You" between snippets of "High Society" and "Chinatown, My Chinatown," showcasing Armstrong as a musical shape-shifter who switches accents on a dime. The footprints Koko and Bimbo track through the jungle abruptly swing about-face even as the hunters examine them—an instance of flip-flopping that suggests those who can't accommodate investigative indirection are bound to be hopelessly misled.

In *The Conjure-Man Dies*, Fisher regularly turns to Africa in order to effect generic distantiation, and so undercuts the narrative logic and ends classical detection resolves to embody. First, when Dr. Archer and Detective Dart inspect the conjure-man's study, they leap into a series of speculations about the dead man's origins. Spotting a set of framed documents on the wall, Archer comments:

> "Bachelor's degree from Harvard. N'Gana Frimbo. N'Gana—"
> "Not West Indian?"
> "No. This sounds definitely African to me. Lots of them have that N'. The 'Frimbo' suggests it, too—mumbo—jumbo—sambo—"
> "Limbo—" (27)

Archer first condenses Frimbo's origins into an associative string of syllables that incorporates first the ritual "babble" of an imaginary Africa and then a low-down epithet for an American slave, following an itinerary of the "Africa-to-Dixie-to-Harlem narrative model" that habitually structured all-black revues of the 1920s (Howland 332)—though Archer stops somewhat short of Harlemese, never arriving at the black metropolis. Instead, Dart's supplement qua interruption, "limbo," suggests a borderland, or intermediary state for the deceased (which, unbeknownst to either Dart or Archer, fairly accurately describes the condition of Frimbo, who only appears to be dead). It also thrusts a wedge in the pattern Archer proposes, which takes its cues from commercial entertainment, rather than Frimbo himself. Indeed, Frimbo embodies such an unusual, far-fetched combination of attributes, "a native African, a Harvard graduate, a student of philosophy—and a sorcerer," that Archer is inclined to dismiss the story outright as one that cannot be told, declaring, "There's something wrong with that picture" (27–28). Dart's interjection, however, advises against such "premature conclusions," and Archer profits from the instruction: days into the investigation, Archer pronounces a decided preference for inductive reasoning over the deductive kind—a preference he claims to have adopted from a "nice fellow . . . even though he was a policeman" (206). And when Dart proceeds to jump to conclusions about the role Harlem's criminal elements might have played in Frimbo's death, Archer reminds the police detective of "the error of letting his imagination, instead of his observation, draw the conclusions," again extolling this "lineal descendant of Francis Bacon—despite their difference of complexion," who demanded facts dictate conclusions, rather than the reverse (206).

These admonitions against a type of narrative prejudice, which apparently operates at the facile level of oral association but is actually rooted in certain transatlantic flows, might be taken as a rebuke of the superficially innocuous grammar of classical detective fiction and the reading practices it prescribes. After all, although the puzzle mystery might be credited with "deautomatizing signification and making things 'strange,'" or illuminating "a rich potentiality of unsuspected meanings" in mundane life that were heretofore inaccessible to the ordinary eye, the detective's interpretative acts are generally motivated by the impulse to reintegrate the newly unfamiliar into "accepted patterns of reality," and thus reinstate customary patterns of meaning, cause, and effect (Hühn 454–55). By foregrounding inductive reasoning as the appropriate investigative route, Fisher suspends the stipulated outcomes that animate genre paradigms in favor of an unanticipated syntax.

The close associates Jinx Jenkins and Bubber Brown also appeal to Africa and its "dark" inhabitants in a series of comic exchanges and insults:

"You ought to be back in Africa with the other dumb boogies."

"African boogies ain't dumb," explained Jinx. "They' jes' dark. You ain't been away from there long, is you?"

"My folks," returned Buber crushingly, "left Africa ten generations ago."

"Yo' folks? Shuh. Ten generations ago, you-all wasn't folks. You-all hadn't qualified as apes." (33)

This procession of abuse—what Fisher calls an "exchange of compliments"—is, in fact, an "elaborate masquerade" that tests and testifies to a hidden but "genuine affection" between the two parties (33). To put this slightly differently, Jinx and Bubber enter into a sort of inverted shadowboxing, a verbal sparring that draws blood and relies on perilous questions of lineal descent—"yo' granddaddy was a hair on a baboon's tail. What does that make you?" (34)—that would under other circumstances trigger "instantaneous violence" in Harlem (33). Their open hostility and derogatory names cannot but be misinterpreted by onlookers (Mrs. Aramintha Snead responds to this verbal jousting with a "cry of apprehension," for instance, while a policeman's "grin of amusement faded" [34]).

Jenkins and Brown are participants in a rite of camaraderie as collaborative deception that takes in even Harlem's long-term residents; they are accomplices in a vernacular that differentiates between signifier and signified, like separating a map from the territory it describes. What we are presumably dealing with, then, is "some degree of meta-communication, *i.e.*, of exchanging signals which would carry the message 'this is play'" (Bateson 179), with the reader kept privy only insofar as Fisher's omniscient narrator pulls back the veil. Stephen Soitos contends that the "'mock' genealogy" of this exchange "strikes two chords and suggests a third": its traffic in apes invokes that exemplary folk creature, the "signifying monkey"; it pokes fun at racist imagery of blacks as brutes and beasts; and finally, it suggests "blacks' pure thirst for their African heritage, which has been degraded, distorted, or erased by white control of their history" (Soitos 112). We might add a literary echo as well: that their genealogical inquiry, insofar as it pitches baboons and apes at the family annals, is a type of "monkey business" that implicitly alludes to detective fiction in one of *its* primordial appearances: Edgar Allan Poe's "The Murders in the Rue Morgue," which hinges on the incentives required for a sailor to claim an orangutan as his rightful property.

But what recompense comes of mobilizing such metacommunicative discourse (whose ostensible subject is African relations) at a historical moment when a reviewer could cite the benefits of the Harlem detective novel as anthropological document "because white folk, not knowing much about them [Negroes], believe them primitively prone to violence" and also offer the evidently deadpan observation that "Negroes are suitable for mystery stories because they are hard to see in the dark"?[12] In play, as in dreams, the difference between map and territory, game strategies and the referential world, fact and fiction, can capsize or become indistinct. Like Bubber and Jenkins, who "come so close to blows that were never offered" (33), Fisher invokes Africa only to dispel his invocation as pure talk, exposing this idiom of "dark insults" and "Africanisms" as utterly detached from reality. Against the puzzle mystery, whose habit of tracing effect to cause or material residue to its source emulates the act of the genealogist, Bubber Brown's and Jinx Jenkins's irreverent cross-examinations highlight the secondary social work achieved by deconstructing one's ancestry, even as Fisher plays with notion of his own text's pedigree as it relates to detective fiction.

Finally, there is Frimbo's story of his own native Buwongo. Dr. Archer is a captive audience before the psychist, who "painted a picture twenty years past and five thousand miles away" of a ceremony witnessed as a child of twelve, shy of manhood, and son of a sovereign (216). This was the Malindo, a "feast of procreation," Frimbo explains, a ceremony of the forty-eight tribes performed at night "at the height of the moon" in the central square of the town of Kimallu, where throngs of drummers conduct a "procession of shadowy figures" carrying a chest into the middle of the square, female torchbearers who kindle a circle of wood into an "unbroken ring of fire, symbol of eternal passion," and an enormous black python, who emerges from the chest. A warrior hurdles through the flames carrying an infant above his head, which he hands to a dancing maiden ("though none has seen it happen"), who dances around the serpent with him, after which she leaps through the blaze and lays the infant at the king's feet (221–23).

"Of all the rites," Frimbo insists, "none is more completely symbolic" (218), but of what exactly? In *To Make a New Race: Gurdjieff, Toomer, and the Harlem Renaissance*, Jon Woodson argues that the procreative feast, Malindo, Frimbo describes is an "inserted text" that represents the ideas of the Greek-Armenian mystic, hypnotist (and to some, charlatan) George Ivanovich Gurdjieff, whose esoteric theories of human existence inspired Jean Toomer's ideas about a raceless society and intrigued Zora Neale Hurston, Wallace Thurman, and George Schuyler, among others. Just as Frimbo's assertions of control over cause and effect are "an allusion to Gurdjieff's Law of the Octave, which describes 'the discontinuity of vibration and . . . the deviation of forces' in the universe," Woodson notes, the Buwongo ritual theorizes how man might manipulate energy to change his state (92–93). Charles Scruggs offers a slightly less erudite and more persuasive interpretation of the Buwongo ritual as a representation of sexual propagation and community regeneration (with the snake as Damballah, the life force, at its center) as a public event in which the entire village is invested (164). More importantly, this communal ritual that Frimbo speaks of so reverentially places procreation equally in the hands of male and female, and so contrasts both with the psychist's vulgar indifference to human sexual contact, which the bachelor Frimbo describes as merely "necessary to comfort, like blowing one's nose" (Fisher 268), and with the underhanded affair he has conducted with Mrs. Crouch (Scruggs 165).

But these explications of Frimbo's Africa must be contrasted against the conjure-man's clearly bizarre "rite of the gonad": Frimbo's slightly disturbing habit of and displaying male sex glands among in his laboratory (most recently, those of his murdered servant N'Ogo Frimbo). To perform this rite and "be master of his past," Frimbo uses the "protoplasm which has been continuously maintained through thousands of generations" in the male sex organ (269). With its heavy-handed sexual primitivism and faux racial id in a jar, not to mention the expressly male-oriented ceremony whose focal point is a biological specimen that apparently embodies the "unbroken heritage of the past," Frimbo's secret rite is pure Freudian parody—a fact Dr. Archer allows for in his description of the whole business as Frimbo "compensatory mechanism" (Fisher 269, 291, Gosselin 616). Though many critics take Frimbo's manifestations of ancestral pride at face value, it is not easy to maintain a straight face when Perry Dart violates Archer's delicately phrased diagnosis of Frimbo's idiosyncrasies, suggesting that the conjure-man killed his kinsman "because he's a nut" (Fisher 290, Gosselin 616). Archer quickly responds with the quick-witted

> Please—not so bluntly. It sounds crude—robbed of its nuances and subtleties. You transform a portrait into a cartoon. Say, rather, that under the influence of certain compulsions, associated with a rather intricate psychosis, he was impelled to dispose of his servant for definite reasons. (290)

Whereas Soitos reads Frimbo's race consciousness and ancestralism as a nonexotic, constructive expression of primitivism, which can "forge a link between Africa and African Americans and redefine Africa as the homeland of racial purity and positive creative energies" (Soitos 97), Archer's surfeit of tact (and Dart's lack thereof) highlight how quickly Frimbo's ancestral pretensions can wither into stereotype—a "cartoon," as it were, that dispels African enchantment—when reiterated in less diplomatic terms. Could it be that the desire for an untrammeled past, an uncontaminated heritage, a coherent community and a clear-cut history are, as the name Malindo suggests, a disease whose remedy is its own form: the bad blues?

RETURN OF THE CONJURE-MAN

> Once the subject is provided with its "*true*" predicate, everything falls into place, the sentence can end.
>
> —ROLAND BARTHES, S/Z

On the back of a letter dated 1924, Rudolph Fisher scrawled a definition of "The Realist": He "combats his black audience" and his "white audience" as well as "what has already been written," acting under the single "conviction that the truth shall make us free, with ruthless reverence for reality."[13] Rather than obliterate a "white-authored" detective fiction—which, during the genre's golden age was precisely enlivened by cross-racial exchange and enthralled by foreign accents that called into questions the notion of racial pedigree—*The Conjure-Man Dies* takes the detective fiction formula as an expressive mode, a vernacular that can convey the varieties of "blackness" in Fisher's "Dark Harlem." Certainly Fisher parts ways with some of the recognizable "vocables" of the genre formula, handling the puzzle mystery as something like a foreign language in its own right as he sketches the modern metropolis. But this is a reciprocal interpolation; in lieu of offering a "proper" image of black life, Fisher deconstructs communal fantasy while destabilizing the puzzle mystery. His "ruthless reverence for reality" risks an antagonistic relationship with a black audience and a white audience whose appeasement was never in the cards. Instead, Fisher exploits and unpacks the sociopolitical imaginary of the locked-room puzzle in a work of literary sociology that hardwires the elimination of that sagacious psychist qua "social technician" N'Gana Frimbo to the materialization of a civil society whose unsociable refrain is, even after the conjure-man's death, "I'll be glad when you're dead, you rascal you."

In *The Conjure-Man Dies*, Fisher finally pulls the whodunit out from under the feet of his amateur sleuth: at the moment Archer neatly negotiates the tidy circuitry of puzzle mystery, Frimbo ensnares the attempted assassin Stanley Crouch (alias Easley Jones, the railroad porter) with a live electric switch. But the psychist has not prepared for every eventuality. Crouch has a gun and shoots Frimbo dead, the revelations of classical detective fiction interrupted by the slug out of the hard-boiled. Gosselin points out that the last scene of the book is reserved for the "street-smart," comic/hard-boiled and self-invented private eye Bubber Brown, "setting the stage" for Chester Himes (617). However, *The Conjure-Man Dies* doesn't mark the end of Fisher's engagement with the detective genre. In fact, his last published story, which appeared in the *Metropolitan Magazine* shortly after Fisher's death in December 1934, revives two investigators from this earlier work. "John Archer's Nose" begins with a phone call that summons Dr. Archer and police detective Dart to the bedside of Sonny Dewey in an apartment on 134th Street—the kind of place where "tenants bring their own locks and take them when they move"—where they find a young man with a pearl-handled knife in his chest (218).[14] This story is bereft of the musical refrain that is the signature device of Fisher's first detective fiction, and it surrenders Bubber Brown and Jinx Jenkins, the "comic relief" in *The Conjure-Man Dies* and *The Walls of Jericho*—though Fisher's unpublished story "One-Month's Wages" brings back that duo in a moment of fiscal despondency for an exercise in slapstick and black camp. But "John Archer's Nose" dispenses with the ratiocinative intensity and the cacophony of voices at the core of *The Conjure-Man Dies*. It fully sheds the optimism of classical detective fiction, which by singling out a culprit exonerates a community. These further deviations from the clue-puzzle conventions of *The Conjure-Man Dies* are not merely indicators of Fisher's hard-boiled bent; "John Archer's Nose" argues for the inevitability of the hard-boiled, with its narrative implosions and ethical uncertainties.

"John Archer's Nose" is a crime solved by olfactory instincts, which come into play after Archer notices a peculiar scent in the boy's room—another scent besides the "discernible—er—fragrance" of alcohol the dead drunk Sonny had "expelled" *before* he was stabbed in his sleep (195). Though Dart humors his colleague, conceding, "I daresay every crime has its peculiar odor," Archer does not speak in jest: "Old stuff," he observes, adding, "They used bloodhounds in *Uncle Tom's Cabin*" (194). Dart, who can't catch a whiff of the scent, nevertheless purports to "smell a rat" and makes Archer out as a bloodhound. This gratuitous punning calls to mind Arthur Conan Doyle's *The Hound of the Baskervilles* (1902), whose scheming Stapletons (a husband and wife who pretend to be siblings) incite a paranormal scare by coating a mastiff in luminescent phosphorous. This allusion and Fisher's pointed reference to slavery announce the themes upon which the story hinges: faulty forms of kinship, supernatural hoaxes, and a history of bondage with some bearing on black experience in Harlem. But the stench in Sonny's room eludes Archer and takes on a life of its own. The physician complains that odors "should be captured, classified and numbered like the lines of the spectrum. We let them run wild" (194). Ineffable and uncataloged, this curious aroma reeks of the occult, or at least its sensory impression has no idiom. Archer remarks, "In a language of a quarter of a million words, we haven't a single specific direct denotation of a smell" (194). The physician's compulsive pursuit of this particular scent also alters the dynamics of detection, breaking away from the hard-and-fast logic of "denotation" to something less precise, an undertone or instinct that informs Archer's activities.

Additionally, Fisher's incessant reprisal of this gag draws our attention to the homophonic echoes in the title of the mystery, which seems to evoke three registers of interpretation at once. First, as I suggested above, it explicitly instantiates Archer as the detective-protagonist of Fisher's tale—as opposed to the actual police detective, Perry Dart. Archer is not only a sleuth who doggedly tracks a scent, however. The physician is also a man who "knows" his Harlemites, perhaps because he can see and think "black," has acquired the "pigmentation of the brain" Fisher attributed to himself. By contrast, *The Conjure-Man Dies* informs us that Dart, who "having himself grown up with the black colony, knew Harlem from lowest dive to loftiest temple," nevertheless operated according to the sensible conventions of ordinary police detection; "the somber hue of his integument in no wise reflected the complexion of his brain, which was bright, alert, and practical within such territory as it embraced" (14).

Yet Archer and Dart remain colleagues in crime-solving and also close friends. They are "complementary" (185)—a promising alternative to the dysfunctional relations between their probable namesakes, detectives Miles Archer and Sam Spade in Dashiell Hammett's *The Maltese Falcon* (1930). (Spade, of course, is romancing his partner's unbearable spouse at the very moment Archer is shot dead by Miss Waverly.) Archer and Dart practice the bachelor banter of an early Holmes and Watson, though their tête-à-têtes in "John Archer's Nose" are chock-full of trivial witticisms and language play. In stark contrast to the repartee of a Bubber Brown and Jinx Jenkins, though, this picture of male friendship sometimes relies on perverse, unpleasant one-liners: at the murder scene itself, for instance, or anticipating the seduction of Petal Dewey, Sonny's sister who arrives at Archer's flat in a pathetic attempt to purloin the murder weapon and protect her family. Their indecorous jokes border on graveyard humor and often fall quite flat, but they also function as a cynical or even misanthropic metacommentary on the state of affairs in Harlem. Or it could be that they are the only defensive mechanism that wards off the truly demoralizing conditions Archer confronts on a daily basis, even if the physician is not capable of the detachment that allows Dart to say, "*Your folks* ... are the most superstitious idiots on the face of the earth" (185, italics mine). Archer hasn't got the heart to argue, having witnessed a young boy die of convulsions earlier that day, precisely because the child's father rejected "new-fangled" X-ray treatments in favor of a charm acquired from a conjure-woman—"a wad of human hair, fried, if you please, in snake oil"—which was in an "evil-smelling packet" around the boy's neck (186–87).

This bleak reality brings us to a final sense of the title: its evocation of de-nial and nay-saying (noes), for this work is suffused with a deep pessimism about urban life and with Archer's despair at the diffuse threat and general malaise that Perry Dart first classifies as "superstition." The triumph of the irrational and the misguided violence it elicits, prefigured in *The Conjure-Man Dies*, is the subject of this story's lamentations, and without the levity of the "low" exploits and rich humor that characterized that earlier detective fiction. McCluskey observes that Fisher's writing takes "seriously an element of traditional experience used more often than not in American fiction for comic effort," but that the scientific-minded author used his detective fic-tions to critique the "survivalism of rural life, which can be regressive and tragic" (McCluskey 29–30). Having played the helpless eyewitness to a child "literally choking to death in a fit," Archer staunchly resolves to identify the source of that peculiar smell in Sonny's room (186). He insists, "I'm going to locate that odor if it asphyxiates me" (213). But we cannot dismiss the possibility that Archer's fixation on conjuration, and the "habit of heckling" that helps him to "dismiss an unpleasant memory," are not themselves the symptoms of self-delusion and denial (187). For if Archer proposes that "Su-perstition" is the perpetrator that compels him to act the pallbearer as much as the physician, Fisher shows us an image of Harlem distressed by much more than faith in the occult.

Where *The Conjure-Man Dies* introduces its reader to "bright-lighted gaiety of Harlem's Seventh Avenue" and "the frequent uplifting of merry voices in the moment's most popular songs," Fisher's picture of the Dewey apartment on 134th Street is uglier and bleaker (3). The only window in Sonny's room looks out onto "the darkness of an airshaft"; when Archer and Dart peer beyond it, they perceive "an occasional lighted window and a blend of diverse sounds welling up: a baby wailing, someone coughing spasmodically, a radio rasping labored jazz, a woman's laugh, quickly stifled" (190). The rough sounds and silences that punctuate the dark space of the airshaft comprise a terse essay on urban malaise. Its somber vortex sucks up the soundscape of the many in this corner of the metropolis, and the Dewey household, otherwise closed off from all others, appears an entity unto itself.[15] There is no locked-room puzzle here; Archer and Dart pains-takingly examine the flat for "some out-of-the-way corner" or a secret hid-ing place where the murderer might have concealed himself, but conclude upon inspection that the apartment "possessed no apparent entrance or exit other than its one outside door, and there was nothing unusual about an arrangement of rooms" (194). Murder, under these circumstances, is a family matter, since each member of the Dewey family, as well as their tenant Red Brown, had ample opportunity to stick a knife into Sonny. Establishing a motive, by contrast, proves more difficult. Though Red Brown, who boards with the family, insinuates that "Ben figured there was somethin' goin' on between Sonny" and Ben's wife Letty, the Dewey family is remarkably mute on the subject (198). Whereas Archer imagines a dozen plausible assassins for N'Gana Frimbo, he finds it more difficult to assign a credible motive to a member of the Dewey family. Still, the physician and the police detective cannot envision an alternative. Urging the Dewey family to turn in the perpetrator, Dart advises, "I should rather expect a flood of accusations . . . unless you are protecting each other" (193).

In contrast to Christie's *Murder on the Orient Express*, where each affiliate of the Armstrong household provided an airtight alibi for another, the force of communal bonds in the Dewey family leads each of its members to turn on himself. Petal delivers Ben's declaration of guilt, warning Dr. Archer that her brother will assault him if he doesn't turn over the murder weapon. But when Archer refuses to bite, Petal changes her tactics and tries to own up to the crime herself, explaining that she mistook Sonny for Red Brown and had attempted to avenge an assault on her virtue. And after Archer and Dart return to the Dewey apartment the following morning, Ma Dewey takes a crack at a confession, declaring that she murdered her son in a sort of dream state and out of mother love, since she could bear to see him suffer from tuberculosis; he would have perished if he didn't go to the "cemetarium" (215). But none of the family stabbed Sonny, Archer discovers, even if Ma Dewey, a sort of snake-oil salesman, is liable for the chain of events that led to his death. Instead, Fisher reveals that Sonny's bedroom *was* accessible from outside. After surveying the premises again, Dr. Archer explains:

> The next apartment is empty. Its entrance is not locked—you know how vacant apartments are hereabouts: the tenants bring their own locks and take them when they move. One room has a window on the same airshaft with Sonny's at right angles to it, close enough to step across—if you don't look down. (218)

Any individual might cross over the pitch-dark space of the airshaft to gain access to the Dewey flat, though he would gamble with his own life in the bargain. This provided the point of entry for Solomon Bright, who came to avenge his clan by murdering each of Ma Dewey's children as punishment for the snake-oil solution she sold him, which did not rescue his infant from death. The killer lacks the wisdom of King Solomon but would, rather than call, raise the wages of death. "Three for one," said the doctor. "Rather unfair, isn't it, Mr. Bright?" (219). Ready to slaughter every one of Ma's children in retaliation for the death of his own son—who might have been saved by modern medicine, John Archer insists—Bright is moved by an irrational, inexorable need for vengeance, which is why Archer proposes that "Superstition" is the true culprit of this crime.

Fisher's story ends on this dark note, with the crazed Solomon Bright taken into police custody, and Dart's initial characterization of Harlemites as "the most superstitious idiots on the face of the earth" yet to be refuted. "Superstition" is made culpable for two deaths in as few days, and buttressed by a treacherous appetite that eviscerates community. Is it easy to forget, then, that before Sonny had a pearl-handled knife in his chest, before "developing bad habits" of drinking and staying out late, his number had already been called? "Tuberculosis both lungs," the autopsy shows; he was "due to go anyway, sooner or later" (214). It is a familiar tragedy, Ma explains, since Sonny's father also contracted the disease and "suffered before he went, and look like when I thought 'bout Sonny goin' through the same thing I couldn' stand it" (216). That it was not superstition, a vestige of rural provincialism, but the urban condition itself that would have claimed Sonny's life, is the substance of Fisher's "ruthless reverence for reality." If *The Conjure-Man Dies* is a crime without a corpse, "John Archer's Nose" is, Solomon Bright notwithstanding, a crime without a proper culprit. Its solution is without justice, or at least it reeks of the hard-boiled since the elucidation of a single crime in a ravaged system of social relations can only be, as Stefano Tani writes of Hammett's *Red Harvest*, "ambiguous and partially unfulfilling" (24). In the cheerless Harlem of "John Archer's Nose," urban contagion and death signal a breakdown in interpersonal relations; they are the symptoms—the substance, too—of the moral contamination of urban existence and an indifferent state.

In *The Conjure-Man Dies*, John Archer proposes to write a murder mystery "that will baffle and astound the world," precisely because "the murderer will turn out to be the most likely suspect" (154). A medical examiner respectfully responds, "You'd never write another" (155). Perhaps "John Archer's Nose" is that story, since it seethes with a cynicism about an urban epidemic that knows no locked rooms and whose only articulated remedy is "the cemetarium." If Fisher's first detective fiction foregrounds an interracial American modernist aesthetic, improvising on the generic edifice of the locked-room mystery to explore the stakes of sociability in "Dark Harlem," Fisher's last published detective story resembles something like a "hidden object" case, as both its amateur sleuth and actual detective are either stymied or tongue-tied against a lethal urban ecology in Depression-era Harlem—what is endlessly in front of Dr. Archer's nose. Like the street or city names that stretch from one end of a map to the other in the game August Dupin describes in "The Purloined Letter," systemic privation can "escape observation by dint of being excessively obvious" (262). In such cases "the physical oversight," Dupin explains, "is precisely analogous with the moral inapprehension by which the intellect suffers to pass unnoticed those considerations that are too obtrusively and too palpably self-evident" (262). Though an indictment lurks beneath the surface and lingers in the interstices of Fisher's last detective story, however, its hard-boiled tendencies need not be read as resignation. Is this Fisher's call, instead, for a leap of sociability—a "pigmentation of the brain," perhaps?—that reads between the lines? Fisher optimistically imagined something like this in his 1927 essay "The Caucasian Storms Harlem" when he mused, "Maybe these Nordics at last have tuned into our wavelength. Maybe they are at last learning to speak our language" (City of Refuge 82).

Conclusion

Dream within a Dream

> I am absolutely frightened to death, and there's something which is happening
> or about to happen that I don't want to face, or let us say, which is an even better
> example, that I have a friend who has just murdered his mother and put her in
> the closet and I know it, but we're not going to talk about it. Now this means
> very shortly since, after all, I know the corpse is in the closet, and he knows I
> know it, and we're sitting around having a few drinks and trying to be buddy-
> buddy together, that very shortly, we can't talk about anything because we can't
> talk about that. No matter what I say I may inadvertently stumble on this
> corpse. And this incoherence which seems to afflict this country is analogous
> to that.
>
> —JAMES BALDWIN, "NOTES FOR A HYPOTHETICAL NOVEL"

> Our chambers were always full of chemicals and of criminal relics which had a
> way of wandering into unlikely positions, and of turning up in the butter-dish
> or in even less desirable places.
>
> —SIR ARTHUR CONAN DOYLE, "THE MUSGRAVE RITUAL"

Like the "curious collection" of keepsakes Sherlock Holmes retains from
"The Musgrave Ritual" (his first case of any significance as a consulting detective), detection's narrative devices were put in safekeeping in conventional
genre texts, in something like Holmes's "small wooden box with a sliding lid
such as children's toys are kept in" (Doyle 605). In this study, I have argued
that though the "relics" in this repository for narrative "playthings" collec-
tively take the recognizable form we call *detective fiction*, they were forged
elsewhere, and of socioeconomic necessity: to address the historical conditions of production and processes of racial formation fundamentally entwined with interracial sociability and interdependencies in the world of
work (605). Like Holmes's "crumpled piece of paper, an old-fashioned brass

key, a peg of wood with a ball of string attached to it, and three rusty old discs of metal," the emergence of these narrative-analytical tools belongs to a complex literary history of the nineteenth and early twentieth centuries, "so much so that they *are* history" (606). Works on the margins of the detective genre (which I have variously referred to as proto-, precursor, and peripheral detective fictions in this study) took these tools as their central narrative tactics, both before and after the generic expectations associated with classical detective fiction took more definite shape. These works on the margins return us to the "latent" content of the genre's conventions, clarify its "intelligence" (the social functions of its various narrative elements), and indicate the fitness of its mechanisms for exploring patterns of interracial sociability and economic interdependencies.

Where there are points of contact and interdependencies between blacks and whites, and where there are questions of labor and profit, the psychodynamics of interracial sociability rise to the surface, and this is absolutely central to understanding what blackness and whiteness have meant in the United States from the early nineteenth century to the mid-twentieth century. This matter is far too complicated to speak of in a few sentences, or to tell as a story. No *fabula* describes it, only the machinery that makes *sjuzhet*. Only certain narrative devices fathom these matters, and American authors seized these devices to represent a sociology of racialized labor, to challenge public fictions of racial separation, and to gauge prospects for interracial sociability.

In precursor and peripheral genre texts, the very presence of these many devices—backward construction, which produces "anticipation in retrospect"; the peculiar combination of metonymy (the clue) with metaphor (imaginative identification); the magnificent riddle of disguise in the dime novel; the locked-room paradox; and so on—point us to a complex interracial history of the nation. They underscore how an anatomy of narrative conventions we now associate with classical detective fiction can open up a history of interracial sociability.

This history of interracial sociability is deeply entwined with a history of work. The histories these proto- and peripheral detective fictions recount have, to borrow the language of Andrew Knighton in his study *Idle Threats: Men and the Limits of Productivity in 19th-Century America*, the effect of "desystematizing labor, unpacking its situatedness, pointing to the arbitrary commitments and marginal distance between an American system of 'interchangeable parts' and the narratives of 'intensified productivity'" (18). Yet

close attention to the interracial dimensions and historically diverse structures of interracial sociability in the world of work also yields an intricate
and frequently shifting project of racial management. As DuBois's sociological treatise "The Study of the Negro Problems" suggests, formulating
any conceptual model of recurrence demands close attention to fluctuating
socioeconomic conditions and developments in American industry, as the
structuring conditions of interracial economic interdependencies morphed
and recoiled only to return in new forms. The "Negro Problem," Du Bois
elaborates, "has changed with the growth and evolution of the nation; moreover . . . it is not one problem, but rather a plexus of social problems, some
new, some old, some simple, some complex" (3). Drawing on detection's devices, the texts I have studied concede the ineradicable fact of interracial
contact, the variegated web of historical contexts that inform it, and the
prospects for interracial sociability these contexts generate.

In this vein, the black and white authors of the proto- and peripheral
works I have examined establish that detective fiction is an eminently *interracial genre*. Indeed, the genesis of detection, its very design and development, is interracial, rather than implicitly ideologically "white," as critics have
generally assumed. Each of these texts refutes simplistic notions about the
"racial formation" of genre, underscoring that, as Andrew Pepper observes,
"To write about black crime fiction, as opposed to white or any other kind of
crime fiction, is to write about a body of writing that does not exist, or rather
does not exist in isolation from, and has not developed outside or beyond
the parameters of, these other kinds of crime fiction" (209).[1] Similarly, this
study requires we rethink the conceptual value of contemporary categories
such as "ethnic detective fiction," given detective fiction's early and continued
investment in interrogating the limits of and possibilities for interracial sociability and economic interdependence.

Recent genre studies, particularly the groundbreaking work of Gina and
Andrew Macdonald, have meticulously differentiated between contemporary varieties of an American "ethnic" detective fiction, arguing that a meaningful ethnic detective fiction is permeated with distinct cultural knowledge
and a worldview that disputes what conventionally constitutes detection.[2]
In a different vein, some critics take the emergence of nonwhite detective
protagonists in the last few decades for a triumph of American liberalism.
According to this logic, "The creation of representative detective heroes has
become an important social ritual for minority groups"—racial, ethnic, or
otherwise—"who would claim a meaningful place in the larger social con-

text" (Cawelti, "Canonization" 8). Alternately, scholars criticize nonwhite authors insofar as their appropriation of the genre is an assimilative tactic. In this case again, an "authentic" ethnic engagement with detective fiction inevitably writes *against* preexisting literary traditions and genre formulas.

I wholeheartedly affirm the social benefits of a publishing industry that does not discriminate against nonwhite authors. Yet the genealogy of precursor and peripheral texts I have assembled makes plain that imagining generic developments through the various lenses of "ethnic" detection belies the historic utility of detective fiction's devices for making sense of interracial sociability. To attribute the recent growth of what we call "ethnic detective fiction" to a liberal project and pursuit of the public sphere ignores that detective fictions' devices are literary products of an interracial modernity grounded in the nineteenth century. Furthermore, judging "ethnic" detective fiction by the standards I described above establishes dubious and inflexible assumptions about what it means to create a nonwhite detective fiction, while implicitly insisting that scientific rationalism is the property of white-authored detective fiction. It also has the effect of reifying the exclusion of nonwhite authors from the domain of scientific-rational thought, reinforcing faulty assumptions about the distinct properties of white-authored and nonwhite-authored detective fictions, and disregarding the varieties of "magical" and pseudoscientific thinking that are pervasive in detective fictions from the nineteenth century on. To speak about a history of detective fiction and examine the genre's peripheral texts in search of its genesis, by contrast, is to discover an interracial history of the nation.

Significantly, varieties of detective fiction that succeeded (but did not replace) the puzzle-mystery cultivated characteristics relevant to an exploration of racialized labor in the twentieth century. Below, I discuss the work of Chester Himes, whose hard-boiled police procedurals of the 1950s and 1960s are dystopic reconfigurations of Rudolph Fisher's Harlem. The high-velocity plot in Himes's *The Big Gold Dream* (1960) is preignited by a violent, interracial past and a present lack of economic opportunity, both anchored in the degradation of work. It takes as its subtext both the fantasy and the failure of gainful employment in a postindustrial inner city, yet Himes's text also experiments with detections' conventions by allocating forms of narrative making to "informants" that unsettle straightforward accounts. And in this case, Himes's Harlem detective novel introduces Dummy, an ex-prizefighter and deaf-mute turned stool pigeon and amateur pimp, as its chief investigating agent when thieves take the lottery winnings of a black maid.

Si vous êtes pris dans le rêve de l'autre, vous êtez foutu!

(If you're trapped in the dream of the other, you're fucked!)

Gilles Deleuze

Both the violence and the design of *The Big Gold Dream* suggest the proximity of Himes's critical tendencies to "noir," "an antigenre that reveals the dark side of savage capitalism," for Raymond Borde and Etienne Chaumeton's seminal inquiry *Panorama du film noir américain* (Naremore 22). Himes's detective fictions incorporate those traits typically associated with noir: "a feeling of discontinuity, an intermingling of social realism and oneiricism, an anarcho-leftist critique of bourgeois ideology and an eroticized treatment of violence" (22). But these characteristics are undoubtedly also an effect of Himes's unapologetic habit of limiting the length of his detective fictions to the bare minimum his contracts required, even if it meant abruptly terminating whatever tale he might have been spinning. As Himes neared the page count, he abandoned syntactic niceties in favor of novelistic shorthand, resorting to fast-paced installments that would bring the plot to closure, rather than adhering to a scrupulous narrative grammar. This habit clearly differentiates Himes's work from classical detective fictions, with their efficient and elegant solutions, and transports him into the world of the hard-boiled. And if there are not bodies lying thick in a Shakespearean finale, we are inevitably dealing with a lopsided, top-heavy, truncated affair that leaves plenty of threads hanging where it does not snip them short.

The remarkable accomplishment of Himes's detective fictions is, however, that tenacious, even perverse causality that galvanizes these texts. Something besides money and sheer force presides in Harlem, and it is the rough geography of Himes's domestic novels, exemplified by the twice-plotted world of *All Shot Up*: "It was ten minutes by foot, if you were on your way to church, about two and a half minutes if your old lady was chasing you with a razor" (21). Himes treats these two setups as topographical equivalents. What serves as their common denominator is an exact distance, a precinct reciprocally calibrated to these particular goings-on, which is to say what measures space is marking time. The opposite is also true—and this is *not* a tautology but something more like the symmetry of double-entry accounting, or an impartial approach to the semantic and syntactic dimensions of the narrative. Of course, this illustration is noteworthy insofar as it brings the violence embedded in Himes's geography to the fore (Cochran 26), but if we appreciate Himes's miniature treatment of Harlem as an allegory for narrative and a model for narrative distance, what is really at issue is whether one ought to differentiate between being compelled to arrive at one's destination rather than propelled toward it.

And the anarchic ends of Himes's detective fictions retroactively generate anarchic beginnings: a horsepower that dashes past the starting gate, sweeping up a cast of characters along its way. This staggering momentum at the outset must too have its provenance, but the police are hamstrung before they ever arrive on the scene. In *The Big Gold Dream*, Himes's policemen Grave Digger Jones and Coffin Ed cannot solve crimes by ordinary police methods. The "modern police techniques," "the Medical Examiner's report, photographs, fingerprints, the findings of the criminal laboratory"— that familiar dossier the police rely upon elsewhere—are to no avail here (58). "Police theories" are out of the question, which sets their game apart from the meticulous, impersonal cogitations of classical detective fiction, but Himes's detectives sometimes steer clear of unadulterated, hard-boiled brawn, since "third-degree methods" can be equally disastrous. Harlem's criminal set know the police routine by rote. Short of eyewitness accounts, Coffin Ed and Grave Digger get briefed by a circuit of informants, petty criminals duty-bound to punch in at appointed posts. With critical information transmitted through a covert constellation of snitches on a "stool pigeon route," it is no wonder that their Sergeant Frick finds the area distressingly indecipherable: "Every time he came to Harlem on a case he got a violent headache" (45). Grave Digger and Coffin Ed piece together partial cases from mismatched narrative scraps collected on street corners, and justice is only improvised.

A contextual deficit in Himes's hard-boiled world sets readers, along with Coffin Ed and Grave Digger, adrift, feeling themselves into a world propelled by an already established but unenunciated logic. Typically, writes Fredric Jameson, hard-boiled violence finally eclipses events "lying half-forgotten in the pasts of the characters before the book begins" (Jameson, "Chandler" 86). According to Jameson, the hard-boiled inevitably sidetracks its reader from the "first plot":

> He [the reader] assumes it to be a part of the dimension of the present, of the events going on before him in the immediacy of his narrated universe. Instead, it is buried in that world's past, in time, among the dead evoked in the memorable closing page of *The Big Sleep*. (86)

Himes's texts incessantly signal that the past has never perished. In *The Big Gold Dream*, what is buried in the world's past resurfaces in the lives of dreamers.

The dreamer in question, or at least the first of many, is Alberta Wright, a "great cook and steady wage earner," and a recent convert to the Church of Wonderful Prayer, whose glitzy, charismatic Sweet Prophet assures his doting congregation that faith is "like a solid gold dream!" (17–18, 7).[3] As a picture puzzle, Alberta's dream is a doozy. "I dreamed I was baking three apple pies," she explains to a "sea of kneeling worshipers" on 117th Street, and "when I took them out the oven and set them on the table to cool the crusts busted open like three explosions and the whole kitchen was filled with hundred dollar bills" (7–8). As far as messages from the Lord go, this seems a fairly elementary cipher, since her fellow worshipers chorus "Money! Money! Money!" when they hear of her dream (8). Alberta has already taken the initiative to stake her last sixty dollars in "the three biggest houses in Harlem" and pulled home a cool profit of thirty-six thousand dollars for her efforts (126).

But Alberta's dream has a double sense, and not merely because her lottery winnings have inexplicably gone missing, or because she soon enters into a convulsive and apparently fatal "religious fervor" in the presence of Sweet Prophet, her body shaking—in the vulgar idiom Himes generally reserves for the religious—"like a nautch dancer" (10). Her dream is also a picture of domestic misuse. Though a "born kitchen mechanic," Alberta cannot make living with her hands. She is (explosive pastry notwithstanding) another economic casualty among the working poor (70). And though she is fully resuscitated from a corpselike state after collapsing at Sweet Prophet's street service (an attack apparently induced by a tainted draught of holy water), she appears ever afterward in terms of her proximate death. Sergeant Ratigan accuses Alberta of "playing dead," and the undertaker Mr. Clay describes her as the body "that came to life" (90, 72). Her work clothes also cast her among the departed. A little girl glimpses the woman "all in white like a ghost" fleeing the police as though her "tight-fitting white maid's uniform" and the white robes of a convert make an apparition or, as with Wilkie Collins's pallid "Woman in White," Alberta's phantasmal presence is the symptom of an inheritance embezzled and a counterfeit past (38).

In this way, the text's "big gold dream" is a sort of Chandlerian "big sleep" Himes tailored to a Harlem for whom death is less appalling than an interminable existence as the walking dead. Religion is, without a doubt, the favored opiate of the people. Sweet Prophet is an accomplished hypnotist who fleeces his flock, Alberta included, all the way to the bank. And plenty of Himes's other characters share a drowsy drug-induced state. Rufus, Alberta's onetime no-good husband, is "on the H" (93). Her erstwhile lover, Sugar Stonewall, spends his days abed and deals Alberta the "Mickey Finn" that puts her temporarily out of commission. The numbers runner Slick spokes opium from a pipe, his flunky Susie is never without a marijuana cigarette dangling from the corner of his mouth, and the mysterious "sepia-colored" blonde Slick keeps in his apartment is a junkie who has "been sniffing it for so long she didn't know what life was without it and couldn't live such a life for one full day" (117). These individuals are dreamers, dream dealers, and they dream mostly of money. In fact, the bed is converted to a bank; the Jewish furniture dealer Abie points out, "The mattress [is] . . . colored people's strongbox, ha" (29). Alberta is convinced that the place for her money is her mattress: "I got to thinking it would be safer if I slept on it" (130).

More importantly, Alberta's bare existence and interminable subjugation signal, as I have suggested above, a history that has been chucked to oblivion, discounted, presumably erased from sight. Her past is a southern past; in *The Big Gold Dream*, the aftereffects of slavery and the Great Migration reveal themselves intermittently and in peculiar forms. When Sugar Stonewall (whose name one must assume is a sarcastic tribute to General Jackson) rummages through Alberta's apartment, he demolishes antiques, discarding "the skeletons of the two overstuffed armchairs" to the side "like the bones of a carcass" (29). The "the Jew" Abie (a character whose acquisitive habits corroborate Himes's typically uncensored anti-Semitism) examines Alberta's still-intact sofa as if "he were assaying a prime beef" (29). Himes's "ur" and only Jewish character in *The Big Gold Dream* is a skilled interpreter of antebellum goods, and he concludes that Alberta's furniture is "Marvelous. More than a hundred years old. Made in New Orleans. Been through the Civil War. Extraordinary!" (29). Having somehow made their way up river, her crummy antebellum furnishings are now prodded, priced, and purchased like chattel. What is more, Abie discovers a thousand hundred-dollar bills in crisp and utterly worthless Confederate currency stashed inside her sofa. This amuses him about as much as the treasure of the Sierra Madre: "Suddenly he bent double, laughing as though he had gone stark raving crazy" (31).

Alberta is saddled with odd remnants of another era. What she possesses once belonged to a past and a place where she might have been a possession. The remains of this realm are a fortune in fool's gold, and Rufus is the fool who kills to get it and is killed for it—drawing Susie, a new fall guy, into the mix. And when Susie flashes his roll of Confederate banknotes to a "chippy," then fails to pay for services rendered, the girl explains to her pimp that "he Georgiaed me!" (56). While Alberta Wright never recovers the jackpot, what is ostensibly its surrogate object in the text (Confederate cash) seems less an uncomplicated proxy for Alberta's money than a far-reaching effect of condensation and displacement, an agglomeration of latent matter that coalesces in a single block of manifest content by associative processes that generate "intermediate thoughts . . . which are often ingenious" (Freud, *On Dreams* 29). This bundle of Confederate notes, a novelistic red herring, is conspicuously joined to a genealogy of violence and a trail of theft: black slavery and civil death, debt peonage, and a migration north, where virtual servitude, economic deprivation, and an urban ghetto are merely the constituent features of new forms of bare life. In Himes's plot, this anachronistic object—"ninety-four years late and in a different country" (103)—strings together a series of misdirected acts into what could only produce a narrative "dead line," a mission punctured of any purpose but to link present and past. Himes pulls this punch line twice. "Bent double" with laughter over the sheaf of hundred-dollar bills, "the Jew" is shot in both arms, blinded with pain and battered to death (31). Later, a receiving teller at Chase National Bank chokes with laughter and explains, "in a strangled voice," to Sweet Prophet's devotee Sister Hopeful that the money is no longer "legal tender," though he "hesitantly" suggests that the bills are "valuable as a souvenir—if you're from the South" (103).

The recurrence of these "dead notes" is not just a gag, however. It is a historical illustration of a narratological tactic. *The Big Gold Dream* hinges on an incident prior to the text and unthinkable inside it. Even before the opening pages, Sweet Prophet's hypnosis has drafted Alberta into a dream state; this dream state has made a dummy of her; she has, for this reason, already delivered her winnings to the Prophet, instrumental in the theft of what is her own; and this theft *avant la lettre* wholly nullifies the novel's course. The counterfeit Confederate cash instructs the reader to register theft in terms of its historical antecedents and as a thing that violently conscripts human bodies. Himes indicates that to follow the narrative is to look before it—or to look awry, by calling upon a vantage point that reconfigures textual authority and sways the direction of the plot and of justice. In *The Big Gold Dream*, this disruptive adjustment requires reallocating the narrativization of crime to those whose practices of enunciation arise from silence, muteness, and blindness.

The Big Gold Dream demands a different kind of storytelling and also a different kind of storyteller, and that job is handed over to Grave Digger and Coffin Ed's best stool pigeon. Dummy is an ex-prize-fighter and deaf-mute who has been beaten within an inch of his life on more than one occasion. Boxing put out his ears ("the racketeers who owned him sent him to the tank so often he got both his eardrums burst" [54]) and gangsters cut out his tongue when he agreed to squeal in front of the state committee. With his "lumpy" face "interlaced with tiny scars" and his "pile hammers for hands," he comes off as a composite Quasimodo taken straight out of *The Killers* (55). Needless to say, Dummy cannot speak in the ordinary sense of the word: swallowing, he sounds like a "baby burping" (118); injured, he is "mewling like a cat" (150); and when asked to make an official statement to the police, "Dummy's mouth flew open, and choking sounds issued from the gruesome cavity" (63). The "gaping black hole where normally a tongue should have been" is an alarming caricature of his muteness, like a cartoon balloon expunged of its contents and blacked out in advance (54). For all these impediments, Dummy's role in the novel is remarkable. He is a writer. He compiles phrases punctuated by slashes with a "dirty scratch pad and stub of pencil" (61), and these bulletins, whether fact or fiction, act as stimulants, prodding the plot forward. Dummy is the informant who advises Slick to be wary of Susie: *"the punk is doublecrossin you"* (113). He also torments Sugar with a preliminary account of Rufus's murder: *"i saw you kill him but i didn't tell"* (83). Coffin Ed and Grave Digger are the recipients of a more detailed version of events:

> *rufus drove up / mugger braced him in car / pulled him out / put knife on throat / pushed him toward outhouse / rufus try to run / mugger stab him in back / keep stabbin / rufus down on hands and knees / crawl into the bush / mugger follow / i didn't see nobody come out* (62)

Dummy's suggestive scribblings and this passage, a sort of storyboard of heterodiegetic proceedings and one of his many selective accounts of events, demonstrate his talents as narrator. More importantly, they indicate the power he wields over others' perceptions. Not only are Dummy's publications concocted to put him at an advantage—though it is certain that he wants, as Slick observes, "to cut himself a piece of the pie" (122)—but his well-advertised cache of local knowledge also makes him a formidable ally. He's got the figures on the furniture scam and is hot on the trail of Alberta's money and, as Sugar comments, "Dummy wasn't the kind to waste his efforts on wild-goose chases" (74). The silent audience to Slick and Susie's latest chicanery, Dummy watches them dupe one of Sweet Prophet's secretaries with a cash-filled manila envelope full of "civil war money."

Of Himes's first project for Marcel Duhamel, *The Five-Cornered Square* (*La Reine des Pommes*, also *For Love of Imabelle*), Jonathan Eburne writes, "The novel is stricken a priori with an epidemic of blindness, both literal and metaphorical, whose manifestations sabotage the possibility of clear vision or metaphysical insight" (255). In *The Big Gold Dream*, blindness has swelled to a chronic condition in a Harlem where Providence is a "blindfolded man" who draws the daily numbers for the Tia Juana house (112). Himes editorializes that "if there were no eyewitness accounts, the detectives had to depend on stool pigeons" (58) and it is true that, in this world of blind men, the deaf and mute dummy is a kind of king. Yet in an extraordinary turn of events, Coffin Ed and Grave Digger Jones also defer to a blind woman's explanation of the murders.

She is nameless, an exotic of indeterminate origin, a composite woman: blonde and "sepia-colored" with distended pupils and eyes slanted "like an Oriental's," attired in a "Chinese gown of deep purple silk" (117). She scarcely speaks, and she moves with a silence so palpable that even Dummy can sense it, "although he couldn't hear it" (119). She is also Slick's mute attendant, administering opium at his bidding while Dummy and Susie look on. Having completed that task, "She flowed silently from the room without having once looked at any one" (118). When Grave Digger and Coffin Ed come by looking for Slick Jenkins, she peers past the chain lock, "but not directly at either of them" and curtly responds, "Slick isn't in" (134). Presently, the detectives return, this time with a typewritten letter they call a "search warrant." They place the paper in front of her, and "her eyes looked down in the direction of the letter but, when she reached for it her hand went aside" (149). Finally Grave Digger presses the document into her hand, but she instantly returns it. "'I see,' she said in a low voice" (149).

This reply is certainly not an attempt to conceal her blindness, since she has already inadvertently played that hand and knows it. Instead, it authorizes the officers' intrusion without question, taking them in at their word. Her "low voice" gives them the go-ahead, and whether or not we can speak of collusion, at some point during the officers' entry and the subsequent fray, she ceases to be a "well-kept" woman and becomes, against all odds, an "eye witness" against Slick Jenkins, on whom she pins the murder of "the Jew." Her testimony is, moreover, accompanied by "substantiating evidence": a billfold identified as the property of one Abraham Finkelstein, and Slick Jenkins's suit, blood-stained in the shoulder where Rufus stabbed him (155). Nevertheless, the two detectives back her statement before Sergeant Frick, having "exchanged" what we can only assume are meaningful "looks" (155), and Coffin Ed tells Grave Digger he is confident that "she'll make it stick" (156). What is more, when Frick worries that her statement won't hold up in a court that bars a woman from testifying against her spouse, the blind woman interrupts:

> "I'm not his wife," she said in that tired, dead voice. "I'm just a woman he blinded, beating me with his fists."
> During the embarrassed silence that followed, no one looked at anybody else. (155)

In the wake of this final declaration, "no one looked at anybody else," a gesture which could not possibly have been made out of respect for the irreversibly injured party, but as if, having failed to see what was before them, they find that the only appropriate penance is to temporarily relinquish their own vision. Ironically, the first penalty Slick faces as the recipient of the blind woman's justice is to be deprived of his sight as well. While waiting for Sergeant Frick to arrive, Coffin Ed and Grave Digger administer a battering severe enough that Slick's "face was swollen, as though he had run into a nest of hornets, and his discolored eyes were almost shut" (153).

As with Dummy's broken sentences, the sightlessness and "dead voice" of a single woman wield an unusual power. She administers a justice that operates outside the realm of empirical evidence and, in the realm of ethical imagination, beyond the law and seemingly from beyond the grave—or is it just on the lower frequencies? Her account is at odds with the facts but supersedes them. It is a record true out of juridical necessity, the alternate story line in a novel that is twice plotted. Himes allows it authority. It is the one that sticks.

> "He had a dream," I says, "and it shot him."
> Mark Twain, *Huckleberry Finn*

Critics have observed that Chester Himes deftly constructs a "fantastic image of society-as-open-market" in his Harlem novels, a society built entirely of "appetitive self-interest" (McCann 283), each citizen conscripted to the frantic pursuit of some alluring but illusory commodity ("Object X") modeled on Dashiell Hammett's *Maltese Falcon* (Soitos 151). Certainly his narratives have the momentum of hard-boiled detective fiction, often accelerating toward predictably grim finales like a cement block dropped off a cliff—assuming that cliff were paved with corpses. And yet these books also race in reverse, irradiating a residue of economic injustice that far precedes the narratives' temporal coordinates, grinding to a halt only when they land in the muck of the nineteenth century. If Himes's books lay out an "unsentimental" critique of the sociopolitical and economic order (Crawford 187), that trawl has bait and a hook: first some criminal relic of the past crops up in some absurd and unexpected place; it reels the reader to a "story of the crime" that is not simply outside the "immediacy of his narrated universe"—to return to Jameson's description of the hard-boiled text—but past what is "buried in *that* world's past," until he regards the past itself ("Chandler" 86, my italics). To put this another way, Himes's detective fictions are inelegant texts set at ungainly angles, awash with narrative paroxysms and ingenious anachronism. There is something outside the world of the narrative that stains it, and this stain becomes the source of an "irritant opacity," a devastating cognitive dissonance or true blind spot, which denotes that "available knowledge serves only to demonstrate that it should no longer serve to sustain the knower" (Godden 5). In *The Big Gold Dream*, the psychodynamics of interracial sociability and a sociology of racialized labor are that latent content situated just beyond the horizon of the narrative. They are something like the closeted "corpse" of James Baldwin's "Notes for a Hypothetical Novel," whose presence is indicated only by a tied tongue, a useless currency, a painful silence.

The fact that a work like *The Big Gold Dream* intermittently admits these stammerings of the unconscious may distinguish it from the typically delimited realms of classical detective fiction, which, in his well-known essay "The Simple Art of Murder," Raymond Chandler eviscerated for its cozy insulation from the world, its "depressing way of minding its own business, solving its own problems and answering its own questions" (977). In spite of its "urban locale, a disordered society, and a final dissolution" (Grella 116), however, hard-boiled detective fiction is, as a genre, no less gentrified than its predecessor. Chandler maintained that "Hammett took murder out of the Venetian vase and dropped it into the alley" (988)—but what is the well-established whiteness of early hard-boiled fiction[4] if not a failure to dedomesticate that housebroken machinery of detective fiction's golden age, a failure to disinter a history of interracial sociability—which, even in Himes, turns up only in what we might call textual somniloquy? "To change the voice, to let the Other speak," Maureen Reddy has argued, requires "replacing the traditional central consciousness with another that does not share the ideology of the racial (or sexual or gender) identity around which the genre formed" (9). Then it is only by forsaking the genre's "central consciousness" and situating ourselves at its margins that we might entertain the not-quite-enunciated proposition that riddles Himes's fictions: that an interracial modernity has left wounds that, however carefully cauterized, return in the form of phantom pains.

In *Black Reconstruction*, DuBois declares that the entire "phantasmagoria" of race subjugation in the United States "has been built on the most miserable of human fictions: that in addition to the manifest differences between men there is a deep, awful and ineradicable cleft which condemns most men to eternal degradation" (705–6). And yet in "The Relations of the Negroes to the Whites in the South," he observes that "the white man as well as the Negro is bound and tied by the color line and many a scheme of friendliness and philanthropy, of broad-minded sympathy, and generous fellowship between the two has dropped still-born" (332). To investigate the origins of classical detective fiction in an American context, I have argued, is to appreciate that the manifest content of recognizable detection texts is subsidiary to the narrative apparatus that organizes them. Assembling a genealogy of detective fiction and its devices in an American context allows us to parse the shape of an American "phantasmagoria," to unleash what James Baldwin calls the "corpse" that "is in the closet," which we may otherwise only "inadvertently stumble on." In this way, exploring an integrated literary canon of proto- and peripheral genre texts alongside popular detective fictions underscores the significance of detective fiction to U.S. literary production. As a repository for a narrative "intelligence" fundamentally entwined with the possibility of an American interracial sociability, it traces an interracial history of the nation—and if "we can't talk about that," to invert Baldwin's proposition, "we can't talk about anything."

Notes

Introduction

1. Early accounts of detective fictions' origins by the likes of Dorothy Sayers and Howard Haycraft trace nearly a direct path from Edgar Allan Poe's Dupin tales to Arthur Conan Doyle's stories in *The Strand*, and credit only a few nineteenth-century authors with contributions to the classical detective novel (e.g., Emile Gaboriau, Charles Dickens and Wilkie Collins, with perhaps a nod to Eugène François Vidocq or James Fenimore Cooper). Recent correctives to this anticipatory, backward-projecting history of detective fiction propose a much vaster set of antecedents for the genre, generally adopting Alastair Fowler's notion of "polygenesis" to establish a potentially diverse provenance for detective fiction in all manner of eighteenth- and nineteenth-century crime writings, as well as gothic and sensation fictions. This inclusive attitude emphasizes the messiness of genre formation. It is also militantly antiteleological. Furthermore, this approach invites new studies of mass culture (e.g., the role of serialized and dime-novel popular fictions' contributions to the development of the detective figure) and encourages recognition of the early contributions of women authors. For early accounts of the genre's origins, see Sayers and also Haycraft; a fine example of more inclusive tendencies is Sussez's *Women Writers and Detectives in Nineteenth-Century Crime Fiction*.

Unfortunately, an inclusive stance risks granting some manner of membership or generic affiliation to representations of crime and mystery whose formal likeness to detective fiction is almost negligible, yielding an agglutinate genre origins that verges on the conceptually useless. The danger of this inclusive, less discriminating genealogy of crime fiction—and especially its concession to the smallest "family resemblance"—is that it can become *too* messy, and ceases to produces meaningful literary categories. And, perhaps counterintuitively, it mobilizes the relative "prestige" of detective fiction to confer legitimacy by association on a diverse set of texts whose historical relevance and social uses may be obscured rather than illuminated if scholarly work on detective fiction supplies a critical agenda. This inadvertent colonization of texts under the auspices of the detective genre paradoxically reinforces the notion that a broad array of popular or mass fictions cannot be legitimate objects of study in their own right. This book undertakes what I believe is a more productive approach: to acknowledge the far-reaching significance of detective fiction and various devices for U.S. literary production in the nineteenth century without indiscriminately insisting that texts that bear some resemblance to the genre ought to be classified as detective fictions. Nevertheless, we might study such peripheral or outsider texts to better grasp the origins of detective fiction's devices.

2. Charles Rzepka designates this activity "analeptic invention": "Detection demands that we cast backwards as many different threads as possible, and try to hang all revealed, as well as all metonymically conceivable, events on each of them, simultaneously" (*Detective Fiction* 28). These "arrays" of possible events are pared to a single "master array," which represents the story of the crime.

3. For a detailed inventory and discussion of narrative conventions associated with detective fiction, see Pyrhönen, *Murder from an Academic Angle*. Sayers compares different approaches to focalization in her introduction to "The Omnibus of Crime." Donna Bennett describes distraction, fragmentation, and narrative ambiguity in detective fiction.

4. In *The Production of Difference*, Roediger and Esch emphasize their indebtedness to Lisa Lowe's *Immigrant Acts*, which "insists both on the centrality of class and on the necessity of transcending any tendency within Marxism to isolate analyses of work from the specifically racialized bodies and histories of those performing it" (Roediger and Esch 8). In this same vein, *Dreams for Dead Bodies* attempts to avoid representing race and class as discrete (rather than entangled and, in certain cases, mutually constitutive) social phenomena.

5. I am not unilaterally differentiating the literary texts examined in this study from works that participate in what Philip Fisher has called the "freezing into place of a situation of hard and irrevocable fact" (25). However, if nineteenth-century American literature had the power to fundamentally alter habits of moral perceptions, to generate space in which "the unimaginable becomes, finally, the obvious" (8), I do think that the self-referential quality of these fictions frequently engenders something akin to distantiation, unsettling or even revoking the very ground upon which all facts are anchored.

6. I also use the term "interracial" to modify "detective fiction" because the genre is, in its unmodified state, implicitly the property of whites, a presumption this study contests. This assumption is evident, for instance, in the frequency with which historians of the genre interpret the emergence of a variety of "ethnic" detective fictions in the United States as part of a liberal project: nonwhite authors' pursuit of the public sphere via the "appropriation" or revision of an ideologically "white" genre. Not only does this discount the markers of ethnic and racial difference in which, I argue, the earliest instances of detective fiction are interested and even invested, but it obscures that the mechanisms of the genre have long been implemented by black and white authors alike—as well

as authors who were neither black nor white. Moreover, the commonplace that detective fiction is "white" solidifies assumptions about whites' presumed purview over the rational and the ratiocinative—a less than sensible move that nevertheless leads critics to cry "false consciousness" when discussing those "ethnic" detectives who do not invent alternative methods for solving mysteries (e.g., a "black" style of detection).

7. Sharon Patricia Holland has insightfully critiqued this reflexive shift from "race and racism" to "racisms" in literary criticism, cautioning us that no perfunctory reallocation of critical attention will engender the multiracial literary criticism it is designed to inaugurate (*Erotic* 7). Rather, Holland points out that, "In calls to abandon the black/white dichotomy for more expansive readings of racism's spectacular effects, critics often ignore the psychic life of racism" (7). She advises literary critics that "to rethink slavery among us is to take seriously the ways in which its logic of property, belonging, and family reshaped each and every one of those concepts irrevocably, as well as the lives of the subjects—black, white, native, Hispanic—who lived within this discursive logic" (31).

8. Leaning upon Foucault's *Discipline and Punish*, most historicizing studies of crime and detective fiction in both British and American contexts have linked literary and generic developments as well as the content of detective fictions to developments within the realm of law enforcement, including courtroom reforms in the late eighteenth century, "real time" reports of crime in newspapers, and the professionalization of police and legal professions. D. A. Miller's *The Novel and The Police* argues that while a mediocre, ineffectual police force is sequestered at the edges of the plot in the nineteenth-century novel, an omniscient narrative style is its ancillary agent. Assigned to the "place of the police in places where the police cannot be," this narrative surveillance is accomplished with the utmost "discretion" (Miller 15–16). The detective would eventually become the supreme envoy of this apparatus of surveillance and a representative of the "pure architectural and optical system" that guaranteed the intelligibility of the social order (Foucault 205). This attention to the detective figure culminates in Ronald Thomas's masterful *Detective Fiction and the Rise of Forensic Science*, which argues that detective fictions materialized as a response to new forensic technologies, and that the detective emerged as the ambassador of "a specialized body of scientific knowledge" that promised to provide narrative order and give meaning and substance to semiotic non-sense and supervise society in its transition from "romantic-autonomous individual" to "the alienated bourgeois agent of the state" (11). More than textual space for the exhibition of new forensic devices, the detective figure it created was independently a device of truth; he introduced a new literacy with forensic approaches that "enable the body to function both as text and as politics" and "often prove to have a political genealogy that becomes inflected into the act of analysis the detective practices and promulgates" (3). See also Haltunnen, Worthington.

An alternate approach to historicizing the detective genre is exemplified by Sean McCann's *Gumshoe America*, which succinctly links the origins of and decisive renovations to the genre to moments of political crisis, illuminating how the classic detective formula dramatizes the central tensions related to classical liberalism, rehearsing the "political myth" of classical liberalism: that "spontaneously created order was nothing more than the combined action of every rationally self-interested member of the community" (7).

9. Those summary executions ascribed to *La Terreur* began when *les enragés*—those revolutionaries who found themselves to the left even of the Jacobins—demanded a low fixed price for bread (*du pain*—a pun revisited in "The Purloined Letter" when Dupin closes a letter of revenge to Minister D. with a seal wrought from a crust). The mythical hoax of Laverna, goddess of thieves, was devised to pocket the grain of two villages. Kopley's *Edgar Allan Poe and the Dupin Mysteries* and DeLombard's *In the Shadow of the Gallows* track down very different historical sources for Poe's plentiful beheadings, which I engage in chapter 2.

10. "The Gold Bug" was simultaneously printed in the Philadelphia *Saturday Courier* on June 24, July 1, and July 8, 1843, very likely with the publishers' permission, since they had taken out a copyright on Poe's text. Moreover, this particular text, which appears as the first story in Poe's collected *Tales* (1845), would be reprinted repeatedly (regardless of copyright) at home, abroad, and in translation during Poe's own lifetime. See *Tales and Sketches* 805–6.

11. Wells places "The Gold Bug" among Poe's tales in the ratiocinative tradition, grouping it with other mystery stories that contain a "cipher interest," though she designates Legrand a "wonder-worker" rather than a detective per se (281, 102). Sayers's "The Omnibus of Crime" presents "The Gold Bug" as Poe's fifth contribution to the development of the detective genre; this tale belongs to the "mark-where-the-shadow-falls-take-three-paces-to-the-east-and-dig variety"—an "Intellectual" path of development for the genre that Sayers contrasts with the "purely Sensational" tendencies of "The Mystery of Marie Rogêt" (82–83).

12. Poe's narrator reports that Wolf's "uneasiness, in the first instance, had been, evidently, but the result of playfulness or caprice, but he now assumed a bitter and serious tone" (213)—an interpretive shift that strains all credulity. Is this equivocation proof of the narrator's pure guilelessness or a spectacular deadpan?

13. Rachel Howells receives far less attention in Brooks's interpretation of "The Musgrave Ritual" than she does in Doyle's text, though Holmes alone attempts to "reconstruct this midnight drama" that ended Brunton's life: "Was it a chance that the wood had slipped and that the stone had shut Brunton into what had become his sepulchre? Had she only been guilty of silence as to his fate? Or had some sudden blow from her hand dashed the support away and sent the slab crashing down into its place?" (621). Following Poe, Doyle preserves a certain ambiguity in the final lines, though he softens the blow: "Of the woman nothing was ever heard, and the probability is that she got away out of England and carried herself and the memory of her crime to some land beyond the seas" (623).

14. I am referring here to Slavoj Žižek's discussion of the *objet petit a* of Lacanian

discourse: the desire that paradoxically "posits retroactively its own cause," that non-existent object which "assumes clear and distinctive features only if we look at it 'at an angle,' i.e., with an 'interested' view, supported, permeated, and 'distorted' by *desire*" (*Looking Awry* 12). Along these lines, the Poe presented here is Doyle's most passionate invention.

15. With Brunton disposed of, Rachel Howells (whose biblical equivalent is "the lamb") disappears entirely—an expurgation that bears out Sean McCann's contention that though its characters are generally "driven by heedless self-interest or primal urges," classical detective fiction manages to "reverse that image by banishing a pair of scapegoats (murderer and victim) who embody the worst of those evils" (8).

16. Other ways of imagining this "anomalous" relation: a blood brotherhood procured by pricked palms clasped together and consecrated with spit; Dorian Gray's likeness (Oscar Wilde's *Portrait* and Arthur Conan Doyle's *The Sign of the Four* both cognates, of course, commissioned by John Marshall Stoddard for the English *Lippincott's* over a luncheon at the Langham Hotel in 1889); a child with a caul; or Lewis Carroll's looking glass world.

17. Indeed, Peter Thoms contends that in nineteenth-century predecessors to classical detective fiction, "the very form that emphasizes the piecing of narrative pattern also incorporates a contradictory impulse that subverts that story making process" (145). There is an internal engine of self-critique by which the books "register discomfort" with the "pleasures of detective fiction" (145).

18. The merging of "creative and resolvent" in the detective-figure traces back to Poe's Dupin. Maurizio Ascari rejects any binary opposition between supernatural revelation and scientific detection; instead, Ascari claims, it is "in the interstices of these dimensions that the appeal of much contemporary crime fiction still resides" (13).

19. Perhaps surprisingly, classical detective fiction has existed in uneasy relation to literary modernism. In "The Professor and the Detective" Marjorie Nicholson designated the clue-puzzle a sanctuary from literary modernism, not because it retained the style and social function of an earlier literary culture, but precisely because it transported the reader to a realm free of introspection and psychology, to a cosmos contained by cause and effect. Michael Holquist also positions classical detective fiction in opposition to "the high art of the novel with its bias toward myth and depth psychology" (162–64). By acknowledging its formal concerns (for instance, its tendency to disclose the constructedness of identity), Stephen Knight draws a more nuanced conclusion, situating the clue-puzzle as "modernist to some degree but also inherently humanist" (90). From the vantage point of the twenty-first century, the rift between detective and "literary" fiction is "often predicated on attempts to construct both detective fiction and modernism in opposition to the postmodern and what is often called 'anti-detective fiction' and invariably rely on partial, limited definitions of what constitutes literary modernism in the first place" (Marcus 252–53).

Chapter 1

1. The genealogy of these works has been a matter for massive speculation, as Twain biographer Albert Bigelow Paine merged the three texts for publication, leading half a century's worth of critics to gauge the temperament of Twain's final years from the happy ending Paine slapped on to the first of the three manuscripts, *The Chronicle of Young Satan*.

2. Hilton Obenzinger observes that No. 44 could easily pass for Satan; he also resembles Jesus, the enfant terrible of the apocryphal "Infancy Gospel of Thomas," which is said to have interested Twain, and he is undeniably a "carnival hybrid of cultural contact, one that absorbs characteristics of the colonized within the colonizer" (178). Furthermore, Obenzinger characterizes No. 44 as an antic "bad-boy" whose typesetter's joke produces a dizzying effect that comments on new sound and film technologies.

3. The mandate of capitalist rationality, by contrast, demands that literature "must grow, and change form, and *never stop*," writes Moretti, and its protagonist "can never stop in space, his adventure can never come to an end in time, as Defoe discovered when writing the last pages of *Robinson Crusoe*. Last, not conclusive: he will immediately have to start writing a second *Robinson*. Yet the problem of how to end the novel is still unsolved: and so a third *Robinson*" (*Way of the World* 26). Defoe only finally extricates himself from this plight by turning to allegory, Moretti notes, "thereby abolishing the problematic of temporality instead of confronting it on its own territory" (26).

4. Houston Baker points to this "entrance examination" to Hampton Institute—as well as other moments in the text when Washington sweeps floors in the company and under the direction of white women as ritual episodes that escape the ordinary configurations of time and space in the South: "Taboos are suspended. We have a form of liminal or transitional instruction as Booker is transfigured from dirty *blackness* into 'Booker Taliaferro Washington'—a 'New Negro,' ahead of his time with respect to 'civilization,' and white womanist intimacy" (48–49).

5. Though industrial democrats essentially argued that the attributes of the political life should apply to market relationships, the practical application of such a theory nevertheless posed distressing implications for some members the middle classes. As Gail Bederman states in her seminal work *Manliness and Civilization*, white middle-class professionals who had in the past characterized themselves as genteel and respectable types were by the last decades of the nineteenth century far removed from the "small-scale, competitive capitalism" of previous generations. Instead, they were saddled with white-collar clerical work and little hope of promotion. These "sons of the middle class" had no guarantee they would ever exercise civic or social authority, and their status as potential "self-made men" was in doubt (Bederman 12). Some middle-class professionals had a genuine fear that political efficacy had migrated to the numerous and visibly muscular members of the working class, whose unionized strength approximated the "consent-as-agency" that middle-class men ought to have possessed. This "challenge to

their manhood" was no figment of the imagination (11); not only did the influx of immigrants and the politics of "New Woman" encroach on their civic authority, nearly seven million members of the working class joined in strikes during the last two decades of the nineteenth century, "an impressive number in a nation whose total work force in 1900 numbered only twenty-nine million" (14). Accordingly, the idea that industrial democracy could be an antidote to social unrest (rather than an exacerbation of it) remained contested. Howell John Harris summarizes: "A synthesis between these two conflicting opinions was possible: that trade unions were a good thing, in theory, and industrial democracy, in the abstract, desirable, though nobody really knew what it meant; but that union power was in practice suspect whenever it showed itself" (54).

6. No. 44's excessive, ironic performances are instances of signifyin(g), since "everything that must be excluded for meaning to remain coherent and linear comes to bear in the process of Signifyin(g)" (Gates 50). As such, signifyin(g) is the Lacanian Other of discourse; Gates also compares it to Bakhtin's "double-voiced word," which contains both the utterance and the speaker's evaluation of that utterance. To put this somewhat differently, we might interpret No. 44's entertainments as of an intensity "precisely beyond the limit at which enjoyment still gives pleasure," such that they exemplify a masochism that can "put in question the Good embodied in the State and common morals" (Žižek, *Sublime* 117).

Chapter 2

1. These tactics would be especially important for classical detection fictions that adhere to the conventions of "fair play," which requires "showing the reader everything yet simultaneously obfuscating its meaning." Pyrhönen, *Murder from an Academic Angle* 18.

2. David Roediger points out that white laborers had already distanced themselves from the perceived degradation associated with black slaves in the early nineteenth century, demanding that designations like "hired hand" or "help" replace servant (an occupation associated with both enslaved and free black workers), thereby making the case that their white labor, unlike that of black workers, was a product or service that could be detached from its owner and put on the market (50). In short, white laborers advanced a linguistic politics with a racialized subtext: "They were becoming white workers who identified their freedom and their dignity in work as being suited to those who were 'not slaves' or 'not negurs'" (49).

3. This line of argument, by which free labor is cleanly divested of the slave's attributes, is an anticipatory repudiation of slavery in concert with Kristeva's concept of the "pre-object" or "*fallen* object": the cause of that "radical revulsion (or *expulsion*) which serves to situate the 'I', or more accurately to *create* a first, fragile sense of 'I' where before there was only emptiness" (Moi in Kristeva 238). Hawthorne's "Truth-teller" censures those who would see utility in comparing themselves to slaves, thereby ranking them-

selves "with four-footed beasts and creeping things," foul, inhuman forms that evoke the wormy corpse of gothic fiction (qtd. in Foner and Shapiro 72). Disavowing resemblance to the slave was an act of differentiation that generated free labor, an identity-conferring renunciation that corresponds, as Anne Williams has suggested in her writings on the gothic, to "that early anxiety about materiality and the borders of the self: between 'me' and the 'improper/unclean' (in French the word *propre* means both 'one's own' and 'clean' as well as the extended 'propriety')" (75).

4. For a discussion of backward construction and the narrative closure it imposes as a form of erasure, see Sweeney, Hühn.

5. Pompey's operations anticipate the work of the fictional detective, particularly the two dominant modes of detection that Marjorie Nicholson identifies as the "Baconian method of Scotland Yard" and the strategy derived from Descartes (126). The "Baconian method" involves the use of material evidence (papers and artifacts) as metonymic traces or clues to reconstruct the story of the crime and to challenge the testimony of witnesses and interested parties (126). Charles Rzepka has linked this mode to the work of the early historians Johann Gustav Droysen and Leopold von Ranke, "the latter of whom once stated that his aim was to describe the past '*wie es eigentlich gewesen*'—'as it really was'" (*Detective Fiction* 43). By contrast, a Cartesian approach to detection depends on imaginative identification with "the mind of the criminal" (44). In the person of Pompey, who pieces together the general's remains and essentially impersonates the Bugaboo and Kickapoo Indians, however, these two facets of detection are mobilized to unseat white hegemonic discourse.

6. For instance, on August 29, the senior editor of the *Constitutional Whig* in Richmond depicted the event as an outburst of irrational violence, juxtaposing the heinous murders perpetrated by Turner's "drunk and desperate" crew with the temperament of their victims, slaveholders "distinguished for [their] lenity and humanity" (Tragle 53). The *Whig* concluded that the murderers "acted under the influence of their leader Nat," and even Turner himself "had no ulterior purpose, but was stimulated exclusively by fanatical revenge, and perhaps misled by some hallucination of his imagined spirit of prophecy" (53). A day later, in Edenton, North Carolina, the *Edenton Gazette* reported that the revolt "is said to have been started by a white man, for some design unknown," and hastened to assure its readers that "we have detected no signs nor symptoms of an insurrectionary spirit; the slaves appear quiet, peaceable and unoffending and while we recommend *vigilance* to our citizens, we would likewise respectfully suggest they should not suffer the present excitement, to cause them to deviate from their accustomed mild and moderate treatment to the slaves" (56).

7. Critically, whatever begins to intimate itself as knowledge enters our perception only as a kind of knowledge that is hidden or has entered into hiding since, as Malcolm Bull explains, "hidden-ness" signals that the determination to be known "was not merely unsuccessful but frustrated in the sense that its defeat is inextricably linked to the proximity of achievement" (19). Thus, the specter of the Kickapoo Indians and white

industrial laborers can be described as "coming into hiding"—made more knowable as the extruded tensions that underlie the tale, and not quite covered over by its superficial content—since being hidden "simply means that when something becomes partially or selectively known the process of becoming accessible to knowledge is simultaneously a coming into hiding" (26).

8. Hawthorne's newspaperman does approximate the sensationalism with which the *Salem Gazette* treated this "Atrocious Assassination," but the storyteller's account only narrowly squares with these events in Salem, and not only because the victim of this "malicious deliberation unparalleled" was bludgeoned in the head and stabbed no less than thirteen times (Joseph White qtd. in Booth 209, Booth 202–3). In fact, the press was perplexed because it could not easily attribute any motive, business or otherwise, to the grisly crime, given that, as the *Salem Gazette* reported, the eighty-two-year-old White "had for years been almost secluded from the world, having long since retired from the active cares of his commercial pursuits." And while it is certainly plausible that the question of each conspirator's accountability (a subject to which the attorney Daniel Webster devoted no little time when he prosecuted the case) intrigued Hawthorne, it is nevertheless the case that Hawthorne differentiates the assassin in each iteration of Mr. Higginbotham's "catastrophe," which is twice told to Pike, then staged before his eyes. See "Atrocious Assassination," *Salem Gazette*, April 6, 1830.

9. Terence Whalen (112) describes Poe's "average racism" as a "strategic construction designed to overcome political dissension in an emerging mass audience," regardless of the author's much-debated perspectives on race. Along similar lines, I strongly doubt we can either exonerate the author or locate definitive proof of Hawthorne's racism in Dominicus Pike's casual use of a racist epitaph or the representations of black and Irish criminality "Mr. Higginbotham's Catastrophe."

10. This interpretation benefits from the insights of whiteness studies; see Ignatiev, Jacobson, Roediger.

Chapter 3

1. I take the notion of the "hidden transcript" from James C. Scott, whose *Domination and the Arts of Resistance* describes a realm of discourse that undercuts the "hegemonic aspirations" of the public transcript while evading the risks incurred by open modes of resistance: a "hidden transcript" or clandestine form of dissent cultivated by the subordinated in order to critique relations of domination. Apparitions of this otherwise undetected speech emerge in what Scott contends is a third realm, a hidden "contrapuntal" discourse (25), a "politics of disguise and anonymity that takes place in public view but is designed to have a double meaning" (19), even if they stop shy of any concrete or symbolic declaration that would overtly disrupt the smooth, homogenized workings of power (8).

2. Until recently, Poe scholars have generally grounded the author's proslavery stance

in the now infamous Drayton-Paulding review, which appeared in the April 1836 *Southern Literary Messenger*. An alarmist reply to slave revolt in the West Indies and to the burgeoning abolitionist movement, the Drayton-Paulding review bemoans antislavery advocates' assault on southern property. Moreover, the review applauds Mr. Paulding, a northerner, for his picture of the South in *Slavery in the United States*, lauding its saccharine romantic racialism and its "accurate" representation of the sentimental attachment between master and slave. In *Poe and the Masses*, Terence Whalen persuasively argues that the review is best ascribed to Beverly Tucker, a professor at the University of William and Mary, though, as John Carlos Rowe has pointed out, this authorship is less a litmus test for Poe's racism than is his "guilt by association." The sheer fact that Poe's writings for the *Southern Literary Messenger* were printed facing articles by well-known proslavery advocates, and that Poe stressed a unique identification with the "Editorial" capacities of the magazine, underscore his complicity in the review's publication. Moreover, the compatibility of Poe's racism with those views expressed in the Drayton-Paulding review is entirely substantiated by articles definitively accredited to Poe, such as his January 1836 review of Ingraham's *The South-West. By a Yankee*, which praises Professor Ingraham's vindication of southern slavery.

3. We might also note that an earlier issue of the *London and Paris Observer* includes an implausible account of "The Monkey Gentleman," an orangutan captured in Borneo who was sold to a French merchant in Chandernague, where he received the "rudiments of a modern polite education"—though he did not entirely cast of his "fashionable accomplishment of swearing" (No. 256 [April 25, 1830], 271). According to the *Observer*, the monkey "would waltz, and dance a quadrille," "was rather partial to riding," and "would spend hours in oiling and curling his moustachoes, and trimming his sidelocks and whiskers!" (271).

4. In essence, Kopley's approach to interpreting "Rue Morgue" differentiates detective fiction from "serious" literature, treating its textual fragments as links in a chain that bring forth narrative coherence. By contrast, "serious" literature requires its readers discover "symbolic depth" in the signifying activities of the text (Pyrhönen, *Murder* 38). Though plainly all narratives can be read superficially or symbolically, Martin Priestman argues that readers of detective fiction cannot make use of both strategies at the same time. Indeed, given the prestige of symbolic depth, he suggests that surface reading supplies a "down-market" explanation scholars use to account for *mass* readership (39).

5. Curiously enough, Kopley's strategy perfectly encapsulates an alternative definition of "morgue": a reference file of old clippings or "miscellaneous material" in a newspaper office, typically used to compose obituaries (OED).

6. This seems to be the interpretive route Arthur Conan Doyle adopted in *The Sign of the Four*, where the "primitive" Tonga, who hails from the Andaman Islands, cheerfully scales a building for his companion Jonatham Small to assassinate Bartholomew Sholto with a poison dart.

7. By contrast, Shawn Rosenheim argues that the "obsessive instances of mutilated

language" in Poe's detective tales (e.g. the "unequal voice" of the orangutan in "The Murders in the Rue Morgue") indicate that "for Poe the disjunction between linguistic and physical identity is always traumatic" (70).

8. In an 1845 unsigned review of his *Tales*, Poe applauds the accuracy of his depiction of Jupiter, remarking, "The negro is a perfect picture. He is drawn accurately—no feature overshaded, or distorted. Most of such delineations are caricatures" ("Edgar Allan Poe" 869). There is little doubt that the depiction of Jupiter subscribes to a humiliating breed of racial stereotypes, since the story implies he cannot function without Legrand, even as he adopts airs of superiority like Zip Coon. Such characterizations observe "the perverse logic of minstrelsy" that instantiates white supremacy (Peeples 41), and indicate Poe's allegiance to antebellum racism and black subordination.

9. Hegel's theory emerged, in all probability, as a reaction to slavery as an *actual* and not a metaphorical social arrangement erected and reinforced in tandem with racial categories. To be sure, Hegel's *The Phenomenology of Mind*, which was written between 1805 and 1806, remains silent on the question of the transatlantic slave trade and on recent events in Haiti. Susan Buck-Morss points out, however, that Hegel brought "into his text the present, historical realities that surrounded it," albeit "in invisible ink": he situated the slave opposite the master—in contrast to his French and British contemporaries, who regarded slavery as the product of a tyrannical state or some other violation of the rights of nature (846). Accordingly, "The actual and successful revolution of Caribbean slaves against their masters is the moment when the dialectical logic of recognition becomes visible as the thematics of world history, the story of the universal realization of freedom" (852).

10. Orlando Patterson's *Slavery and Social Death* disputes this insight, pointing out that the category of "worker qua worker has no intrinsic relation to slave qua slave"— that, in fact, even when the master class did not profit from the labor of its slaves, or experienced slaves as economic deadweight, slaveholders were amply rewarded in esteem from other slave owners as well as free nonslaveholding persons, all of whom could share in the timocratic values that depended on the social death of the slave (99). Accordingly, "The poorest free person took pride in the fact that he was not a slave" and the master class was recognized as "those most adorned with honor and glory" (99). Even if slave owners conceded the mutually degrading consequences of slavery for master and slave alike, Patterson argues, masters either "dropped all pretension to culture and civilization and simply indulged their appetites," resorting to a regime of brutal physical and sexual assault, or they abandoned the source of sullied wealth for some metropolis where their profits would confer honor and recognition (100).

11. C. B. Macpherson distinguishes "possessive individualism" as integral to nineteenth-century liberal democratic ideals; "possessive individualism" is what "regards the individual as human in his capacity as proprietor of his own person" and protects that individual "from any but self-interested contractual relations with others" in a market-based economy (151).

12. For this reason, Malcolm Bull argues that the dual articulation of consciousness inherent to mesmerism influenced Hegel's interpersonal *and* intrapersonal conception of the master-slave dialectic (233). Hegel's challenge to the unity of the soul, and his adoption of the bi-part soul (at once self-less and universal), relied on a theory of mesmeric relations. The upshot of this influence, Bull suggests, is Hegel's argument that "the potentially dominant pole of the subordinated individual remains, not of course fulfilling a dominant role, but as an unfulfilled potential or ineffectual residuum," which is activated through the bondsman's work (237). Moreover, the nascent potential Hegel attributes to the bondsman indicates "how being enslaved, like being magnetised, might paradoxically be a step towards universality and freedom" (Bull 239).

13. In his review of the novel, Poe reasons that a text like *Sheppard Lee* must contrive to present a multiplicity of narrators, yielding a sort of crazy-quilt version of the picaresque. Or, better yet, it must dramatize an assortment of events, but anchor them in a common denominator: the perspective of a single narrator. In this way, "The chief source of interest in each narrative is, or should be, the contrasting of these varied events, in their influence upon a character unchanging—except as changed by the events themselves" ("Sheppard Lee" 137).

14. Mesmer's ideas made their way across the Atlantic in the person of hydrographer Count Antoine-Hyacinthe Anne de Chastenet de Puysegur (a younger brother to Mesmer's prominent disciple the Marquis de Puysegur), who introduced animal magnetism to Haiti in June 1874 (Regourd 313). Incredibly, colonists soon entertained the possibility that Haitian slaves had appropriated magnetism to put its powers to malevolent purpose; slaves that participated in nocturnal ceremonies in the mountainous Marmalade district were brought to trial in 1786 for wielding mesmeric powers. The words "magnetised" and "mesmerize" appear in the trial records, yet Francois Regourd argues that this terminology "never appeared in judiciaries sources of that time in Saint Domingue as anything other than European words used by white judges for describing various parts of Vodou rites," which had been already independently documented in other sources (324). The very idea of a "black mesmerism," Regourd explains, was at the time merely a "smokescreen set between the traditionality of French judges, and the frightening manifestations of black Vodou nocturnal ceremonies," as well as an effort to delegitimize the idea of an autonomous "black occult knowledge" (324). There is little evidence that a hybrid, religio-scientific mix of mesmerism and voodoo ever existed. Nevertheless, the superimposition of de Puysegur's vocabulary on black voodoo practices had the effect of forever linking Mesmer's science with black slave religion and revolt (324).

15. Curiously, Bird's sequence on "negro insurrection" does not end with "the hanging of Nigger Tom," as Poe suggests in his review. After they are hanged and buried, Tom and his associates are exhumed by a group of young anatomists who propose to perform galvanic experiments on the corpses with a battery, hypothesizing that the dead slaves, when stimulated with electrical energy, will immediately perform those tasks they were most accustomed to in life. The musician Zip, or Scipio, when charged with that "ex-

traordinary fluid," presented "the lively spectacle of a man playing the fiddle in death" (2:212); Sam, "notorious for nothing so much as a great passion he had for butting with his head against brick walls, or even stone ones, provided they were smooth enough" (2:212), responds with "a jerk of propulsion equal in force to the butt of a battering-ram" (2:213), while Tom, in life habituated to playing the horse with young Tommy, does not go "galloping about the table" as expected but is instead entirely revived and runs from the room, seeking escape (2:213)!

16. Poe dismisses this dream denouement, however, asking, "What difficulty, or inconvenience, or danger can there be in leaving us uninformed of the important facts that a certain hero did not actually discover the elixir vitae, could not really make himself invisible, and was not either a ghost in good earnest, or a bona fide Wandering Jew?" ("Sheppard Lee" 139).

Chapter 4

1. According to Stephen Kern's *The Culture of Time and Space*, the great benefits of Edison's invention were to "to exercise greater control over what would become the historical past," and "to speak 'forward' in time to the unborn and listen 'backwards' to the dead" (38–39). In the decade before Hopkins's novel appeared, philosophers such as William James, Henri Bergson, and Edmund Husserl asserted the absolute necessity of introducing time and memory into each act of perception, without which, Kern explains, "melody would appear as a series of discrete sounds unrelated to what had gone before, understanding of ourselves would be chopped into unconnected fragments, and it would be impossible to learn a language or follow an argument" (43). Bergson went so far as to conceptualize the present as the "invisible progress of the past gnawing into the future," while he characterized duration as a rapacious beast that "gnaws on things and leaves on them the mark of its tooth" (qtd. in Kern 43).

2. Stephen Soitos also emphasizes Johnson's use of intuition and guesswork to solve the case; he argues that these talents fall outside the realm of Detective Henson's empirical skills and "seem directly related to Aunt Henny's hoodoo second sight, which may have been passed down to Venus" (66). Whereas Henson "functions much like an FBI director and seems to be modeled on a Pinkerton agent," Johnson's undercover success classifies her as a "double-conscious detective" (65). She demonstrates mastery of a "liberating manipulation of masks and a revolutionary *renaming*," an achievement Houston Baker calls "a primary move in Afro-American discursive modernism" (qtd. in Soitos 36), and one that she uses constructively, "to move in and out of the white world with safety and profit" (Nathan Huggins qtd. in Soitos 36).

3. Ronald Thomas convincingly shows that nineteenth-century forensic technologies had a "political genealogy." That is, the function of these "devices of truth" was to regard the body "as text and as politics," and forensic innovation was generally put in service of establishing and policing racial and national differences (3). The advent of fingerprint-

ing in particular was a remarkable addition to police science. Not only did Sir Francis Galton's 1892 work on the subject suggest an economical substitute for "anthropometry" or "signaletics," Alphonse Bertillon's elaborate set of physical measurements that was widely used at the time, but fingerprinting also had distinct implications for policing the body politic (201–3). The photographer Isaiah West Tauber, for example, had advocated the use of fingerprinting to monitor Chinese immigrants in San Francisco as early as the 1880s (204). The best-known literary illustration of this scientific novelty is, of course, Mark Twain's *Pudd'nhead Wilson* (1899). Twain had enthusiastically perused Galton's *Finger Prints*, which publicized the usefulness and permanence of these "physiological autographs" (Gillman 451). When Twain's protagonist David Wilson avails himself of the newfangled technology, he ends by distinguishing a free white man from a Negro slave—thereby fulfilling Galton's unrealized dream of implementing the fingerprint as a gauge of racial difference only a few years after *Plessy v. Ferguson* had chiseled that difference into law and public policy (Thomas 242).

4. Charles Sumner was notorious for his abolitionist convictions. The senator's 1856 speech "The Crime Against Kansas," a strongly worded indictment of proslavery forces, so affronted South Carolina representative Preston Brooks the latter responded by accosting Sumner with a cane on the Senate floor and beating him severely. Brooks's infamous assault was nothing less than "a plantation ritual in the highest halls of Congress," argues historian Manisha Sinha; the scandal brought home the South's brutal policies and "crystallized the black critique of racial slavery as an affront to American freedom and republican government" (236, 235).

5. For instance, the prominent northern businessman Arthur G. Sedgwick argued that "every deposit in a savings-bank is worth ten votes to him. His color will be forgotten as soon as he is 'respectable,' and to be 'respectable' in modern times means to exhibit the faculty of acquiring independent wealth" (qtd. in Cohen 74). During and after Reconstruction, the economic character of the freedman was to be assessed against these precepts. "Political Economy," the proslavery social theorist George Fitzhugh argued in 1866, "stands perplexed and baffled in the presence of the negro," to whom Fitzhugh attributed indolence and parasitism (qtd. in Fabian 127–28).

6. In *Petroleum V. Nasby*, David Locke also associates the exploitation of black bodies to fiscal speculation. The extremely limited curriculum of Nasby's Classikle, Theologikle, and Military Institoot demanded students devote their attention to "considerin the various texts wich go to show that Afrikin slavery is not only permitted by the skripters, but especially enjoined"—a scriptural account of slavery that banked on a traditional defense ("the cuss uv Noer"), and also adopted an evolutionary-biblical method of inquiry that would prove "the Afrikin nigger wuz reely the descendents uv Ham" (Locke 365). But the second duty of the institution was to train its students in the talents of the "troo Southern gentlemen": to "draw poker," "pitchin dollars," and so forth (366).

7. Mikhail Bakhtin presents the carnivalesque as antagonistic toward that which

"seeks to absolutize a given condition of existence or a given social order" (*Dostoevsky* 160); this razing of hierarchies is directly opposed to "consecration of inequality" Bakhtin associates with the despotism of official rites (*Rabelais* 10).

8. I will, of course, concede the very legitimate protest that readers of *Colored American Magazine* could not possibly have been and were not expected to make this association, while pointing out that in *Hagar's Daughter*, as in many detective narratives, signs reveal their proper meaning and sense only when they are revisited.

Chapter 5

1. In his autobiography *The Big Sea*, Langston Hughes confesses that he eschewed his doctor's advice to go to Rudolph Fisher for X-ray photographs of his ailing stomach and "went to another Harlem specialist I did not know," simply because he was intimidated by Fisher's brilliant sense of humor (245). Hughes was certain that the X-ray specialist and physician "would be full of clever witticisms of a sort that I could never find repartee for when I was in a normal state of mind, let alone now—with my mind in the far-off spaces and my stomach doing flops" (245).

2. Rudolph Fisher, "White Writers of Current Black Fiction" and Notes: Handwritten manuscript, undated, Rudolph Fisher Papers, MS-1U-F5, Brown University Archives, Box 2, Folder 14.

3. Miriam Thaggert contends that arguments about the aesthetic mediocrity of black writing by the late 1920s have become "another paradigmatic cliché" in critical conversations surrounding the Harlem Renaissance (17). By the end of that decade, she argues, critiques of an "earlier tepid, predictable writing" of novels calculated to "proclaim the worthiness of the Negro" at the expense of groundbreaking artistic expression (e.g., Walter White's *Fire in the Flint* [1924] and Jessie Fauset's *There Is Confusion* [1924]) indicate precisely "a growing awareness, a growing maturity" and *not* an end to the Renaissance, while short-lived journals such as Wallace Thurman's *Harlem* and *Fire!!!* endeavored to create space for ambitious artistic expressions, revealing a broad "desire for more nuanced depictions of black life and dissatisfaction with simplistic characters and tropes" (17–18).

4. Norman Klein, "Harlem Doctor Produces Dusky Sherlock Holmes," *New York Evening Post* (July 27, 1932), Rudolph Fisher Papers, MS-1U-F5, Brown University Archives, Box 4, Folder 44.

5. Rufus Gillmore, "Omnibus of Crime," *Time* (August 1, 1932), Rudolph Fisher Papers, MS-1U-F5, Brown University Archives, Box 4, Folder 44.

6. Eric Walrond, "At Home in Harlem," *New York Herald Tribune Books* (August 26, 1928), Rudolph Fisher Papers, MS-1U-F5, Brown University Archives, Box 4, Folder 36.

7. As an appendix to *The Walls of Jericho* (1928), Fisher included "An Introduction to Contemporary Harlemese, Expurgated and Abridged," which supplies translations of

many of the figures of speech and slang that appear in the novel—no doubt a rejoinder to the more ostentatious and formal "Glossary of Negro Words and Phrases" at the end of Carl Van Vechten's *Nigger Heaven* (1926). Significantly, Fisher's lexicon attaches idioms to place ("Harlemese") rather than race, as Van Vechten's does ("Negro Words"). Fisher includes a definition and etymology for "ofay": "A person who, so far as is known, is white. *Fay* is said to be the original term and *ofay* a contraction of "old" and "fay" (299); a dickty is both an adjective ("Swell") and a noun ("High-toned person") (298), while a rat is the "Antithesis of *dickty*" (298–99).

8. Ronald Thomas compares *Murder on the Orient Express* with Dashiell Hammett's *The Maltese Falcon*, arguing that Agatha Christie's detective Hercules Poirot is repeatedly aligned with the ideals of "European collective nationalism" and the League of Nations in the interwar period, in contrast to the "American isolationist policies" embodied by Hammett's Sam Spade (271). Thomas contends that the *Europeans* aboard the *Calais Coach* perceive America as "at once a savage and a progressive place," a site of "violence, irrationality, and crass materialism beneath whatever façade of civility it might present to the world" (272). Along these lines, Christie takes an "infamous event in American criminal history"—the kidnapping of Daisy Armstrong, which indisputably evokes the Lindbergh kidnapping—as "the originary crime that led to the narrative's complicated murder on a train" (269–70). While this view of America as "a frightening post-nationalist world of social and moral dislocation" captures the attitudes of the various passengers, it is worth pointing out that those suspects attached to the Armstrong household deliberate distance themselves from the United States to conceal their affiliation with the Armstrongs, and so ward off suspicion, while in reality they are a well-oiled machine that collaborates in a collective administration of vigilante justice. In other words, their colonization of the *Calais Coach* for the purposes of justice suggests less a "post-nationalist world of social and moral dislocation" as a portable nation-state, and a population whose communal bonds (cemented in the wake of crime) far transcend their superficial differences (272). In this light, the murder of Ratchett (alias Casetti) presumes a nation-state and a collectivity—unanticipated, perhaps, because of its internal diversity but nevertheless foreign to most European nations—that longs to expunge him. Their anti-American attitudes are a masquerade, as are the American stereotypes cultivated by the private detective (heavy-handedly named Cyrus Hardman) and by Mrs. Hubbard (Linda Arden, the famous actress and the Mother Goose who orchestrates the affair). The substance of America—and the household that is the metaphor for the relations between Americans—is a passionate, collective desire to administer justice albeit by disregarding the laws of other nations.

9. Harry Hansen, "A Corpse and Hocus Pocus in Harlem," *New York World News—Telegram* (Wednesday, July 27, 1932), Rudolph Fisher Papers, MS-1U-F5, Brown University Archives, Box 4, Folder 44.

10. Gremin Zorn, ed., "A Mystery that is Different," *Long Island Daily Press* (August 21, 1932), Rudolph Fisher Papers, MS-1U-F5, Brown University Archives, Box 4, Folder 44.

11. While challenging the pervasive and insidious representations of the Chinese American detective Charlie Chan—whom Frank Chin has called an "Asian Uncle Tom"—in the white popular imagination, Charles Rzepka argues that Earl Derr Biggers's first Chan novel, *The House without a Key* (1925) uses the detective genre to disrupt racist representational convention, enlisting the genre's "very tendencies toward racism to question racial stereotyping, even as he [Biggers] played the game of detection according to the genre's own rules" ("Race, Region, Rule" 1464). Moreover, while Rzepka discounts white writers' authority to depict "Asian humanity," he points out that Biggers's book avails itself of "a radically counterintuitive regionalist prototype," using urban Honolulu as a racially heterogeneous and inclusive "cultural grid" that dramatically undermines the sensationalized caricatures of sinister, all-male Chinatowns, ethnic enclaves that were themselves the effect of U.S. immigration policies and other discriminatory laws that systematically exploited the Chinese (1463–64, 1469).

12. Rufus Gillmore, "Omnibus of Crime," *Time* (August 1, 1932), Rudolph Fisher Papers, MS-1U-F5, Brown University Archives, Box 4, Folder 44.

13. Rudolph Fisher, handwritten note on the back of a letter from H. Brickhead at the Emmanuel Church Parish House in Baltimore, Mary 24, 1924, Rudolph Fisher Papers, MS-1U-F5, Brown University Archives, Box 4, Folder 1.

14. In his introduction to *City of Refuge: The Collected Stories of Rudolph Fisher*, John McCluskey Jr. contends that Fisher anticipated writing at least two sequels to *The Conjure-Man Dies*. At the time of his death, Fisher had already embarked upon the second novel in this series, provisionally titled "Thus Spake the Prophet" (McCluskey 28).

15. Though Fisher's depiction of the airshaft is decidedly dismal, the airshaft itself is an acoustic emblem of black urban experience, typified, for instance, in Duke Ellington's observation that "so much goes on in a Harlem air shaft. You get the full essence of Harlem in an air shaft. You hear fights, you smell dinner, you hear people making love. You hear intimate gossip floating down. You hear the radio. An air shaft is one great big loud-speaker" (qtd. in Thompson 131). In his unpublished story "Across the Airshaft," Fisher again characterizes the desolation of the airshaft: it is "deep, utter blackness, soft, impenetrable, measureless," though in this case it doubles as a space of fantasy and fairy tale (*City of Refuge* 277). After peering into this "abysmal emptiness," Fisher's fleeced, broke, and desperate rent-collector Rip Halliday discovers a vision across the airshaft: the beautiful, down-and-out Betty Green, whom he rescues (with the help of a clothesline) from the thug Buck Martin, whose business is "high-jackin' rent-collectors" (277, 283).

Conclusion

1. Pepper concedes, however, that the genre's "codes and conventions have, largely, been shaped by a set of white, male discourses" that potentially holds heavy sway over an exercise in the genre (210); this study rejects Pepper's conventional understanding of detective fiction's origins.

2. The least valuable of these fictions, Gina and Andrew Macdonald argue, are those whose exploitative engagement with ethnic and racial difference consists of forays into the exoticized terrain of the "Other." Nevertheless, they contend that meaningful "ethnic" detective fictions must also do more than textualize cultural difference.

3. *The Big Gold Dream* also incorporates what George Grella calls "the motif of the magical quack" in the person of Sweet Prophet, a street preacher whose "pseudoreligious fakery" and profession of "fleecing the credulous" place him among the cultish charlatans of hard-boiled fiction (114).

4. For a thorough discussion of the whiteness of hard-boiled detective fiction, see Reddy.

Bibliography

Adams, Henry. "Napoleon I. at St. Domingo." *Historical Essays*. New York: Charles Scribner's Sons, 1891. 122–77.

Althusser, Louis. *Lenin and Philosophy and Other Essays*. New York: Monthly Review Press, 1972.

Altman, Rick. *The American Film Musical*. Bloomington: Indiana University Press, 1989.

Anderson, Maureen. "The White Reception of Jazz in America." *African American Review* 38.1 (Spring 2004): 135–45.

Aptheker, Herbert. *American Negro Slave Revolts*. New York: International Publishers, 1963.

Ascari, Maurizio. *A Counter-history of Crime Fiction: Supernatural, Gothic, Sensational*. New York: Palgrave Macmillan, 2007.

Baker, Houston A. *Turning South Again: Re-thinking Modernism / Rereading Booker T*. Durham, NC: Duke University Press, 2001.

Bakhtin, M. M. *The Dialogic Imagination: Four Essays*. Ed. Michael Holquist. Trans. Caryl Emerson and Michael Holquist. Austin: University of Texas Press, 1981.

Bakhtin, M. M. *Problems of Dostoevsky's Poetics*. Ed. and trans. Caryl Emerson. Minneapolis: University of Minnesota Press, 1984.

Bakhtin, M. M. *Rabelais and His World*. Trans. Hélène Iswolsky. Bloomington: Indiana University Press, 1984.

Baldwin, James. "Notes for a Hypothetical Novel." *Baldwin: Collected Essays*. Ed. Toni Morrison. New York: Library of America, 1998. 222–30.

Barrett, Lindon. *Blackness and Value: Seeing Double*. New York: Cambridge University Press, 1998.

Barrow, David. "The Bound Apprentice." *Mark Twain Journal* 29.1 (1991): 13–21.

Barthes, Roland. *S/Z*. New York: Hill and Wang, 1974.

Bateson, Gregory. *Steps to an Ecology of Mind*. San Francisco: Chandler, 1972.

Bauer, William R. "Louis Armstrong's 'Skid Dat De Dat': Timbral Organization in an Early Scat Solo." *Jazz Perspectives* 1.2 (2007): 133–65.

Bauer, William R. "Scat Singing: A Timbral and Phonemic Analysis." *Current Musicology* 71–73 (2001): 303–23.

Beaney, Michael. *Frege: Making Sense*. London: Duckworth, 1996.

Bederman, Gail. *Manliness and Civilization: A Cultural History of Gender and Race in the United States, 1880–1917*. Chicago: University of Chicago Press, 1995.

Bennett, Donna. "The Detective Story: Towards a Definition of Genre." *PTL: A Journal for Descriptive Poetics and the Theory of Literature* 4 (1979): 233–66.

Bennett, Tony. *Outside Literature*. New York: Routledge, 1990.

Bensel, Richard Franklin. *Yankee Leviathan: The Origins of Central State Authority in America, 1859–1877*. New York: Cambridge University Press, 1990.

Berlin, Ira. *Slaves without Masters: The Free Negro in the Antebellum South*. New York: Pantheon, 1974.

Beuka, Robert A. "The Jacksonian Man of Parts: Dismemberment, Manhood, and Race in 'The Man That Was Used Up.'" *Edgar Allan Poe Review* 3.1 (Spring 2002): 27–44.

Biggers, Earl Derr. *Charlie Chan: Five Complete Novels*. New York: Avenel Books, 1981.

Bird, Robert M. *Sheppard Lee: Written by Himself*. New York: Harper and Brothers, 1836.

Blackmon, Douglas A. *Slavery by Another Name: The Re-enslavement of Black People in America from the Civil War to World War II*. New York: Doubleday, 2008.

Blight, David. *Beyond the Battlefield: Race, Memory, and the Civil War*. Amherst: University of Massachusetts Press, 2002.

Booth, Robert. *Death of an Empire: The Rise and Murderous Fall of Salem, America's Richest City*. New York: St. Martin's Press, 2011.

Borshuk, Michael. *Swinging the Vernacular: Jazz and African American Modernist Literature*. New York: Routledge, 2006.

Breu, Christopher. "Freudian Knot or Gordian Knot? The Contradictions of Racialized Masculinity in Chester Himes' *If He Hollers Let Him Go."* *Callaloo* 23.6 (Summer 2003): 766–95.

Brooks, Peter. *Reading for the Plot: Design and Intention in Narrative.* New York: A. A. Knopf, 1984.

Brown, Lois. *Pauline Elizabeth Hopkins: Black Daughter of the Revolution.* Chapel Hill: University of North Carolina Press, 2008.

Brown, William Wells. *Clotel; or, The President's Daughter.* London: Partridge and Oakey, 1853.

Buchanan, Joseph. *Outlines of Lectures on the Neurological Systems of Anthropology.* Cincinnati: Office of Buchanan's *Journal of Man,* 1854.

Buck-Morss, Susan. "Hegel and Haiti." *Critical Inquiry* 26.4 (Summer 2000): 821–65.

Bull, Malcolm. *Seeing Things Hidden: Apocalypse, Vision and Totality.* New York: Verso, 1999.

Bussey, Susan Hays. "Whose Will Be Done? Self Determination in Pauline Hopkins's 'Hagar's Daughter.'" *African American Review* 39.3 (Fall 2005): 299–313.

Caillois, Roger. "The Detective Novel as Game." *The Poetics of Murder: Detective Fiction and Literary Theory.* Ed. Glenn W. Most and William W. Stowe. New York: Harcourt Brace, 1983. 1–12.

Camfield, Greed. "A Republican Artisan in the Court of King Capital: Mark Twain and Commerce." *A Historical Guide to Mark Twain.* Ed. Shelley Fisher Fishkin. New York: Oxford University Press, 2002. 95–126.

Cappetti, Carla. *Writing Chicago: Modernism, Ethnography, and the Novel.* New York: Columbia University Press, 1993.

Cawelti, John G. *Adventure, Mystery, and Romance: Formula Stories as Art and Popular Culture.* Chicago: University of Chicago Press, 1976.

Cawelti, John G. "Canonization, Modern Literature, and the Detective Story." *Theory and Practice of Classic Detective Fiction.* Westport, CT: Greenwood Press, 1997. 5–16.

Chandler, Raymond. "The Simple Art of Murder." *Later Novels and Other Writings.* New York: Library of America, 1995. 977–92.

Christie, Agatha. *Murder on the Orient Express.* New York: Dodd, 1968.

Chu, Patricia. *Race, Nationalism, and the State in British and American Modernism.* Cambridge: Cambridge University Press, 2007.

Cohen, Nancy. *The Reconstruction of American Liberalism, 1865–1914.* Chapel Hill: University of North Carolina Press, 2002.

Copjec, Joan. "The Phenomenal Nonphenomenal: Private Space in Film

Noir." *Shades of Noir: A Reader*. Ed. Joan Copjec. New York: Verso, 1993. 167–98.

Coviello, Peter. "Poe in Love: Pedophilia, Morbidity, and the Logic of Slavery." *ELH* 70.3 (Fall 2003): 875–901.

Davis, Lennard J. *Factual Fictions: The Origins of the English Novel*. New York: Columbia University Press, 1983.

DeLombard, Jeanine Marie. *In the Shadow of the Gallows: Race, Crime, and American Civic Identity*. Philadelphia: University of Pennsylvania Press, 2012.

Denning, Michael. *Mechanic Accents: Dime Novels and Working-Class Culture in America*. New York: Verso, 1987.

Dew, Thomas Roderick. "Professor Dew on Slavery." *The Pro-Slavery Argument, as Maintained by the most Distinguished Writers of the Southern States*. Philadelphia: Lippincott, Grambo, 1853. 287–490.

Douglass, Frederick. "The Color Question." July 5, 1975. MS. Frederick Douglass Papers at the Library of Congress. *Library of Congress*. Web. November 11, 2013. http://www.loc.gov/item/mfd000413.

Dove, George N. *The Police Procedural*. Bowling Green, OH: Bowling Green University Popular Press, 1982.

Doyle, Sir Arthur Conan. *Sherlock Holmes: The Complete Novels and Stories*. Vol. 1. New York: Bantam Dell, 2003.

DuBois, W. E. B. *Black Reconstruction in America: An Essay toward a History of the Part Which Black Folk Played in the Attempt to Reconstruct Democracy in America, 1860–1880*. New York: Russell and Russell, 1962.

DuBois, W. E. B. *The Philadelphia Negro: A Social Study*. Philadelphia: University of Pennsylvania Press, 1996.

DuBois, W. E. B. "The Study of the Negro Problems." *Annals of the American Academy of Political and Social Science* 11 (January 1898): 1–23.

Eburne, Jonathan P. *Surrealism and the Art of Crime*. Ithaca, NY: Cornell University Press, 2008.

Edwards, Brett Hayes. "Louis Armstrong and the Syntax of Scat." *Critical Inquiry* 28.3 (Spring 2002): 618–49.

Elbert, Monica. "Nathaniel Hawthorne, *The Concord Freeman*, and the Irish 'Other.'" *Eire-Ireland* 29.3 (1994): 60–73.

Elmer, Jonathan. *Reading at the Social Limit: Affect, Mass Culture, and Edgar Allan Poe*. Stanford, CA: Stanford University Press, 1995.

Fabian, Ann. *Card Sharps, Dream Books, and Bucket Shops: Gambling in 19th-Century America*. Ithaca, NY: Cornell University Press, 1990.

Faust, Drew Gilpin, ed. *The Ideology of Slavery: Proslavery Thought in the Antebellum South, 1830–1860.* Baton Rouge: Louisiana State University Press, 1981.

Felski, Rita. "Context Stinks!" *New Literary History* 42.4 (Autumn 2011): 573–91.

Felski, Rita. "Suspicious Minds." *Poetics Today* 32.3 (Summer 2011): 215–34.

Fields, Barbara J. "Ideology and Race in America." *Region, Race, and Reconstruction: Essays in Honor of C. Vann Woodward.* Ed. J. Morgan Kousser and James M. McPherson. New York: Oxford University Press, 1982. 143–77.

Fisher, Philip. *Hard Facts: Setting and Form in the American Novel.* New York: Oxford University Press, 1985.

Fisher, Rudolph. *The City of Refuge: The Collected Stories of Rudolph Fisher.* Ed. John McCluskey Jr. Columbia: University of Missouri Press, 2008.

Fisher, Rudolph. *The Conjure-Man Dies: A Mystery Tale of Dark Harlem.* Salem, NH: Ayer, 1992.

Fisher, Rudolph. *The Walls of Jericho.* New York: A. A. Knopf, 1928.

Fisk, Theophilus. "Capital against Labor." *Workingman's Advocate.* July 25, 1835: 1.

Foner, Philip Sheldon. *History of the Labor Movement in the United States.* New York: International Publishers, 1947.

Foner, Philip Sheldon. *Organized Labor and the Black Worker, 1619–1973.* New York: Praeger, 1974.

Foner, Philip Sheldon, and Ronald L. Lewis. *Black Workers: A Documentary History from Colonial Times to the Present.* Philadelphia: Temple University Press, 1989.

Foner, Philip Sheldon, and Herbert Shapiro. *Northern Labor and Antislavery: A Documentary History.* Vol. 157. Westport, CT: Greenwood Press, 1994.

Foucault, Michel. *Discipline and Punish: The Birth of the Prison.* New York: Vintage, 1995.

Fredrickson, George. *The Black Image in the White Mind.* New York: Harper & Row, 1971.

Freud, Sigmund. *On Dreams.* Trans. James Strachey. New York: Norton, 1952.

Freud, Sigmund. "The Uncanny." *The Standard Edition of the Complete Psychological Works of Sigmund Freud.* Vol. 17. Trans. James Strachey. London: Hogarth, 1953. 219–52.

Fuller, Robert C. *Mesmerism and the American Cure of Souls.* Philadelphia: University of Pennsylvania Press, 1982.

Fulton, Joe B. *The Reverend Mark Twain: Theological Burlesque, Form, and Content.* Columbus: Ohio State University Press, 2006.

Gates, Henry Louis. *The Signifying Monkey: A Theory of Afro-American Literary Criticism.* New York: Oxford University Press, 1988.

Gibson, Arrell Morgan. *Kickapoos: Lords of the Middle Border.* Norman: University of Oklahoma Press, 1963.

Gillman, Susan. "'Sure Identifiers': Race, Science, and the Law in *Pudd'nhead Wilson.*" *Pudd'nhead Wilson and Those Extraordinary Twins.* Mark Twain. Ed. Sidney E. Berger. New York: Norton, 2005. 445–64.

Ginsberg, Lesley. "Slavery and the Gothic Horror of Poe's 'The Black Cat.'" *American Gothic: New Inventions in a National Narrative.* Ed. Robert K. Martin and Eric Savoy. Iowa City: University of Iowa Press, 1998. 99–128.

Ginzburg, Carlo. *Clues, Myths, and the Historical Method.* Trans. John Tedeschi and Anne C. Tedeschi. Baltimore: John Hopkins University Press, 1989.

Girard, Philippe R. *The Slaves Who Defeated Napoleon: Toussaint L'Ouverture and the Haitian War of 1801–1804.* Birmingham: University of Alabama Press, 2011.

Godden, Richard. *William Faulkner: An Economy of Complex Words.* Princeton, NJ: Princeton University Press, 2007.

Goddu, Teresa A. "Hawthorne and Class." *What Democracy Looks Like: A New Critical Realism for a Post-Seattle World.* Ed. Amy Schrager Lang and Cecelia Tichi. New Brunswick, NJ: Rutgers University Press, 2006. 131–43.

Gosselin, Adrienne Johnson. "The World Would Do Better to Ask Why Is Frimbo Sherlock Holmes? Investigating Liminality in Rudolph Fisher's *The Conjure-Man Dies.*" *African American Review* 32.4 (Winter 1998): 607–19.

Grella, George. "Murder and the Mean Streets: The Hard Boiled Detective Novel." *Detective Fiction: A Collection of Critical Essays.* Ed. Robin W. Winks. Englewood Cliffs, NJ: Prentice-Hall, 1980. 103–20.

Haddock, Joseph. *Psychology, or The Science of the Soul, Considered Physiologically and Philosophically.* New York: Fowlers and Wells, 1850.

Haltunnen, Karen. *Murder Most Foul: The Killer and the American Gothic Imagination.* Cambridge, MA: Harvard University Press, 1998.

Hammett, Dashiell. *The Maltese Falcon*. New York: First Vintage Crime, 1992.

Hammond, James Henry. "Hammond's Letters on Slavery." *The Pro-Slavery Argument, as Maintained by the Most Distinguished Writers of the Southern States*. Philadelphia: Lippincott, Grambo, 1853. 99–174.

Harris, Howell John. "Industrial Democracy and Liberal Capitalism, 1890–1925." *Industrial Democracy in America: The Ambiguous Promise*. Ed. Nelson Lichtenstein and Howell John Harris. New York: Cambridge University Press, 1993. 43–66.

Hartman, Saidiya V. *Scenes of Subjection: Terror, Slavery, and Self-Making in Nineteenth-Century America*. New York: Oxford University Press, 1997.

Hawthorne, Nathaniel. "Mr. Higginbotham's Catastrophe." *Twice Told Tales*. Boston: American Stationers Co., John B. Russell, 1837. 149–67.

Hawthorne, Nathaniel. "The Story Teller No. I. At Home." *New-England Magazine* 7 (November 1834): 352–58.

Hawthorne, Nathaniel. "The Story Teller No. II. The Village Theatre" *New-England Magazine* 7 (December 1834): 449–59.

Haycraft, Howard. *Murder for Pleasure: The Life and Times of the Detective Story*. New York: Carroll & Graf, 1979.

Hegel, Georg Wilhelm Friedrich. *Phenomenology of Spirit*. Trans. Arnold V. Miller. New York: Oxford University Press, 1977.

Himes, Chester B. *All Shot Up*. Chatham, NJ: Chatham Bookseller, 1973.

Himes, Chester B. *The Big Gold Dream*. Chatham, NJ: Chatham Bookseller, 1973.

Himes, Chester B. *The End of a Primitive*. New York: Norton, 1997.

Hoffman, Daniel. *Poe Poe Poe Poe Poe Poe Poe*. New York: Paragon House, 1990.

Holcombe, William M. *A Mystery of New Orleans: Solved by New Methods*. Philadelphia: J. B. Lippincott, 1890.

Holland, Sharon Patricia. *The Erotic Life of Racism*. Durham, NC: Duke University Press, 2012.

Holland, Sharon Patricia. *Raising the Dead: Readings of Death and (Black) Subjectivity*. Durham, NC: Duke University Press, 2000.

Holquist, Michael. "The Whodunit and Other Questions: Metaphysical Detective Stories in Post-war Fiction." *The Poetics of Murder: Detective Fiction and Literary Theory*. Ed. Glenn W. Most and William W. Stowe. New York: Harcourt Brace Jovanovich, 1983. 149–74.

Hopkins, Pauline E. *The Magazine Novels of Pauline Hopkins*. New York: Oxford University Press, 1988.

Hoppenstand, Gary, ed. *The Dime Novel Detective*. Bowling Green, OH: Bowling Green University Popular Press, 1982.

Horton, Carol A. *Race and the Making of American Liberalism*. New York: Oxford University Press, 2005.

Howe, Daniel Walker. *What Hath God Wrought: The Transformation of America, 1815–1848*. New York: Oxford University Press, 2007.

Howland, John. "'The Blues Get Glorified': Harlem Entertainment, Negro Nuances, and Black Symphonic Jazz." *Musical Quarterly* 90 (2008): 319–70.

Huang, Yunte. *Charlie Chan: The Untold Story of the Honorable Detective and His Rendezvous with American History*. New York: Norton, 2010.

Hughes, Langston. *The Collected Works of Langston Hughes: The Big Sea. Autobiography*, vol. 13. Ed. Joseph McLauren. Columbia: University of Missouri Press, 2002.

Hühn, Peter. "The Detective as Reader: Narrativity and Reading Concepts in Detective Fiction." *Modern Fiction Studies* 33.3 (1987): 451–66.

Hull, Richard. "Puns in 'The Gold-Bug': You Gotta Be Kidding." *Arizona Quarterly* 58.2 (Summer 2002): 1–18.

Hutchinson, George, ed. *The Cambridge Companion to the Harlem Renaissance*. New York: Cambridge University Press, 2007.

Ignatiev, Noel. *How the Irish Became White*. New York: Routledge, 2009.

Irwin, John T. *Doubling and Incest / Repetition and Revenge: A Speculative Reading of Faulkner*. Baltimore: Johns Hopkins University Press, 1996.

Irwin, John T. *The Mystery to a Solution: Poe, Borges, and the Analytic Detective Story*. Baltimore: Johns Hopkins University Press, 1994.

Jacobson, Matthew Frye. *Whiteness of a Different Color: European Immigrants and the Alchemy of Race*. Cambridge, MA: Harvard University Press, 1998.

Jameson, Fredric. "Modernism and Imperialism." *Nationalism, Colonialism, and Literature*. Minneapolis: University of Minnesota Press, 1990. 43–68.

Jameson, Fredric. *The Political Unconscious: Narrative as a Socially Symbolic Act*. Ithaca, NY: Cornell University Press, 1981.

Jameson, Fredric. "On Raymond Chandler." *The Critical Response to Raymond Chandler*. Ed. J. K. Van Dover. Westport, CT: Greenwood Press, 1995. 65–87.

Jameson, Fredric. *Seeds of Time: Utopia, Modernism, and Death*. New York: Columbia University Press, 1994.

Johnson, Barbara. "The Frame of Reference: Poe, Lacan, Derrida." *The Purloined Poe: Lacan, Derrida, and Psychoanalytic Reading*. Ed. John P. Muller and William J. Richardson. Baltimore: Johns Hopkins University Press, 1988. 173–212.

Kayman, Martin. *From Bow Street to Baker Street: Mystery, Detection, and Narrative*. London: Macmillan, 1992.

Kempton, Daniel. "The Gold/Goole/Ghoul Bug." *ESQ: A Journal of the American Renaissance* 33.1 (1987): 1–19.

Kern, Stephen. *The Culture of Time and Space, 1880–1918: With a New Preface*. Cambridge, MA: Harvard University Press, 2003.

Kirstein, Lincoln. *Lay this Laurel; an Album on the Saint-Gaudens Memorial on Boston Common, Honoring Black and White Men Together, Who Served the Union Cause with Robert Gould Shaw and Died with Him July 18, 1863*. Alt. Authors Richard Benson and Augustus Saint-Gaudens. New York: Eakins Press, 1973.

Knight, Stephen. "The Golden Age." *The Cambridge Companion to Crime Fiction*. Ed. Martin Priestman. Cambridge: Cambridge University Press, 2003. 77–94.

Knighton, Andrew. *Idle Threats: Men and the Limits of Productivity in 19th-Century America*. New York: New York University Press, 2012.

Knox, Ronald A. "Detective Story Decalogue." *The Art of the Mystery Story*. Ed. Howard Haycraft. New York: Biblio and Tannen, 1976. 194–96.

Kojève, Alexandre, and Raymond Queneau. *Introduction to the Reading of Hegel*. Ithaca, NY: Cornell University Press, 1980.

Kopley, Richard. *Edgar Allan Poe and the Dupin Mysteries*. New York: Palgrave Macmillan, 2008.

Kristeva, Julia. *The Kristeva Reader*. Ed. Toril Moi. New York: Columbia University Press, 1986.

Lacan, Jacques. *Écrits*. Trans. Alan Sheridan. New York: Norton, 1977.

Lacan, Jacques. "Seminar on 'The Purloined Letter.'" *The Purloined Poe: Lacan, Derrida and Psychoanalytic Reading*. Ed. John P. Muller and William J. Richardson. Baltimore: John Hopkins University Press, 1988. 28–54.

Larson, John Lauritz. *The Market Revolution in America: Liberty, Ambition, and the Eclipse of the Common Good*. New York: Cambridge University Press, 2010.

Lemire, Elise. "'The Murders in the Rue Morgue': Amalgamation Discourses and the Race Riots of 1838 in Poe's Philadelphia." *Romancing the Shadow:*

Poe and Race. Ed. Liliane Weissberg and J. Gerald Kennedy. New York: Oxford University Press, 2001. 177–204.

Levine, Robert S. *Dislocating Race and Nation: Episodes in Nineteenth-Century American Literary Nationalism.* Chapel Hill: University of North Carolina Press, 2008.

Lewis, Nathaniel. *Unsettling the Literary West: Authenticity and Authorship.* Lincoln: University of Nebraska Press, 2003.

Lichtenstein, Alex. "Racial Conflict and Racial Solidarity in the Alabama Coal Strike of 1894: New Evidence for the Gutman-Hill Debate." *Labor History* 36.1 (1995): 63–76.

Locke, David Ross. *The Struggles (Social, Financial and Political) of Petroleum V. Nasby [Pseud.] . . . Embracing His Trials and Troubles, Ups and Downs, Rejoicings and Wailings; Likewise His Views of Men and Things. Together with the Lectures "Cussed be Canaan," "The Struggles of a Conservative with the Woman Question," and "In Search of a Man of Sin."* Boston: Lee and Shepard, 1872.

Macdonald, Andrew, and Gina Macdonald. "Ethnic Detectives in Popular Fiction: New Directions for an American Genre." *Diversity and Detective Fiction.* Ed. Kathleen Gregory Klein. Bowling Green, OH: Bowling Green State University Popular Press, 1999.

Macpherson, C. B. "Revolution and Ideology in the Late Twentieth Century." *Revolution.* Ed. Carl Joachim Friedrich. New York: Atherton Press, 1966. 139–53.

Marcus, Laura. "Detective and Literary Fiction." *The Cambridge Companion to Detective Fiction.* Ed. Martin Priestman. New York: Cambridge University Press, 2003. 245–68.

Marx, Karl. *Capital: A Critique of Political Economy.* New York: Modern Library, 1906.

McCann, Sean. *Gumshoe America: Hard-Boiled Crime Fiction and the Rise and Fall of New Deal Liberalism.* Durham, NC: Duke University Press, 2000.

McDougall, Walter A. *Throes of Democracy: The American Civil War Era, 1829–1877.* New York: Harper, 2008.

McNamara, Kevin R. *Urban Verbs: Arts and Discourses of American Cities.* Stanford, CA: Stanford University Press, 1996.

Michelson, Bruce. *Printer's Devil: Mark Twain and the American Publishing Revolution.* Berkeley: University of California Press, 2006.

Mihm, Stephen. *A Nation of Counterfeiters: Capitalists, Con Men, and the*

Making of the United States. Cambridge. MA: Harvard University Press, 2007.

Miller, D. A. *The Novel and the Police.* Berkeley: University of California Press, 1988.

Miller, Jacques-Alain. "Suture (Elements of the Logic of the Signifier)." *Screen* 18.4 (Winter 1977–78): 24–34.

Miller, Russell. *The Adventures of Arthur Conan Doyle.* New York: St. Martin's Press, 2008.

Mink, Louis O. "History and Fiction as Modes of Comprehension." *New Literary History* 1.3 (1970): 541–58.

Mittell, Jason. *Genre and Television: From Cop Shows to Cartoons.* New York: Routledge, 2004.

Montgomery, David. "Industrial Democracy or Democracy in Industry? The Theory and Practice of the Labor Movement, 1870–1925." *Industrial Democracy in America: The Ambiguous Promise.* Ed. Nelson Lichtenstein and Howell John Harris. New York: Woodrow Wilson Center Press, 1993. 20–42.

Moretti, Franco. *Signs Taken for Wonders: On the Sociology of Literary Forms.* New York: Verso, 2005.

Moretti, Franco. *The Way of the World: The Bildungsroman in European Culture.* London: Verso, 1987.

Morrison, Toni. *Playing in the Dark: Whiteness and the Literary Imagination.* Cambridge, MA: Harvard University Press, 1992.

Morson, Gary. *Narrative and Freedom: The Shadows of Time.* New Haven, CT: Yale University Press, 1996.

"Mr. Mark Higginbotham's Case of Real Distress." *New Monthly Magazine and Literary Journal.* London: Henry Colburn, 1825. 290–93.

Naremore, James. *More Than Night: Film Noir in Its Contexts.* Berkeley: University of California Press, 1998.

Nelson, Dana D. *National Manhood: Capitalist Citizenship and the Imagined Fraternity of White Men.* Durham, NC: Duke University Press, 1998.

Nicholson, Marjorie. "The Professor and the Detective." *The Art of the Mystery Story: A Collection of Critical Essays.* Ed. Howard Haycraft. New York: Biblio and Tannen, 1976. 110–27.

North, Michael. *The Dialect of Modernism: Race, Language, and Twentieth-Century Literature.* New York: Oxford University Press, 1994.

O'Malley, Michael. *Face Value: The Entwined Histories of Money and Race in America.* Chicago: University of Chicago Press, 2012.

O'Malley, Michael. "Specie and Species: Race and the Money Question in Nineteenth-Century America." *American Historical Review* 99.2 (April 1994): 369–95.

O'Meally, Robert G. "Checking Our Balances: Louis Armstrong, Ralph Ellison, and Betty Boop." *Uptown Conversation: The New Jazz Studies*. Ed. Robert G. O'Meally, Brent Hayes Edwards, and Farah Jasmine Griffin. New York: Columbia University Press, 2004. 278–96.

Obenzinger, Hilton. "Better Dreams: Political Satire and Twain's Final 'Exploding' Novel." *Arizona Quarterly* 61.1 (2005): 167–84.

Olwell, Robert. *Masters, Slaves, and Subjects: The Culture of Power in the South Carolina Low Country, 1740–1790*. Ithaca, NY: Cornell University Press, 1998.

Painter, Nell Irvin. "Thinking about the Language of Money and Race: A Response to Michael O'Malley, 'Specie and Species.'" *American Historical Review* 99.2 (April 1994): 396–404.

Pamplin, Claire. "'Race' and Identity in Pauline Hopkins's *Hagar's Daughter*." *Redefining the Political Novel: American Women Writers, 1797–1901*. Ed. Sharon M. Harris. Knoxville: University of Tennessee Press, 1995. 169–83.

Patterson, Orlando. *Slavery and Social Death: A Comparative Study*. Cambridge, MA: Harvard University Press, 1982.

Pauly, Thomas H. "'Mr. Higginbotham's Catastrophe': The Story Teller's Disaster." *American Transcendental Quarterly* 14 (Spring 1972): 171–74.

Peach, Linden. *Masquerade, Crime and Fiction: Criminal Deceptions*. New York: Palgrave Macmillan, 2006.

Peeples, Scott. "Love and Theft in the Carolina Lowcountry." *Arizona Quarterly* 60.2 (Summer 2004): 33–56.

Pepper, Andrew. "Black Crime Fiction." *The Cambridge Companion to Crime Fiction*. Ed. Martin Priestman. New York: Cambridge University Press, 2003. 209–26.

Perry, Lewis. *Boats against the Current: American Culture between Revolution and Modernity, 1820–1860*. New York: Oxford University Press, 1993.

Pinkerton, Allan. *The Molly Maguires and the Detective*. New York: G. W. Dillingham, 1877.

Poe, Edgar Allan. "Edgar Allan Poe." *Essays and Reviews*. New York: Literary Classics of the U.S., 1984. 868–73.

Poe, Edgar Allan. "The Gold Bug." *Selected Tales*. Ed. David Van Leer. New York: Oxford University Press, 1998. 198–229.

Poe, Edgar Allan. *The Letters of Edgar Allan Poe.* Ed. John Ward Ostrom. Vol. 2. New York: Gordian Press, 1966.

Poe, Edgar Allan. "Maelzel's Chess Player." *The Complete Works of Edgar Allan Poe.* London: Chesterfield Society, 1908.

Poe, Edgar Allan. "The Man That Was Used Up." *Burton's Gentleman's Magazine.* Ed. William E. Burton and Edgar Allan Poe. Philadelphia: William E. Burton, 1839. 66–70.

Poe, Edgar Allan. "The Murders in the Rue Morgue." *Selected Tales.* Ed. David Van Leer. New York: Oxford University Press, 1998. 92–122.

Poe, Edgar Allan. "The Purloined Letter." *Selected Tales.* Ed. David Van Leer. New York: Oxford University Press, 1998. 249–65.

Poe, Edgar Allan. "Sheppard Lee: Written by Himself." *The Complete Works of Edgar Allan Poe.* Vol. 10. Ed. James A. Harrison. New York: AMS Press, 1965. 126–39.

Poe, Edgar Allan. *Tales and Sketches.* Vol. 2: *1843–1849.* Ed. Thomas Mabbott. Cambridge, MA: Harvard University Press, 1978.

Poe, Edgar Allan. "Thou Art the Man." *The Complete Works of Edgar Allan Poe.* Vol. 5. Ed. James A. Harrison. New York: AMS Press, 1965. 290–309.

Porter, Dennis. *The Pursuit of Crime: Art and Ideology in Detective Fiction.* New Haven, CT: Yale University Press, 1981.

Pyrhönen, Heta. "Criticism and Theory." *A Companion to Crime Fiction.* Ed. Charles J. Rzepka and Lee Horsley. Malden, MA: Wiley-Blackwell, 2010.

Pyrhönen, Heta. *Mayhem and Murder: Narrative and Moral Problems in the Detective Story.* Toronto: University of Toronto Press, 1999.

Pyrhönen, Heta. *Murder from an Academic Angle: An Introduction to the Study of the Detective Narrative.* Columbia, SC: Camden House, 1994.

Rachman, Stephen. "Poe and the Origins of Detective Fiction." *The Cambridge Companion to American Crime Fiction.* Ed. Catherine Ross Nickerson. New York: Cambridge University Press, 2010. 17–28.

Reddy, Maureen. *Traces, Codes, and Clues: Reading Race in Crime Fiction.* New Brunswick: Rutgers University Press, 2003.

Reed, Touré. *Not Alms but Opportunity: The Urban League and the Politics of Racial Uplift, 1910–1950.* Chapel Hill: University of North Carolina Press, 2008.

Regourd, François. "Mesmerism in Saint Domingue: Occult Knowledge and Vodou on the Eve of the Haitian Revolution." *Science and Empire in the Atlantic World.* Ed. James Delbourgo and Nicholas Dew. New York: Routledge, 2007. 311–32.

Ricardou, Jean. "Gold in the Bug." *Poe Studies* 9.2 (1976): 33–39.

Ritchie, L. David. *Metaphor*. New York: Cambridge University Press, 2013.

Robinson, Forrest G. "Dreaming Better Dreams: The Late Writing of Mark Twain." *A Companion to Mark Twain*. Ed. Peter Messent and Louis J. Budd. Malden, MA: Blackwell, 2005. 449–65.

Robinson, Forrest G. *In Bad Faith: The Dynamics of Deception in Mark Twain's America*. Cambridge, MA: Harvard University Press, 1986.

Roediger, David R. *The Wages of Whiteness: Race and the Making of the American Working Class*. New York: Verso, 1991.

Roediger, David R., and Elizabeth Esch. *The Production of Difference*. New York: Oxford University Press, 2012.

Rogin, Michael Paul. *Blackface, White Noise: Jewish Immigrants in the Hollywood Melting Pot*. Berkeley: University of California Press, 1996.

Rogin, Michael Paul. *Fathers and Children: Andrew Jackson and the Subjugation of the American Indian*. New York: Knopf, 1975.

Rohrbach, Augusta. "To Be Continued: Double Identity, Multiplicity and Antigenealogy as Narrative Strategies in Pauline Hopkins' Magazine Fiction." *Callaloo* 22.2 (Spring 1999): 483–98.

Rosenheim, Shawn. *The Cryptographic Imagination: Secret Writing from Edgar Poe to the Internet*. Baltimore: Johns Hopkins University Press, 1997.

Rowe, John Carlos. "Poe, Antebellum Slavery, and Modern Criticism." *Poe's Pym: Critical Explorations*. Ed. Richard Kopley. Durham, NC: Duke University Press, 1992. 117–38.

Rubin, Gayle. "The Traffic in Women." *Literary Theory: An Anthology*. Ed. Julie Rivkin and Michael Ryan. Malden, MA: Blackwell, 2004. 770–93.

Rzepka, Charles J. *Detective Fiction*. Malden, MA: Polity, 2005.

Rzepka, Charles J. "Race, Region, Rule: Genre and the Case of Charlie Chan." *PMLA* 122.5 (2007): 1465–81.

Said, Edward. *Culture and Imperialism*. New York: A. A. Knopf, 1993.

Saint-Arnaud, Pierre. *African American Pioneers of Sociology: A Critical History*. Trans. Peter Feldstein. Toronto: University of Toronto Press, 2009.

Saint-Amand, Pierre. *The Laws of Hostility: Politics, Violence, and the Enlightenment*. Minneapolis: University of Minnesota Press, 1996.

Salerno, Roger A. *Sociology Noir: Studies at the University of Chicago in Loneliness, Marginality and Deviance, 1915–1935*. Jefferson, NC: McFarland, 2007.

Sallis, James. *Chester Himes: A Life*. New York: Walker, 2000.

Sayers, Dorothy. "Aristotle on Detective Fiction." *Detective Fiction: A Collection of Critical Essays*. Ed. Robin W. Winks. Woodstock, VT: Countryman Press, 1988.

Sayers, Dorothy. "The Omnibus of Crime." *The Art of the Mystery Story: A Collection of Critical Essays.* Ed. Howard Haycraft. New York: Biblio and Tannen, 1983. 71–109.

Scaggs, John. *Crime Fiction.* New York: Routledge, 2005.

Scandura, Jani, and Michael Thurston. "Introduction: America and the Phantom Modern." *Modernism, Inc.: Body, Memory, Capital.* New York: New York University Press, 2001. 1–18.

Schatz, Thomas. *Hollywood Genres: Formulas, Filmmaking, and the Studio System.* Philadelphia: Temple University Press, 1981.

Schneider, Linda. "The Citizen Striker: Workers' Ideology in the Homestead Strike of 1892." *Labor History* 23.1 (1982): 47–66.

Scott, James C. *Domination and the Arts of Resistance: Hidden Transcripts.* New Haven, CT: Yale University Press, 1990.

Scruggs, Charles. "Sexual Desire, Modernity, and Modernism in the Fiction of Nella Larsen and Rudolph Fisher." *The Cambridge Companion to the Harlem Renaissance.* Ed. George Hutchinson. New York: Cambridge University Press, 2007. 155–83.

Sedgwick, Eve Kosofsky. *Between Men: English Literature and Male Homosocial Desire.* New York: Columbia University Press, 1985.

Sellers, Charles Grier. *The Market Revolution: Jacksonian America, 1815–1846.* New York: Oxford University Press, 1991.

Shell, Marc. "The Gold Bug." *Money Talks: Language and Lucre in American Fiction.* Ed. Roy R. Male. Norman: University of Oklahoma Press, 1980.

Silber, Nina. *The Romance of Reunion: Northerners and the South, 1865–1900.* Chapel Hill: University of North Carolina Press, 1993.

Sinha, Manisha. "The Caning of Charles Sumner: Slavery, Race, and Ideology in the Age of the Civil War." *Journal of the Early Republic* 23.2 (2003): 233–62.

Soitos, Stephen F. *The Blues Detective: A Study of African American Detective Fiction.* Amherst: University of Massachusetts Press, 1996.

Sollors, Werner. *Neither Black nor White yet Both: Thematic Explorations of Interracial Literature.* New York: Oxford University Press, 1997.

Standish, Burt L. "Dick Merriwell, Mediator; or, The Strike at the Plum Valley Mine." *Tip Top Weekly.* New York: Street and Smith, 1911. 1–29.

Steeves, Harrison R. "A Sober Word on the Detective Story." *The Art of the Mystery Story: A Collection of Critical Essays.* Ed. Howard Haycraft. New York: Biblio and Tannen, 1976. 513–26.

Stephen, James. *The History of Toussaint Louverture.* Printed for J. Butterworth and Son, 1814.

Stockton, Kathryn Bond. *Beautiful Bottom, Beautiful Shame: Where "Black" Meets "Queer".* Durham, NC: Duke University Press, 2006.

Sundquist, Eric J. *To Wake the Nations: Race in the Making of American Literature.* Cambridge, MA: Belknap Press of Harvard University Press, 1993.

Sussez, Lucy. *Women Writers and Detectives in Nineteenth-Century Crime Fiction: The Mothers of the Mystery Genre.* New York: Palgrave Macmillan, 2010.

Sweeney, S. E. "Locked Rooms: Detective Fiction, Narrative Theory, and Self-Reflexivity." *The Cunning Craft: Original Essays on Detective Fiction and Contemporary Literary Theory.* Ed. Ronald G. Walker and June M. Frazer. Macomb: Western Illinois University Press, 1990. 1–14.

Takaki, Ronald T. *Iron Cages: Race and Culture in Nineteenth-Century America.* New York: Knopf, 1979.

Tani, Stefano. *The Doomed Detective: The Contribution of the Detective Novel to Postmodern American and Italian Fiction.* Carbondale: Southern Illinois University Press, 1984.

Thaggert, Miriam. *Images of Black Modernism: Verbal and Visual Strategies of the Harlem Renaissance.* Amherst: University of Massachusetts Press, 2010.

Thomas, Ronald. *Detective Fiction and the Rise of Forensic Science.* New York: Cambridge University Press, 2004.

Thompson, Ann, and John Thompson. "Not So Much "Whodunnit" as "Whoizzit." *Theory and Practice of Classic Detective Fiction.* Ed. Jerome H. Delamater and Ruth Prigozy. Westport, CT: Greenwood Press, 1997. 51–60.

Thompson, Emily Ann. *The Soundscape of Modernity: Architectural Acoustics and the Culture of Listening in America, 1900–1933.* Cambridge, MA: MIT Press, 2004.

Thoms, Peter. *Detection and Its Designs: Narrative and Power in 19th-Century Detective Fiction.* Athens: Ohio University Press, 1998.

Tihanov, Galin. *The Master and the Slave: Lukács, Bakhtin, and the Ideas of Their Time.* New York: Oxford University Press, 2000.

Todorov, Tzvetan. *The Poetics of Prose.* Ithaca, NY: Cornell University Press, 1977.

Torlasco, Domietta. *The Time of the Crime: Phenomenology, Psychoanalysis, Italian Film.* Stanford, CA: Stanford University Press, 2008.

Townshend, Chauncy Hare. *Facts in Mesmerism, with Reasons for a Dispas-*

sionate Inquiry into It. New York: Harper and Brothers, 1841. New York: Da Capo, 1982.

Tragle, Henry Irving, ed. *The Southampton Slave Revolt of 1831: A Compilation of Source Material.* Amherst: University of Massachusetts Press, 1971.

Trouillot, Michel-Rolph. *Silencing the Past: Power and the Production of History.* Boston, MA: Beacon Press, 1995.

Turner, Frederick Jackson. *The Frontier in American History.* New York: Henry Holt, 1921.

Twain, Mark. *Following the Equator and Anti-imperialist Essays.* New York: Oxford University Press, 1996.

Twain, Mark. *The Mysterious Stranger Manuscripts.* Ed. William M. Gibson. Berkeley: University of California Press, 2005.

Underwood, Grant. "'Dark and Bloody Mystery': Mark Twain's Relationship with Detective Fiction." Diss., University of Alabama, 1990.

Van Dine, S. S. *Philo Vance: Four Complete Novels.* New York: Avenel Books, 1984.

Van Dover, J. K. *Making the Detective Story American: Biggers, Van Dine and Hammett and the Turning Point of the Genre, 1925–1930.* Jefferson, NC: McFarland, 2010.

Van Peebles, Melvin. "His Wonders to Perform." *Yesterday Will Make You Cry.* Chester Himes. New York: Norton, 1998. 11–21.

Victor, Metta Victoria Fuller. *The Dead Letter.* New York: Beadle, 1867.

Wiegman, Robyn. *American Anatomies: Theorizing Race and Gender.* Durham, NC: Duke University Press, 1995.

Weinstein, Cindy. *The Literature of Labor and the Labors of Literature: Allegory in Nineteenth-Century American Fiction.* New York: Cambridge University Press, 1995.

Weissberg, Liliane. "Black, White, and Gold." *Romancing the Shadow: Poe and Race.* Ed. J. Gerald Kennedy and Liliane Weissberg. New York: Oxford University Press, 2001. 127–56.

Wells, Carolyn. *The Technique of the Mystery Story.* Springfield, MA: Home Correspondence School, 1913.

Whalen, Terence. *Edgar Allan Poe and the Masses: The Political Economy of Literature in Antebellum America.* Princeton, NJ: Princeton University Press, 1999.

White, Hayden. *The Fiction of Narrative: Essays on History, Literature, and Theory, 1957–2007.* Baltimore: John Hopkins University Press, 2010.

White, Phillip M. *The Kickapoo Indians, Their History and Culture: An Annotated Bibliography*. Westport, CT: Greenwood Press, 1999.

Williams, Anne. *Art of Darkness: A Poetics of Gothic*. Chicago: University of Chicago Press, 1995.

Wonham, Henry B. *Playing the Races: Ethnic Caricature and American Literary Realism*. New York: Oxford University Press, 2004.

Woodson, Jon. *To Make a New Race: Gurdjieff, Toomer, and the Harlem Renaissance*. Oxford: University of Mississippi Press, 1999.

Worthington, Heather. *The Rise of the Detective in Early Nineteenth Century Popular Fiction*. New York: Palgrave Macmillan, 2005.

Žižek, Slavoj. *Looking Awry: An Introduction to Jacques Lacan through Popular Culture*. Cambridge, MA: MIT Press, 1991.

Žižek, Slavoj. *The Sublime Object of Ideology*. New York: Verso, 1989.

Žižek, Slavoj. *Violence: Six Sideways Reflections*. New York: Picador, 2008.

Index

Althusser, Louis, 23
American Federation of Labor, 40
anomalous kinship, 20, 22–23, 148, 219n16
Ascari, Maurizio, 219n18
assimilation, 58, 75, 138, 153–54, 169, 176
automaton, 52, 116, 117, 161
avenger detective, 31, 44, 45, 47–48, 49
"average racism," 91, 223n9

Baker, Houston, 220n4, 227n2
Bakhtin, Mikhail, 33, 35, 221n6, 228n7
Baldwin, James: "Notes for a Hypothetical
    Novel," 201, 213, 214
Barrett, Lindon, 103
Barrow, David, 54
Barthes, Roland: S/Z, 193
Beadle and Adams Company, 44
Bederman, Gail: Manliness and Civilization,
    220n5
Biggers, Earl Derr, 187; The Chinese Parrot,
    187; The House without a Key, 186, 231n11
bildungsroman, 32, 35, 36, 37, 38, 61
Bird, Robert Montgomery: Sheppard Lee, 11,
    26, 96, 98, 119–20, 121, 123, 124, 125–27, 128,
    129, 130, 226n15
Blackmon, Douglas A., 39
blackness, 7, 78–79, 100, 165, 194, 202, 220n4
Brewster, M.: Letters on Natural Magic, 116
Brooks, Peter, 14, 15, 19, 218n13
Brooks, Preston, 228n4
Brown, Lois, 135
Brown, William Wells: Clotel, 144

Bruce, J. E.: Black Sleuth, 164
Buchanan, Joseph, 98
Bull, Malcolm, 147, 222n7, 226n12
Burke, Kenneth, 96
Burton's Gentleman's Magazine, 74

Cable, George Washington, 160
Caillois, Roger, 182, 183
Calhoun, John C., 10, 69
Calloway, Cab, 180, 185
Cappetti, Carla: Writing Chicago, 179
Cawelti, John, 79, 157, 168
Chandler, Raymond: "The Simple Art of
    Murder," 213
Christie, Agatha, 30, 182; Murder on the Ori-
    ent Express, 172, 173, 174, 198, 230n8
chronotope, 31, 33, 35
Chu, Patricia: Race, Nationalism, and the State
    in British and American Modernism, 50,
    52–53
Clarke, Cottrell, 16
classical liberalism, 172, 217n8
Coleman, Edward, 101
contrapuntal discourse, 7, 223n1
Cooke, Philip Pendleton, 93–94
Copjec, Joan, 170–72, 173, 174
Coviello, Peter, 71

Darley, Felix O. C., 16
Defoe, Daniel: Robinson Crusoe, 220n3
Deleuze, Gilles, 205; "The Philosophy of
    Crime Novels," 95

DeLombard, Jeanine Marie, 101–2; *In the Shadow of the Gallows*, 218n9

Denning, Michael, 43–44, 139; "Simon Wheeler, Detective," 29; "The Stolen White Elephant," 29

detection, 4–5, 8, 9, 10, 12, 16, 21, 22, 24–25, 26–27, 29, 66, 88, 96, 98, 120, 129, 130, 131, 132, 135, 136–37, 140, 147, 157, 158, 161, 172, 178, 179, 184, 195, 201, 203–4, 214, 216n2, 221n1, 222n5, 231n11; black-authored, 165, 216n6; dime-novel, 48, 58; double-conscious, 164; Eurocentric classical, 165

Devyr, Thomas, 69

Dew, Thomas Roderick, 95–96; "Abolition of Negro Slavery," 127

Dickens, Charles, 215n1; *The Mystery of Edwin Drood*, 95

dime novel, 10, 25, 29, 30–31, 32, 38, 43–44, 45–48, 55, 58–59, 61, 139, 202, 215n1

Dollar Newspaper, 16, 17

Douglass, Frederick, 150; "The Color Question," 157

Doyle, Arthur Conan, 165, 181, 215n1; *The Adventures of Sherlock Holmes*, 15–16; *The Hound of the Baskervilles*, 195; "The Musgrave Ritual," 13, 14–16, 18, 20–21, 201, 218nn13–14; "a Scandal in Bohemia," 20; *The Sign of the Four*, 16, 219n16, 224n6; *A Study in Scarlet*, 16

Droysen, Johann Gustav, 222n5

DuBois, W. E. B., 130; *Black Reconstruction*, 70, 96, 214; *Dark Princess*, 164; *The Philadelphia Negro*, 174, 175; "The Propaganda of History," 133, 140; *The Souls of Black Folk*, 181; "The Study of the Negro Problems," 203

Duhamel, Marcel: *The Five-Cornered Square* (*La Reine des Pommes*; *For Love of Imabelle*), 211; *La Série Noire*, 3

Elbert, Monica: "Nathaniel Hawthorne, *The Concord Freeman*, and the Irish 'Other,'" 91; Elmer, Jonathan, 74

Esch, Elizabeth, 4–5; *The Production of Difference*, 216n4

ethnic detective fiction, 12, 186–87, 203–4, 216n6, 232n2

Fabian, Ann, 150

"fair play," 221n1

Fauset, Jessie: *The Chinaberry Tree*, 163; *Plum Bum*, 163; *There Is Confusion*, 229n3

Fields, Barbara J.: "Ideology and Race in America," 147–48

Fisher, Charles: *The American Farmer*, 71

Fisher, Rudolph, 229n1; "Across the Airshaft," 231n15; "The City of Refuge," 168–70; *The Conjure-Man Dies*, 12, 26, 164, 165–68, 170, 174, 177, 178, 179, 180–81, 182–84, 187–99, 231n14; "John Archer's Nose," 12, 166, 194, 195, 196, 199–200; "The Lindy Hop," 163; "Negro Life as Literary Material," 163; "The Realist," 194; Rudolph Fisher Papers, 163; "Situation in American," 163–64; "Skeeter," 163; *The Walls of Jericho*, 167, 169–70, 229n7; "White Writers of Current Black Fiction," 163

Fisher, Philip, 216n5

Fisk, Theophilus, 69

Fleischman Brothers: *I'll Be Glad When You're Dead, You Rascal, You*, 188

Foucault, Michel, 24; *Discipline and Punish*, 217n8

Fowler, Alastair, 215n1

Freedman's Savings and Trust Company, 149, 150

Frege, Gottlob: *Grundlagen der Arithmetik*, 171

Freud, Sigmund: "A Child Is Being Beaten," 147

Galton, Francis: *Finger Prints*, 227n3

gambling, 149–50

Ginsberg, Lesley, 77

Ginzburg, Carlo: "Clues," 131

Girard, René, 103; *Deceit, Desire, and the Novel*, 156

Godden, Richard, 8, 67, 111

Goddu, Teresa, 91

Gosselin, Adrienne, 194; "Dusky Sherlock Holmes," 164–65

Gowen, Franklin B., 47

Graham's Magazine, 16

Green, Anna Katherine: *The Leavenworth Case*, 25, 167

Green, Gene: "From Here to Shanghai," 185

Grella, George, 232n3

Guess Who's Coming to Dinner?, 53

Gurdjieff, George Ivanovich, 192
Gypsy Frank, the Long Trail Detective, 45

Halperin, Victor: *White Zombie*, 52–53
Haltunnen, Karen, 8
Hammett, Dashiell: "Dead Yellow Woman,"
   185; *The Maltese Falcon*, 185, 196, 213, 230n8;
   Red Harvest, 199
Hammond, James Henry, 96; "Letter to an
   English Abolitionist," 95
Hansen, Harry: "A Corpse and Hocus Pocus
   in Harlem," 174
hard-boiled detective fiction, 2, 12, 44, 166,
   183, 185, 194, 195, 199, 200, 205, 206, 213,
   232nn3–4
Harris, Howell John, 220n5
Hartman, Saidiya, 95, 110–11
The Haunted Churchyard, 44
Hawthorne, Nathaniel, 62, 94; "Mr. Higgin-
   botham's Catastrophe," 11, 63, 79–82, 85, 89,
   90–93, 223nn8–9; "The Story Teller," 93;
   "Truth-teller," 221n3; *Twice Told Tales*, 81
Haycraft, Howard, 215n1
Hegel, Georg Wilhelm Friedrich, 111, 126–27;
   Phenomenology of Spirit, 8, 225n9, 226n12
Heyward, DuBose: *Porgy*, 163
"hidden transcript," 98, 223n1
Himes, Chester, 12, 194; *All Shot Up*, 205; *The
   Big Gold Dream*, 204, 205–10, 211, 212–14,
   232n3; *The End of a Primitive*, 1, 2, 3; *The
   Five-Cornered Square*, 211; *Yesterday Will
   Make You Cry*, 2
Hoffman, Daniel, 19, 105
Holcombe, William H.: *A Mystery of New
   Orleans*, 12, 26, 131, 132–33, 157–61
Holland, Sharon Patricia, 10, 217n7
Holquist, Michael, 219n19
Hopkins, Pauline, 23; "Famous Men of the
   Negro Race," 135; *Hagar's Daughter*, 9, 12,
   131, 132, 134–59, 164, 227n1
Hoppenstand, Gary, 44
Hughes, Langston: *The Big Sea*, 229n1; *Not
   Without Laughter*, 163

imaginative identification, 4, 11, 21, 96–97, 98,
   101, 103, 104, 106, 119, 120, 123, 124, 128, 129,
   202, 222n5
incest, 143, 153
interracial: affinity, 53; cooperation, 30;

dependency, 7, 10, 18, 23, 68, 130; detective
   fiction, 216n6; economic dependency, 11;
   genre, 5, 203; industrial democracy, 12;
   marriage, 145, 156, 160; modernism, 187;
   mutuality, 86; sociability, 3, 4, 5–6, 7–9, 10,
   11, 12, 13, 22, 23, 26, 27, 31, 41, 63, 64, 78, 88,
   91, 94, 96, 97, 98–99, 106, 112, 120, 129, 131,
   134–35, 140, 158, 165, 201, 202, 203, 204, 213,
   214; tension, 29; union, 144, 153–57, 158,
   161; working-class, 92
Irwin, John, 9, 117; *The Mystery to a Solution*,
   128

Jackson, Andrew, 10, 79, 97, 208
Jacksonian America, 94
Jacksonian democracy, 74
Jacksonian manhood, 64, 65
Jacksonian political culture, 78
Jacksonian vision of citizenry, 65
Jameson, Frederic, 34, 206, 213
Johnson, Barbara, 20

Kempton, Daniel, 106, 107, 110, 115
The Kennel Murder Case, 186
Kern, Stephen: *The Culture of Time and
   Space*, 227n1
Klein, Norman: "Harlem Doctor Produces
   Dusky Sherlock Holmes," 166
Knight, Stephen, 219n19
Knighton, Andrew: *Idle Threats*, 202
Knights of Labor, 54
Knox, Ronald A., 185–86
Kojève, Alexandre, 8, 111
Kopley, Richard, 101, 224nn4–5; "Deliber-
   ate Murder in Broadway, at Midday," 101;
   Edgar Allan Poe and the Dupin Mysteries,
   218n9

labor, 5, 28, 30, 35, 38, 39–41, 46, 90, 91,118; antebellum, 69, 109; black, 71, 78, 109; body,
   115; bonded, 71, 112; bound, 10, 62, 64, 65,
   70, 108; desystematizing, 202; disputes, 10,
   31, 41, 61; exploitation, 150; free, 70–71, 77,
   112, 143, 149, 154, 221n3; honest, 98, 121, 122,
   126, 138; industrial, 70, 78, 222n7; physical
   bodily, 112; racialized, 3, 12, 41, 48–49, 98,
   166, 202, 204, 213, 221n2; right's, 119; slave,
   8, 10, 50, 52–55, 62, 71, 78, 92, 111, 126, 141,
   225n10; trauma, 8, 67; union, 33, 54;

labor (continued)
    white 65, 70, 71, 221n2. See also American
    Federation of Labor; New England Asso-
    ciation of Farmers, Mechanics, and Other
    Workingmen
Lacan, Jacques, 58, 72, 107, 171, 218n14, 221n6
Larsen, Nella: Passing, 163
Lemire, Elise, 100, 101
The Liberator: "Difference Between a Free
    Laborer and a Slave," 70–71
Literary Journal, 79
Locke, Alain, 163
Locke, David R.: "Instittoot uv Confedrit X
    Roads," 144; "Petroleum V. Nasby," 142–44,
    228n6
locked room, 4, 13, 44, 164, 165, 170, 171, 172,
    173, 174, 188, 194, 197, 200, 202
Long Island Daily Press, 180, 181
Longstraw, Zachariah, 124, 125
Lost Cause ideology, 11, 135

Macdonald, Andrew, 203, 232n2
Macdonald, Gina, 203, 232n2
Macpherson, C. B., 225n11
Malaeska, the Indian Wife of the White
    Hunter, 44
Manfred, the Ventriloquist Detective, 45
Marx, Karl: Capital, 106
Marxism, 216n4
McCann, Sean: Gumshoe America, 219n15
McCluskey, John, Jr., 170, 179, 197, 231n14
McDuffie, Geo, 69
McParland, James (James McKenna), 46, 47
Mechanics' Union of Trade Association, 70
Meister, Wilhelm, 36, 38
mesmerism, 98, 122, 226n12, 226n14
metaphor, 4, 13, 21, 51, 70, 96–97, 98, 101, 102,
    103, 104, 106, 115, 119, 124, 128, 129, 139, 170,
    183, 202, 211, 225n9, 230n8; collapsed, 15
metonymy, 4, 26, 96–97, 102, 103, 104, 106, 115,
    119, 128, 129, 202
Michelson, Bruce, 30; Printer's Devil, 54
Miller, D. A., 8; The Novel and The Police,
    217n8
Miller, Jacques-Alain, 171
Mink, Louis, 72
modernity, 28, 35, 36, 38, 50, 52–53; American,

26, 27; cultural, 27; industrial, 32, 53, 59,
    188; interracial, 214
Molly Maguires, 46–47
Monte-Cristo Ben, the Ever-Ready Detective,
    45
Moretti, Franco, 21, 23, 24, 35, 181–82,
    220n3
Morrison, Toni, 6, 17, 41
Morson, Gary, 146
narrative contiguity, 11–12, 131–62
National Laborer, 70
"negro insurrection," 226n15
New England Association of Farmers, Me-
    chanics, and Other Workingmen, 92
New Monthly Magazine, 79
Nicholson, Marjorie, 222n5; "The Professor
    and the Detective," 219n19
Nullification Crisis, 10

Obenzinger, Hilton, 220n2
Olwell, Robert, 112
O'Meally, Robert, 188

Paine, Albert Bigelow, 220n1
Park, Robert, 176
"passing" plots, 12, 131
Patterson, Orlando, 108; Slavery and Social
    Death, 225n10
Pepper, Andrew, 203, 231n1
Phantasy-Pieces, 74
Philadelphia Saturday News, 101
Pinkerton, Allan: The Molly Maguires and the
    Detectives, 47
Pinkerton detectives, 10, 31, 46
Plessy v. Ferguson, 227n3
Poe, Edgar Allan: Eureka, 28; "The Gold Bug,"
    11, 13, 16–19, 20–22, 23, 96, 97, 98, 104, 106,
    107, 109, 112, 113, 117–21, 129, 218nn10–11;
    "Maelzel's Chess Player," 116; "The Man
    That Was Used Up," 11, 62–65, 67, 70, 74,
    78, 79, 81–82, 84–85, 87, 94; "The Murders
    in the Rue Morgue," 13–14, 17, 20, 28, 94,
    97, 99, 173, 191, 224n7; "The Premature
    Burial," 71–72; Prose Romances, 74; "The
    Purloined Letter," 17, 20, 77, 103, 107, 200,
    218n9; Tales of the Grotesque, 74, 218n10;
    "Thou Art the Man," 68

Porter, Dennis, 8, 13, 79, 157; *The Pursuit of Crime*, 62
"possessive individualism," 112, 123, 225n11
proletarian detective, 44

Rachman, Stephan, 94
Reddy, Maureen, 185, 214
Regourd, François 226n14
reunion discourse, 155
Ricardou, Jean: "Gold in the Bug," 105–6
Robeson, Paul, 163, 180
Robinson, Bill, 180
Robinson, Forrest, 28–29, 37
Roediger, David, 4–5, 221; *The Production of Difference*, 216n4
Rogers, H. H., 28
Rohrbach, Augusta, 138, 141, 153
Rosenheim, Shawn, 224n7
Rubin, Gayle, 155
Rush, Benjamin: "Of the Mode of Education Proper in a Republic," 62
Rzepka, Charles, 15, 24–25, 84, 100, 101, 216n2, 222n5, 231n11

Saint-Amand, Pierre, 103
Salem Gazette, 79, 223n8
Salerno, Roger: *Sociology Noir*, 178–79
Sayers, Dorothy, 66, 215n1, 218n11; "The Omnibus of Crime," 153, 216n3
Schumann, Robert: "Humoresque," 146–47
Schuyler, George, 192; *Black No More*, 164
Scott, James C., 67; *Domination and the Arts of Resistance*, 223n1
Sedgwick, Arthur G., 228n5
Sedgwick, Eve: *Between Men*, 155
selective focalization, 4
Shell, Marc, 109
Smith, Greenhough, 16
Soitos, Stephen, 164, 167, 191, 193, 227n2
Sollors, Werner: *Neither Black nor White yet Both*, 5–6, 7
Standish, Burt L.: *Dick Merriwell, Mediator*, 47
Steeves, Harrison R.: "A Sober Word on the Detective Story," 180
Stephen, James: *The History of Toussaint Louverture*, 100

Stevenson, Robert Louis, 113
The Strand, 16, 215n1
Sumner, Charles, 145, 148; "The Crime Against Kansas," 228n4
Sumner, William Graham, 145, 148
Sundquist, Eric: *To Wake the Nations*, 6

Takaki, Ronald, 77, 112
Tani, Stefano, 199; *The Doomed Detective*, 148
temporal reconstruction, 11, 81, 131–62
Thaggert, Miriam, 118, 229n3
Thomas, Ronald, 8, 25, 173, 185, 227n3, 230n8; *Detective Fiction and the Rise of Forensic Science*, 217n8
Thomas, W. I., 176
Thoms, Peter, 219n17
Thurman, Wallace, 192; *The Blacker the Berry*, 163; *Fire!!!*, 229n3; *Harlem*, 229n3
Toussaint-Louverture, François-Domique, 100
Townshend, Chauncy Hare: *Facts in Mesmerism, with Reasons for a Dispassionate Inquiry into It*, 122–23
Trouillot, François, 59
Turner, Frederick Jackson: "The Significance of the Frontier in American History," 154
Turner, Nat, 76–77, 95–96, 127, 222n6
Twain, Mark: *A Connecticut Yankee in King Arthur's Court*, 54; *The Chronicles of Satan*, 36–37; *Huckleberry Finn*, 212; "The New Dynasty," 54; *No. 44, The Mysterious Stranger*, 10, 26, 28–43, 45–46, 61, 220n2, 221n6; *What is Man?*, 37, 52

Underwood, Grant, 29
Urban League, 176, 177

Van Dine, S. S., 186; *The Benson Murder Case*, 167, 182
Van Dover, J. K., 186
Van Peebles, Melvin, 2
Van Vechten, Carl: *Nigger Heaven*, 164, 229n7
Victor, Metta Fulla: *The Dead Letter*, 25, 45
Vidocq, Eugène François, 100–101, 215n1
von Ranke, Leopold, 222n5

Walker, Amasa, 149

Walrond, Eric: "At Home in Harlem," 167
Washington, Booker T., 138, 220n4
Washington, George, 96
Weber, Max, 178–79
Whalen, Terence: *Poe and the Masses*, 223n9
White, Hayden: "The Nineteenth Century as
    Chronotope," 63
whoizzit mode, 12, 131, 148, 157–58

Williams, Anne, 221n3
Wonham, Henry: *Playing the Races*, 58, 59
Woodson, Jon: *To Make a New Race*,
    192
Workingman's Advocate, 69
Worthington, Heather, 8

Žižek, Slavoj, 146–47, 218n14